New Overtures

Originally published in
Journal of Race, Ethnicity, and Religion
Volume 3, Issue 2

www.raceandreligion.com

Miguel A. De La Torre, editor

New Overtures

Asian North American Theology in the 21st Century

Essays in Honor of Fumitaka Matsuoka

Eleazar S. Fernandez, editor

Sopher Press
Upland, California

© 2012 Sopher Press
Please direct inquiries to info@sopherpress.com.
ISBN 978-1-935946-02-1

TABLE OF CONTENTS

Acknowledgments xi

Contributors xiii

Prelude: Introduction
Orchestrating New Theological Overtures:
Heterogeneity, Dissonance, and Fluidity
vis-à-vis Imperial Monophony 3
   Eleazar S. Fernandez

Part One
Reading the Past and Setting the Notes
for the New Theological Overtures

1. Asian North American Theology in the 21st Century:
   A Personal Reflection 29
      Fumitaka Matsuoka

2. From Classical Tradition Maintenance to Remix *Traditioning*:
   Revisioning Asian American Theologies for the 21st Century ... 51
      Jonathan Y. Tan

Part Two
Sight (Site) Reading:
Voicing our Songs of Laments, Struggles, and Hopes

3. Revisiting the Question Concerning
   (Theological) Contextualization 73
      Lester Edwin J. Ruiz

4. Theological Counterpoints:
   Transnationalism and Political Theology in the Asia Pacific 93
      Kwok Pui-lan

5. Postcolonial in Fugue:
   Contrapuntality of Asian American Experience 111
      Wonhee Anne Joh

6. Elegies of Social Life:
   The Wounded Asian American 133
      James Kyung-Jin Lee

7. Collaborative Dissonance:
   Gender and Theology in Asian Pacific America 149
      Nami Kim

8. A Three-Part Sinfonia:
   Queer Asian Reflections on Trinity 171
      Patrick S. Cheng

Part Three
Our Repertoire:
Perspectives from Various Disciplines

9. Composing Integrity:
   A Method for Moral Agency for Asian North Americans 193
      Sharon M. Tan

10. Singing Bluegrass in a Mother Tongue:
    An Asian North American Pedagogy 219
       Boyung Lee

11. Informality, Illegality, and Improvisation:
    Theological Reflections on Money, Migration,
    and Ministry in Chinatown, NYC, and Beyond 243
       Amos Yong

12. Should the Pedal Point always Bring Dissonance
    Back into Harmony?
    Interrogating *missio Dei* from an Asian American Perspective 267
       J. Jayakiran Sebastian

13. Discordant Notes:
    Proselytism in an Age of Pluralism 287
    J. Paul Rajashekar

Part Four
Orchestrating and Conspiring with Others:
Conversations with Companions on the Journey

14. Requiem Mess:
    The Bitter Medicine of Religious Change 307
    James Treat

15. A *Bembe* for Chino Cubanos 325
    Miguel A. De La Torre

16. Suffering We Know:
    The Hermeneutic of *Han* and the Dilemma of
    African American (Religious) Experience 339
    Anthony B. Pinn

Conclusion: Postlude
Worlds Made a Part 355
    David Kyuman Kim

Acknowledgements

There are always more things to do and deadlines to beat, even if at times I am not sure if all of them really matter. As I look back at the years passed and raise my gaze toward the future, I have become more selective as to where to give my time and energies. Offering a tribute to a person who has contributed much to concerns I deeply care about is worthy of such a gift of time and commitment. Fumitaka Matsuoka, the honoree of this book, deserves such a precious gift. My personal and professional life has been blessed because of my encounter with Fumitaka. I cannot recall when I first met him, but I remember engaging with him on various occasions, both in the U.S. and Asia. I was drawn to his humble demeanor, hospitable spirit, words of wisdom, commitment to the least, and prophetic vision. Throughout his professional life, Fumitaka has mentored new generations of church leaders, teachers, scholars, and community leaders. I should not let the days pass without giving honor to a friend, a mentor, a great teacher and scholar, and a church and community leader who has given so much to the academy, the church, and the wider society.

An edited book in his honor would be a fitting tribute, I thought to myself. I carried this project in my mind but was reluctant to pursue it until May of 2009 at the Asian Theological Summer Institute (ATSI) of the Lutheran Theological Seminary at Philadelphia. There, I shared my idea with Kwok Pui-lan and Tat-siong Benny Liew. Not only were they excited, they also helped me plan this book project. I am grateful in particular to Benny's suggestion for the title (*New Overtures*) of this anthology and to Pui-lan's timely and wise advice. I also express my gratitude to the essay contributors to this volume. They have graced this volume with essays that offer rigorous critique and profound insights. Likewise, my gratitude belongs to the anonymous peer-reviewers.

I also would like to express my deep appreciation to generous and gifted individuals who helped me in the editing process: Chris Kliesen Wehrman and Zoe Kuester, who gave much of their precious time. The project also benefited from the editing skills of Karen Hering and Gage Church. My appreciation goes as well to United Theological Seminary of the Twin Cities for the financial support in the editing process and, in particular, to a very supportive dean, Richard Weis. I am thankful to Jon Berquist, founder of Sopher Press, for the encouragement, editorial skills, and for providing a venue for this work to become public, and to Miguel A. De La Torre, editor of the *Journal of Race, Ethnicity, and Religion*. Finally, my gratitude goes to my wife, Jo, for taking much of the household work so I can edit this book.

Fridley, Minnesota
In the bleak of winter 2011

Contributors

Patrick S. Cheng is the Assistant Professor of Historical and Systematic Theology at the Episcopal Divinity School in Cambridge, Massachusetts. His current research relates to LGBT Asians and the intersections of postcolonial and queer theologies. Cheng is the author of *Radical Love: An Introduction to Queer Theology* and the forthcoming *From Sin to Amazing Grace: Discovering the Queer Christ*. He also contributes to the *Huffington Post*. Cheng holds a Ph.D., M.Phil., and M.A. from Union Theological Seminary in New York, a J.D. from Harvard Law School, and a B.A. from Yale College. For more information, please see his website at www.patrickcheng.net.

Miguel A. De La Torre is Professor of Social Ethics at the Iliff School of Theology in Denver. He has written numerous articles and more than fourteen books, including the award-winning *Reading the Bible from the Margins* (Orbis, 2002), *Santería: The Beliefs and Rituals of a Growing Religion in America* (Wm. B. Eerdmans, 2004), and *Doing Christian Ethics from the Margins* (Orbis, 2004). Within the academy, he is a director of the Society of Christian Ethics and the American Academy of Religion. He is the editor of *Journal of Race, Ethnicity, and Religion* (www.raceandreligion.com) and a founder of the Society of Race, Ethnicity, and Religion. A scholar-activist, Dr. De La Torre has written numerous articles in popular media and has served on several civic organizations.

Eleazar S. Fernandez is Professor of Constructive Theology at United Theological Seminary of the Twin Cities, New Brighton, Minnesota. He is currently a member of the Interfaith Relations Commission of the National Council of Churches of Christ, USA. His published works include *Burning Center, Porous Borders: The Church in a Globalized World*, *Reimagining the Human: Theological Anthropology in Response* *to Systemic Evils, Realizing the America of our Hearts: Theological Voices of Asian Americans* (co-edited with Fumitaka Matsuoka), *A Dream Unfinished: Voices from the Margins* (co-edited with Fernando Segovia), and *Toward a Theology of Struggle*.

Wonhee Anne Joh is Associate Professor of Systematic Theology at Garrett-Evangelical Theological Seminary in Evanston, Illinois. She is the author of *Heart of the Cross: A Postcolonial Christology*. Her research interests are at the intersection of theology, critical race, sexuality and gender studies, Asian American studies, and post-colonialism. Her forthcoming book is titled *Terror, Trauma and Hope: A Postcolonial Spectrality of the Cross*.

Nami Kim is Associate Professor of Religious Studies in the Department of Philosophy and Religious Studies at Spelman College. Her publications include a co-edited special issue of *Journal of Feminist Studies in Religion* 25, no.1 (Spring 2009); "Engaging Afro/black-Orientalism: A Proposal," *Journal of Race, Ethnicity, and Religion* 1, no. 7 (June 2010); and "A Mission to the 'Graveyard of Empires'? Neocolonialism and Contemporary Evangelical Missions of the Global South," *Mission Studies* 27, no. 1 (2010).

David Kyuman Kim is Associate Professor of Religious Studies and a member of the Associated Faculty in the Program in American Studies at Connecticut College, where he was also the inaugural director of the College's Center for the Comparative Study of Race and Ethnicity from 2005 to 2008. In 2006, he became a board member and creative consultant/dramaturge and scholar-in-residence for David Dorfman Dance. In 2009, Kim was Inaugural Visiting Professor of the Humanities at Brown University. Since 2009, he has served as Senior Advisor at the Social Science Research Council (SSRC) and Editor-at-Large of The Immanent Frame, the SSRC's blog on secularism, religion, and public life. With John L. Jackson Jr., Kim co-edited in 2011 *Race, Religion, and Late Democracy*, a special issue of the *ANNALS of the American Academy of Political and Social Science*. He is also co-editor with John L. Jackson Jr. and Rudy Busto of the new Stanford University Press book series *RaceReligion*. He is also co-editor with Philip Gorski, Jonathan VanAntwerpen, and John Torpey of the collection of essays *The Postsecular in Question*. Kim is the author of *Melancholic Freedom:*

Agency and the Spirit of Politics. His current book project is *The Public Life of Love.*

Kwok Pui-lan is William F. Cole Professor of Christian Theology and Spirituality at Episcopal Divinity School, Cambridge, Massachusetts. Her books include *Postcolonial Imagination and Feminist Theology, Introducing Asian Feminist Theology,* and *Discovering the Bible in the Non-Biblical World.* She is the editor of the major reference work *Women and Christianity* (4 vols.), from Routledge.

Boyung Lee, a native of Korea, is Associate Professor of Educational Ministries at Pacific School of Religion, Berkeley, California. The breadth of her educational preparation extends from Korea to the United States. Among her published works are "From a Margin Within the Margin: Rethinking the Dynamics of Christianity and Culture from a Postcolonial Feminist Perspective" (in *Journal of Theologies and Cultures of Asia*), "Realities, Visions, and Promises of a Multicultural Future" (co-authored with Mary Elizabeth Moore *et al.*, in *Religious Education*), "Caring-self and Women's Self-esteem: A Feminist's Reflection on Pastoral Care and Religious Education of Korean-American Women" (in *Pastoral Psychology*), "Teaching Justice and Living Peace: Body, Sexuality and Religious Education in Asian American Communities" (in *Religious Education*). She is the author of *Restoring Community in the Mainline: A Pedagogical Guide to Communal Faith and Ministry* (Westminster John Knox Press, forthcoming).

James Kyung-Jin Lee is Associate Professor of Asian American Studies and English at the University of California, Irvine, and is the author of *Urban Triage: Race and the Fictions of Multiculturalism* (University of Minnesota Press, 2004). He serves as an associate editor for *American Quarterly* and sits on the editorial board of the *Heath Anthology of American Literature.* He is also a postulant for the Episcopal priesthood, and is currently pursuing a Master of Divinity at Claremont School of Theology.

Fumitaka Matsuoka is Robert Gordon Sproul Professor of Theology Emeritus at Pacific School of Religion and was Vice President for Academic Affairs/Dean and Professor of Theology at Pacific School of Religion and at Bethany Theological Seminary. He also served as the director of the Institute for Leadership Development and the Study of

Pacific and Asian North American Religion at Pacific School of Religion. His books include *Learning to Speak a New Tongue* (Pickwick, 2011), *Out of Silence: Emerging Theological Themes of Asian American Churches* (Cleveland: United Church Press, 1995), and *The Color of Faith: Building Community in a Multiracial Society* (Cleveland: United Church Press, 1998). He is currently working on the *Encyclopedia of Asian American Cultures & Religions* (co-edited with Jane Iwamura) (ABC/CLIO).

Anthony B. Pinn is the Agnes Cullen Arnold Professor of Humanities and Professor of Religious Studies at Rice University. He is the author or editor of twenty-six books, including *The End of God-Talk: An African American Humanist Theology* (Oxford University Press, 2012) and *Embodiment and the New Shape of Black Theological Thought* (New York University Press, 2010). His research and teaching cover a variety of areas including religious aesthetics, liberation theologies, religion and popular culture, and humanism. He is the founding director of the HERE Project, a program fostering innovative relationships between Houston and Rice through creative research collaborations and engaged pedagogical approaches. Pinn is also the director of research for the Institute for Humanist Studies (Washington, DC), and a member of the Meadville Lombard Theological School Board of Trustees.

Lester Edwin J. Ruiz is Director, Accreditation and Institutional Evaluation of the Association of Theological Schools in the US and Canada (ATS) and the Commission on Accrediting (COA). He is co-editor of four published works, including *Re-Framing the International: Law, Culture, Politics*, with Richard Falk and R.B.J. Walker. He has contributed numerous chapters to books and has been widely published in journals and other periodicals. He serves on the editorial committees of a number of journals including *Alternatives: Global, Local, Political*. His areas of interest include peace and world order studies, and the relationship between politics, ethics, theological education and transformation.

J. Jayakiran Sebastian is H. George Anderson Professor of Mission and Cultures and Director of the Multicultural Mission Resource Center at the Lutheran Theological Seminary in Philadelphia. He is a Presbyter of the Church of SouthIndia, and has been Professor in the Department of Theology and Ethics at the United Theological College, Bangalore, India, where he served as Chairperson of the Department and also Dean of Doctoral Studies. His most recent publication is *Enlivening the Past: An Asian Theologian's Engagement with the Early Teachers of Faith.*

Jonathan Y. Tan is Senior Lecturer at Australian Catholic University Faculty of Theology & Philosophy and author of *Introducing Asian American Theologies* (Orbis, 2008) and 50 essays, book chapters, and encyclopedia/dictionary entries on Asian American Theologies, Asian Theologies, Missiology, World Christianity, and World Religions. He holds an LL.B. (Honors) from the National University of Singapore Law School, a Master of Arts degree from the Graduate Theological Union, and a doctoral degree from The Catholic University of America.

Sharon Tan is McVay Associate Professor of Christian Ethics at United Theological Seminary of the Twin Cities, New Brighton, Minnesota. She holds J.D. and Ph.D. degrees from Emory University. Her publications include: *The Reconciliation of Classes and Races: How Religion Contributes to Politics and Law* (Edwin Mellen Press, 2009); "Satyagraha and Reconciliation," *Journal of Interreligious Dialogue* (Vol. 1 No. 1, 2009); and "Human Rights and Confucianism: Religious Liberty in China," with Hong Qu in *Journal of Ethics in Leadership* 1, no. 2 (2005).

James Treat teaches courses on indigenous religious and ecological traditions in the Department of Religion at the University of Illinois. He is the author of *Around the Sacred Fire: Native Religious Activism in the Red Power Era* (Palgrave Macmillan/St. Martin's Press, 2003) and the editor of three other books exploring the native encounter with Christianity in the contemporary period. His research and writing now focus on American Indian environmental issues, especially in the context of anthropogenic climate change. One of his current projects is "Mvskoke Country," a monthly column published in the *Muscogee Nation News* and archived at http://mvskokecountry.wordpress.com/.

Amos Yong is J. Rodman Williams Professor of Theology at Regent University, Virginia Beach, Virginia. He has authored or edited eighteen books, one of the most recent of which is, *Afro-Pentecostalism: Black Pentecostal and Charismatic Christianity in History and Culture*, in New York University Press's Religion, Race, and Ethnicity Series. He holds a doctoral degree from Boston University.

Introduction

Introduction

Orchestrating New Theological Overtures: Heterogeneity, Dissonance, and Fluidity *vis-à-vis* Imperial Monophony

Eleazar S. Fernandez

It was January 2008, in Berkeley, California, when Fumitaka and I had a conversation about his plan to retire from Pacific School of Religion. We had a great conversation about retirement, but it was hard for me to imagine he would be retiring soon. If my memory serves me well, I even said, "As a retired person you can take *more risks*!" He laughed as we continued walking to a nearby restaurant. I surely miss, as many do, his presence at some of the academic and church events, but I am glad he now has the freedom to pursue some of his other interests. He has more time for his family and playtime with his grandchildren. However, with his love for the church, theological education, Asian North American communities, and transformative community involvement, I cannot imagine Fumitaka hiding in retirement isolation. I am not surprised when from time to time I hear news about his new adventures and theological overtures.

In gratitude for Fumitaka Matsuoka's significant contribution to theological education, the church, religious studies, Asian and Asian American studies, and interdisciplinary studies, Asian North American scholars and friends have undertaken a book project. Honoring Matsuoka's visionary projects and courageous initiatives, this book project is also visionary in its direction and audacious in its moves. It aims not only to take account of the accomplishments and continuing struggles of Asian North Americans but also articulates strategic and creative responses to new challenges. Because the sociopolitical-religious space that Asian North Americans navigate is wide, involving multiple forms of negotiation and subject-agents and demanding interfaith and interdisciplinary approaches, this book addresses a wide range of topics: contextualization, empire and geopolitics, diaspora and racial minority formation, sexuality, class, gender, Asian North American theologies, postcolonialism, biblical studies, mission and ministry, pedagogy, interfaith relations, transnationalism, and more. In the spirit of companionship and dialogue, this book also has a section devoted to African American, Latino/a, and Native American voices.

On Music Metaphor: New Overtures

Music is something that is already in the air waiting for creative spirits to catch its tune and rhythms and its various expressions. Such is the case with the title of this book: New Overtures. The title came as if waiting for receptive and reflective individuals to welcome it into the world of words and prose. It emerged out of my conversation with Kwok Pui-lan and Tat-siong Benny Liew. Contributors to the volume have used various musical metaphors— notes, melody, syncopation, counterpoint, fugue, *sinfonia*, composition, improvisation, bluegrass, pedal point, remix, elegy, requiem, *bembe*, etc.—to articulate their views. With the skillful transposition of the authors, these musical metaphors have explanatory and revelatory powers: to disclose the intricate web of social relations and articulate new possibilities of dwelling and acting.

Music is an apt metaphor for use in this project. It conveys many of the key ideas presented by various authors regarding social harmony, dissonance, contrapuntality, change, fusion, creativity, adaptation, cooperation, construction, fluidity, hybridity, lament, tradition, option for the least, etc. The complicated and complex nature of harmony, polyphony, and counterpoint makes musical metaphor particularly fitting. Creative and delightful compositions often include pleasing harmonies as well as discordant notes and dissonance. The Chinese composer Tan Dun, notes Kwok, uses counterpoint to bring ancient and modern, Eastern and Western, sound and silence together to create imaginative musical works that resist easy classification. Fugue offers an example of counterpoint or contrapuntal expression. A composition of counterpoint in which many voices enter, fade, overlap, and reenter, fugue is an appropriate metaphor for postcolonial contrapuntal reading strategy—a reading strategy that has been an effective ally of subaltern communities.

Writers in this volume convey deep respect for tradition, for classical music of various times and climes. Patrick Cheng, for example, employs *sinfonia,* a term originating in the late Renaissance to introduce various kinds of pieces, usually vocal. By the 1700s, it was sometimes used to designate the three-movement Italian overture, which Cheng adopts for his articulation of the trinity. Nonetheless, even as contributors to the volume show deep respect for tradition, they approach tradition as a living heritage that needs constant engagement and re-interpretation in relation to new challenges. Jonathan Tan speaks of moving beyond tradition maintenance to traditioning-remix as a much-needed posture in order to take account of historical movement as well as of fluidity and multiplicity. Similarly, Boyung Lee employs the bluegrass form, which showcases each musician one-by-one; instruments and singers take turns playing or singing the melody and improvising. As part of a whole, each one plays an active role and does not simply conform to established harmony, authority, or tradition.

Context: Asia, Transnationalism, and Asian America as Geopolitical Place and Space

The greater freedom claimed by later generations of Asian North American theologians to use pieces from various places and cultural traditions to compose new overtures, reflects not only a greater embrace of the dynamic, shifting, and fluid character of realities but also a new understanding of our global context—particularly our global connectivity. To be sure, each musician has a geographic provenance, birthed and shaped by specific localities. Johann Sebastian Bach is a child of Germany (West) as Tan Dun, widely known for his scores for the movies *Crouching Tiger* and *Hidden Dragon,* is of China (East). Similarly, we can say that an Aristotelian classic is a child of the West as a Confucian classic is of the East. But what is Germany or China, Europe or Asia? There was not even a nation-state called Germany when Bach was born! Where is the demarcation line that separates the East from the West? Who draws the line and for what purpose? Boundaries are constructs that people determine and, in many instances, change. Bach belongs to the West as Tan to the East (where is the reference point?) as they both belong to the earth and to humanity. Tan did not learn music solely from his village in Hunan, China, but also in New York as a graduate student at Columbia University studying composition with Chou Wen-Chung, a Chinese American composer, who in turn worked with composer Edgard Varèse, an immigrant from France. Tan encountered the works of composers such as Philip Glass (trained in harmony and counterpoint), John Cage, and Steve Reich, to name a few.

In a spirit like Tan Dun's, Asian American theologians have exercised growing freedom in fusing horizons to compose new theological overtures. This is not simply because no one can own a single horizon, but because the well-being of one locality or group is connected to another. With a fluid and unstable construal of borders and an expansive sense of belonging, the new generation of Asian North American theologians has become more daring in transgressing constructed boundaries of various sorts, whether geographic, racial/ethnic, nation-state or fields of discipline. They fuse horizons for the sake of that which promotes life. Appropriating Michel de Certeau's poacher who trespasses on the private properties of others, Liew speaks of drawing "resources available from various sites and transits liberally and flexibly, without pledging to any cultural, racial, or national canons or canonical standards, *for the sake of justice making.*"[1]

Essentialist, territorial-based thinking served an important purpose in the era of the formation of nation-states and their struggles for national independence. While geographical territory is a given reality, it is not simply geography that defines the life of nation-states. Much of what defines the quality of life and people's interaction within a nation-state is a construct, a geopolitical construct. There is a geographical place called Asia to be sure—discourse exists in relation to geographic place; nothing exists in thin air—but the term "Asia" and how Asians experience life in relation to the rest of the world is a geopolitical

---

[1] Tat-siong Benny Liew, "Introduction: Intervening on the Postcolonial," in *Postcolonial Intervention: Essays in Honor of R. S. Sugirtharajah*, ed. Tat-siong Benny Liew (Sheffield: Sheffield Phoenix Press, 2009), 15. Emphasis mine.

construct. There is Asia because Asia or Asia Pacific has been constructed: it is a construct in relation to Europe, the United States of America, and in relation to what Michael Hardt and Antonio Negri call "Empire," a network of power relations that transcends nation-states even if it is enforced and propagated by more powerful nation-states, especially the United States.[2]

Asia as a context is a construct of the Euro-American sociopolitical imaginary. Japan tried to claim it but was not successful when its interest collided with the interest of the West, particularly of the United States. Edward Said calls this Western sociopolitical imaginary of Asia Orientalism. Asia is a creation of a Western Orientalizing gaze; it is a mirror of Western fantasy, fears, and desires. For the West, Asia is the wild, the barbaric, the exotic, and the alien that must be subjugated, tamed, rejected, and/or appropriated. From a geopolitical point of view, Asia serves the political and economic interests of the United States. In cultural and religious matters, it is considered a resource for bottled spirituality to rejuvenate spiritually-sapped Westerners. Asia in the Western imaginary offers what it desires, provided the objects of its desire are first tamed and domesticated.

As a geopolitical construct—non-bounded space—much of what is Asia lies beyond its geographic confines. Much of what is Asia is transnational and relational. As a constructed relational concept much of what Asia experiences—poverty, economic prosperity, conflict, etc.—is a product of this transnational relationship. Global relationship as it is seen through geopolitics is constitutive of what is Asia and Asian reality. There is no such thing as Asia apart from this geopolitically framed relationship, and this geopolitically framed relationship shapes the interaction of nation-states within the Asian region and its interaction without, with such entities as Europe and the United States. The exchange of communications, financial transactions, goods, services, and ideas make up Asia and the context of Asia. When Asia is viewed as a construct, a fluid, shifting, porous, and expansive reality, it is no longer tenable to speak of Asia in essentialist-purist terms. Asia is a hybridized reality. The "Asian critical principle" that Asian theologians speak about

---

[2] Michael Hardt and Antonio Negri, *Empire* (Cambridge: Harvard University Press, 2000).

is "critical" only when it is critical of its closely-bounded geographic framework and of its essentialist, purist, and nativistic premises.

Seeing Asia as a constructed geopolitical discourse (not a unified and bounded unit) liberates us from territorial/sociocultural essentialism, and it helps us understand the relationship between Asian and Asian American. If Asia as a construct is a reality beyond the geographic confines of the Asian region, we can say that being Asian is not completely identical with remaining physically in the land called Asia and embodying traditional/essential markers of "Asianness," whatever they may be. This runs counter to the insistence of some Asian scholars that those who are physically at home in Asia are true (or more) Asian than those in the diaspora.[3] I contend that in the era of massive global diaspora, Asia is where its people are: the majority of its inhabitants have stayed at home but many are scattered around the globe and are finding spaces, creating or constructing the Asian. The Asian is mobile, not simply bounded by national soil. The Asian, even if not in the Asian territory, is connected to Asia and affected by what happens to Asia. This is clearly the case in the relationship between the United States and Asia. Whatever relationship the United States has with Asia at a particular moment in history has a corresponding effect on how the U.S. society is in relationship with Asian Americans. Asia as a constructed context is not a stable reality, but subject to the vicissitudes of global politics. In this regard, when Asians and Asian North American theologians articulate what the Asian context and, by extension, being Asian is, they must move beyond geography to the realm of geopolitics and social imaginary.

Multiple Subjectivities and Belongings:
Multiple Expressions of Struggle

If we speak of Asia as a complex, broad, transnational, porous, hybrid, fluid, unstable, and contested geopolitical space, we must do the same when we speak of Asian identity and subjectivity. Musical

---

[3] Cf. Gerald O. West, "What Difference Does Postcolonial Biblical Criticism Make? Reflections from a (South) African Perspective," in Liew, *Postcolonial Interventions: Essays in Honor of R. S. Sugirtharajah*, 256-273.

metaphors that express freedom, movement, fluidity, and multiplicity are reflective of the prevailing understanding among Asian North American scholars and theologians that Asian American identity is socially constructed, fluid, shifting, complex, and multiple. The homogenous Asian does not exist except in the Orientalist imaginary. Asians and Asian North Americans are humans assuming multiple identities, subjectivities, and belongings. This multiplicity is true not only *between* nation-states in Asia, but even *within* nation-states. Moreover, there are multiple subjectivities at the individual level. An individual may be Chinese by ethnicity, born in Malaysia, adopted by white Canadians, and an immigrant to the United States. We may add other categories: gender, sexuality, class, and religious affiliation. If this person is gay or lesbian, she or he may seek affinity with white gays and lesbians, but may also encounter racism within that group. On the other hand, while she or he may feel at home ethnically with Asian North Americans, she or he may experience marginalization in the Asian North American communities because of her or his sexual identity.

With heightened transnational connection brought about by the compression of time and space and extension of reach, we must articulate an anthropology that takes serious account of translocal identity. There is a need to speak of identity not only in terms of multiplicity but also in terms of translocality. The translocal is not simply an adjective we attach to a person: it is constitutive of a person's identity, an evolving form of identity. It is a particular way of being and a particular way of dwelling. The translocal is a self that is porous to the interweaving of the many localities in the self. This person is locally rooted and globally winged. A translocal is one who experiences the interweaving, the tension, and the possibilities of one world of many worlds.

Complexifying the multiplicity, fluidity, and unstableness of identity is what Matsuoka calls "amphibolous" life. He speaks of himself as one living with an amphibolous faith, not completely at home in one religion such as Christianity. A person or community with an amphibolous faith embodies more than one epistemological and cosmological orientation. Most often the Eurocentric-Christian worldview expects or forces the individual to make an either-or decision, but diverse orientations do not submit to easy compromise. Thus the diverse person or community experiences tensions with the wider society as well as tension within. There have been tensions within white churches that see Hmong members, for example, embodying their indigenous and Buddhist religious practices as baptized Christians. Tension results from the expectation that Hmong members must stick to a single Christian, if not Eurocentric, worldview.

Given the constructed, multiple, and constantly shifting character of identity and subjectivity, Asian North American theologians have realized that they cannot continue in silence for the sake of harmony within Asian North American communities. Harmony cannot be maintained at the expense of muted identities and subjectivities of other members within Asian American communities, especially if these identities and subjectivities have become occasions of oppression. Asian North American theologians of later generations are increasingly cognizant of this reality; hence, they have become more open and daring in speaking about dissonance within the Asian North American communities. One's experience of pain cannot be muted for the sake of harmony. As there are multiple identities and various experiences of marginalization, so must the expressions of struggle be multiple.

"We must work with many fronts at once," says Charlotte Bunch, because people are oppressed by multi-dimensions of issues in different degrees. She continues, "While we may say at any given moment that one issue is particularly crucial, it is important that work be done on other aspects of the changes we need at the same time."[4] Aida Hortado states a similar point: "All forms of oppression afflicting . . . groups have to be taken into account simultaneously."[5] Subaltern women, in response to white feminists' homogenizing discourse which assumes generic women's experience, point to the necessity of dealing with forms of oppression that are particular to specific groups. Instead of conceptualizing gender subordination from the sole point of women's experience, which homogenizes and imperializes, Hortado, along with Patricia Zavella and other feminists of color, proposes that "social structure should be the analytical focus, which allows for profound differences among women."[6] This insight is

---

[4] Charlotte Bunch, "Going Public with Our Vision," in *Experiencing Race, Class, and Gender in the United States,* ed. Virginia Cyrus (Mountain View, Calif.: Mayfield Publishing Company, 1993), 389.

[5] Aida Hortado, *The Color of Privilege: Three Blasphemies on Race and Feminism* (Ann Arbor: The University of Michigan Press, 1996), 42.

[6] Ibid.; Patricia Zavella, "The Problematic Relationship of Feminism and Chicana Studies," *Women's Studies* 17:123-134.

useful not only in women's discourse but also in negotiating, articulating, and advancing coalitional politics for global democracy.

Even as dissonance and differentiated response is affirmed, Asian North Americans know that collaboration is critically important. Collaboration and dissonance are not antithetical. Collaboration has integrity when dissonance has its place. This includes dissonance within Asian communities and dissonance in relation to the wider society. Artful collaboration, like bluegrass or jazz, allows each participant to take a turn in playing the melody and, at other moments in the performance, the accompaniment. Each contributes to the performance, taking leadership and fading away in turn, to produce a marvelous performance in spite of or because of their distinctness, because they share something in common: the performance of beautiful music. Naming the "common" is critical for collaboration or coalition building. The crucial question becomes: What is the "common"?

Naming and Producing the "Common": Collaboration/Coalition

The common is often understood in generic, general, and essentialist terms. It is frequently associated with the traditional notion of community or public. In legal terms the "common" is public domain that is owned and managed by the state. This is not what "common" means here. The "common," as Hardt and Negri contend, is not an entity controlled by the state but something that is named and produced through the communication and collaboration of the singularities.[7] The common is an expression of an "ethical notion of performativity": it is the performance of the singularities in their acts of naming the common that they share (they live on the same earth, struggle under capitalist regimes of production and exploitation, and share hopes for a better life) and, through the process of communication, also produce the common. The common they produce is, in turn, also productive: the common produces the common. This dual understanding of the common—that which is *produced* as well as that which *produces*—is a critical key to understanding economic and social activity.[8]

---

[7] Michael Hardt and Antonio Negri, *Multitude: War and Democracy in the Age of Empire* (New York: Penguin Books, 2004), 206.

What is the common that already exists and which Asians and Asian American theologians must produce? Where must we focus our gaze to start building the common? Where do differences intersect, and how shall we discern the common in the intersection?

Aside from the general notion of the common that Asians and Asian North Americans share with each other and with the rest of humanity—such as the shared earth and globally shared vulnerabilities and hopes—Asians have come to share (or have been forced to share) something in common by virtue of geopolitical destiny in relation to the interest of the West or the global North. Asian Americans share a common plight as racialized/minoritized groups within the white dominant society. To be sure the common they share is fluid, volatile, and shifting, but what they share in common provides a strategic, tactical point for collaboration or coalition. Multiple identities and belonging complicate the shape of the common: there are differences that cannot be muted. How shall we take the differences, particularly those that are locations of pain?

One way to interpret the intersection of differences is to recognize the various forms of oppression as inseparable even as they are distinct. This is what I have argued elsewhere as the interlocking structure of systemic evils.[9] It means that the configuration of one's experience of a specific form of oppression and exploitation is influenced by the extent to which one is affected by other forms of oppression, a reminder that while differences exist, interconnections also exist. Lines of differences are present (e.g., class lines, racial lines, and gender lines), and it is "between" such lines, says Cherríe Moraga, that "the truth of our connection lies."[10] When lines of differences connect, attract, and relate, the common is being produced, and coalitional praxis is being born.

The lines of differences and oppression intersect and interlock and the multiple forms of marginalization must be addressed singly and integrally. But what is needed is more than the coming together of different interests interconnected by pain. There is a broader reality and

---

[8] Ibid., 28.

[9] Eleazar S. Fernandez, *Reimagining the Human: Theological Anthropology in Response to Systemic Evil* (St. Louis: Chalice Press, 2004).

[10] Chela Sandoval, *Methodology of the Oppressed* (Minneapolis: University of Minnesota Press, 2000), 59.

frame that people with distinctive pains share; this is the imperial condition. We need to see the distinctive pains and struggles through this larger frame: global democracy in the face of imperial hegemony. Identity politics in Asian America needs to be seen in relation to empire, which, as I noted earlier, is a network of power relations at a global level. Without this larger perspective ethnic groups can easily be subverted and pitted against each other, as was the case between African Americans and Asian North Americans in South Central Los Angeles.

Transgressing Boundaries, Bridging Various Disciplines and Publics

If geographic regional formations are constructs, so are various academic disciplines. If Asia is a construct based on geopolitical interest, so are Asian studies and Asian American studies. Geopolitical interest has shaped their academic formation. This is the case, Kwok argues, with area or regional studies which traditionally divided Asia into regions: East Asia, Southern Asia, and South Asia. Each area studies developed "experts" (including "native informants") who gathered and accumulated a body of knowledge for the consumption of the global North. Area studies served the function of providing information on enemy nation-states and strategic regions. The influence of geopolitics in the formation of academic fields reminds us of Michel Foucault's discourse on power-knowledge.[11] In the case of Asia regional studies, the hegemonic power of the global North assumed the form of knowledge; it possessed an aura of academic neutrality and legitimacy.

The emergence and status of Asian American studies, as Matsuoka's essay reminds us, is also reflective of the larger politics; it mirrors the plight of Asian American communities. Like other fields of study, its institutionalization as an academic discipline intertwined with the politics of higher education, the politics of the wider society, and the question of its contribution to the cultural capital. Asian American studies emerged out of the clamor from the community for a relevant academic program and with a strong participation from members of the

---

[11] Michel Foucault in *Power/Knowledge: Selected Interviews and Other Writings 1972-1977*, ed. Colin Gordon (New York: Pantheon Books, 1980).

community. Pressures from the university to conform to academic autonomy, which is considered essential for research, led to its distancing from the community at large. Asian American studies gained academic legitimacy, but it resulted in separation—being split off—from the interest of the wider community, particularly Asian North American communities.

Asian American studies, including theological studies, contends Matsuoka, need to constantly question the relationship between academic legitimacy and accountability to our communities, particularly to the challenges Asian North Americans face. Theological education must do the same. The academic integrity of Asian American studies or theological studies needs to be maintained, but academic fields do not exist for themselves alone. We need to know how they are contributing to the cultural capital of the wider society in general and to Asian and Asian North American communities in particular. We need to find out how Asian North American theological discourse is informing our faith communities. Is it a postcolonial theology without a church? Asian American studies and Asian North American theologies must not only maintain their legitimacy in the academic world, they must also exercise critical presence in academic settings—questioning content, method, pedagogy, policies, and institutional structures that promote marginalization—and they must articulate transformative practices.

Global complexity, geographic/geopolitical deterritorialization and re-territorialization, border crossings, threshold dwelling, transnationality, fluidity, and hybridity must bear on how we construct fields of disciplines. The academic community has abundant institutional forms of insistent individualism (such as disciplinary fields) that have become specialty silos. These specialty fields, says John Cobb, Jr., "constitute self-contained communities of research whose selection of topics is little affected by any needs but their own."[12] The "hands-off" agreement among specialty fields breeds a kind of indifference to common concerns that everyone must address.[13] Writers in this volume

---

[12] John Cobb Jr., cited in John B. Bennett, *Academic Life: Hospitality, Ethics, and Spirituality* (Boston: Anker Publishing Company, Inc., 2003), 15.

[13] Joseph Bessler, "Seminaries as Endangered Habitats in a Fragile Ecosystem: A New Ecology Model," in *Revitalizing Practice: Collaborative Models for Theological Faculties* (New York: Peter Lang, 2008), 9.

have recognized the need for interdisciplinary work that, in the prevalence of sacralized disciplinary silos, requires the unholy act of transgression. This volume embodies theologies that transgress disciplinary boundaries: boundaries that make academic disciplines captive to hegemonic interests; boundaries that are of little use in the life and practice of communities; boundaries or disciplinary silos that make scholars prisoners of their academic disciplines. Matsuoka is a model of bridging the various publics—civil society, academy, and the church—of Asian American studies and Asian North American theological discourse, as well as of various fields of discipline. He is a public intellectual, a church leader, an academic administrator, a scholar, and a teacher.

Engaging the Public and Creating Counterpublics

The dreams and voices of Asian Americans need to find a place in the wider public square if they are to contribute to the shaping of our public life. The dominant public sphere is, however, elitist and exclusionary: it favors the wealthy and denies participation to a significant number of groups such as the poor majority, common laborers, women and children, and migrants or non-citizens, to name but a few. The notion of public discourse based on the force of better argument only serves to hide the advantage of those who have educational credentials and economic and political means. It is naïve to start a dialogue or conversation as if sociopolitical inequalities do not exist. The official, dominant global public as we know it is controlled by powerful economic and political interests.

The official public sphere not only excludes subaltern voices, in many ways it is also inhospitable to religious voices, including the theological production of the subaltern. Although there is growing recognition of the positive role that religion plays in society, many subaltern progressive movements do not readily welcome the contributions of religious communities except for tactical purposes, "renting a clerical collar" or clothing mobilization work with "moral garments" in order to provide a "passport of morality."[14] This should

---

[14] Saul Alinsky, *Rules for Radicals: A Practical Primer for Realistic*

not, however, be a reason to give up working with progressive movements or give up participation in the wider public sphere. Asian American theologians perform an important role in articulating political or public theologies that address our common life.

Given multiple exclusions and inequalities, it is imperative that the official public be challenged. Even more, Asian North American theological communities must create counterpublics. The struggle is not simply for inclusion into the single official public, as if it were good in itself, but because multiple publics are necessary for participatory democracy.[15] Any adequate theory of the public must allow for the multiplicity of publics, especially publics that have been sidelined and silenced by the larger public. These alternative publics are not meant to be "separatist, except periodically, for health," says Alice Walker.[16] Counterpublics provide a space for the subaltern multitude to regroup, re-imagine, re-energize and re-strategize so as to engage and subvert the larger exclusionary public, as well as to construct a new and better tomorrow. The vision of a new world—a world symbolized by the Pentecost, or a world in which there is room for many worlds (*un mundo donde quepan muchos mundo*), or following U.S. feminists of color, of *Otro Mundo Zurdo* (the left-handed world)—needs a counterpublic to dream, subvert the status-quo and launch differential-oppositional-coalitional praxis.[17]

Organization of the Book

In addition to the Introduction and the Postlude this book has four parts: Reading the Past and Setting the Notes for the New

---

Radicals, First Edition (New York: Random House, 1971), 36, 44.

[15] Nancy Fraser, *Justice Interruptus: Critical Reflections on the "Poststructuralist" Condition* (New York: Routledge, 1997), 69-98.

[16] Cited in Sandoval, *Methodology of the Oppressed*, 41.

[17] Gloria Anzaldúa, "La Prieta," in *This Bridge Called My Back: Writings by Radical Women of Color*, eds. Cherríe Moraga and Gloria Anzaldúa (Watertown, Mass.: Persephone Press, 1981), 208-209. Also see Analouise Keating, "Forging El Mundo Zurdo: Changing Ourselves, Changing the World," in *This Bridge We Call Home: Radical Visions for Transformation,* eds. Gloria Anzaldúa and Analouise Keating (New York: Routledge, 2002), 519-530.

Theological Overtures (Part 1); Sight (Site) Reading: Voicing our Songs of Laments, Struggles, and Hopes (Part 2); Our Repertoire: Perspectives from Various Disciplines (Part 3); and Orchestrating and Conspiring with Others: Conversations with Companions on the Journey (Part 4). Let me spell out the basic direction of each Part and then proceed to take a brief rendering of the distinctive notes of each essay composition.

Part 1, Reading the Past and Setting the Notes for the New Theological Overtures, attempts to take account of the history of Asian American experience: the struggles and hopes of previous generations, the shifting contours of Asian American studies in response to shifting political dynamics in the wider U.S. context, and the evolving faith praxis of the people, particularly those who have given shape to the theological discourse of the time. Based on critical retrieval and re-reading of historical developments, the essays in Part 1 attempt to articulate the basic shape and direction that Asian and Asian North American theological reflection must take in the twenty first century. The two essays in Part 1 are from Matsuoka, "Asian North American Theology in the 21st Century: A Personal Reflection," and Jonathan Tan, "From Classical Tradition Maintenance to Remix *Traditioning*: Revisioning Asian American Theologies for the 21st Century."

Asian North Americans cannot move forward without learning where they have been and without embracing the pains, struggles, and hopes of the previous generations. Their ability to name and give voice to the history of their people is possible only if they have learned to care and have cared enough to learn and listen. Second generation theologians know that their current position in the world of theological discourse owes much to the labors of an earlier generation. It is with profound gratitude that they exercise a critical assessment of the past as they seek to move forward.

Matsuoka, a pioneer among second generation Asian North American theologians and the honoree of this anthology, highlights both this gratitude and critical assessment of the past even as he seeks to articulate what he believes should be the new direction for Asian and Asian North American theology. Matsuoka's posture in relation to the past and the present coheres with the way he sees his life's journey, a journey made up of self-conscious decisions within the larger framework of a historical context he did not choose. Perhaps this is what we call destiny, as Matsuoka does. He sees destiny not as the iron jacket of history that stifles agency, but rather the setting of his experience of life "on the boundary;" it is "grace entangled." From this personal starting point Matsuoka takes a cursory account of the development of Asian American studies and, more explicitly, of theological studies. He then proceeds to name the themes of Asian North American theologies and articulates the scaffolding of Asian North American theologies for the twenty first century.

Providing a hinge connecting Matsuoka and the rest of the essays is Tan's work. Tan does a brief historical critique of the works of first generation theologians, highlighting the significance of their struggles against racism and various forms of discrimination as well as their claim for a place in church and society, while pointing out the limitations of their theoretical frameworks, particularly their essentialist thinking and assimilationist stances. He then articulates the theological project of the next generation, which takes account of the multivalent and complex intertwining of sociopolitical, economic, cultural, religious, ecological, and sexual identities. Tan adopts a lens of traditioning-remix *vis-à-vis* tradition maintenance, an approach he believes is best suited to dealing with multiple subjectivities and concerns in a globalized world.

Part 2, Sight (Site) Reading: Voicing our Songs of Laments, Struggles, and Hopes, critiques the context of the Asian North American experience, one which is multidimensional and simultaneously local and global, as well as transnational. Attentiveness to the local is possible only by being attentive to the global, which is not simply the world out there but a reality constituted by the interweaving of various localities. With this wider frame setting the context, essays in Part 2 name the multidimensional aspects of Asian North American identity and experience and bring to the forefront matters that call for serious engagement not only within Asian North American communities but also in the wider public, such as gender, sexuality, diaspora, racial inequality, and the persistence of hegemonic-colonializing practices. Opening Part 2 is the essay of Lester Edwin Ruiz, followed by essays of Kwok Pui-lan, Wonhee Anne Joh, James Kyung-Jin Lee, Nami Kim, and Patrick S. Cheng.

Ruiz's essay, "Revisiting the Question Concerning (Theological) Contextualization," provides an appropriate opening for Part 2. His account of contextualization sets the stage or framework for taking account of the context of Asian North American theological discourse.

No doubt contextualization calls us to take context seriously, but what does taking it seriously mean? Before this question can be adequately addressed, a more fundamental question needs to be asked: What do we mean by contextualization? In an attempt to answer this question Ruiz calls us to revisit the question concerning contextualization. Situating the context of contextualization in the world of empire, diaspora, and multiple ways of dwelling, Ruiz brings up the significant multiple nuances of contextualization, exploring its depth and width. Subverting essentialist premises, he speaks of contextualization as an act or practice of re/producing insurrectionary knowledge, liberating ways of being, empowering politics, world-forming practices, etc.

Kwok's "Theological Counterpoints: Transnationalism and Political Theology in the Asia Pacific" demonstrates that relevant political theology must account for shifts in the conceptualization of the in-between space and in the relationship between Asia and America. She calls for a serious examination of the older Western imaginaries of Asia, which often fail to consider the changing geopolitical dynamics, particularly the rise of China and India as global economic powers. We cannot continue to ignore this new reality if political theology must speak prophetically to the challenges of our increasingly globalized and transnationalized context. In addition to taking Asian geopolitics as context seriously, Kwok argues that categories such as empire, nation, citizenship, and transnationalism must be integral to theological discourse, along with race, class, gender, sexuality, and other forms of identity. Kwok calls for an approach to theologizing that accentuates counterpoint as a way of experimenting with what she names new theological aesthetics.

Interweaving and complementing Kwok's theological counterpoint is Joh's "Postcolonial in Fugue: Contrapuntality of Asian American Experience." Joh deploys fugue as a musical metaphor to speak, following Edward Said, of contrapuntality in postcolonial discourse. The characteristics of fugue—a polyphonic composition in which many distinct voices enter, fade, re-enter, overlap, interweave, and assume a certain texture—is akin to a postcolonial contrapuntal composition. As a postcolonial metaphor, fugue, argues Joh, points to a way of reading that blurs or transgresses the traditional binary line of center/periphery, East/West, citizen/non-citizen, etc. With postcolonial fugue, Joh points to a way of doing theology that opens the possibility of singularity and plurality coming together to form a promising social textuality.

After Kwok and Joh have introduced us to the larger context of geopolitics and postcolonial ways of reading such as counterpoint/contrapuntality, Lee presents in his "Elegies of Social Life: The Wounded Asian American," a reading of the pain of Asian North Americans through the hermeneutic lens of "woundedness." What if, Lee asks, instead of theorizing damage as injury inflected upon otherwise healthy Asian North Americans by the dominant white society, we see Asian North American experience as fundamentally that of woundedness, one that is intrinsic to its social body history? Perhaps, Lee ventures, in such a reframing we might be able to reimagine justice not as an elusive revolutionary fantasy but as a life practice in which we become more attentive to the limits and capacities of social institutions and the contingencies of wounded bodies that inhabit our sociopolitical habitat. It may be, contends Lee, that the dominant narrative or the fundamental starting point of health is a problem in itself, and that we need to subvert the hegemony of the normal so as to liberate ourselves from its grip.

Building on the works of Asian North American scholars, Kim's essay, "Collaborative Dissonance: Gender and Theology in Asian Pacific America," pursues and articulates the crucial importance of gender in doing theology in the Asian Pacific American context. Without a doubt, putting gender at the front and center of theology creates tensions and conflicts within Asian North American communities, but this matter cannot be skirted to preserve superficial unity. Recognizing the need for collaboration even in the midst of conflict, Kim proposes "collaborative dissonance" as a posture for theologizing in the Asian North American context. Collaborative dissonance does not seek to resolve differences, but sees the constructiveness of difference and multiplicity in the re/production of theological knowledge.

Cheng's essay, "A Three-Part Sinfonia: Queer Asian Reflections on Trinity," pursues further the intersectionality of various forms of oppression and exploitation, particularly as it relates to the experience of queer Asian North Americans. Queer Asian North Americans are caught in the dehumanizing middle: the heterosexism of Asian North American communities and the racism of white lesbian, gay, bisexual, and transgender communities. Wrestling with this context, Cheng correlates the queer Asian North Americans' three-fold experience of sexuality, race, and spirituality with the perichoretic interaction within the trinitarian God-head. If the three-fold experience of sexuality, race, and spirituality mirrors the interaction in the Divine life itself, then, Cheng argues, queer Asian North Americans are made in the image and likeness of God, although in a distinctive melodic key. This trinitarian rendering of queer Asian North American experience is Cheng's attempt to bring wholeness not only to queer Asian North American communities but also to the wider world in need of transformation.

Part 3, Our Repertoire: Perspectives from Various Disciplines, articulates and presents the various repertoires that Asian North Americans scholars have developed and advanced in response to the challenges they face. Part 3 includes essays from the fields or disciplines of ethics, education and pedagogy, biblical studies, theology (particularly mission), ministry, and interfaith relations.

The first essay under Part 3 is "Composing Integrity: A Method for Moral Agency for Asian North Americans," by Sharon Tan. "Simple integrity," which Tan describes as a past-oriented, dogmatic consistency of belief, voice, and action, is not adequate to the complex identity experience of Asian North Americans that intertwines racism and partial privilege. Instead of simple integrity Tan composes and proposes what she calls "complex integrity." This notion of complex integrity, Tan contends, acknowledges multiple sources of moral knowledge and responsibilities, and it composes integrity by weaving multiple sources and narratives into a desired moral future seeking to respond to the challenges of the present. For those who are both victims of marginalization and recipients of partial privilege, Tan envisions the direction of complex integrity to be that of reconciliation and justice: right relation and the flourishing of all, particularly in U.S. society.

Following Tan is Boyung Lee's "Singing Bluegrass in a Mother Tongue: An Asian North American Pedagogy." Lee appropriates bluegrass, though not native to Asia, as an apt metaphor for articulating the distinctive features of Asian North American religious education. In contrast to a kind of music in which all instruments play the melody together or one instrument consistently leads while others follow, bluegrass allows each musician to take turns in leading, playing the melody and improvising on it. Transposing the old-music and the bluegrass metaphors to Asian North American communities, Lee points out the old-music emphasis in Asian North American communities in which community members are expected to sing the community's tune, often at the expense of their own. The emphasis on communal harmony in many instances silences dissonance. Lee is not debunking the old-music, but is seeking balance: motherland's strong communal music balanced by encouraging each member to take a turn playing the melody and, sometimes, to improvise. Lee proposes this balance for Asian North American religious education.

The theme of the next essay, "Informality, Illegality, and Improvisation: Theological Reflections on Money, Migration, and Ministry in Chinatown, NYC, and Beyond," is ecclesiology in relation to economy, migration, and religion. Amos Yong calls our attention to the socioeconomic plight of Asian Americans—particularly to the lives of many undocumented Fuzhounese in New York City who are struggling to survive under Chinatown's informal economy—as an entry point to thinking about the church. With insights from ethnographic research that highlight the interweaving of globalization, migration, and religion, Yong explores their impact on how we may re-imagine church and ministry. Deploying the lens of informal economy, he re-reads the socioeconomic experience of the early apostolic church to articulate a model of mission and ministry, one that is particularly responsive to the plight of diasporized and marginalized people. Without a doubt, what he calls a migration model presents challenges, but it also offers immense possibilities for the church's wider engagement with economic globalization.

Following an ecclesiological focus and a theologizing that does not run away from dissonance, J. Jayakiran Sebastian's essay, "Should the Pedal Point always Bring Dissonance Back into Harmony? Interrogating *missio Dei* from an Asian American Perspective," examines the dominance of *missio Dei*, the direction of the pedal point in the understanding and practice of mission in the past few decades. In introducing the possibility of dissonance to the established harmony, Sebastian moves in the spirit of critical scholarship that is fully cognizant of the constant temptation to create regimes of truth. He is not discounting the significance of *missio Dei*, but wants us to see how the concept has played out in empirical terms. With probing questions, Sebastian asks: Without completely denying its Divine inspiration, by granting it Divine origin are we not covering up the harsh realities that have been done in the name of mission? Are we downplaying human responsibility in mission?

Sebastian's essay offers a great segue to J. Paul Rajashekar's "Discordant Notes: Proselytism in an Age of Pluralism." The reality of religious pluralism that has been part of Asian reality is now increasingly a global reality. The migration of people has changed the religious demographics of various places, including countries of the global North. Given our increasingly plural religious context, Rajashekar explores some issues related to proselytism. When religion is understood as integral to the life of the whole society, proselytism may be seen as an assault to identity and rights, and can therefore, contends Rajashekar, be socially disruptive. He is not suggesting that Christian churches abandon evangelism or the possibility of conversion, but puts evangelism in tension with the challenges of pluralism. Rajashekar's highly nuanced essay does not offer closure to the conversation, but leaves us with discordant notes.

Asian Americans need to articulate their distinctive narratives, their struggles, hopes, and dreams of a new and better tomorrow, but they know that they have companions and they need companions. They share many challenges with other marginalized voices, such as African American, Latino American, and Native American. Part 4, Orchestrating and Conspiring with Others: Conversations with Companions in the Journey, provides a space for companions to share their thoughts as Asian North American theologians articulate new theological overtures.

James Treat's essay, "Requiem Mess: The Bitter Medicine of Religious Change," presents a Native American voice and perspective. Treat forewarns his readers that, much as he finds affinity with the plight of Asian Americans, Native Americans are not Asia's second sons sent packing across the Bering land bridge, and they are not another American minority group. There is no easy or simple solidarity between indigenous people and diasporized communities. With this warning, Treat recounts through the story of Christian boarding schools how Christian mission has given bitter medicine to Native Americans. In the wake of the considerable misery Native Americans have experienced from Christian mission, what redeeming grace does Christianity have to offer? Perhaps, contends Treat, this is the aspect most troublesome with Christian faith: its "concern for culpability before the practice of charity." Is pitifully begging forgiveness the best act Western Christians can offer in relation to Native Americans?

The next essay is Miguel A. De La Torre's "A *Bembe* for Chino Cubanos." *Bembes*, says De La Torre, are Afro-Cuban dance rituals in which humans become one with gods and attain wisdom. He adopts the *bembe* metaphor to speak of the dance that must be performed to gain an understanding of the Asian (Chino) roots in Cuba and the intersection of Asian Cuban identity with race, ethnicity, and nationhood. In an account that is itself reflective of the wisdom derived from dancing with the gods, De La Torre takes his readers to the intricate web of intra-Hispanic (Cuban) oppressive structures, especially as they shed light on the plight of Chino Cubanos. His account has the power of revelation: it discloses insights that have not been given much attention before, and it explores the complex and fluid discourse of identity and marginalization.

The last essay of Part 4 is Anthony Pinn's, "Suffering We Know: The Hermeneutic of Han and the Dilemma of African American (Religious) Experience." Pinn uses Nella Larsen's novel (*Quicksand*) and her portrayal of the fictional character, Helga Crane, as an entry point in dealing with the complex, multidimensional, highly nuanced, and paradoxical experience of the suffering of African Americans, which does not easily fit the common grand design of black and womanist theological discourses. Instead of a clear trajectory from oppression to resistance and the teleology of liberation, Helga's suffering and struggle reflect a deep sense of woundedness. It is in this regard that Pinn sees the Asian concept *han* as a helpful category in taking account of the suffering that African Americans have experienced.

The closing essay by David Kyuman Kim, "Worlds Made a Part: An Essay in Honor of Fumitaka Matsuoka," provides an excellent ending, a postlude if you will, to this anthology project. Kim's account of critical nostalgia and the point he makes about exercising freedom or agency while recognizing that we are products of history resonates with Matsuoka's account of his own journey and his sense of vocation. Matsuoka speaks of the actions he made in freedom while recognizing that "we exercise our freedom in the midst of values and powers we have not chosen but by which we are bound." Beyond recognizing that agency is exercised between freedom and destiny, Kim speaks of critical nostalgia that Matsuoka embodies, as the unstoppable search for humanizing possibilities. Kim's excellent tribute to Matsuoka is a fitting postlude.

Part One

Reading the Past and Setting the Notes for the New Theological Overtures

Chapter 1.

Asian North American Theology in the 21st Century: A Personal Reflection

Fumitaka Matsuoka

My Faith Journey: Grace in an Entangled Story

H. Richard Niebuhr in *Christ and Culture* talks about the shaping power of history and the historical context of human choices. Though we choose our actions in freedom, we are not independent, for we exercise our freedom in the midst of values and powers we have not chosen but by which we are bound. Niebuhr writes:

> Before we choose to live we have been chosen into existence... have been elected members of humanity.... We have not chosen the time and place of our present, but we have been selected to stand at this post at this hour of watch or of battle. We have not chosen our culture ... there has always been a choice prior to our own, and we live in dependence on it.... The history of culture illustrates in myriad ways this dependence of our freedom on consequences we do not choose.[1]

As I look back in hindsight at the vocational path I have taken, I am amazed at the truth of Niebuhr's words about the presence of "a choice

---

[1] H. Richard Niebuhr, *Christ and Culture* (New York: Harper & Row, 1951), 249-51.

prior to [my] own, and [my life] dependence on it." Ministry, let alone theological education, was not on the horizon of my vocational choice in my youth. When I finished my college education, my desire was to work in international relations. In fact, at first I took a job in the airline industries. The war in Vietnam led me to a seminary to follow the path of conscientious objection to war. Even then, my purpose in seminary education was to wait for an opening in an alternative service. The language of theology was totally foreign to me when I entered seminary. But something about the inquiry into the meaning of Christian faith and life fascinated me. That was forty some years ago. I ended up devoting these years of my life to ministry and theological education. My vocational life and the freedom of choice I exercised were indeed dependent on "consequences" I did not choose. In his writing, Niebuhr points out that in choosing freedom we attend to our religious situation as well as to the value structures that condition our lives. There are values, beliefs, or dispositions that are woven into the very fabric of our life and thoughts that shape whatever choices we make. There are values or dispositions of mind and modes of response which we hold simply because it has been our common force to come into existence in a particular geocultural and historical context. Perhaps my dependence on consequences I did not choose is the real meaning behind Calvin's concept of predestination. Surely I was not predetermined to be a minister or a student of theology. But I was nudged "to stand at this post at this hour of watch or of battle."

Niebuhr's notion of the historical contexts of human choice suggests another mark of my vocational life: being on the boundary. In his autobiography, Paul Tillich characterizes his life as being "on the boundary."[2] Tillich relates how his life has been straddling the boundaries between theology and philosophy, the church and society, Europe and America, Protestantism and Catholicism, liberalism and neo-orthodoxy, and so on. In a similar fashion I find that my life has been "on the boundary" of one sort or another ever since my birth. I was born in 1943 during the height of World War II in Tokyo. The cultural marks of old Japan were still present in my family life at the time of my birth. The impact of old Japan is evident in my name, Fumitaka, which means "faithful filial piety." In my early years, I lived in the midst of the birth

---

[2] Paul Tillich, *On the Boundary* (New York: Scribner, 1966).

of modern Japan. My personal identity is also on the boundary between my country of birth and my new home where my spouse, Sharon, and my children and grandchildren live. Among other boundaries on which I live perhaps the most acute is the boundary between my Christian faith and Asian faith traditions. I am truly "amphibolous" in faith—a term I will explain later in this essay.

Life on the boundary is nomadic in character. There is no stability and permanency in life on the boundary. It is "not being at home in one's own home," as Theodore Adorno puts it.[3] It is an exhausting life. But it is also, strangely, a rich and gratifying life. Such values as trust, interdependence, and honesty are very important for me even in the midst of the temptation for stability, safety, and predictability that I also crave. Early in my childhood at an annual ritual of *obon* (the return of the dead), I memorized a phrase I heard a priest recite from the Buddhist sutra: "the rosy cheek of today turns to a white skull of tomorrow." In life on boundary I learned that impermanence is not to be resisted.

As I look back at my life, each turning point speaks of the "Alphabet of Grace."[4] If we learn to listen to the message of each turning point in our entangled lives, we hear the holy and elusive word that is spoken out of the depths—the word of grace. God speaks words of grace to me through each turning point. My personal reflection on Asian North American theology is really my attempt to witness to the presence of grace in my entangled life.

Construction of the Asian North American Cultural Capital

To begin, I would like to describe the establishment of Asian North American cultural capital in academy. I believe one of the critical challenges facing Asian American studies today (with its inclusion of Asian North American theology) is the question of how the political nature of a particular discipline becomes institutionalized as an academic field and what the consequences of this transformation might mean to institutions of higher learning in the United States. The issue of cultural capital is always associated with the emergence of a new discipline.

---

[3] Theodore Adorno, *The Adorno Reader* (Oxford: Blackwell, 2006).
[4] Frederick Buechner, *Alphabet of Grace* (New York: Harper One, 1989).

Asian North American Studies, including theological studies, is no exception. Any form of cultural or intellectual activity can gain entry into the academic field only if it produces some form of cultural capital, which can be understood on a basic level as any kind of information or knowledge that possesses some value.

The recent publication of *The Cultural Capital of Asian American Studies: Autonomy and Representation in the University* by Mark Chiang treats this subject quite persuasively.[5] Chiang traces the inception of Asian American Studies to the 1968 student-led strike at San Francisco State University. Although his studies are located within the U.S. context, his insights will probably also apply to the Canadian context to a certain extent. The field of Asian American Studies was founded as a result of student and community protests that sought to make education more accessible and relevant to the American public. Chiang recounts how non-academic members of the Asian American communities initially served on department advisory boards to help plan and develop areas of the curriculum. But university pressures eventually dictated their expulsion. Chiang argues that the program threatened the principles of faculty autonomy and self-governance that were essential to the modern research university. The necessity of institutional survival forced the new program to conform to the rest of the university and therefore to exclude non-faculty members from any participation in program design and execution. Chiang says that at that moment in history, the intellectual work of the field was split off from its relation to the community at large, giving rise to the entire problematic of community representation in the academic sphere.

Needless to say, the original established goals for the field of Asian American Studies have been variously redefined since the time of San Francisco State's protest movement. Asian American Studies now finds itself in a radically altered sociopolitical landscape in universities and seminaries. I believe it is fair to say that Asian American Studies has achieved a certain degree of academic legitimacy and respectability. This also means that it has a very different relation to those features of seminaries and universities that many of its founders opposed: faculty autonomy and the primacy of research.

---

[5] Mark Chiang, *The Cultural Capital of Asian American Studies: Autonomy and Representation in the University* (New York, NYU Press, 2009).

And yet, the issue of representation and accountability of the field still remains. Insofar as seminaries, universities, and colleges are the primary institutions engaged in the determination and reproduction of the value of cultural capital, Asian North American studies necessarily had to convert itself into a form of cultural capital in order to be institutionalized in them. At the same time, such a cultural capital still needs to be accountable to Asian North American communities including the Asian North American faith community. Asian North American studies is an organic discipline that is reflective of what is going on in Asian American communities. I believe the question of how to negotiate between the legitimacy in academy and the accountability in our communities is one of the primary challenges facing Asian North American studies including theological enterprise.

This is to say that every aspect of Asian North American studies has been impacted by the relative position and circumstances of Asian North Americans in the wider North American society. Even as Asian American studies as an overall field remains committed to the political project of ethnic studies, its relation to other fields of minority studies is complicated. Many factors such as the model minority image and the perceived success of Asian North Americans in North American society; the "overrepresentation" of Asian North American students and faculty at colleges, universities, and seminaries in comparison to their percentage of the general population; and the rapid rise of some Asian economies in the global system distinguish Asian North American studies from other minority fields. Despite being much fewer in number than either Latinos or African Americans, Asian North Americans as a group face greater challenges in forging political unity. Although as ethnically heterogeneous as Latinos, Asians lack a unifying language or colonial history, and are more divided along class lines—not only within particular ethnic communities, but also among them. At many schools, for example, students from poorer Southeast Asian and Pacific Islander communities are grouped together with more affluent East Asian and South Asian students and so are excluded from affirmative action and financial aid programs. Asian North American studies has had to grapple with the consequences of both real and perceived success. Ironically, this has meant in some ways that the field has less political and academic capital because it has seemed not as crucial for many Asian American students, who appear to be doing just fine without it. This may also explain the fragile nature of Asian North American centers in seminaries. With the exception of a few historically strong Asian North American centers, many are marginal in universities and seminaries. On the other hand, it also seems apparent that the tremendous growth of the Chinese and Indian economies has resulted in a resurgence of interest in Asian Studies that is pulling the two fields more closely together and potentially away from the U.S. national context that originally defined Asian North American Studies. The cultivation of Asian American studies' cultural capital in schools of higher learning continues to pose new and renewed challenges.

The Historical Development of Asian North American Theology: Voices and Visions: Sojourners in Asian North American Ministries

Now I would like to turn more explicitly to the development of Asian North American theology. Theology can be said to be an "imaginative construction" of a comprehensive and coherent picture of humanity in the world under God in theistic religious traditions.[6] Within the Asian North American context, Christian scholars, ministers, and many writers have been engaged in theological construction from the early 1900s. Theology emerged in Asian North American religious communities in order legitimize them and to assert these communities' hopes and promises for their future. Lately, Asian North American scholars of other religious traditions have begun to join in theological discourse because of an inclusive understanding of "theology" beyond the traditional theistic definition. One of the first issues in Asian North American theology is to note the fluid and sometimes hybrid nature of theistic, non-theistic, and polytheistic readings of faith traditions. Even though the monotheistic faith orientations of the Abrahamic faith traditions still predominate the assumed cosmology of Asian North American theology, the boundary between the theistic and extra-theistic religious traditions is not as clearly defined as for other racial and ethnic theological enterprises.

---

[6] Gordon Kauffman, *An Essay on Theological Method*, 3rd edition (American Academy of Religion Book, 1995).

In the early stage of Asian North American religious tradition building (*actus tradendi*), which spanned the first several decades of the twentieth century, the theological writings of Asian North Americans appeared mainly in community newsletters and sermons collections of the Christian churches. For example, Japanese Christian leaders who were interred in concentration camps during World War II produced numerous reflective writings on the meaning of their faith in that difficult era. The first notable collection of Asian North American theological construction appeared in *The Theologies of Asian Americans and the Pacific Peoples: The Reader*, an unpublished collection of theological reflective essays in 1976 compiled by Bishop Roy Sano, then the director of Center of Pacific and Asian American Center for Theology and Strategies (PACTS) in Berkeley, California.[7] The contributors of *The Reader* included Christians and Buddhists, both ministers and lay leaders. What is noteworthy about this endeavor is the wide representation of women as contributors. Since the compilation of *The Reader*, there have been numerous books and essays on theology written by contemporary Asian North American theological religious leaders.[8] We should note that *The Reader* and its companion volume, *Contours and Currents: Theologies of Pacific and Asian Americans* (1976),[9] have never been published in spite of the important roles they played in the Pacific and Asian American theologies.

The first wave leaders have their own particular ethnic experiences but also share in corporate experiences that can be appropriated into one's own being as "learned memory." Asian North Americans' experiences are part of the "learned memory" of the people of God to be appropriated by the whole church.

---

[7] Roy Y. Sano, ed., *The Theologies of Asian Americans and the Pacific Peoples: The Reader* (Berkeley, CA: Center for Pacific and Asian American Theology and Strategies, 1972).

[8] A recent representative publication is Viji Nakka-Cammauf and Timothy Tseng, eds., *Asian American Christianity: A Reader* (Pacific and Asian American and Canadian Christian Education Project & The Institute for the Study of Asian American Christianity, 2009).

[9] Roy Y. Sano, ed., *Contours and Currents: Theologies of Pacific and Asian Americans* (Berkeley, CA: Center for Pacific and Asian American Theology and Strategies, 1976).

A few sample representative theological topics that appeared in the first wave of Asian North American theological constructions during the 1960s and 1970s are: "Sojourners: In Asian-American and Biblical History" by Wesley Woo;[10] "Cultural Heritage of Asian Americans" by Joseph Kitagawa;[11] "The Role of Religion in Asian American Communities by William Mamoru Shinto;[12] and "Asian Americans: A Forgotten Minority Comes of Age," prepared by the Joint Strategy and Action Committee Inc.[13]

In these writings the word "sojourners" was prominent. The early theological reflections focused on the meaning of sojourners as: those who value memory as an indispensable key to identity formation; those who shape a particular posture towards relating with others; and those who develop a distinct "angle of vision" toward the future. In the past, Asian North American usage of the term "sojourner" was an epithet. A more positive meaning has evolved in light of Asian North American religious leaders' sojourn experiences in the changing world, and this new understanding is redefining their beings and behaviors. Feelings of discomfort or uneasiness in North American societies and feelings of not quite fitting in can be channeled towards a new vision of human relatedness rather than a search for personal security and acceptance into society.

It is no surprise that the first wave of Asian North Americans used the term "sojourner" to describe the history of Asian North Americans. The biblical reference of the term is obvious. What is important to note by the choice of the term "sojourner" is the gnawing sense that Asian North Americans live with a different yardstick from what is taken for granted as the common values and life orientations that are all around them. While racial and ethnic experiences were first considered to be the primary source of Asian North American identity, there was also a growing sense that there was something Asian North

---

[10] Wesley Woo, *Sojourners in Asian-American and Biblical History: Adult*, 2-9 (This article originally appeared in *Asian-American Christian Education Curriculum Project*, 1979: The Office of Ethnic and Urban Church Affairs & the Office of Education, Golden Gate Mission Area, Synod of the Pacific, United Presbyterian Church, U.S.A., San Francisco, California).

[11] Joseph Kitagawa, *Contours & Currents*, 1-29.

[12] "William Mamoru Shinto, *A Reader*, 16-27.

[13] Joint Strategy and Action Committee, Inc., *The Reader*, 437-439.

American about the experience that was shared with other ethnic communities. That "something" is the shared experience of being a sojourner, the experience of being "a stranger within." This realization led the first wave of Asian and Pacific Americans to embrace a particular kind of life orientation and value system that speaks of what they experience: "Holy Insecurity." Being a stranger at home means to look for ways of life which help Asian and Pacific Americans to live with basic insecurity and to find, paradoxically, the security of Christian faith in this state of insecurity. That is their interpretation of the biblical meaning of "sojourner."[14] The following passage appeared in the Centennial Worship Celebration of Japanese Christian Mission in North America (October 9, 1977) reflects the significance of the theological theme of sojourner.

> Though arriving at the end of our first century and celebrating it, we still are seekers, looking for whatever it is we are looking for. We will are a pursuing church, or the pilgrim of God in the wilderness, or the dispersed like the first century Christians, or simply call it *search* – we are all on the way, together. But we are not alone, nor helpless. Our fathers crossed over the Pacific for a new life in this land; they were immigrants, away from their homes. They found what the life of sojourners was like, and yet, wherever they were, they were not away from the Lord's field. They met him, and built their churches.[15]

Other sample writings of Asian North American theology in its first wave are:

---

[14] Wesley Woo, "Sojourners: In Asian-American and Biblical History" (This article originally appeared in *Asian-American Christian Education Curriculum Project*, 1979: The Office of Ethnic and Urban Church Affairs & the Office of Education, Golden Gate Mission Area, Synod of the Pacific, United Presbyterian Church, U.S.A., San Francisco, California).

[15] From: The Centennial Worship Celebration, Japanese Christian Mission in North America (October 9, 1977).

- The question of what impelled Asian North American theologians to express their voices and visions.
    "The Role of Religion in Asian American Communities"—William Mamoru Shinto (*The Reader*, pp.16-27)
    "Asian Americans: A Forgotten Minority Comes of Age"—Joint Strategy and Action Committee, Inc (*The Reader*, pp.437-439)
    "Problems and Promise of Filipinos In Hawaii"—Ben Junasa (*A Reader*, pp. 415-423)
    "Ethnic Liberation Theology: Neo-Orthodoxy Reshaped or Replaced?"—Roy I. Sano (*Mission Trends* No. 4: *Liberation Theologies in North America and Europe*, eds. Gerald H. Anderson & Thomas F. Stransky, C.S.P. Paulist Press: New York/Ramsey/Toronto & Wm. B. Eerdmans Publishing Co., Grand Rapids, 1979), 247-258

- The question of how they saw themselves then.
    "In Remembering"—(*The Reader*, pp. 468-469)
    "Perspective"—Joann Miyamoto (*The Reader*, p.1)
    "Amazing Grace"—Violet Masuda (*The Reader*, pp. 2-3)
    "My Spiritual Pilgrimage"—Jitsuo Morikawa (*The Reader*, pp.4-9)
    "There Are Giants in the Land"—Teruo Kawata (Harold V. Jensen Lecture, First Baptist Church, Seattle, October 17, 1993)
    "The Right to Struggle for Ourselves"—Marilyn J. Mar (*The Reader*, pp. 214-219)
    "Theological Understanding of Women"—Eun Ja Kim Lee (*The Reader*, pp. 361-367)
    "From Silence to Sounds"—June I. Kimoto (*The Reader*, pp. 368-373)
    "Between Black and White: The Asian In America"—Lawrence H. Mamiya (*Contours & Currents*, pp. 232-265)
    Asian American Ethnic Identity--Paul M. Nagano, "Asian American Ethnic Identity for Community" (*Asian American Theology: Multicultural Communities* 1992, pp. 151-188)

- The voices and visions of these theologians thirty Years later.
    "Resistance, Rebellion, and Defiance: Examples of Christian Activities Against Domination "—Roy Sano (APARRI, 2006)
    "Crossing Boundaries: Our Common Journey"—Lloyd Wake, (APARRI 2003 Plenary address)
    Paul Nagano, "From Authoritative Christianity to Universal Pluralistic "Agape" (love) Faith" (unpublished document)

Representative Themes in Asian North American Theology Today

What is the current state of Asian American theological construction? To respond to this question, we need to articulate a working definition of what it means to be an Asian North American. The term "Asian North American" is relatively young one, just a hair over forty years old, with its first recorded public usage occurring at the University of California Berkeley, the gravitational center of 1960s student activism. As noted earlier in the section on "Asian North American Cultural Capital," the role played by the student-led demonstrations at San Francisco State University is significant. In those days, being "Asian North American" was an act of passion and a statement of purpose. The lack of a stated history and definition around the term were a source of freedom, not concern, offering a chance to build a brand new way to be American or Canadian. The emergence of Asian North American theology was no doubt influenced by this political climate.

Four decades later, however, I believe the situation is more complicated. I like Jeff Yang's description:

> ...bringing together Asian Americans has often seemed like herding cats, if those cats were randomly mixed in with, say, dogs, sheep and giraffes—a metaphor that reflects the staggering diversity of our community, which incorporates dozens of nationalities, each with multiple linguistic, religious and ethnic subsets, and a varying historical record of immigration to the United States.[16]

No community has been more impacted by multiracialism, transnationalism and panculturalism than the Asian North American community. Lisa Lowe talks about Asian North American cultural identity in terms of "heterogeneity, hybridity, and multiplicity."[17] I believe Asian North Americans represent something of a beta test for the future meaning of "peoplehood" in the United States. I believe the definition of peoplehood and the question of what brings people together in an increasingly interrelated and yet fractured nation is the context in which Asian North American theology needs to be placed. Asian American theology needs to contribute to the coherence of people in a world that is becoming simultaneously closer to and more distant from each other.

A number of themes continue to challenge and shape the future of Asian North American theology. These include the theological meaning of "sojourner" (a theme that emerged in an early stage of the development of Asian North American theology); liminality; the politicization and racialization of faith; the intersection of gender and sexuality in this racialized society of ours; and the need for a shift from the monotheism-centered theology to a reflection of Christian faith among pluralistic cosmologies of lived faiths. At the same time, I believe Asian North Americans also participate in the traditioning process of Christian faith, *actus tradendi*, that has been unfolding in history. Our present theological activities are fashioned toward a future that has already been signaled by the decisive event of Christ in history. In theology we explore and name the meaning of the promised signals for humanity as revealed in the Christ event. In this sense, I believe we Asian North Americans are co-sojourners with all the other people of faith in the *actus tradendi* that began a long time ago. Ultimately, as H. Richard Niebuhr so aptly describes the purpose of the church and ministry and thus theological enterprise, theology participates in the common journey to "increase the love of God and neighbor."[18]

---

[16] Jeff Yang, "What does it mean to be Asian American?" San Francisco Chronicle, June 4, 2009.

[17] Lisa Lowe, *Immigrant Acts: On Asian American Cultural Politics* (Durham and London, Duke University Press, 1996) 60-83.

[18] H. Richard Niebuhr, *The Purpose of the Church and Its Ministry* (San

The Three-fold Epistemological Scaffold of Asian North American Theological Construction

Finally, I would like to summarize my personal theological reflection as a person who has lived in the United States for nearly fifty years and considers both Japan and the United States as my homes. (A more comprehensive version of my theological thoughts was published in 2011.[19]) I should say my work here is more a prolegomena for a theological construction than theology itself. What I offer is my own reading of the epistemological scaffold that sets the context of an Asian American theological construction; I am limiting my work to a U.S. context. This scaffold is three-fold: (1) the translocal meaning of race; (2) the spirit of dissonance and dissent; and (3) "amphibolous" faith orientation.

Race as Translocal

The first pillar of the epistemological scaffold that I propose is the meaning of race experienced and interpreted by Asian Americans. Historian Gary Okihiro poses the question, "Is Yellow Black or White?"[20] This question reflects the ambiguous role Asian Americans hold in this racialized society. It is a well-known observation that when race relations are a black and white binary, whites render Asian Americans, American Indians, Latina/os, and Pacific Islanders invisible. At the same time, it is equally true that Asian Americans share with African Americans the status and repression of nonwhites as the "Other." Therein lies what Okihiro terms the "debilitating aspect of Asian-African antipathy" and, at the same time, the liberating nature of African-Asian unity.[21] We also need to note that the ambivalence associated with the position of Asian

---

Francisco: Harper Collins, 1977).

[19] Fumitaka Matsuoka, *Learning to Speak a New Tongue* (Eugene, Oregon: Pickwick Publications, 2011).

[20] Gary Okihiro, *Margins and Mainstreams* (Seattle: University of Washington Press, 1994).

[21] Gary Y. Okihiro. "Is Yellow Black or White?" in *Asian Americans: Experiences and Perspectives,* ed. Timothy P. Fong & Larry H. Shinagawa. New York: Prentice Hall, 2000. 63.

Americans in the U.S. racial landscape is exacerbated by viewing Asian Americans as a "model minority" on the one hand and "foreigners within" on the other.

This contradiction originates from how Asian Americans have been treated in the history of the United States, a history that has contributed to our unique racial formation in the United States. To complicate this history, Asian Americans have been variously lumped together with whites or blacks, depending on the value for the dominant culture. For example, there were periods in American history when both African and Asian work forces were seen as one in so far as they were essential for the maintenance of white supremacy. Okihiro says "…they were both members of an oppressed class of 'colored' laborers, and they were both tied historically to the global network of labor migration as slaves and coolies."[22]

On the other hand, Asian Americans were sometimes paradoxically classified as whites in order to insulate whites from African Americans. The "model minority" perception of Asian Americans maintains the assumption that Asian Americans are "near whites" or "whiter than whites," even though in this minority stereotype we continue to experience racism like African Americans and other racially disfranchised groups of people. This ambiguous state of race classification of Asian Americans has resulted in a confused image of who we are in the racial hierarchy of the United States and, simultaneously, created opportunities for an alliance with other racially oppressed groups of people. Asian American scholar Lisa Lowe points out that Asian Americans live in "the *contradictions* of Asian immigration, which at different moments in the last two centuries of Asian entry into the United States have placed Asians 'within' the U.S. nation-state, its workplaces, and its markets, yet linguistically, culturally, and racially marked Asians as 'foreign' and 'outside' the national polity."[23]

Because of the conflicting perceptions placed upon Asian Americans, we experience race to be *translocal*; there is no fixed locus for our race experiences. This translocal racial identity produces cultural and religious expressions in response to the prevailing desires of

---

[22] Ibid.

[23] Lowe, *Immigrant Acts: On Asian American Cultural Politics*, 8.

America to domesticate and assimilate us into the wider society. Translocality is the cultural and religious context of navigating the conflicting and contradicting treatments of Asian Americans by America. Asian Americans are often *not at home in our own home, displaced in the very society we live*. The translocal race experiences of Asian Americans have produced a particular cultural and religious value orientation, if you will, a nomadic morality. This nomadic value orientation is akin to what Theodor Adorno calls an exilic morality.[24] We are not at home in our own home.

But our translocal racial experiences say to us that race could be a site not only for an alternate value orientation—the morality of "not being at home in one's own home"—as much as the locus of a particular cultural and religious identity. Race, in other words, is a site to create a new set of conventions, a second tongue, for interpreting "the reality [Asian Americans] share within the majority through the institutions it creates or infiltrates."[25] When life is translocal, what is valued is trust, intimacy, and honesty that arise out of the importance of relationship-building. Stability, security, and insurance, on the other hand, are not as much of a value because they can be taken away at anytime. We realize that our translocal racial identity is fragile and its transmission to subsequent generations is by no means guaranteed. This nomadic orientation helps Asian Americans to recognize other folks and communities that are not at home in our own society.

Sensitivity to Pathos

The second pillar of the threefold epistemological scaffold I propose is the sensitivity to pathos that has grown out of a culture of dissonance and dissent. Asian American culture is dissonant and irresolute within the prevailing dominant societal and cultural milieu.

---

[24] Theodore Adorno, *Minima Moralia: Reflections from Damaged Life* (London: New Left Books, 1951), 38-39. Quoted in Said, *Reflections on Exile*, 564–565. "Dwelling, in the proper sense, is now impossible. The traditional residences we grew up in have grown intolerable: each trait of comfort in them is paid for with a betrayal of knowledge, each vestige of shelter with the musty pact of family interests…. The house is past… it is part of morality not to be at home in one's home."

[25] Ibid.

Language as an indispensable means of expressing culture reveals both dissonance and irresolution for Asian Americans. As Frantz Fanon points out, "To speak means to be in a position to use a certain syntax, to grasp the morphology of this or that language, but it means above all to assume a culture, to support the weight of a civilization."[26]

The language of dissonance and dissent is prevalent in Asian American literature. In Theresa Hak Kyung Cha's book *Dictee,* for example, the language of dissonance and dissent is clearly expressive. The protagonist of the book writes poorly, stutters, stops, and leaves verbs un-conjugated. She adulterates the Catholic catechism by mocking the expression that human beings are created in "God's likeness" as duplication, counterfeiting, carbon copying, and mirroring. She dissents and resists the pressure to mimic the powerful religion that is forced upon her from outside. The language of dissonance and dissent points to yet another and deeper epistemological significance for Asian Americans: the emergence of a distinct angle of vision with sensitivity toward pathos in life arising out of the dissonant culture. Carlos Bulosan in his work, *America Is in the Heart,* captures this sensitivity:

> Why was America so kind and yet so cruel? Was there no way to simplify things in this continent so that suffering would be minimized? Was there no common denominator on which we could all meet? I was angry and confused and wondered if I would ever understand this paradox.[27]

The juxtaposition of the publicly-owned ideal of a democratic nation and Bulosan's experience of suffering, sorrow, and exclusion from the ideal, which is replicated many times over by Asian immigrants, represents the real America. "We are America!"—without any resolution or reconciliation between the ideal and the contradicting reality experienced by Asian immigrants—is the well-spring of the sensitivity to pathos that is deeply ingrained in Asian Americans. The movement of the spirit of dissent out of dissonance is ritualized and

---

[26] Franz Fanon, *Black Skin, White Masks* (New York: Grove Press, 1967), 17-18.

[27] Carlos Bulosan, *America Is in the Heart* (Seattle, Washington: reprint, University of Washington Press, 1943), 147.

traditioned into a reliable cultural referential point within the community. The Asian American language of dissonance and dissent is located in a "storied place" where lost memories are reinvented and the unlike varieties of silence emerge into spoken words connecting intergenerationally through the past of the living and the dead into the present in community. In other words, storied places such as the immigration station barrack museum of Angel Island and the sites of Japanese American internment camps during World War II (Manzanar, Tule Lake, and other sites) are sacred spaces where "that which is rejected is ploughed back for a renewal of life,"[28] as my colleague Joanne Doi tells us. Thus, the spirit of dissonance and dissent in Asian Americans, collectively as well as individually, moves us in much the same way as a ritual pilgrimage to a storied site.

Asian Americans' translocal identity leads to our conscious positioning in society that is a willful dissent against the officially prescribed history of America. This positioning emerges out of the historical experiences of disruption, pain, and dissonance that await our excavation and retrieval. Ritualized acts of excavation and retrieval of these referential points in our history are indeed the dissenting acts that serve as communal glue to bind Asian Americans together. The historical injuries and our experiences of dissonance carry the memory of a rehabilitative meaning both in regard to Asian Americans ourselves and also to those who have undergone similar experiences. These experiences uncover "hidden histories" that fuel the emergence of important social movements of the time. In this sense, the spirit of dissent born out of our dissonance with the dominant racial and cultural group is both subversive and constructive. The spirit of willful dissent is a powerful driving force to move Asian American communities toward the future as a "people on the way" in the company of other marginalized "people on the way." It acts as the seedbed for an alternate set of sacred conventions—a bond, a second tongue—that brings people together.[29]

---

[28] Mary Douglas, *Purity and Danger: An Analysis of the Concepts of Pollution and Taboo*, (London & New York: Routledge, 1966), 162.

[29] David Ng, ed., *People on the Way: Asian North Americans Discovering Christ, Culture, and Community* (Valley Forge, Pennsylvania: Judson Press, 1996).

Amphibolous Faith

The third pillar of the epistemological scaffold for Asian Americans as I see it is what I call an *"amphibolous"* faith. For Asian Americans, faith is likely to be expressed within a myriad of conflicting religious traditions that force us to live in a state of dis-identification with any singular religion. Simply put, amphibolous faith is the simultaneous existence of radically different epistemological and cosmological orientations in a person or in a community. These orientations are materially lived as well as spiritually expressed. The contradiction of these diverse orientations does not readily settle for resolution or compromise.

In his D.Min. project at the Pacific School of Religion, Yoshiki Morita talked about the meaning of memorial services among the newly arrived Japanese immigrants who come the Sycamore United Church of Christ in El Cerrito, California, where he is the Japanese language pastor. One of the illustrative images he introduced was a picture of a *butsudan*, a Buddhist altar known as a "Buddha Box." This is a family altar honoring deceased members. The photograph that pastor Morita exhibited was a *butsudan* with a cross in the middle and a place just under the cross for the picture of the deceased—as is common in the Buddhist practice. This is a graphic image of an amphibolous faith.

An "amphibolous faith" is, to a certain extent, akin to the term *aporia* as defined by Jacques Derrida. For him, the term speaks of "difficulty in choosing," "doubt," or, more precisely, a blockage: "no road" in the context of justice.[30] Amphibolous faith entails for Asian Americans an interminable experience like the experience of the "undecidable," a "blind spot" (Derrida) of both in metaphysics and in

---

[30]Jacques Derrida, *Deconstruction and the Possibility of Justice*, ed. Drucilla Cornell et al. (New York: Routledge, 1992), 24-26. Here Derrida treats the history of justice. He stresses the Greek etymology of the word "horizon": "As its Greek name suggests, a horizon is both the opening and limit that defines an infinite progress or a period of waiting." Justice, however, even though it is un-presentable, does not wait. A just decision is always required immediately. It cannot furnish itself with unlimited knowledge. The moment of decision itself remains a finite moment of urgency and precipitation. The instant of decision is then the moment of madness, acting in the night of non-knowledge and non-rule. Applied in the notion of amphibolous spirituality, there is the "ghost of the undecidable" is always present in amphiboly.

religion. In other words, amphiboly is an experience of a non-singular vision with an unresolved state of non-complimentary cosmologies and faith traditions existing within a person or in a community. This domain of contradictions becomes particularly acute for Asian American Christians who are assumed to embrace the monotheistic claims of historical Christian faith and, at the same time, are inclined to live with the non-theistic cosmologies embedded in the Asian religious traditions we inherit as our cultural DNAs.

For Asian Americans, epistemology begins with the notion that reality is multiple, and not *e pluribus unum,* (out of many one) or unity in diversity. The Christian use of *butsudan,* the Buddhist family altar, points to this difference. The depth-reality is not one but many. Asian Americans live with *aporia,* "undecidable," a refusal to be acquiesced into a singular vision precisely because of the contradiction inherent between the "foreigner within" and "model minority." In other words, we Asian Americans live in an amphibolous state both spiritually and materially. The crucial point to understand is that those whose faith is amphibolous understand the pressure to mimic the dominant ideology, and, at the same time, are driven by the desire to reassemble their broken history into a new whole. People for whom faith is amphibolous are aware that such restoration and rehabilitation are likely to be unattainable given the histories of failed attempts to establish restored communities by other groups such as Native Americans, Palestinians, and Asian Americans ourselves. Thus, our expressions of faith exist in a precarious state of being without any assurance of a glorious future. But those who embrace the amphibolous faith still *provisionally* insist and believe in "planting an apple tree even if the world comes to its end tomorrow." The pathos of amphibolous faith indelibly etches its mark on the life of Asian American Christians.

The amphibolous faith suggests that the alternative to an exclusive belief is not simply unbelief but a different kind of belief, one that embraces irresoluteness, disruption, and even uncertainty and yet enables the believer to respect that which we do not understand. In a complex world, wisdom is knowing that one does not really know for certain so that the believer can keep the future open with a provisional stance of faith as the only guide. The person of amphibolous faith longs, most of all, for bridge-building amidst disrupted and estranged relationships, bridge-building whose real meaning is an "interpretation of the worlds" through the grammar of amphiboly.

The Courage to Imagine Life as Others Live

What is needed today for reclaiming a societal coherence—that is, peoplehood—is the nurturing of another tongue, a second tongue, in order to have the courage to imagine life as others live it. As George Semaan, editor of the London-based Arabic language newspaper, *Al Hayat,* commented after the horrendous events of 9/11, the need for another tongue is to

> change [our] perspective on how [we] build [our] interests and now [we] defend them by building a network of relationships that take into consideration the interests of others who are weak and who have rights but are incapable of imposing these interests or these rights.[31]

In our increasingly diverse population, not only in terms of race, culture, and religion, but equally in terms of wealth, class, and power, we need a capacity to see life contrapuntally. "With the lives of the diverse characters starkly juxtaposed—in constant counterpoint...[to create] a world that offers both biting criticism and profound sympathy" says Edward Said.[32] Such a contrapuntal task for the renewal of peoplehood seeks mutual consideration of otherwise incongruent social, economic, and political practices of culture and of history with particular attention given to the practices, cultures, histories and faiths that have been neglected and undervalued. Amphibolous faith with its own epistemological view of the world provides a glimpse of such a counter-perspective of our collective life.

A new peoplehood may have a chance to be born in a world where another tongue is readily spoken, a tongue that welcomes an

---

[31] George Semaan, editor of the London-based Arabic-language newspaper, *Al Hayat,* in *The Christian Century* (September 26-October 3, 2001), 45.

[32] Edward Said, *Huxley's Point Counter Point Celebrates 75th Anniversary* (Center for Book Culture.org May 2003).

amphibolous faith in which eluding certainty becomes the value which propels us into action—especially in those contexts where exploitation of those on the underside of life is palpable. From this responsible reaction to the diminishment of fellow human beings, it is not difficult to perceive that amphiboly has its place. What is now needed is the commitment to allow our imaginations to transform our minds and hearts, inform our lips and hands, and inspire our thoughts and action so that an amphibolous faith is recognized and valued for what it offers: that *when we think we have grasped reality, whatever our intentions be, the reality passes through our minds, in front of us, eludes us and goes on its way.* The future of peoplehood may well be a gathering of all people who are on the way together.

Conclusion

The future of peoplehood in the United States speaks of what Ronald Takaki calls the creation of a "larger memory." His thoughts would probably also speak to Canadians to a certain extent:

> Our expanding ethnic diversity of this century, a time when we will all be minorities, offers us an invitation to create a larger memory of who we are as Americans and to reaffirm our founding principle of equality. Let's put aside fears of the "disuniting of America" and warnings of the "clash of civilizations." As Langston Hughes sang, "Let America be America, where equality is in the air we breathe."[33]

I believe that the creation of what Takaki terms as a "larger memory" in light of the divine presence in the world is a necessary task facing Asian North American theological construction. Theology is uniquely accountable to the past and to the future, not simply to the present. Theology encompasses both memory and hope. The creation of a larger memory is at the same time our pursuit of hope, or for Christians, our faith in and living out the signals of the promised humanity that was

---

[33] Ronald Takaki, 2001 WashingtonPost.com interview, quoted by Jeff Yang, "What does it mean to be Asian American?" SFGate, June 2, 2009.

revealed in the Christ event. Theological construction is about learning that molds a lifetime, learning that transmits the heritage of millennia, learning that shapes the future in light of this promise. Asian North American theological communities are stewards of this living tradition where learning and knowledge are pursued because they define what has over centuries made the faithful pursue a larger memory of who we are as human.

Chapter 2.

From Classical Tradition Maintenance to Remix *Traditioning*: Revisioning Asian American Theologies for the 21st Century

Jonathan Y. Tan

In this chapter, I would like to examine the implications of hybridities, multiple belongings, and multiple border crossings on Asian American theological reflections in twenty-first century United States. First, I would like to argue that early Asian American theologies emphasized the ideals of cohesive group identity and overarching intra-group consensus and harmony, while downplaying the challenges of hybridities and conflicts that are caused by emerging generational shifts from immigrant to American-born Asian Americans and multiple border crossings that arise from outmarriages and adoptions. Second, I would like to make the case that the essentialized categories of racial-ethnic and cultural identities have to be deconstructed and remixed in new keys and forms to address the implications of hybridities and multiple border crossings among the 1.5 generation and American-born Asians, bi/multiracial Asian Americans, and Asian adoptees. Third, I would like to propose that Asian American theologies move away from classical *tradition maintenance* to the creative remix of *traditioning*, i.e., from theologies that uncritically reinscribe the past to theologies as creative and dynamic endeavors that seek to address the multiplicity of heterogenized, hybridized, and conflicting constructions of faith and identity within a multidimensional daily living in a pluralistic society.

What is "Asian American"?

Before we proceed with our exploration, we need to be aware that the term "Asian American" is often used in contemporary discourse as a generic and convenient shorthand to categorize all Americans of Asian ancestry and heritage, with their diverse languages, cultures, and traditions. In so doing, the term "Asian American" masks distinct racial-ethic communities under the facade of a homogenous and monolithic pan-Asian American identity that exists more in theory than in reality. In truth, the category of "Asian Americans" encompasses groups of peoples of diverse languages, cultures, spiritual traditions, worldviews, socio-economic classes, and generational levels, such that all attempts at generalizations run the significant risk of error. Instead of viewing the Asian American identity in rigid and normative terms, perhaps this identity is better understood as diverse and multiple, constantly in flux and being shaped by, as well as shaping, historical, social, cultural, and political contexts. The Asian American scholar Lisa Lowe explains the implications of Asian American heterogeneity as follows:

> What is referred to as "Asian American" is clearly a heterogeneous entity. From the perspective of the majority culture, Asian Americans may very well be constructed as different from, and other than, Euro-Americans. But from the perspectives of Asian Americans, we are perhaps even more different, more diverse among ourselves. . . . As with other diasporas in the United States, the Asian immigrant collectivity is unstable and changeable, with its cohesion complicated by intergenerationality, by various degrees of identification and relation to a "homeland," and by different extent of assimilation to and distinction from "majority culture" in the United States.[1]

---

[1] Lisa Lowe, "Heterogeneity, Hybridity, Multiplicity: Marking Asian

More significantly, the label "Asian American" is a double-edged sword. On the one hand, it is a useful label to define a panethnic identity that serves to unite disparate ethnic Asian American communities under a common umbrella in contemporary sociopolitical discourse, giving them a united and collective voice vis-à-vis the dominant White mainstream. On the other hand, it is also problematic insofar as its categories break down when confronted with American-born, adoptees, and bi/multiracial Asian Americans who are the products of interracial marriages. Indeed, the presence of adoptees and bi/multiracial Asian Americans challenges the uncritical presumption of a normative, monolithic, and static notion of "Asianness." The incongruity arising from their presence serves as a reminder that identity is negotiated and constructed, neither given nor born, and neither static nor fixed. Are the American-born, adoptees, and bi/multiracial Asian Americans authentically Asian Americans? Would they be able to do authentic Asian American theological reflections? Are they legitimate subjects of Asian American theologizing?

Asian American Theologians and their Theologizing

The initial wave of Asian American theologians who emerged in the 1960s and 1970s were exclusively Japanese American, Korean American, and Chinese American men who carried out their theologizing from within mainline Protestant traditions and who also struggled from outside the mainstream theological establishment to challenge the entrenched racism and discrimination of mainstream U.S. society and Christian institutions. These theologians sought to address issues of race relations, faith and culture, and social justice with which the Japanese American, Korean American, and Chinese American communities were confronted.

In response to the challenges of their social location and the historic racial shifts that were occurring in the 1960s and 1970s, prominent early Asian American theologians such as Japanese American theologians Roy Sano,[2] Paul Nagano,[3] and Jitsuo Morikawa,[4] Korean

---

American Differences," *Diaspora* 1 (1991): 27.

American theologians Jung Young Lee[5] and Sang Hyun Lee,[6] and

---

[2] See Roy I. Sano, "Cultural Genocide and Cultural Liberation Through Amerasian Protestantism," in *The Theologies of Asian Americans and Pacific Peoples: A Reader*, comp. Roy I. Sano (Berkeley, California: Asian Center for Theology and Strategies, Pacific School of Religion, 1976), 28-50; "Ministry for a Liberating Ethnicity," in Ibid., 281-295; "Yes, We'll Have No More Bananas In Church," in Ibid., 51-54; "This Matter of Integration," in Ibid., 262-263; "The Church: One Holy Catholic and Apostolic," in Ibid., 264-280; "The Bible and Pacific Basin Peoples," in Ibid., 296-309; *From Every Nation Without Number: Racial and Ethnic Diversity in United Methodism* (Nashville, Tennessee: Abingdon Press, 1982); and "Shifts in Reading the Bible: Hermeneutical Moves Among Asian Americans," *Semeia* 90/91 (2002): 105-118.

[3] See Paul M. Nagano, "The Japanese Americans' Search for Identity, Ethnic Pluralism, and A Christian Basis of Permanent Identity," in Sano, *Theologies of Asian Americans and Pacific Peoples*, 225-253; "Biblical and Theological Statement For The Asian American Baptist Caucus," in Ibid., 450-456; "My Theological and Identity Odyssey," *Journal of Asian and Asian American Theology* 1 (1996): 4-9; and "A Japanese-American Pilgrimage: Theological Reflections," in *Journeys at the Margin: Toward an Autobiographical Theology in American-Asian Perspective*, eds. Peter C. Phan & Jung Young Lee (Collegeville, Minnesota: Liturgical Press, 1999), 63-79.

[4] See Jitsuo Morikawa, *My Spiritual Pilgrimage* (New York: Ministers and Missionaries Benefit Board of the American Baptist Churches, 1973) and "Toward an Asian American Theology," *American Baptist Quarterly* 12 (1993): 179-189.

[5] See Jung Young Lee, *A Theology of Change: A Christian Concept of God in Eastern Perspective* (Maryknoll, NY: Orbis Books, 1979); "Marginality: A Multi-Ethnic Approach to Theology from an Asian-American Perspective," *Asia Journal of Theology* 7 (1993): 244-53; *Marginality: The Key to Multicultural Theology* (Minneapolis: Fortress Press, 1995); *The Trinity in Asian Perspective* (Nashville, Tennessee: Abingdon Press, 1996); and "A Life In-Between: A Korean-American Journey," in Phan and Lee, *Journeys at the Margin*, 23-39.

[6] See Sang Hyun Lee, "Called to be Pilgrims: Toward a Theology Within the Korean American Context," in *The Korean Immigrant in America*, eds. Byong-suh Kim and Sang Hyun Lee (Montclair, NJ: Association of Korean Christian Scholars in North America, 1980), 37-74; "Called to be Pilgrims: Toward an Asian-American Theology from the Korean Immigrant Perspective," in *Korean American Ministry: A Resource Book*, ed. Sang Hyun Lee (Princeton: Princeton Theological Seminary, 1987), 90-120; "Korean American Presbyterians: A Need for Ethnic Particularity and the Challenge of Christian Pilgrimage," in *The Diversity of Discipleship: Presbyterians and Twentieth Century Christian Witness*, eds. Milton J. Coalter, John M. Mulder, and Louis B. Weeks (Louisville: Westminster/John Knox Press, 1991), 312-330; "How Shall

Chinese American theologians Wesley Woo[7] and David Ng[8] were very interested in issues of marginality and liminality that arose as a result of the racism and discrimination within the United States society in general and the United States church in particular. They challenged their White American counterparts about the ethnocentrism of U.S. Christianity and U.S. theologians. In their theological responses to the challenges posed by White American ecclesiastical and theological institutions, idealized and essentialized biological and cultural notions of what constituted "Asian" and "American" identities were commonly adopted by these early Asian American theologians to undergird their theological reflections. While these constructs proved useful to define and frame the

---

We Sing the Lord's Song in a Strange Land?" *Journal of Asian and Asian American Theology* 1 (1996): 77-81; "Pilgrimage and Home in the Wilderness of Marginality: Symbols and Context in Asian American Theology," in *Korean Americans and Their Religions: Pilgrims and Missionaries from a Different Shore*, ed. Ho-Youn Kwon, Kwang Chung-Kim, and R. Stephen Warner (University Park, Pennsylvania: Pennsylvania State University Press, 1996), 55-69; and "Marginality as Coerced Liminality: Toward an Understanding of the Context of Asian American Theology," in *Realizing the America of Our Hearts: Theological Voices of Asian Americans*, eds. Fumitaka Matsuoka and Eleazar S. Fernandez (St Louis, Missouri: Chalice Press, 2003), 11-28.

[7] See Wesley S. Woo, *The History of Pacific and Asian American Churches in Their Communities: Study Guide* (Berkeley: Pacific and Asian American Center for Theology and Strategies, 1977) and *Chinese American Christian Identity and Calling* (Berkeley: Pacific and Asian American Center for Theology and Strategies, 1979).

[8] See David Ng, "The Chinaman's Chances Are Improving," in Sano, *Theologies of Asian Americans and Pacific Peoples*, 153-155; *Developing Leaders for Youth Ministry* (Valley Forge, Pennsylvania: Judson Press, 1984); *Youth in the Community of Disciples* (Valley Forge, Pennsylvania: Judson Press, 1984); "Sojourners Bearing Gifts: Pacific Asian American Christian Education," in *Ethnicity in the Education of the Church*, ed. Charles R. Foster (Nashville, Tennessee: Scarritt Press, 1987), 7-23; "Working with Pacific Asian American families," in *Faith and Families: A Parish Program for Parenting In Faith Growth*, eds. Thomas Bright and John Roberto (New Rochelle, New York: Catholic Family Series, 1992), ch. 5; "Introduction," in *People on the Way: Asian North Americans Discovering Christ, Culture and Community*, ed. David Ng (Valley Forge, Pennsylvania: Judson Press, 1996), xv-xxix; "Varieties of Congregations or Varieties of People," in Ibid., 281-300; and "A Path of Concentric Circles: Toward an Autobiographical Theology of Community," in Phan and Lee, *Journeys at the Margin*, 81-102.

theological issues of assimilation, dislocation, and discrimination vis-à-vis the ethnocentrism of White American ecclesial and theological perspectives, it also unfortunately downplayed differences and particularities within Asian American realities that arise from generational differences between immigrant and American-born, and Asian Americans with hybridized identities.

Since the 1980s, American-born Asian Americans, feminist theologians, biblical scholars, Evangelical, Pentecostal, and Catholic thinkers, theologians from other Asian racial-ethnic communities, e.g., Filipino American, Vietnamese American, Thai American, Indian American are chiming in with their contributions, resulting in the emergence of an increasingly diversified and pluralistic range of creative and innovative Asian American theological approaches that seek to engage with church, community, and society at large. This has resulted in a broad range of diverse, complex, and nuanced theological reflections that belie easy categorization. Compared to the early Asian American theologies of the 1960s and 1970s which focused on issues of liberation and equality for Asian American Christians vis-à-vis their White Christian American counterparts, since the 1980s an increasing number of Asian American theologians have demonstrated a willingness to grapple with the ambiguities that emerge when the blurring of the boundaries is giving rise to an increasingly multivalent and complex intertwining of social, cultural, sexual, communal, and religious identities. What follows below is an introduction to a broad cross-section of emerging Asian American theologians whose theological contributions reveal the diversity and plurality of contemporary Asian American theologies.

For example, the Korean American theologian Andrew Sung Park's theological reflection on the aftermath of the 1992 Los Angeles riots that pitted Blacks against Korean Americans challenges the Korean American Christian community in Los Angeles to reexamine their own culpability in their attitudes toward Blacks. He goes on to articulate a theology of transmutation, i.e., a mutual cooperation, marked by mutual enrichment and mutual challenge, among the various racial groups in the United States amid much racial diversity. In the process of doing so, the challenges of racism and discrimination are overcome, interracial relations are strengthened, and past hurts and sufferings (i.e., *han*) of victims of racism and discrimination are healed.[9]

Similarly, the Japanese American biblical scholar Frank Yamada questions the uncritical privileging of essentialized notions of what constitutes "Asian American," arguing that identity constructions are shaped by forces of hybridity and heterogeneity. Specifically, he asserts that cultural identity for third and later generations of American-born Asian Americans is messy, complicated, and conflicting. He contends that Asian American theologians "must move beyond idealized and essentialist notions of culture" and a tendency to utilize the immigrant experience of marginality and liminality as normative of all Asian Americans to "emphasize particularity, contradiction, and complexity in order to counter oversimplified personifications of what constitutes Asian American."[10] In particular, Yamada insists that themes of marginality and liminality are based upon stable, essentialized notions of what it means to be Asian and American.[11] As a result, he stresses hybridity and heterogeneity over the essentialism, with the later generations breaking down fixed boundaries and "pure" notions of culture that earlier generations have uncritically assumed.[12]

The Asian American biblical scholars Mary Foskett and Henry Morisada Rietz have critiqued the essentialism of the category of "Asian American" in their theological reflections, especially with regard to the life experiences of Asian Americans who fall outside conventionally defined categories, challenging the uncritical privileging of certain

---

[9] See discussion in Andrew Sung Park, *Racial Conflict and Healing: An Asian-American Theological Perspective* (Maryknoll, N.Y.: Orbis Books, 1996); "Church and Theology: My Theological Journey," in Phan and Lee, *Journeys at the Margin*, 161-172; "A Theology of Transmutation," in *A Dream Unfinished: Theological Reflections on America from the Margins*, eds. Eleazar S. Fernandez and Fernando F. Segovia (Maryknoll, N.Y.: Orbis Books, 2001), 152-166; "A Theology of *Tao* (Way): Han, *Sin, and Evil*," in Matsuoka and Fernandez, *Realizing the America of Our Hearts*, 41-54; and *From Hurt to Healing: A Theology of the Wounded* (Nashville, Tennessee: Abingdon Press, 2004).

[10] See Frank M. Yamada, "Constructing Hybridity and Heterogeneity: Asian American Biblical Interpretation from a Third-Generation Perspective," in *Ways of Being, Ways of Reading: Asian American Biblical Interpretation*, ed. Mary F. Foskett and Jeffrey Kah-Jin Kuan (St Louis, Missouri: Chalice Press, 2006), 166.

[11] Ibid., 169.

[12] Ibid., 172-3.

biological traits that purport to define Asian American identity. In particular, they highlight the tension between the *biological* reproduction vis-à-vis *cultural* reproduction in the construction of Asian American communities, and challenge all Asian American theologians to confront the invisibility and double marginalization of Asian Americans who are adopted by White Americans (Foskett) and biracial and multiracial Americans with some Asian ancestry or heritage (Rietz).

In her essay entitled "The Accidents of Being and the Politics of Identity: Biblical Images of Adoption and Asian Adoptees in America,"[13] Foskett, an ethnic Chinese who was adopted by a White American family, explores the question of Asian American adoptees of White American families, an in-between group that has historically been ignored by Asian American community activists and theologians alike. According to Foskett, Asian American adoptees not only have to contend with the ambiguity and confusion of defining their identity, but also their invisibility and double marginalization to the wider Asian American communities. She rejects the essentialism of the category of "Asian American" that many Asian American theologians and scholars have taken for granted in their theological reflection, confronting headlong the tension between the biological reproduction vis-à-vis cultural reproduction in the construction of Asian American communities. In her rereading of Exodus 2:1-22 (Moses becoming the adopted son of an Egyptian princess), she offers a new vision of Moses' lost identity being replaced by a newly gained identity through his adoption by the Egyptian princess, as well as the bicultural socialization that resulted in him having to confront painful choices. By interpreting Moses' story as an adoptee's struggle to come to terms with his own identity and purpose in life, Foskett challenges Asian Americans to overcome their indifference toward the plight of Asian American adoptees in the United States and discover ways of defining Asian American identity without essentializing cultural and bloodline identities.

Similarly, in his autobiographical essay "My Father Has No Children: Reflections on a *Hapa* Identity Toward a Hermeneutic of Particularity,"[14] Henry Morisada Rietz focuses attention on himself as a

---

[13] *Semeia* 90/91 (2002): 135-144, cf. "Obscured Beginnings: Lessons from the Study of Christian Origins," in Foskett and Kuan, *Ways of Being*, 178-191.

[14] *Semeia* 90/91 (2002): 145-157; cf, "Living Past: A *Hapa* Identifying with

biracial *hapa-haole* who claims German and Japanese ancestries. Rietz acknowledges that his mixed heritage precludes him from claiming one specific identity completely, such that he is the "Other" to both Asian Americans and White Americans. He asserts that his *hapa* identity reveals the limitations of essentialism and homogeneity in Asian American identity constructions that are usually based on boundaries defined by the commonalities of the members, while at the same time accentuating their differences from biracial and multiracial Asian Americans who do not fit neatly into traditional constructions. In doing so, Rietz unmasks the painful tension between *inherited* (i.e., biological or "blood") reproduction and *constructed* reproduction. He challenges the privileged position of the former by articulating the controversial view that the Asian American identities could be *constructed* without reference to inherited biological ("blood") reproduction. As a solution, he proposes a new model of identity construction that is modeled on *differences* or *particularity* as the basis for community and communication, emphasizing that Asian American identities are not transmitted by inheritance, but shaped by the dynamic process of identity construction politics.

In other words, the increasing hybridity and heterogeneity in Asian America is exemplified not only by the increasing presence of Asians adoptees of White American families (as Foskett points out), but also by Asian Americans who outmarry and end up with bi/multiracial identities (as discussed by Rietz). Foskett and Rietz do not fit neatly into essentialized and clearly demarcated, biologically defined racial ethnic categories of Asian Americans. Indeed, Rietz's writings reveal that he considers himself both Asian and White American. Would that make him any less Asian or White American?

A handful of Asian American theologians, e.g., Kwok Pui-Lan,[15]

---

the Exodus, the Exile, and the Internment," in Foskett and Kuan, *Ways of Being*, 192-203.

[15] See Kwok Pui-Lan, "Asian and Asian American Churches," in *Homosexuality and Religion: An Encyclopedia*, ed. Jeffrey S. Siker (Westport, Connecticut: Greenwood Press, 2007), 59-62; "Finding Ruth a Home: Gender, Sexuality, and the Politics of Otherness," in Kwok Pui-Lan, *Postcolonial Imagination and Feminist Theology* (Louisville: Westminster John Knox Press, 2005), 100-21; and "Gay Activism in Asian and Asian-American Churches," *The Witness* 87/20 (May 21, 2004): 28.

Patrick Cheng,[16] You-Leng Leroy Lim,[17] Eric H. F. Law,[18] and Tat-Siong Benny Liew,[19] have begun reflecting theologically on the life experiences of, and challenges faced by, Queer Asian Pacific Americans (QAPAs). As the QAPA theologian Patrick Cheng explains, QAPAs face much pressure to conform to a heterosexual ideal of marriage and family life.[20] Another QAPA community activist, Eric Wat, points out that many Asian Americans view "being Asian and being gay as mutually exclusive," because being gay is "a white disease."[21] As a result, the tremendous suffering inflicted upon many QAPA youth by their own families and pastors often leads to suicidal thoughts, wishes, and acts.[22]

---

[16] See Patrick S. Cheng, *Radical Love: An Introduction to Queer Theology* (New York: Seabury, 2011); "Rethinking Sin and Grace for LGBT People Today," in *Sexuality and the Sacred*, Second Edition, eds. Marvin M. Ellison and Kelly Brown Douglas (Louisville: Westminster John Knox Press, 2010); "Reclaiming Our Traditions, Rituals, and Spaces: Spirituality and the Queer Asian Pacific American Experience," *Spiritus* 6/2 (Fall 2006): 234-40; "Unclean Spirits," *PersuAsian* 23 (Spring 2006): 27-28, 31; "Jesus Comes Out," *PersuAsian* 22 (Summer 2005): 23, 26-27; "Response, Roundtable Discussion: Same Sex Marriage," *Journal of Feminist Studies in Religion* 20/2 (Fall 2004): 103-07; "Multiplicity and Judges 19: Constructing a Queer Asian Pacific American Biblical Hermeneutic," *Semeia* 90/91 (2002): 119-33; and "Jesus, Mary, and the Beloved Disciple: Towards a Queer Asian American Christology" (M.A. thesis, Union Theological Seminary, 2001).

[17] See You-Leng Leroy Lim, "'The Bible Tells Me to Hate Myself': The Crisis in Asian American Spiritual Leadership," *Semeia* 90/91 (2002): 315-22; and "Webs of Betrayal, Webs of Blessings." in *Q&A: Queer in Asian America*, ed. David L. Eng and Alice Y. Hom (Philadelphia: Temple University Press, 1998), 323-334.

[18] See Eric H.F. Law, "A Spirituality of Creative Marginality," in *Que(e)rying Religion: A Critical Anthology*, ed. Gary David Comstock and Susan E. Henking (New York: Continuum, 1997), 343-46.

[19] See Tat-siong Benny Liew, "Queering Closets and Perverting Desires: Cross-Examining John's Engendering and Transgendering Word across Different Worlds," in *They Were All Together in One Place? Toward Minority Biblical Criticism*, ed. Randall C. Bailey, Tat-siong Benny Liew, and Fernando F. Segovia (Atlanta: Society of Biblical Literature, 2009), 251-88.

[20] Cheng, "Multiplicity and Judges 19," *Semeia* 90/91 (2002): 126-127.

[21] "Preserving the Paradox: Stories from a Gay-Loh," in *Asian American Sexualities: Dimensions of the Gay and Lesbian Experience*, ed. Russell Leong (New York: Routledge, 1996), 75.

[22] Lim, "Webs of Betrayal, Webs of Blessings," 328-31.

Not surprisingly, many QAPAs find it difficult, if not impossible, to come out to their parents and families about their sexual orientation, although they may have no problem coming out to their close friends.[23] It is ironic that when Asian American children come out of the closet, their families go into a closet to avoid stigmatization by their ethnic and church communities. Indeed, several Asian American ethnic heritage organizations and churches publicly campaigned in support of Proposition 8, which sought to amend the California State Constitution by adding a new section 7.5: "Only marriage between a man and woman is valid or recognized in California."

Nonetheless, QAPA community activists and their heterosexual supporters are coming forward to work for change in Asian American communities. For example, the Pacific, Asian, and North American Asian Women in Theology and Ministry (PANAAWTM) devoted its 2004 annual meeting to discussing sexual diversity and embodiment, with Asian American women sharing their coming out experiences and their struggles to be accepted by their families, congregations, and seminaries and panelists challenging churches to "rethink the meaning of marriage and to recognize the gifts gay, lesbian, bisexual, and transgender people bring to the church."[24]

The QAPA theologian Patrick Cheng has challenged the politics of dominant heterosexual privilege in Asian American communities and churches that seek to control and even eliminate the problematic Asian American identities of QAPAs. He compares the plight of QAPAs as "radical sexual and geographical outsiders" to the story of the unnamed concubine in Judges 19 who was gang-raped and dismembered, arguing that like the concubine, QAPAs are "radical sexual and geographical outsiders who experience multiplicity in a number of ways, including multiple naming, multiple silencing, multiple oppression, and multiple fragmentation."[25] As Cheng argues, QAPAs not only "remain outsiders, particularly in the theological academy,"[26] they also have to contend with

---

[23] See the extended discussion in Connie S. Chan, "Issues of Identity and Development among Asian-American Lesbians and Gay Men," in *Psychological Perspectives on Lesbian and Gay Male Experiences*, ed. Linda D. Garnets and Douglas C. Kimmel (New York: Columbia University Press, 1993).

[24] Kwok, "Gay Activism in Asian and Asian-American Churches."

[25] Cheng, "Multiplicity and Judges 19," 129.

[26] Ibid., 125.

the racism of the predominantly white queer community, e.g., the "'rice queens' within the white queer community who 'fetishize Asian men' and engage in the 'predatory consumption' of queer Asians as 'boy toys'," as well as the orientalism of many white queers who objectify QAPAs as the exotic "other."[27]

The Challenges of Globalization and Transnationalism

Several Asian American theologians have begun to address the implications of globalization, continuing im/migration, the growing presence of undocumented Asians in America, and growing transnational ties among Asian American communities in their theological reflections. For many Asian Americans, immigration is no longer a one-way street that entails an absolute, conclusive break from the old country, uprooting Asian immigrants and transplanting them in the United States. This paradigm shift from the absolute and unidirectional migration patterns of the past to the dynamic and multidirectional transnational movements of the present marks a momentous Copernican turn for Asian Americans, leading to a multiplicity of heterogenized, hybridized, and conflicting constructions of identity and relations in relation to the dominant White American mainstream.

Since the 1990s, transnationalism has emerged as a social phenomenon that has far-reaching implications for Asian Americans as they discover and define their identities. In an essay entitled "From International Migration to Transnational Diaspora,"[28] the Korean American sociologist John Lie asserts that the classic immigration narrative that the "sojourn of immigrants entails a radical, and in many cases a singular, break from the old country to the new nation," leading to their uprooting and "shorn of premigration networks, cultures, and belongings," is no longer tenable or viable in view of a world that is becoming increasingly global and transnational.[29] As an alternative, he invites his colleagues to focus on transnational movements and networks:

---

[27] Ibid., 126.
[28] John Lie, "From International Migration to Transnational Diaspora," *Contemporary Sociology* 24/4 (1995): 303-306.
[29] Ibid., 303.

> It is no longer assumed that immigrants make a sharp break from their homelands. Rather, pre-immigration networks, cultures and capital remain salient. The sojourn itself is neither unidirectional nor final. Multiple, circular and return migrations, rather than a singular great journey from one sedentary space to another, occur across transnational spaces. People's movements, in other words, follow multifarious trajectories and sustain diverse networks.[30]

As he explains, new advances in transportation and communication also subvert the "unidirectionality of migrant passage; circles, returns, and multiple movements follow the waxing and waning structures of opportunities and networks."[31]

More importantly, the rapid convergence of the forces of globalization, affordable international air travel, advanced telecommunications and broadband technology means migration is no longer a one-way departure from birth country to adopted country. Instead of a permanent boundary crossing that ruptures the ties with one's birth country, many immigrants and their descendants are increasingly engaging in *multiple border crossings* between two or more locations either physically (e.g., by air travel) or virtually (e.g., using cheap international telephone calls, e-mail, instant messaging, or VOIP technology), initiating and nurturing transnational networks with extended families, clans, business partners, and friends.

On the one hand, many people often equate Asian American transnationalism with education, wealth, and privilege. For example, Aihwa Ong's classic study on the transnationalism of diasporic Chinese communities dealt with middle- and upper-class Chinese who could afford to move back and forth between locations.[32] But on the other hand, Kenneth Guest's ethnographical study of Fuzhounese Chinese in New York's Chinatown highlights the fact that many *undocumented*

---

[30] Ibid., 304.
[31] Ibid., 305.
[32] Aihwa Ong, *Flexible Citizenship: The Cultural Location of Transnationality* (Durham, North Carolina: Duke University Press, 1999).

Fuzhounese who were smuggled into the United States by "snakeheads," finding themselves "systematically marginalized in the United States, discriminated against because of their economic skills, legal status, language, and even ethnicity," turn to transnational activities in order to "build identities that transcend their dead-end jobs, their transient lifestyles, and their local marginalization."[33] Guest's groundbreaking study debunks the commonly held view[34] that Chinese transnationalism is characteristic of middle- and upper-class Chinese who possess the economic resources to live, work, and travel in different places. In Guest's words:

> For the majority of the Fuzhounese, their transnationalism is much more nascent, grassroots, and fragile; an ocean-borne transnationalism of the working poor, not the jet-set transnationalism of the elite. Unlike the transnational entities so often discussed that transcend the state, most Fuzhounese immigrants mobilize small-scale transnational networks from a position deep within and vulnerable to state structures. As workers, many of them undocumented, they are disciplined by economy and state alike. ... Through these [transnational] networks, they seek to transcend regulated national boundaries and construct broader notions of citizenship and participation. They utilize their emerging transnational religious networks to articulate an alternative existence and identity in the fact of the homogenizing influences of global capitalism and the U.S. labor market. Their participation in the life of their home communities – encouraged, facilitated, and

---

[33] Kenneth Guest, "Religion and Transnational Migration in the New Chinatown," in *Immigrant Faiths: Transforming Religious Life in America*, eds. Karen I. Leonard, Alex Stepick, Manuel A. Vasquez, and Jennifer Holdaway (Lanham, Maryland: AltaMira Press, 2005), 159. Cf. Kenneth Guest, *God in Chinatown: Religion and Survival in New York's Evolving Immigrant Community* (New York: New York University Press, 2003).

[34] See the discussions in Aihwa Ong and Donald Nonini, eds., *Ungrounded Empires: The Cultural Politics of Modern Chinese Transnationalism* (New York: Routledge, 1997) and Aihwa Ong, *Flexible Citizenship*.

rewarded through religious networks – assists in creating and enhancing a transnational identity which may in fact serve as an alternative to immigrant incorporation in the host society.[35]

As Asian Americans cross the threshold of the twenty-first century, they are increasingly developing transnational networks beyond the United States to their ancestral countries or elsewhere, constructing new identities and maintaining close ties that transcend national boundaries. They are able to build and nurture familial, socio-cultural, economic, political, and religious bonds with their ancestral lands with relative ease, rather than breaking away and seeking assimilation into an aspirational lifestyle defined by White Americans. This is true not just of Asian-born Americans, but also second and later generations of American-born Asians who are rejecting uncritical assimilation and searching for identity in the midst of their ancestral roots. As a result, there is a blurring of boundaries between geographic space on the one hand, and social and experiential space on the other. Instead of a linear Asian American identity, we are now confronted with a hybridized, nuanced, and multidimensional transnational Asian American identities that are simultaneously rooted in the United States while reaching out and becoming attached to other social, familial, and religious contexts in Asia.

In turn, these transnational developments mean that Asian Americans are no longer interested or willing to give up their ethnic identity by complete assimilation. Instead, we find Asian Americans becoming creative and adept at negotiating multiple belongings and loyalties, developing a hybridized sense of belonging simultaneously to the United States as well as countries that they or their forebears have left. For example, many Vietnamese Americans display both the Stars and Stripes and the South Vietnamese flags with pride in Little Saigon communities, remit money home to their extended family or clan in Vietnam, and travel back and forth between Vietnam and the United States, forging and renewing deep-rooted familial and kinship ties. In a similar vein, Korean Americans joyously celebrate both Korean and

---

[35] Guest, "Religion and Transnational Migration in the New Chinatown," 160, 161.

United States holidays, while an increasing number of third-, fourth-, and fifth generation Chinese Americans and Japanese Americans are learning their ancestral languages and cultures.

These transnational developments have significant implications for understanding the present situation and future directions of Asian American Christianity. Indeed, contemporary scholars of religion are increasingly emphasizing the important roles that religion plays in shaping and maintaining transnational ties and networks. Kenneth Guest's ethnographic study of undocumented Fuzhounese in New York's Chinatown reveals, among other things, the deep involvement of Chinese American Churches in nurturing transnational networks between China and the United States for undocumented Fuzhounese immigrants.[36] Fenggang Yang's research on Chinese American Evangelical Churches reveals how they are forging multiple transnational ties with churches and parachurch organizations in Mainland China, Taiwan, and the wider Chinese Diaspora.[37] Thao Ha's study on Vietnamese Catholics and Buddhists in Houston focuses attention on the institutional dimensions of the transnational relations that these Vietnamese temples and churches have forged with their counterparts in Vietnam.[38]

As a result, second generation Asian American theologians are moving beyond idealized and essentialized notions of identity and culture to reflect critically on conflict, particularity, and hybridity, and how these notions affect and shape their theological endeavors. They realize that bipolar dichotomies such as insider-outsider, homeland-host country, center-margin, and so forth are no longer tenable. While it is easy to challenge these uncritical bipolar constructs today, we must realize that these constructs made perfect sense for first generation Asian American theologians who were dealing with issues of assimilation, dislocation, and discrimination. In their minds, they were fighting for Asian Americans to get their rightful positions and entitlements in church and society. With the benefit of hindsight, we now see that this uncritical

---

[36] Guest, *God in Chinatown*, 201-206.

[37] Fenggang Yang, "Chinese Christian Transnationalism: Diverse Networks of a Houston Church," in *Religions Across Borders: Transnational Immigrant Networks*, ed. Helen Rose Ebaugh and Jane Saltzman Chafetz (Walnut Creek, California: AltaMira Press, 2002), 129-148.

[38] Thao Ha, "The Evolution of Remittances from Family to Faith," in Ebaugh and Chafetz, *Religions Across Borders*, 111-128.

assimilationist perspective presumed not only a stable and normative view of identity construct, but also the presumption that rights and privileges of White Americans were the ideals of the "American Dream" that they should aspire to, without challenging their inequities and other exploitative or questionable aspects.

From Tradition Maintenance to Traditioning

How do Asian American theologians go beyond essentialist and normative views of Asian cultural traditions and heritage to include the concerns, hopes, and dreams of the 1.5 generation and American born Asians, the bi/multiracial Asian Americans, and Asian American adoptees? In response, I would like to propose that contemporary Asian American theologies move away from *tradition-maintenance* in favor of what I would call *traditioning*. By *tradition-maintenance*, I mean clinging on to ethnic-bound traditions and customs from the "Old World" at all costs. I define *traditioning* as the largely unconscious and ongoing process of shaping, constructing, and negotiating new traditions and practices that seek to address the issues and questions confronting all Asian Americans, be they immigrant, American-born, bi/multiracial, or adoptees. On the one hand, *tradition-maintenance* is akin to a classical symphony in that both emphasize the ideals of overarching group harmony and unity subsuming differences. On the other hand, I see *traditioning* as comparable to *remixing* that is transforming the contemporary music scene, i.e., both *traditioning* and *remixing* challenge and deconstruct essentialized categories, theological and musical, yet reshaping them in new keys and forms. As the contemporary musical scene shifts away from the ahistorical essentialism of the classical symphony to embrace the creativity and dynamism of remixing, so too Asian American theologies are shifting away from *tradition-maintenance* of age-old cultural ideals to creative *traditioning*, giving birth to new theological insights that address contemporary concerns.

The theological process of *traditioning* is not something completely new. Other theologians such as Dale Irvin,[39] Simon Chan,[40]

---

[39] Dale Irvin, *Christian Histories, Christian Traditioning: Rendering Accounts* (Maryknoll, N.Y.: Orbis Books, 1998).

Amos Yong,[41] Orlando Espin,[42] Nancy Pineda-Madrid,[43] Theresa Torres,[44] and Carmen Nanko-Fernandéz[45] have reflected about various aspects of *traditioning* in other contexts in their theological writings. For example, the Singaporean Chinese theologian Simon Chan observes that *traditioning* ensures that the Pentecostal faith tradition is handed down to a new generation "in a way that *takes account of the new context of a new generation of faithful.*"[46] In the context of Latino/a pastoral ministry, Carmen Nanko-Fernandéz observes that *traditioning* is an ongoing process that not only "occurs in the daily and is integral to the process of constructing identity, personally and collectively," but also requires "a habit of learning how to read across contexts in order to avoid absolutizing or universalizing the particular."[47] Hence, the process of *traditioning* is based upon the premise that tradition is not fixed and static, but rather, it is dynamic, always changing, and deeply contextual.

More importantly, *traditioning* rejects all attempts at fossilizing or archaizing the present in a state of theological *stasis*, as well as challenging any notion that theologizing is ahistorical, atemporal, and independent of sociocultural changes. Instead, *traditioning* entails critical

---

[40] Simon Chan, *Pentecostal Theology and the Christian Spiritual Tradition* (London: Sheffield Academic Press, 2000).

[41] Amos Yong, *Spirit-Word-Community: Theological Hermeneutics in a Trinitarian Perspective* (Burlington, Vermont: Ashgate, 2002).

[42] Orlando Espin, "Traditioning: Culture, Daily Life and Popular Religion, and their impact on Christian Tradition," in *Futuring Our Past: Explorations in the Theology of Tradition*, eds. Orlando O. Espin and Gary Macy (Maryknoll, N.Y.: Orbis Books, 2006), 1-22.

[43] Nancy Pineda-Madrid, "Traditioning: The Formation of Community, the Transmission of Faith," in *Futuring Our Past*, 204-226.

[44] Theresa L. Torres, "La Quinceañera: Traditioning and the Social Construction of the Mexican American Female," in *Futuring Our Past*, 277-298.

[45] See Carmen Nanko-Fernandéz, "Traditioning latinamente: A Theological Reflection on la lengue cotidiana," unpublished paper; "Language, Community and Identity," in *Handbook of Latino/a Theologies*, eds. Edwin Aponte & Miguel de la Torre (St Louis, Missouri: Chalice Press, 2006), 265-275; and "Handing on Faith en su propia lengua," in Carmen Nanko-Fernandéz, *Theologizing en Espanglish: Context, Community, and Ministry* (Maryknoll, N.Y.: Orbis Books, 2010), 61-76.

[46] Chan, *Pentecostal Theology*, 20, emphasis added.

[47] Nanko-Fernandéz, "Traditioning latinamente: A Theological Reflection on la lengue cotidiana."

theological reflections about a community's present and future. By going beyond mere replication of historical theological precedents, *traditioning* seeks to retell, reinterpret, and give nuance to one's theological reflections with new layers of meaningfulness that address the concerns of the present context. *Traditioning* also pursues strategic, dynamic, creative, and contextualized interpretations of the Christian Gospel, mediating between historical theological precedents and current concerns, thereby endeavoring to create a coherent theology that unites the rich legacy of historical theological precedents with contemporary needs and challenges.

In other words, *traditioning* is dynamic and flexible. It is open to life realities, as well as healthy theological renewal and change that are integral to a community's social location and context, while remaining "in conversation with the past." Rather than looking for a single normative and essentialistic meaning in theologizing, *traditioning* seeks hybridized and multiple *meaningfulness*, embodying and integrating differences and consensus, past and present, precedent and innovation, and authority and creativity, thereby facilitating the articulation of new meanings for the present and future. As a result, the theological tradition is constantly being renegotiated, renewed, and given nuance.

Conclusion: Asian American Theologies as Traditioning Theologies

I see *traditioning* as enabling Asian American theologians to mediate contradictions that arise from multiple subjectivities that Asian Americans constantly negotiate in their daily lives as they grapple with fragmented selves and mixed allegiances to many places, spaces, persons, and groups, all of which generate intersecting subjectivities, hybridities, and heterogeneous identifications. In addition, *traditioning* provides the impetus for Asian American theological reflections to be dynamic, situational, and strategic, differentiating between elements, as well as privileging the faith development of "a new generation of faithful." Through the process of *traditioning*, Asian American theologians are able to engage in, nuance, and redefine theologies in a creative, strategic, flexible, and innovative manner to empower Asian Americans in their effective engagement with the joys and pathos of the postmodern conditions of their daily living, helping them to engage with the world around them where they are constantly being reminded that they are out of line and not wanted, or at best, tolerated.

Part Two

Sight (Site) Reading:
Voicing Our Songs of
Laments, Struggles, and Hopes

Chapter 3.

Revisiting the Question Concerning (Theological) Contextualization

Lester Edwin J. Ruiz

Situating Contextualization

Essentially, contextualization, particularly *theological* contextualization exercised under the sign of Christianity, is concerned with how the Gospel and culture—broadly and contingently conceived—relate to one another across space, time, and place. By definition, as much as in practice, contextualization cannot be extricated from the diversity and plurality of personal, political, historical, and sacred being that marks human experience.

Biblically, theologically, and pastorally, the metaphor for contextualization is not only the Incarnation but also *Kenosis*.

However, if the reader expects to find this essay engaging directly in theological contextualization, he or she will be disappointed. While important, that task is currently beyond my competence or interest. Mine is a more modest goal, at least in this essay: that is, to "revisit" the *question* concerning contextualization, by which I mean simply identifying those issues with which one ought to be concerned if one wishes to embark on a project of theological contextualization adequate to the present world situation. In fact, the title of this essay is a play on Martin Heidegger's reflection on technology, in which he explored "the conditions of understanding" under the dispensation of (technological) being. The connection with this essay is suggestive, if not metaphorical, but methodologically congenial: what are the conditions under which theological contextualization is being done today?—hence, the title of this essay, "the question concerning contextualization."

Stephen Bevans' four models of contextualization: translation, anthropological, praxis, and synthetic—provide a useful theoretical occasion for revisiting the question concerning contextualization. In fact, Bevans may be read as pointing to at least four underlying, inextricably-related characteristics of contextualization. First, contextualization is always and already an act of interpretation that combines thinking, feeling, and acting—involving speculative and practical forms of reason as well as desire; it is not mere cogitation. Second, contextualization is inextricably related to transformation, the creation and nurture of the fundamentally new, which is also fundamentally better.[1] Third, contextualization is almost always an event of competence: it has structure, process, and (human) agency. And finally, contextualization, particularly *theological* contextualization, is unavoidably "locational/positional." Here, "the local" is not so much a question of "origin" or "trajectory" but a "site" of engagement; and "position" is not exclusively "subjective" but comprehensively "discursive" (an apparatus or *dispositif*, if you will)—both always and already intimately related to how one encounters the multistranded diversities and pluralities of space, time, and place—not unlike what Foucault called a "practice."[2]

---

[1] Manfred Halpern, translated by David Abalos, *Transforming the Personal, Political, Historical and Sacred in Theory and Practice* (Scranton: University of Scranton Press, 2009).

[2] Situated in the context of a post-positivist, post-empiricist, post-structuralist tradition, I deploy the term "practice" much in the same way Michel Foucault used the term dispositive—"a resolutely heterogeneous assemblage, containing discourses, institutions, architectural buildings, reglementary decisions, scientific statements, philosophical, moral, philanthropic propositions… said as well as non-said…" to signify the delightful and frustrating entanglements between "theory" (speculative reason) and "praxis" (practical reason), and their interplay with the personal, the political, the historical, and the sacred—in the service of transformation. See Michel Foucault, ed., Colin Gordon, "The Confession of the Flesh," in *Power/Knowledge: Selected interviews and other writings* (New York: Pantheon, 1980), 194-228.

In the Asian context, not excluding the Asian Diaspora, contextualization has been a vital part of the theological landscape. Thinkers including Shoki Coe, M.M. Thomas, D.T. Niles, Emerito Nacpil, Kosuke Koyama, and C.S. Song, as well as Virginia Fabella, Marianne Katoppo, and Maryjohn Mananzan, have pioneered what Huang Po Ho has called a "Contextual Theology movement in Asia." In my own generation, we saw *Minjung* theology from Korea, Homeland theology and Theology of *Chhut Thau Thin* from Taiwan, theologies of struggle from the Philippines, and theologies of religion from India. Institutions like The Commision on Theological Concern of the Christian Conference of Asia, the Program for Theology and Cultures in Asia (PTCA), the Ecumenical Association of Third World Theologians (EATWOT), the Asian Church Women's Conference (ACWC), and, the Association for Theological Education in South East Asia (ATESEA)—all may be understood as part of this vital movement. From the Asian Diaspora one might include the post-positivist, post-empiricist, post-colonial work of Eleazar Fernandez, Kwok Pui Lan, Tat-siong Benny Liew, and R. S. Sugirtharajah.

The *Asianist* contribution to the larger work of theological contextualization cannot be underestimated. Indeed, anyone who may be interested in developing both a "general" theory and "specific" practice of contextualization cannot evade having to engage these movements in (geographical) Asia and its Diaspora. As I will argue in this essay, however, one's location and positionality are decisive, not to mention constitutive, not only in the selection of the manner in which one engages with these movements but also in the choices both of conversation partners and substantive, methodological, metathereotical, and political/institutional problems. To put the matter simply, if polemically, being an *Asian-in-Diaspora* by choice, it would be the height of *hubris* to even begin to engage these "Asian" discourses from my current location because of the difficulties of representation implicated in the asymmetries of power, privilege, and access between the global south and the global north, as well as the very real limits of one's capacity to understand or evaluate the competing or even incommensurable claims made by these *Asianist* thinkers. Less important, but by no means inconsequential, is that I am not entirely convinced that the production and reproduction of *new* knowledge where theological contextualization is concerned must necessarily travel the pathways of these pioneering works. A fuller, transdisciplinary, trans-*Asianist* engagement with different, if not wider global contexts, seems to be an equally important "conditionality" for articulating a more robust understanding of theological contextualization. This is where I intentionally locate myself.[3]

The Context of Contextualization

Location, Positionality, Critique: The Methodological Importance of "Fallibility"

My own understanding of theological contextualization, first and foremost, is shaped fundamentally by my own context, where my location and positionality require an acknowledgement of the methodological importance of "fallibility" for understanding.

The intellectual production, reproduction, and representation in which I am engaged, as much as it may desire the sublime, is still the discourse of a privileged male *flaneur*, if not *bricoleur*, however personally innocent—and even though I might aspire towards a Gramscian "organic intellectual." Michel Foucault observes that because *all* intellectual work is a passage through privilege, it is fraught with both dangers and possibilities: dangers because, on the one hand, we are a species marked not only by reason, or by freedom, but also by error; and, on the other hand, possibilities because the history of thought read as a critical philosophy appreciative of "fallibility" can become a "history of trials, an open-ended history of multiple visions and revisions, some more enduring than others."[4]

Contextualization, in fact, is such a form of production, reproduction, and representation. Here, recognition of location, not to

---

[3] A more systematic discussion of my perspective can be found in Lester Edwin J. Ruiz, "Recovering the "Body Politics": When the Question of "Race" and Power Migrates" in Dietrich Werner, David Esterline, Namsoon Kang, Joshva Raja, eds. *Handbook of Theological Education in World Christianity: Theological Perspectives, Ecumenical Trends, Regional Surveys* (Oxford: Regnum Books International, 2010), 85-103.

[4] James D. Faubion, ed., *Michel Foucault: Aesthetics, Method and Epistemology, Essential Works of Foucault*, vol. 2 (New York: The New Press, 1998), 476.

mention positionality and maneuver, is not only politically necessary given the radical plurality of human history; it is also methodologically decisive for the production and reproduction of knowledge as a passage to transformation.

The affirmation of self-critical accountability rests in no small measure on an affirmation of the necessity of a kind of contextualization that is constantly challenged by what in my earlier work, following many of Latin American theologians of liberation, I called the "hermeneutical privilege of the poor and oppressed," but which, I now want to argue, is unavoidably shaped, not to mention *inspired*, by the "hermeneutical *significance* of the victim."

Jacques Derrida notes that a "victim" is "one who cannot even protest... [who] cannot even identify the victim as victim... [who] cannot even present himself or herself as such. He or she is totally excluded or covered over by language, annihilated by history." [5] Derrida goes on to note that being a "victim" involves a certain kind of

> unreadability that stems from the violence of foreclosure, exclusion, all of history being a conflictual field of forces in which it is a matter of making unreadable, excluding, of positing by excluding, of imposing a dominant force by excluding... not only by marginalizing, by setting aside the victims, but also by doing so in such a way that no trace remains of the victims, so that no one can testify to the fact that they are victims or so that they cannot even testify to it themselves.[6]

Derrida invokes the image of "cinders" which is a "trope that comes to take the place of everything that disappears without leaving an identifiable trace." The difference between the trace "cinder" and other traces, according to Derrida, is that the body of which cinders is the trace has totally disappeared; it has totally lost its contours, its form, its colors, its natural termination; it can no longer be identified, and forgetting itself is forgotten.[7]

---

[5] Jacques Derrida, *Points...: Interviews, 1974-1994*, ed. Elizabeth Weber (Stanford: Stanford University Press, 1995), 387-391.
[6] Ibid.
[7] Ibid.

I am convinced that one of the religio-moral dimensions, not to mention challenges, of the *project* of contextualization today is not only the discovery of how contextualization is embodied and/or situated but also the clarification of where the *hope* that animates it lies. It is particularly critical to explore this embodiment and hope in the context of this forgetfulness of victimization—something which Gayatri Spivak very early on explored in her thoughtful piece, "Can the Subaltern speak?" We need not only to find again the power of a transformative philosophy of contextualization but also to articulate the conditions of its possibility as a transformative practice. It is not only important to proclaim the legitimacy of the struggles of the marginalized and excluded against their victimization, but also to nurture and defend their struggles as the expression of their hope, not only for liberation but for *liberative* meaning, significance, and change. At the same time, it is critical to be mindful that while these expressions, at their best, are ruptures in the geographies of tradition that give birth to our own desires for contextualization, our own responses, at their worst, often colonize the struggles and hopes to which the marginalized, the excluded, and the victims aspire. In other words, how "fallibility" becomes methodologically necessary for theological contextualization, is a task to which one must always attend.

Moreover, part of what is at stake is finding new and better languages for struggle and hope (which is part of the discursive strategies of contextualization) which give birth to new and better understandings and practices of contextualization. Both the context of and challenge for contextualization is to move towards the cultivation of what Foucault long ago called the "(insurrection of) subjugated knowledges"— discursive strategies and formations that have been conceptually, historically, philosophically, and institutionally excluded or eclipsed from theorizing heretofore—in the hope that they will contribute to both new knowledge, practice and discursive proximity.[8] Here, genealogy yields to cartography, by which I mean the strategic deployment of local knowledges, the goal of which is to illumine, if not understand, alternative pathways to biblical, theological, and pastoral practice.

---

[8] Michel Foucault, *"Society Must be Defended": Lectures at the College de France, 1975-1976*, trans. David Macey (New York: Picador, 2003), 7.

Diaspora, Global Capital (or Empire), and Strangeness

Second, my understanding of theological contextualization is shaped fundamentally by my historical experience of Diaspora, global capital, or empire as the formative grounds for strangeness, which is a condition of possibility for contextualization.

In his analysis of modern international politics and global capitalism, Michael Dillon notes that states as regimes of sovereignty and governmentality together with transnational capitalism and the environmental degradation of the planet have not only rendered millions of people radically endangered strangers in their own homes, but have criminalized or anathemized them in the places to which they have been forced to seek refuge. The modern international state system, in fact, is a *panopticon* of manufactured estrangement.[9]

In the Philippine context, this estrangement is clearly demonstrated by the migration of Filipinos, today numbering over ten million, to other parts of the planet. Such migration is characterized not only by dispersal, displacement, and dislocation,[10] but also of what Nikos Papastergiadis has innovatively and insightfully called, turbulence, suggesting by its use not mere motion, activity, or movement, but disruptive, unpredictable, volatile speed.[11]

---

[9] Michael Dillon, "Sovereignty and Governmentality: From the Problematics of the 'New World Order' to the Ethical Problematic of the World Order" *Alternatives: Social Transformation and Humane Governance* 20/3 (Spring 1995), 323-368.

[10] Epiphanio San Juan, "Fragments from a Filipino Exile's Journal," *Amerasia Journal* 23/2 (Winter 1997): 1-25. See also Jonathan Okamura, *Imagining the Filipino American Diaspora: Transnational Relations, Identities, and Communities* (New York: Garland Publishing, Inc., 1998); Oscar Campomanes, "The New Empire's Forgetful and Forgotten Citizens: Unrepresentability and Unassimilability in Filipino-American Postcolonialities," *Critical Mass* 2: 2 (Winter 1995): 145-200. Cf. Epiphanio San Juan, Jr., "Configuring the Filipino Diaspora in the United States," *Diaspora* 3/2 (Winter 1994): 117-133; Epiphanio San Juan, *From Exile to Diaspora: Versions of the Filipino Experience in the United States* (Boulder: Westview Press, 1998).

[11] Nikos Papastergiadis, *The Turbulence of Migration: Globalization, Deterritorialization, and Hybridity* (Cambridge: Polity Press, 2000), 3-21. See Avtar Brah, *Cartographies of Diaspora: Contesting Identities* (New York: Routledge, 1996).

Moreover, the experience of "Diaspora" is not only about the dispersal, displacement, and dislocation of those "outside" the homeland. In fact, Diaspora dissolves not only the geopolitical, geostrategic, and territorial boundaries of "inside" and "outside," but also their epistemological and ontological foundations. The Filipino Diaspora today is emblematic of a more comprehensively human condition that has produced new forms of belonging and identity as well as novel understandings of contemporary politics and culture. Diaspora evokes and provokes images of "border crossings" as well as invasions, of estrangements as well as of hybridities. It reveals global de-territorializing trajectories as well as local re-territorializing surges or insurgencies, especially under the conditions of transnational capital.[12] Diaspora underscores contradictions and antagonisms, while intensifying the asymmetries of political, economic, and cultural structures and processes."[13]

The reality of "Diaspora" also raises a question not only about subjecthood, but also about subjectivity. This is the question of "the Subject:" not only who the subject is, but also what being a subject entails.[14] The contested plurality of subjects and subjectivities presupposed by a "Diaspora" directs us not only to the question "What is to be done?" but also to the questions of "Who we are, what we hope for, and where we go?" In short, "What does it mean to be a people under the conditions of turbulent, volatile dispersal, displacement, and dislocation?" Posing the issue as a question of community places theological contextualization at the heart of the struggles for transformation and in the context of the "hermeneutical significance of the victim."

The reality of "Diaspora" also identifies the locus of struggle and hope at the intersection of self, other, and world. Of no small methodological and political significance, locating the question at the nexus of a peoples' cultural practices—defined broadly as those concrete, sensuous realities embodied in rhetorical forms, gestures,

---

[12] Ibid.

[13] Nevzat Soguk, *States and Strangers: Refugees and Displacements of Statecraft* (Minneapolis: University of Minnesota Press, 1999).

[14] Eduardo Cadava, Peter Connor, and Jean-Luc Nancy, eds., *Who Comes after the Subject?* (New York: Routledge, 1991).

procedures, modes, shapes, genres of everyday life: discursive formations and/or strategies, if you will, which are radically contingent arenas of imagination, strategy, and creative maneuver[15]—not only challenges the narrow confines of conventional understandings of struggle and hope, but also foregrounds their most comprehensive point of departure: a peoples' pluralistic, and therefore always and already contradictory, antagonistic and agonistic histories, which are expressed in their stories, songs, poetry, and arts; embodied in their political struggles; and articulated in their economic institutions. Another way of stating the point is to suggest that "Diaspora" ruptures the pretensions of modernity's appetite for intellectual idealism as the unitary foundation for human thought and action and re-positions them as articulations of the "interstitial."[16]

It is here that the "nativist" temptation is most forcefully raised. The work of scholars like Kwok Pui Lan and Tat-Siong Benny Liew, in fact, may be interpreted as suggesting that contextualization needs to move through its *Asianist*, if not Asian-*centric* pre-occupations, to engage with a radically-extended notion of "Asian" which goes beyond a homogenous or unitary notion arising not only out of its multistranded contexts, but also will have multiple, intersectional accounts: biological, cultural, psychic, and political.[17] This abbreviated, admittedly oversimplified, summary of the "nativist" temptation that assumes a somewhat geographically-essentialist understanding of "the Asian" describes the fundamental divide between the proponents of "Asian as social construction" and the proponents of "Asian as biology" that continues to cast its long, if epistemologically-flawed, shadow on present-day discourses on contextualization. Moreover, it suggests that the discussion on contextualization cannot be extricated from socio-historical and physicalist/geographical considerations of "the Asian,"

---

[15] Michael Ryan, *Politics and Culture: Working Hypotheses for a Post Revolutionary Society* (Baltimore: Johns Hopkins University Press, 1989).

[16] See Avta Brah and Ann Phoenix, "Ain't I a Woman? Revisiting Intersectionality," *Journal of International Women's Studies* 5:3 (2004): 75-86.

[17] As Brah and Phoenix note, the concept of intersectionality signifies "the complex, irreducible, varied, and variable effects which ensue when multiple axis [sic] of differentiation—economic, political, cultural, psychic, subjective and experiential—intersect in historically specific contexts" (76). Diaspora is such a reality.

precisely because the perspectives noted previously rely on *Asianist* (read racialized) physical, morphological, and geographical traits assumed to be "ontologically-different." It also points to ongoing discussions, as in the work of Kwok, Liew, and Fernandez, that the notion of "Asian" not only continues to change over time, but also that contextualization (in the Asian context) may be more productively understood by the "effects" of this "contingent Asian" rather than by its already established conceptually-dominant definitions—hence, the methodological importance of "Diaspora."

If "Diaspora" is the geographic/strategic condition of contextualization, then the strangeness that it creates is its methodological occasionality, alongside the Stranger—the Other—who embodies such strangeness, which is its methodological and religio-moral challenge. For indeed, "Diaspora," as a creature of both modernity and postmodernity,[18] methodologically radicalizes the experience of the Stranger or of Otherness in our time, and the existence of the Stranger in our midst raises for us the problems, prospects, and possibilities of both fundamentally new and better forms of knowledge and being, as well as of their interpretations. Similarly, strangeness, not to mention marginalization, it seems, is a condition of possibility both for community and interpretation: it is its constitutive outside. At the same time, if the Stranger is the constitutive *outside*, then its constitutive *inside* is hospitality. Because hospitality—the inclusion of the Stranger into a community not originally his or her own—is that which "arrives at the borders, in the initial surprise of contact with an other, a stranger, a foreigner"[19] it ruptures the boundaries that seek to contain migration and

---

[18] The modern-postmodern divide is a profoundly contested one. By placing them in proximity, as I do in this essay, I want to suggest that these structures of meaning are best understood in both their continuities and discontinuities of method, cultural form, and political practice. Thus, I understand modernity and postmodernity less as periodizations and more as "conditions," "sensibilities," and "practices." My own orientation, sensibility, and location are probably more congenial with the theory and practice of postcoloniality than with modernity or postmodernity. See, for example, Bill Ashcroft, Gareth Griffiths, and Helen Tiffin, eds., *The Post-Colonial Studies Reader* (New York: Routledge, 1995).

[19] This I take to be the philosophical significance of Jacques Derrida's January 1996 Paris lectures on "Foreigner Question" and "Step of Hospitality/ No Hospitality," published in Jacques Derrida and Anne Dufourmantelle, *Of*

immigration in the name of state sovereignty, if not national integrity. It asks of us how we treat the stranger in our midst; and in that question, our identities begin to be articulated.

Of course, danger lies in the fact that both the Stranger and the giver of hospitality are not immune to the desire or temptation for "sameness" or uniformity—or even coercion and domination—even as the long experience of the condition of strangeness and hospitality often breeds certain fetishes for such strangeness and hospitality, including desires for the exotic. Moreover, hospitality does not always aspire towards genuine compassion or unconditional plenitude. Hospitality itself, when implicated in the perpetuation of power and privilege, tends to cast its long shadow on the struggle for a "genuine" hospitality that seeks to offer both the Stranger and the giver of hospitality the opportunity to live well together in the context of their shared differences. Indeed, the very structure of hospitality often must posit the existence of strangers "in need of hospitality," requiring therefore, the legitimation of structures and processes that exclude before they include. Such exclusionary logics, for example of race, gender, and class, migrate on to the structures of "hospitality" without being overcome or transformed. Put differently, one must be open to the possibility that strangeness and hospitality (i.e., "Diaspora") are necessary though insufficient conditions for the creation and nurture of radically inclusive communities of struggle and hope. Hence, writing from the perspective of the religio-moral, contextualization requires that we gesture toward resistance and solidarity. At the same time, since the religio-moral cannot be extricated from the methodological, the fundamental question for contextualization is: how can it be rendered methodologically (read "structurally") hospitable? What may be said of the Stranger and of hospitality are equally true for theological contextualization.

Elsewhere I have argued that Diaspora is not a stranger to global capital and empire. Here, let me note only in passing, its importance as a context for contextualization.

Global capital cannot be reduced to "empire," but neither can "empire" be extricated from transnational capital.[20] Both, whatever their

---

Hospitality, trans. Rachel Bowlby (Stanford: Stanford University Press, 2000).
    [20]Charles Amjad-Ali and Lester Edwin J. Ruiz, "Betrayed by a Kiss: Evangelicals and US Empire," in Bruce Ellis Benson and Peter Goodwin

raisons d'etre, are fundamentally articulations of power. In fact, both transnational capital and "empire" are implicated in a narrative of modernity that in turn reproduces global capital and "empire." By "modernity" I mean, following Richard K. Ashley's lead, the "multifaceted historical narrative rooted in the Enlightenment, dominant in Western society, expressed in rationalist theory, and centering on the progressive unfolding of universalizing reason and social harmony via science, technology, law, and the state."[21] Where Ashley assists us in identifying the *philosophical* contours of this multifaceted historical narrative, Anthony Giddens provides a useful *institutional* cartography of modernity, arguing in *The Consequences of Modernity* that there are four institutional dimensions of modernity: capitalism, i.e., capital accumulation in the context of competitive labor and product markets; industrialism, i.e., the transformation of nature or the development of the 'created environment'; surveillance, i.e., the control of information and social supervision; and, military power, i.e., the control of the means of violence in the context of the industrialization of war.[22]

What is important to understand about the narrative of modernity is its logocentric disposition, the tendency to regard all thought, feeling, and action as grounded in some fundamental identity, principle of interpretation, or necessary thinking substance which is itself regarded as unproblematic, nonhistorical, and hence, in no need of critical accounting. This principle of interpretation and practice is conceived as existing in itself as a foundation or origin of history's making, not a contingent effect of political practices within history. Such a disposition

---

Heltzel, eds., *Evangelicals and Empire: Christian Alternatives to the Political Status Quo* (Grand Rapids, MI: Brazos Press, 2008), 54-66. The academic literature on this is extensive. See for example, Michael Mann, *Incoherent Empire* (London: Verso, 2003), David Harvey, *The New Imperialism* (London: Oxford University Press, 2003), Gopal Balakrishnan and Stanley Aronowitz, eds., *Debating Empire* (London: Verso, 2003).

[21] Richard Ashley, "The Geopolitics of Geopolitical Space: Toward a Critical Social Theory of International Politics," *Alternatives: Social Transformation and Humane Governance* 2: 4 (1987), 403-434.

[22] Anthony Giddens, *The Consequences of Modernity* (Stanford: Stanford University Press, 1991). Cf. Michael Hardt and Antonio Negri, *Empire* (Cambridge: Harvard University Press, 2000)); Michael Hardt and Antonio Negri, *Multitude: War and Democracy in the Age of Empire* (New York: Penguin Press, 2004).

has become a principle of articulation, if not a ground for domination that creates and re-creates human life in its own image.

Hence, William Connolly rightly notes that the West at its imperial best, the US being a clear example, arrogates to itself the power and privilege of the interrogator, consistently negating or demeaning the role of other peoples in civilizational, socio-cultural, political and economic history, while claiming the same history as an exclusively Western possession.[23] At the same time the West is very quick to hyperbolize and render pathological the imperial powers, practices and ambitions of others: All that is good, it is argued, is of Western origin and all that is wrong is part of the larger tragic human condition which is external to the West.

Thus, any project of contextualization cannot avoid addressing the dangers of being absorbed into this US-led western project.[24]

At the same time, it is no longer sufficient, empirically if not analytically or philosophically, to explain "the world" in terms of US-led "empire." There is enough evidence to suggest that the very states that have historically challenged US hegemony, for example, China, India, and even the EEU, are themselves engaged in their own versions of "empire-building," albeit within the larger frame of global capital. This multi-polar view of the world is enough to suggest that the fundamental *problematique* to which theological contextualization needs to attend are the dynamics of power and privilege that accompany these multiple realities of empire-building, and not only the dominant historical form that they take.

---

[23] William E. Connolly, *Identity/Difference: Democratic Negotiations of Political Paradox* (Ithaca: Cornell University Press, 1991), 61. See generally Paul A. Passavant and Jodi Dean, eds., *Empire's New Clothes: Reading Hardt and Negri* (New York: Routledge, 2004). See especially Ernesto Laclau, "Can Immanence Explain Empire?" in Passavant and Dean, *Empire's New Clothes*, 21-30. Cf. Mark Taylor, *Religion, Politics, and the Christian Right: Post 9/11 Powers in American Empire* (Minneapolis: Fortress Press, 2005); and Sharon Welch, *After Empire: The Art and Ethos of Enduring Peace* (Minneapolis: Fortress Press, 2004).

[24] Catherine Keller, et al., eds. *Postcolonial Theologies: Divinity and Empire* (St. Louis: Chalice Press, 2004).

Challenges to Contextualization

The future of theological contextualization as a discursive formation and strategy may require at least three tasks. First, contextualization needs to continue to recognize, affirm, and articulate different ways of producing and reproducing knowledge (epistemology): here, not only is this about situated knowledges and partial perspectives, but also of subjugated and insurrectionary knowledges and agents of knowledges, and the ways in which they are related. Even more important, however, is the need to consistently focus, among other things, on the fundamental situatedness and partial character of our ways of organizing thinking, feeling and acting, and on the necessity, if not desirability, of rethinking the relationship between reason and desire, and knowledge and politics, in the construction of interpretive frameworks for theological contextualization that demonstrate the mutually constitutive rather than oppositional relationship between them.[25] Here it will be important to pay very close attention to the epistemological implications of, say Giorgio Agamben's work on "apparatus" (and certainly of Foucault on genealogy), particularly as they frame the realities of "situated knowledges and partial perspectives."[26]

Second, theological contextualization needs to continue to recognize, affirm, and articulate different modes of being (ontology). Here discourses on the "body" are useful guides to understand what is at stake. For example, not only is this about thinking, feeling, and acting as relational practices, but also about "volatile bodies," i.e., of re-figuring and re-inscribing bodies, of moving through and beyond the conventional divide of gender as socially-contructed, on the one hand, and of sex as biologically-given, on the other hand, to "our bodies our selves."[27]

---

[25] Allison Jaggar, "Love and Knowledge: Emotion in Feminist Epistemology" in Sandra Kemp and Judith Squires, eds. *Feminisms* (New York: Oxford University Press, 1997); cf. Fernando Segovia and Mary Ann Tolbert, eds., *Reading from this Place: Social Location and Biblical Interpretation in Global Perspective* (Minneapolis: Fortress Press, 1995).

[26] Georgio Agamben, *"What is an Apparatus?"* (Stanford: Stanford University Press, 2009).

[27] Elisabeth Grosz, *Volatile Bodies: Towards a Corporeal Feminism* (St. Leonard's, NSW: Allen and Unwin, 1994). Cf. Lester Edwin J. Ruiz, "Recovering the Body: When Race and Power Migrate," in Werner, et al,

Feminists have suggested that the "male (or female) body can no longer be regarded as a fixed, concrete substance, a pre-cultural given. It has a determinate form only by being socially inscribed... as a socio-historical 'object'." They continue,

> The body can no longer be confined to biological determinants, to an immanent 'factitious', or unchanging social status. It is a political object par excellence; its forms, capacities, behaviours, gestures, movements, potential are primary objects of political contestation. As a political object, the body is not inert or fixed. It is pliable and plastic material, which is capable of being formed and organized.[28]

One may ask, therefore, "How does one contextualize concrete, sensuous bodies?" But perhaps more important, we will need to ask what, how, and where are the *embodied* forms of theological contextualization?

Third, theological contextualization needs to continue to recognize, affirm, and articulate different empowering practices (politics). Not only is this about the importance and power of self-definition, self-valuation, nor of self-reliance and autonomy, but also about transformation and transgression, of finding safe places and voices in the midst of difference, and of making the connections. Chandra Talpade Mohanty summarizes this point quite well. She notes,

> ...third world women's writings on feminism have consistently focused on (1) the idea of the simultaneity of oppressions as fundamental to the experience of social and political marginality and the grounding of feminist politics in the histories of racism and imperialism; (2) the crucial role of a hegemonic state in circumscribing

---

Handbook of Theological Education in World Christianity: Theological Perspectives, Ecumenical Trends, Regional Surveys, 85-103.

[28] Elisabeth Grosz, "Notes towards a corporeal feminism," *Australian Feminist Studies* 5 (1987): 2. Michel Foucault, "Nietzsche, Genealogy, History," in Paul Rabinow, ed., *The Foucault Reader* (New York: Random House, 1984), 83. See also Michel Foucault, *The Birth of the Prison*, trans. Alan Sheridan (New York: Pantheon, 1977). Cf. Judith P. Butler, *Bodies that Matter: On the Discursive Limits of Sex* (New York: Routledge, 1993).

their/our daily lives and survival struggles; (3) the significance of memory and writing in the creation of oppositional agency; and (4) the differences, conflicts, and contradictions internal to third world women's organizations and communities. In addition, they have insisted on the complex interrelationships between feminist, antiracist, and nationalist struggles...[29]

Contextualization as World-Forming Practices: Dialogue, Diversity, and the Creation of "One World, Many Worlds"

I suggested at the beginning of this essay that contextualization is fundamentally a hermeneutical event, an act of understanding, which arises in the "fusion of horizons" (*Horizontverschmelzung*)—or of bringing that which is "strange" into proximity with that which is "not-strange"—which is a relationship that is constituted both by the reality of history and of historical understanding. Hans-Georg Gadamer called this "effective historical consciousness" (*Wirkungsgeschichtliches Bewußtsein*), where the "reality of history" presents itself "so much in terms of our own selves that there is no longer a question of self and other."[30] It is within this hermeneutical *practice* that contextualization must be articulated. What elements are required for such a re-articulation?

My intuition returns to the ancient notion of dialogue (dia-*logos*)[31] or moving together through multiple universes of meaning—understood

---

[29] Chandra Talpade Mohanty, Anna Russo, and Lourdes Torres, eds. *Third World Women and the Politics of Feminism* (Bloomington: Indiana University Press, 1991), 10. Cf. Judith P. Butler and Gayatri Chakravorty Spivak, *Who Sings the Nation-State? Language, Politics, Belonging* (Calcutta: Seagull Books, 2007).

[30] Hans Georg Gadamer writes, "Understanding is not to be thought of so much as an action of one's subjectivity, but as the placing of oneself within a process of tradition, in which past and present are constantly fused." Hans Georg Gadamer, *Truth and Method* (London: Sheed and Ward, 1975), 258. Cf. pages 267ff. See also Hans-Georg Gadamer, "Text and Interpretation" in Diane P. Michelfelder and Richard Palmer, eds., *Dialogue and Deconstruction: The Gadamer-Derrida Encounter* (New York: SUNY Press, 1989), 21-51.

[31] I am grateful to Professor Charles Amjad-Ali of Luther Seminary in Minneapolis, Minnesota for drawing my attention to dialogue as more than a

as the "transformation of play into structure."³² Here dialogue has a fourfold process that moves from the evanescent immediacy of proximal engagement ("the encounter"), to the narrative of biography ("my story"), then to history ("our people's story"), and finally to cosmology ("the story of the universe"). To be sure, this is not an inexorable teleological unfolding of some Hegelian *Geist*, but rather the "play of differences" where dialogical ruptures often result in unexpected historical repetitions or sometimes profound Nietzschean-like repudiations of hallowed traditions, but where the encounter with the "totally-transpersonal-other-than-me" is always mediated through the engagement with what Emmanuel Levinas describes as the Other, and where the way through the *Logos* (or *logoi*) cannot evade fallibility, and therefore, must affirm the self-critical accountability of those engaged in theological contextualization.

I am almost convinced that the practice of contextualization will work only if there is a genuine identification with particular "communities of transformation" where the play of differences is affirmed as constitutive of being-in-a-community-of-shared-difference, and where this "shared difference," understood as "conviviality," reaches not only for diversity but for "radical inclusion," where persons see all of humankind (and, possibly all of creation) as *possible* fellow sojourners towards a world of meaning and significance who realize that their destinies are inextricably-woven to their capacities to learn how to live together on the one planet that is our common heritage (the ethical demand), and who intentionally move towards a common and abiding refusal to understand self, other, and world as being constitutively dependent on the gaze of a subject-of-the-world (the philosophical demand). For while the human condition arises out of "difference" and returns to difference, its normative, if not necessary challenge, is not how the difference can be overcome, but rather how and under what conditions is it possible for us not only to live together, but to live together well *finally*.³³

"conversation" between two individuals.

³² See Gadamer, 102ff., fn 30.

³³ This is how I read Jacques Derrida's *The Last Interview: Learning to Live Finally*, translated by Pascale-Anne Brault and Michael Nass (Hoboken: Melville House Press, 2007), where one's death, when understood as the quintessential *aporia* which is both limit and rupture (Spivak), presents the possibility of being thrown back on to life not as mere existence but as living

Put differently, contextualization is not an end in itself; it is a passage through difference into *living well* differently. Here, difference and "limits" embrace, not unlike life and death, *Eros* and *Thanatos*. Thus, I am more than convinced that theological contextualization, which by its very structure is a fallible, if not fumbling (i.e., contingent), Gadamerian "conversation," requires a commitment to some minimal form of "mutuality" or reciprocity and self-criticality that intentionally and purposively reaches from the ground of humility for the "fundamentally new which is also fundamentally better."

Moreover, contextualization is not only a contingent conversation that aspires to the ethical and the philosophical. In fact, it is a creative act of *forming* a world. Gadamer brings the "transformation of play into structure" and the "fusion of horizons" into discursive proximity—both of which constitute our (human) "being-in-the-world." It is here where the significance of forming a world arises for "contextualization." Not only do these acts of interpretation cast suspicions on construals of grand theories of contextualization as "totality grasped as [an indistinct] whole," but more important, they also force such theorizing into a process of differentiation and formation that "maintains a crucial reference to the world's horizon as a space of human relations... of meaning held in common... of signification or possible signification"[34] that no longer conceives of theological contextualization as merely an object of representation.

When articulated against this multi-stranded background, dialogue and diversity as conditions of possibility press towards a non-representational *practice* that is simultaneously critical interpretation, effective performance, purposive formation, and transformative contextualization.[35] Here dialogue, diversity, and the formation of "one world,

---

fully well.

[34] Jean-Luc Nancy's path breaking distinction between globalization and *mondialisation* illustrates the methodological move I am making. See especially, Jean-Luc Nancy, *The Creation of the World or Globalization*, translated by Francois Raffoul and David Pettigrew (Albany: State University of New York, 2007), 2ff. See also, R.B.J. Walker, *After the Globe: Before the World* (New York: Routledge, 2010).

[35] The terminology of this four-fold practice is adapted from Charles Foster, et al, *Educating Clergy: Teaching Practices and Pastoral Imagination* (San Francisco: Jossey-Bass, 2006).

many worlds," as well as of "the play of differences," conviviality, the dialogical non-binary commitment to unconditional and principled openness and reciprocity, the goal of transformation or the "creation of the fundamentally new which is also fundamentally better"—all provide the fundamental elements for theological contextualization.

Conclusion: Contextualization as Transformation

I want to conclude by returning to the fundamental and necessary challenge that gives rise to the question of "contextualization" with which I began this essay: the need for biblical, theological, and pastoral contextualization resting on the metaphors of both Incarnation and Kenosis. The need is as simple as it is profound. The human condition under the sign of "Diaspora" is essentially about the familiar becoming strangely unfamiliar with uneven consequences depending on one's location and positionality. This "strangeness" which some would prefer to call "estrangement" requires both interpretation and transformation if one wants not only to live but to *live well*. Unfortunately, what is becoming clear to me is that the assertion of the desirability or normative character of "theological contextualization" is almost always accompanied by a fundamental subterranean epistemological temptation to "represent" the world as an act of a "subject of history." The conditions of our world—even this postcolonial world—so powerfully captured in Martin Heidegger's image of the "the age of the world as picture," conspire to preserve this temptation. Reality is surrendered to the determination of a subject, particularly of a "possessive individual."[36] Such representation is not only the quintessential repetition of the Cartesian aspiration for that *fundamentum inconcussum* that guarantees knowledge, but also its consequences have become fundamentally flawed, if unsustainable, in a postmodern, postcolonial world where both incommensurability and the *possibility* of understanding cannot be evaded, and the asymmetry of power and privilege resists transformation.

My wager, at least at the intuitive and philosophical level, is that by bringing contextualization into discursive proximity with trans-

---

[36] C. B. Macpherson, *The Political Theory of Possessive Individualism: From Hobbes to Locke* (New York: Oxford University Press, 1962).

formation as "the creation of the fundamentally new that is also fundamentally better," understood as a particular kind of practice, the inherently *ontotheological* or representational character of our inherited notions of contextualization might be greatly reduced to a place where the locations and positionalities of critique become questions not of epistemology, but of (ontological) worldliness.[37] Here contextualization is not only an "impossible possibility," it becomes a necessary strategy for the survival of the world.

Such ontotheological assertions betray a fundamental subterranean epistemological dichotomy between "church" and "world" (theology and human science) which functions as a "Trojan Horse" for the privileging of the former in theological contextualization. This is the quintessential repetition of that heresy around the Incarnation with which the Christian churches have wrestled throughout its almost 2000-year history. I want to suggest that for as long as the dichotomy is maintained, "contextualization" will simply be a principle that regulates Christian thought and practice, a creature of incremental change that undermines the possibility of fundamental change itself. For Christians, this bringing into proximity can only be achieved by moving from their *ontotheological* assertions to their "worldly" locations and positionalities.

It was Dietrich Bonhoeffer who started me on my theological journey towards a *non-representational* contextualization when he declared in his *Letters and Papers from Prison*, dated July 21, 1944, the profound this-worldliness of Christianity. It may be that Christians today must aspire to this *Diesseitigkeit des Christentums* not as an assertion of the eternal relevance of the mission of Christianity and therefore, the imperative for contextualization, but rather, as Christian faith's unavoidable and necessary *arche* and *telos*—where the practice of contextualization is one of the key strategic conditions for becoming finally "fully human" in a non-representational "one world, many worlds." This may prove to be Christianity's greatest challenge yet.

---

[37] This is the burden of Martin Heidegger's "The Question Concerning Technology" and "The Age of the World Picture." Martin Heidegger, *The Question Concerning Technology and Other Essays*, translated by William Lovitt (New York: Harper and Row, 1977). Gadamer addresses similar concerns about the ontotheological character of modern philosophy in terms of his notions of "effective historical consciousness," "the fusion of horizons," and, "transformation of play into structure."

Chapter 4.

Theological Counterpoints: Transnationalism and Political Theology in the Asia Pacific

Kwok Pui-lan

On August 16, 2010, the headline of *The Wall Street Journal* said China is on track to overtake Japan as the world's second-largest economy.[1] Ever since China overtook Germany as the third-largest economy in 2007, observers have predicted that China would sooner or later catch up with Japan. It would take decades before China would overtake the United States as the world's biggest economy, for the gap between China's $7 trillion economy and the United States' nearly $15 trillion is huge. Nevertheless, this is a significant turning point in global economy. By virtue of its sheer size and collective national wealth, China would be in a position to exert political clout in global politics.

Not coincidentally, the headline on the cover of the British journal *The Economist* the following week read: "Contest of the Century: China v India."[2] The phenomenal economic growth of China and India has journalists busy talking about modernization with "Asian characteristics" and its impact on the rest of the world. To sustain their pace of growth China and India have voracious appetites for oil, coal, iron ore, and other natural resources from Africa, Latin American, and

---

[1] Andrew Batson, Daisuke Wakabayashi, and Mark Whitehouse, "China Output Beats Japan," *The Wall Street Journal*, August 19, 2010, sec. A, 1.

[2] *The Economist*, August 21-27, 2010.

other countries. The dramatic new trend in South-South economic relations has already disrupted traditional patterns of economic development. Some African countries have redirected their trade and other relationships from the North Atlantic to India and China.[3] These two countries, with about forty percent of the world's population, will play decisive roles in shaping the rules that will govern the twenty-first century.

The rise of India, China, Brazil, and other emerging markets challenges Western hegemony and shifts the economic balance of the world. Indian American journalist Fareed Zakaria has predicted a "Post-American world" in which the United States will no longer dominate global economy, orchestrate geopolitics, or exert disproportional influences over culture.[4] Perceptions about the rise or fall of Asia have always had direct impact on how Americans look at Asian Americans. In the 1980s, keen competition from Japan, especially by Japanese automakers, led to widespread anti-Japanese feelings. Vincent Chin, a Chinese American, was beaten to death in Detroit by two white autoworkers, because he was mistaken to be Japanese. As trade imbalance between China and the United States continues to grow and negative criticism about China fills the airwave, the old myth of "yellow peril" might be revived.

How should theologians respond to the rise of Asia and changes in geopolitics around the Pacific? Although there has been a resurgence of interest on the relationship between the political and the theological, most of these discussions focus on the European tradition and experience in Western countries. Few of these debates touch on the Asia Pacific as a regional formation poised to change the world. This article attempts to probe the contours of a transnational political theology amidst the hyper-capitalist flow, ingenious hybridity, and shifting religious and cultural identities in the Asia Pacific.

---

[3] Harry G. Broadman, *Africa's Silk Road: China and India's New Economic Frontier* (Washington, D.C.: World Bank, 2007).

[4] Fareed Zakaria, *The Post-American World* (New York: W. W. Norton, 2008).

Asia Pacific as a Space for Political Theology

Political theology, as Jan Assman suggests, concerns the "ever-changing relationships between political community and religious order, in short, between power [or authority: Herrschaft] and salvation [Heil]."[5] Political theology has a long history in Western Christianity. In *The City of God*, Augustine contrasts the city of God with an earthly city and refuses to sacralize the Roman Empire. In the medieval period the issue of church and state loomed large due to power struggles between the papacy and secular rulers. During the Reformation Luther proposed the theory of the "two kingdoms": the spiritual regiment concerned with the soul and the inner person, and the worldly regiment concerned with the body and the world. The Treaty of Westphalia (1648) marked the collapse of "Christendom" and gave secular authorities the power to determine matters of religion in their own state. The authority of the church was further undermined during the Enlightenment, when philosophers pushed for the separation of religion from public affairs. In the development of modern states in the West politics is typically considered to be public, while religion is relegated to the private domain.[6]

This brief historical background helps us understand the surge of interest in political theology in the West, for religion has not disappeared but has entered the public domain and policy discussions, both nationally and internationally. After September 11, religion has been on the forefront of discussions on the "war on terror," global peace, and reconciliation. Presidents and world leaders, policy-makers, social and political scientists, journalists, cultural critics, and philosophers have commented on religion and observed it with both fascination and—sometimes—frustration. Prominent critics and theorists such as Jacques Derrida, Jean-Luc Nancy, Terry Eagleton, Slavoj Žižek, and Alain Badiou have joined the fray. Some among them have even explicitly discussed Christian faith.[7] There is clearly a change of attitude in the

---

[5] Jan Assmann, *Herrschaft und Heil: Politische Theologie in Altägypten, Israel und Europa* (Munich: Carl Hanser, 2000), 15, as quoted in Hent de Vries, "Introduction," in *Political Theologies: Public Religion in a Post-Secular World*, ed. Hent de Vries and Lawrence E. Sullivan (New York: Fordham University Press, 2006), 25.

[6] See the discussion in Michael Kirwan, *Political Theology: A New Introduction* (London: Darton, Longman and Todd, 2008), 55-104.

secular state and in the public domain with respect to the enduring impulses of religion and religious communities. Some have called this the post-secular world. Weber's notion of the disenchantment of the world has been cast aside as some begin to speak of the "permanence" of the theologico-political.[8] However, there is hardly any consensus or unitary theory to explain the relation between the theological and the political. Hent de Vries notes that, while religion can be a "potential source of inspiration and democratic openness, it simultaneously—inevitably?—presents a danger of dogmatism and hence of closed societies and mentalities."[9] Political theology flourishes in the current lively debates on secularism and the post-secular world in the West.

If the climate for political theology is "post-secular" in the North Atlantic, the context for political theology in Asia Pacific is "post-colonial" and "de-imperial." First of all, "Asia Pacific" was a regional structure formed as a result of colonial impetus. Arif Dirlik calls it a dominantly Euro-American formation. He observes:

> Entering the Pacific from the west or the east, the Portuguese, the Spaniards, the Dutch, the Russians, and the English, as well as their colonists in the Americas, all contributed in turn to the creation of a regional structure, in which Asian and Pacific societies provided the building blocks and the globalized interests of Euro-American powers furnished the principles of organization.[10]

It is therefore not surprising to find that many of the progressive Asian theologies developed in the twentieth century were politically charged. In the 1930s, during foreign encroachment on China, Wu Yaozong advocated radical social revolution as a means to save China

---

[7] For example, Slavoj Žižek, *The Fragile Absolute, or Why the Christian Legacy Is Worth Fighting For* (London: Verso, 2000); Terry Eagleton, *Reason, Faith, Revolution: Reflections on the God Debate* (New Haven: Yale University Press, 2010).

[8] Claude Lefort, "The Permanence of the Theologic-Political," in de Vries and Sullivan, *Political Theologies*, 148-87.

[9] De Vries, "Introduction," 3.

[10] Arif Dirlik, "The Asia-Pacific Idea: Reality and Representation in the Invention of a Regional Structure," *Journal of World History* 3 (1992): 66.

and transform the world. He criticized the aggression of capitalist powers, which led to war and conflicts in China and other parts of the world. He declared that the Christian church should not support the status quo, but should actively participate in social change. His use of Marxism in social analysis and his critique of idealist Christianity anticipated liberation theologies to come decades later.[11] After the Second World War when Asian countries engaged in intense struggles for political independence, M. M. Thomas of India emerged as one of leading voices among Asian theologians. In his book *Christian Response to Asian Revolution*, published in 1966, he criticized Western imperialism and the identification of the Gospel with Western culture.[12] With a strong nationalist sentiment Thomas argued that the Asian revolution enabled us to see the transcendence of the Gospel over all cultures. For Thomas, Jesus Christ is a model of new humanity, providing the spiritual foundation, renewal, and ultimate fulfillment of the struggle for full humanity. His view of Jesus was clearly anti-colonial, as he contrasted the messianism of a conquering king with the crucified servant Christ.[13]

On the other side of the Pacific the Civil Rights movement and the protest against the Vietnam War aroused the political consciousness of Asian Americans. From a few small, disconnected and largely invisible ethnic groups, they organized to form a self-identified racial group and they refused to be treated as second-class citizens. Out of these intense political movements Asian American theology arose, during a time when anti-racism in the United States was much linked to Third World liberation. Jonathan Tan points out that the pioneers of Asian American theologians, "engaged in debates with their Caucasian counterparts about the ethnocentrism of U.S. Christianity and U.S. theologies. The significance of their struggles lies in the creation of Asian American Christian identity and theologizing."[14] Race, nation, and citizenship were important concerns, as Asian Americans were seen as

---

[11] Ng Lee-ming, "A Study of Y. T. Wu," *Ching Feng* 15/1 (1972): 5-54.

[12] M. M. Thomas, *Christian Response to the Asian Revolution* (London: SCM, 1966).

[13] See the discussion in Sathianathan Clarke, "M. M. Thomas," in *Empire and the Christian Tradition: New Readings of Classical Theologians*, ed. Kwok Pui-lan, Don H. Compier, and Joerg Rieger (Minneapolis: Fortress, 2007), 430.

[14] Jonathan Y. Tan, *Introducing Asian American Theologies* (Maryknoll, N.Y.: Orbis, 2008), 93.

"perpetual foreigners." They were targeted by the Chinese Exclusive Act of 1882 and were ineligible for citizenship until 1952, not to mention the internment of hundreds of thousands of Japanese Americans during the Second World War. As Asian American theologians reclaim their rightful place as Americans, they have also to negotiate their hyphenated "Asian-American" identity in relation to both sides of the Pacific.

The 1970s saw the rise of the Pacific Rim discourse following the economic success of Japan and the rapid development of the newly industrialized countries such as Korea, Taiwan, Hong Kong, and Singapore. Since the late 1970s, American trade across the Pacific surpassed trade with Europe. The twenty-first century was dubbed the "Pacific Century," with PBS airing a ten-hour documentary on the topic in 1993. But as Christopher L. Connery has pointed out, the Pacific Rim discourse was a transnational American construct emanating from the spread of multinational capitalism and colored by the Cold War imaginary. The late Cold War required a "new spatial mythology for U.S. international capital," Connery notes.[15] As an extension of America the Pacific was imagined as a place where capital would freely transverse the ocean.

While the Asia Pacific was restructured into a space for the fluidity of capital and commodities, political theology from the region, which developed in the 1970s and 1980s, offered a counter-mapping by articulating the aspiration of the Asian and Pacific peoples. Emerging in the 1970s, Minjung Theology from South Korea offered a political hermeneutic of the Bible and argued that people are subjects of history. Living under Japanese colonial rule and then under suppression of the Kuomingtang, Taiwanese theologians articulated the demand for self-determination in their Homeland Theology. The theology of struggle in the Philippines expressed the ferment and protest of Filipinos against a dictatorial regime; the People's Power Revolution finally toppled the Marcos government in 1986. In the Pacific churches and theologians spoke out against dependence theory and for the protection of the natural and cultural environment of the Pacific. Indigenous theologians across the Asia Pacific articulated the need for social equality, cultural survival, and the freedom to articulate theology in their own idioms. Although

---

[15] Christopher L. Connery, "Pacific Rim Discourse: The U.S. Global Imaginary in the Late Cold War Years," *boundary 2* 21/1 (1994): 40.

shaped by their particular context and demand, these theologies are linked internationally, as the United States plays a crucial role in the geopolitics of the region.

The term "Asia Pacific" proposed by capitalist managers and military strategists, is inadequate to describe the multifaceted and persistent people's struggle for democracy. Under the veneer of the "Asian miracle," Asia becomes the factory of the world, and low wage labor enables capitalist entrepreneurs to make great profit. Political theology in the region offers one counter-hegemonic space to reflect on the past and imagine a different possible future. With the rise of China and India and the current financial crisis in Europe and the United States, such reimagining is more urgent than ever. As Rob Wilson and Arif Dirlik, two veteran scholars of the Asia Pacific, write, we must begin to "historicize, question, and *undo* those conceptual categories, maps, imaginary geographies, master narratives, self-evident discourses, and configurations of Western knowledge/power," that threaten the freedom and welfare of peoples living in this vast area.[16]

Cultural Imaginary and Political Theology

As Antonio Negri and Michael Hardt have pointed out, today's Empire has no territorial center of power, as there are no fixed boundaries, and center and periphery are constantly shifting.[17] Within the Asia Pacific region one of the most astute theorists of Empire and deimperialization is Chen Kuan-Hsing, a professor of cultural studies in Taiwan. He elucidates why the process of decolonization is long and tortuous. Because of the uneven distribution of capital and power, some Asian countries might go through a decolonizing process, while at the same time collude with imperial interests. Thus, Asians cannot point fingers at Western colonial powers without going through a painstaking self-analysis and critique. In his groundbreaking volume *Asia as Method*, Chen points to the important roles cultural studies can play in this region:

---

[16] Rob Wilson and Arif Dirlik, "Introduction: Asia/Pacific as Space of Cultural Production," *boundary 2* 21/1 (1994): 6. Emphasis the authors.

[17] Michael Hardt and Antonio Negri, *Empire* (Cambridge, Mass.: Harvard University Press, 2000), xii.

"To further the progress of decolonization, the task of cultural studies is to deconstruct, decenter, and disarticulate the colonial cultural imaginary, and to reconstruct and rearticulate new imaginations and discover a more democratic future direction."[18]

Chen says the legacy of colonialism has transfigured the inner structure of the cultural imaginary of both the colonizers and colonized. Decolonizing the cultural imaginary involves the following: (1) placing colonialism at the center of analysis, (2) revealing hidden Eurocentrism such that a more balanced account of different regional formation of the world can be presented and (3) emphasizing the relative autonomy of local history and paying attention to the specificities of the historical and the geographical. The shape of the cultural imaginary in a specific time and space depends on the interaction between the colonial, the historical, and the geographical.[19] Since the nation-state is no longer sufficient to explain the workings of the globalized world, Chen proposes we focus on geographical spaces to develop a more appropriate understanding of the formerly colonized world in the neoliberal economy.

Chen's book identifies three components in reconstructing the cultural imaginary from the particular situations of his East Asian context. The first is decolonization, in which he engages the work of Frantz Fanon, Albert Memmi, and Ashis Nandy to discuss postcolonial subjectivity and their critique of nationalism, nativism, and civilizationalism. The second is de-cold war, because the entanglement of colonialism and the cold war disrupted the evolution of political structures in the Asian region and heightened conflicts within the nation. The third is deimperialization, which involves an honest and soul-searching analysis of the desire to identify with the Empire and to support imperialist projects. In case after case decolonization quickly turned into recolonization or neocolonization, because the imperialist cultural imaginary was effortlessly inherited by the colonized without critical reflection. Chen calls Korea, Taiwan, and Hong Kong "subimperial spaces," because they were lured by and colluded with the imperialist desires of the Japanese and American empire. Today, the image of a "Greater China Economic Sphere" looms large on the

---

[18] Kuan-Hsing Chen, *Asia as Method* (Durham, N.C.: Duke University Press, 2010), 112.

[19] Ibid., 108.

horizon, and the Chinese leadership's slogan of a "peaceful rise" does nothing to ease the anxiety of neighboring countries.

Theologians can contribute to the process of deimperialization by participating in the critique and reformulation of cultural imaginary. I would like to give examples of the ways theologians and conscientious intellectuals are engaging in this process in the United States and China. Although Chinese leaders have said that China does not want to become a superpower, commentators have coined the term "Chinamerica" and suggested a G2 that would put China and the United States at the head of international affairs. On the American side, Japanese American theologian Rita Nakashima Brock has emerged as a leading theological voice critiquing the American empire. Founder and director of Faith Voices for the Common Good, Brock is a seasoned activist in the women's movement and in the grassroots movement to stop the Iraq war. Beginning with her first book, *Journeys by Heart*,[20] Brock's theology has been shaped by her concerns for social outcasts and those who toil under multiple oppressions of society, including the abused child, prostitutes and sex-workers, and victims of domestic and military violence.

Brock traces the founding myths of the United States to the Puritan imperative to build a new Eden—a new paradise—in the New World. The Puritans saw the Indians either as innocent or childlike, the original inhabitants of Eden, or as Canaanites, illegitimate occupants of the Promised Land. Most often Indians were seen as agents of Satan to be annihilated to make room for God's chosen people. Puritan theology condoned war to eradicate evil, and Puritans lived by what historian Richard Slotkin calls "the myth of regeneration through violence."[21] Such a myth absolved the settlers from the sins of killing Indians and taking over their lands and possessions. Genocide, white hegemony, and environmental exploitation were the engines of the nation's expansion.

Brock links imperial nostalgia for the vanquished Indians to the exoticizing and Orientalizing of Asians in white imagination. In this colonial fantasy, Asian men are stereotypically seen as servile and

---

[20] Rita Nakashima Brock, *Journeys by Heart: A Christology of Erotic Power* (New York: Crossroad, 1988).

[21] Richard Slotkin, *Regeneration through Violence: The Mythology of the American Frontier, 1660-1860* (Middletown, Conn.: Wesleyan University Press, 1973).

effeminate and Asian women as desired objects, submissive and yet sexually sophisticated.[22] In the book *Saving Paradise*, Brock and Rebecca Ann Parker argue that as long as the crucifixion and Jesus' suffering on the cross remain central for salvation, Christianity can easily be used to condone suffering and violence.[23] Their detailed study documents that the first images of crucifixion emerged in the tenth century, a time when Christians used violence to force pagans into conversion. In the first decade, Anselm of Canterbury developed the satisfaction theory of atonement in his *Cur Deus Homo*. Jesus' death became an offering to pay for human's debt of sin, and satisfy God's honor. Violence was no longer seen as sinful. Instead, killing in the name of Christ became a holy act, sanctioned by the Christian Church and championed by bishops and theologians.

Brock and Parker offer a counter-hegemonic cultural imaginary, focusing not on Jesus' sacrificial death, but on his resurrection and paradise. The early theologians drew their concepts of paradise from the Bible and Greek, Roman, and Persian thought. They associated paradise with the resurrection of Jesus Christ. Depictions of paradise in Christian art were various: the four rivers of Eden and the Jordan, fecund trees, green meadows, and Jesus appearing as the Good Shepherd. Baptism was immersion into the waters of paradise sanctified by the Holy Spirit, and Eucharist was a feast of abundant life. Instead of salvation through redemptive violence, Brock and Parker reconstruct the idea that salvation is paradise in this world and in this life. Brock writes:

> Life in paradise was maintained through doing divine deeds, such as healing the sick, feeding the poor, working for justice, practicing non-violent resistance to oppression, teaching the ignorant, and loving each other as friends of God. The Eucharist trained the senses for love of beauty and appreciation for

---

[22] Rita Nakashima Brock, "Paradise in the Exotic Asian 'Other'" (paper presented at the annual meeting of Pacific, Asian, and North American Asian Women in Theology and Ministry, Chicago, April 2, 2009).

[23] Rita Nakashima Brock and Rebecca Ann Parker, *Saving Paradise: How Christianity traded Love of This World for Crucifixion and Empire* (Boston: Beacon, 2008).

creation as blessed, and guided virtue toward the ethical standards of the church.[24]

While Brock and Parker have developed a theology of redemptive beauty to challenge the glorification of suffering and sacrifice in the service of the empire, intellectuals and theologians in China describe the loss of faith in Marxist ideology. The sixtieth anniversary of the founding of the People's Republic of China on October 1, 2009, was celebrated with much fanfare and a spectacular military parade. Just months before the anniversary, Liu Peng, a researcher at the Chinese Academy of Social Sciences, published an important essay on the crisis of "faith" behind China's rise. By "faith" he does not mean "religion," but the spiritual and moral foundation of the country and the individual. He said that Marxism, treated as a religion, has been the official ideology in China for the past sixty years. Further, slogans of "liberation" and "class struggle" helped mobilize the masses to participate in the "revolutionary enterprise," but since the late 1970s, with economic reforms and open-door policies, the major concern for the Chinese people has been to be become rich as fast as possible. Social and moral problems in China are, therefore, rampant as the result of a spiritual vacuum and a crisis of faith. In short, Liu implies that the cultural imaginary promulgated by the Chinese Communist Party can no longer serve the new China, and calls for the government to adopt more open policies toward religion, since religion can serve important functions in civil and moral education and the satisfaction of spiritual needs.[25]

Chinese Christian writer and dissident Yu Jie argues that while the government boasts the "rise of the big country" (*daiguo jueqi*), China is plagued by huge inequities of wealth, a corrupted bureaucracy, a weak legal system, and rampant violence and hatred. He believes that Christianity can contribute to the construction of a new value system, social morality, and cultural institutions in Chinese society. He notes that a small minority of Christian public intellectuals has emerged in China

---

[24] Brock, "Paradise in the Exotic Asian 'Other.'"
[25] Liu Peng, "Zhongguo jueqi de ruanlei: xinyang" (The weak link of China's rise: faith), *Newsletter of the Centre for Christian Studies, Chinese University of Hong Kong* 7 (October 2009): 1-9. This is a shorter version of an article first appeared in *Lingdaozhe* (Leaders), June 2009.

who are addressing social issues in the public square.[26] Yu and other intellectuals have argued that grassroots Christian organizations can contribute to the construction of civil society in China. "Civil society" has also been called the "voluntary sector," "nonprofit sector," and "voluntary sector," which is separate from the state and capital. The discussion of civil society has captured the attention of Chinese scholars and China observers abroad since the 1990s, especially after the Tiananmen incident and the pro-democracy movement in 1989. According to Yang Fenggang, civil society has often been conceptualized as antagonistic to the state in Western theories. But it needs not be so in China, and Christianity can play a crucial role in enlarging civil society and paving the way for a modern, healthy, and pluralistic society.[27]

Chinese intellectuals and theologians have also discussed the need to develop public theology in China. For a long time the audience for theology has been limited to the Chinese church and Christians, but with the establishment of religion departments and research institutes in China and growing interest in religion among the Chinese, theology must address different publics: the academy, the church, and secular society. As a public discourse theology must address critical issues of common concern, such as contemporary Chinese social conditions, religious pluralism, and globalization. Its purview includes religious, cultural, and social dimensions.[28] Public theology need not shy away from critiquing Chinese politics and its global impacts. Hong Kong theologian Lai Pan-Chiu argues that the mission of Chinese theology involves the critique of cultural hegemony and serving as a catalyst for cultural transformation.[29]

---

[26] Yu Jie, "Zhongguo jiating jiaohui de gongkaihua ji Jidutu gonggong zhishi fenzi de chuxian" (Chinese house churches becoming public and the emergence of Christian public intellectual community), *Newsletter of the Centre for Christian Studies, Chinese University of Hong Kong* 6 (May 2009): 7-12.

[27] Fenggang Yang, "Civil Society and the Role of Christianity in China," in *Civil Society as Democratic Practice*, ed. Antonio F. Perez, Semou Pathé Gueye, and Fenggang Yang (Washington, D.C.: Council for Research in Values and Philosophy, 2005), 197-211.

[28] See the discussion in Xie Zhibin, "Hanyu shenxue 'gonggong' zhi keneng" (The possibility of Chinese theology being "public"), in *Gonggong shenxue yu chuanjiuhua* (Public theology and globalization) (Beijing: Zongjiao wenhua chuban she, 2008), 259-78.

If Brock and Parker offer paradise as a vision of hope and healing, Chinese theologians participate in the discussion of Christianity and the construction of harmonious society. Chinese leaders promote the building of a harmonious society as a way to bridge gaps and ease contradictions between rich and poor, urban and rural, men and women, the majority Han and ethnic minorities. Theological faculties in China gathered in Nanjing in 2007 to discuss how Christianity might contribute to this national effort. For them, the construction of a harmonious society depends on harmonious relation between God and humans, between human beings, and between humans and nature. God's love, manifested in the death and reconciliation of Jesus Christ, motivates Christians to create a harmonious earth and society and peace and reconciliation among religions.[30]

Theological Counterpoints

In 2003 the Academy Award winning Chinese composer Tan Dun conducted the premiere of *The Map* in Boston, a work commissioned by the Boston Symphony Orchestra. Inspired by rural and ritual music Tan heard as a child in Hunan, China, this multimedia event featured video recordings of folk musicians playing within the context of a Western symphonic piece. In a workshop prior to the performance Tan talked about his music, which commentators have said creatively blends the East and the West. He said Bach has created magnificent and sophisticated counterpoints. Going a step further, Tan sought to create counterpoints across the divide of East and West, sound and silence, image and sound. Taking the cue from Tan Dun then, the idea of theological counterpoints can mean creating sound, resonance, and echoes of diverse theological voices from different social and geographical locales. The public space in and from which a theologian speaks is not defined or bounded by the immediate social context in

---

[29] Lai Pan-chiu, "Cong wenhua shenxue zaisi hanyu shenxue" (Rethinking Chinese theology from cultural theology), cited in ibid., 263-64.

[30] Gao Ying, ed., *Judijiao yu goujian kexie shehui* (Christianity and the construction of harmonious society) (Nanjing: Nanjing Union Theological Seminary, 2008).

which he or she lives and works. Our theological imagination will be stretched if we can develop the capacity to hear and appreciate the stone cymbals in rural China and the cello at the same time. Just as listening to music across time and space can create new musical genres, theology in the transnational age needs to experiment with new forms and new imaginary.

Given the colonial past, the construction of "the West and the rest" still influences our discussion of political theology in the Asia Pacific to a large extent. The structure of global power is uneven, and Western countries continue to dominate in economics and knowledge production. In terms of political theology, European Christianity has a much longer and rich history than Asian Christianity. But as Chen Kuan-Hsing has noted, global and regional changes have produced impetus and possibilities to break through this binary. He proposes an alternative strategy that "posits the West as bits and fragments that intervene in local social formations in a systematic, but never totalizing way."[31] Within such a framework, the West is considered a fragment within the local and a cultural resource among many others, instead of an opposing force to be constantly negated and resisted. To overcome the constant pressure to make the West the reference point, Chen suggests inter-referencing, fostering dialogues and communications within Asia and with the Third World to create new imaginary horizons for comparison.[32] In doing so, we will construct multiple frames of reference unconfined by nativist or Eurocentric viewpoints.

The need to move beyond binary and stabilized constructions of identities, cultures, and geographies is emphasized by Asian and Asian American theologians. Korean theologian Namsoon Kang notes that Asian feminist theology is still largely defined by a sharp contrast between Asia and the West. She argues that a nativist approach will confine Asian feminist theology within *"geographically deterministic* and *culturally essentialist* discursive boundaries."[33] Instead, she proposes

---

[31] Chen, *Asia as Method*, 223.

[32] Ibid.

[33] Namsoon Kang, "Re-constructing *Asian* Feminist Theology: Toward a *Glocal* Feminist Theology in an Era of Neo-Empire (s)," in *Christian Theology in Asia*, ed. Sebastian C. H. Kim (Cambridge: Cambridge University Press, 2008), 221. Emphasis hers.

a *glocal* feminist theology in which the global and local contexts are combined to resist empire(s) of all forms and to strengthen solidarity with women, the marginalized, and the displaced. The task of feminist theology in Asia within this *glocal* purview has two prongs. The first is the internal critique of kyriarchical structures in theologians' own local cultures and societies. The second is to link theologians' local realities and the hybrid experience of Asian women in their own contexts with global geopolitical reality.[34]

Jonathan Tan notes that the Asian American theologians of the first generation have largely directed attention to external racism and discrimination, which they encountered in the church and society. They have paved the way for the second generation, who represent a much broader cross-section of Asian Americans, disciplines, religious backgrounds, and ecclesial affiliations. These theologians came into prominence in the 1990s and 2000s and applied interdisciplinary approaches to theologizing on a variety of issues. In addition to issues of reconciliation and community transformation, they are interested in the relations between faith, Bible, evangelism, ethnicity, and culture. Since Asian American theology has been more or less accepted by the mainstream institutions, the second generation theologians have freedom and space to address internal challenges within the Asian American communities. Newer voices, such as those from Asian American feminist theologians, gay and lesbian theologians, Asian adoptees, and Evangelical and Pentecostal theologians, are being heard.[35] Lester Edwin J. Ruiz further notes, "[W]hile not oblivious to the call to engage with the claims of a Pacific and global world, second generation Asian Americans have a clear, substantive, methodological, and political/institutional commitment to their particular locations and positionalities that sees the 'local' and the 'global' as co-constitutive."[36]

A theological horizon that sees local history and positionalities as closely related to changing global realities would require us to conceptualize nation, continent, territory, and race with a new imaginary.

---

[34] Ibid., 221-22.

[35] Tan, *Introducing Asian American Theologies*, 99-101.

[36] Lester Edwin J. Ruiz, "Recovering the 'Body Politic': Racialized and Gendered Diaspora in Accredited Graduate Theological Education," *Journal of Race, Ethnicity, and Religion* 1/6 (2010): 34.

In the debates on postcolonial biblical criticism tensions exist between those scholars who "work@home" (anaphora) and those who live in diaspora. Gerald O. West from South Africa has argued that postcolonial criticism done by diasporic scholars in metropolitan centers should not elide those who remain @home and who get their hands dirty in actual postcolonial contexts.[37] While I agree that we cannot elide the differences of the concerns and starting points of work@home and diasporic scholars, I want to problematize any stabilized concepts of "home" and "diasporic." In the Asian Pacific diasporic experience refers not only to those who leave Asia to go to the West, but also successive waves of migration of Asians, such as the Indians and Chinese, to other Asian countries and Pacific islands. In the age of globalization, when the local is constantly impinged upon by the global, one may feel diasporic even if one lives @home. To complexify the picture, many Asian Americans are treated as perpetual foreigners even though they may be second or third generation Americans and are constantly being asked the question, "Where do you come from?"

I agree with Joseph Duggan, who says we need to push established boundaries and "create multiple dialogical openings that foster porosity, interstitial relationships, and hybridity."[38] With the help of technology he hopes to create a public space so that theologians and activists@home, in diaspora, and in metropolitan centers can be in proximity to one another and exchange views. [39] My notion of theological counterpoint is to encourage us to hear our own theological voice as a part of the theological symphony, and not isolated from one another. We will all be diminished if there is only one hegemonic voice,

---

[37] Gerald O. West, "What Difference Does Postcolonial Biblical Criticism Make: Reflections from a (South) African Perspective," in *Postcolonial Interventions: Essays in Honor of R. S. Sugirtharajah*, ed. Tat-siong Benny Liew (Sheffield: Sheffield Phoenix Press, 2009), 270.

[38] Joseph Duggan, "The Performance and Embodiment of Hybridity, Porosity, and Interstitial Relationships: A Vision for the Journal of Postcolonial Theory and Theology," *Journal of Postcolonial Theory and Theology* 1/1 (October 2010): 3.

[39] Duggan operates a Postcolonial Theology Network on Facebook and a Postcolonial Networks Web site (www.postcolonialnetworks.com), and he founded the online *Journal of Postcolonial Theory and Theology* (www.postcolonialjournal.com).

or when there are multiple voices with one dominant all the time. In the development of transnational political theology in the Asia Pacific it is critical for Asian, Pacific, and Asian American theologians to maintain dialogue, so that we can learn to hear each other's rhythm, discern the coming and emerging horizon, and be open to self-critique.

Fumitaka Matsuoka, who has done much to promote conversations on Asian American theology, speaks of the "monopoly of imagination" when a dominant group uses power to guard and enforce its norms, virtues, and worldviews to the exclusion of others'.[40] He laments that Asian Americans are often anxious that they will remain a "minor key," irrelevant and insignificant in the eyes of the mainstream. Yet it is in the liminal space of "in-betweenness" that one remains intensely alert and refuses to accept easily what is regarded as common sense. He writes, "A person in a liminal world is poised in uncertainty and ambiguity between two or more social constructs, reflecting in the soul the discords and harmonies, repulsions and attractions."[41] I believe transnationalism and globalization have thrust many people into living in such "holy insecurity,"[42] as Matsuoka calls it. We stand at the threshold of a new age, in which technology and the information highway would radically transform our understanding of theological community and enable us to hear counterpoints that we might not have imagined before.

---

[40] Fumitaka Matsuoka, *The Color of Faith: Building Community in a Multiracial Society* (Cleveland: United Church Press, 1998), 76.

[41] Fumitaka Matsuoka, *Out of Silence: Emerging Themes in Asian American Churches* (Cleveland: United Church Press, 1995), 54.

[42] Ibid., 53.

Chapter 5.

Postcolonialism in Fugue: Contrapuntality of Asian American Experience

Wonhee Anne Joh

My memories of Korea
They seem so strange sometimes
Like they are about someone else's childhood
That I had stolen...
So I try to look for bridges,
To give meaning to my short existence in Korea
Before I became a hyphenated duality.
Someday I will go back to Korea
And look at my past in the face.
Try to reconcile my past and my present.
Figure out why my memories keep haunting me still and
Maybe mourn for the person
I could have been if I had never been planted
Somewhere else.
Julie Kim, Red and Yellow Dreams

No matter how I tried, I could not remember the alphabet. I cried out of sheer frustration and feelings of stupidity. Not knowing English was making my life miserable. In the time it took for my family to travel across the Pacific Ocean to the United States, I lost my voice and even, according to kids at the new school, my intelligence. I wanted to learn English quickly. When I went to school, not only were children making fun of me for not knowing how to speak English, but even Korean children were malicious. This betrayal felt unexpectedly humiliating and confusing. Some of them even tricked me. One Korean boy gave me his nickels and took my dimes. He said the bigger nickel was valued more than the smaller dime. About a week after our arrival in this country, we did the mile run and that I could do. I couldn't speak English but I could run so I ran my heart out. Once I began feeling the wind in my hair I could not stop running. All my pent-up emotions poured out in tears as I ran. I ran right off the track and ran all the way to my grandmother's home and told her I wanted to go back to Korea. That was back in 1976.

Feelings of Being "Out of Place":
Haunting and Contrapuntality of Asian American Experience

Memories of the past are always with us even as they are not static but always remembered differently; that difference appears in microscopic changes, say, in the smell associated with that memory. While some parts may be crystal clear and sharp, other parts remain unfocused and hazy, much like a dream as it fades with each waking moment. Eventually I did return to Korea for a visit but by then I knew that my identity was already changed by my life in the United States. I did not feel at home in Korea, but I still do not feel at home in the United States. Between this present moment and 1976 are reference points—multiple, complex and dynamically moving—and they continue to influence the way I experience and know the spectrum of belonging and not belonging.

How do our still-present pasts continue to haunt us? How is it that the place one has left continues to haunt even as one tries with every effort to belong to a new place, despite its latent and sometimes overt hostility? History presents forms of powerful spectral reality and forms of spectral witnessing (for example feelings of being 'out of place,') that help us to recognize dormant ghosts of our past lives. No totalizing reach of dominant forces can ultimately and permanently repress or erase other truths and realities.[1] Haunting memories allow us to re-member these

---

[1] William V. Spanos, *American Exceptionalism in the Age of Globalization: The Specter of Vietnam* (New York: State University of New York Press, 2008).

always vibrating, simmering, and shadowed spectral presences. During my doctoral studies, I came across Edward Said's memoir, *Out of Place*. Since my head was buried in reading postcolonial theory, it was a real joy and delight to find his memoir. Said's memoir stirred memories that I had long forgotten or had buried as I trudged through my immigrant life. Though he wrote as a Palestinian exile his recollections found resonance in my life and experience as a Korean American immigrant. I, too, have often felt the desolate feeling of not belonging, of being here but not quite here, visible but not quite visible, accepted but not quite accepted, not quite white but not brown enough. Like Said, for whom the history of Palestine was and is fraught with a sense political ambush by dominant powers, I am also haunted by the colonial pasts of Korean history and Korea's struggle with dominating powers. Though I have lived most of my life in the United States and did not directly experience Japanese colonization of Korea, the traumas of the Korean War, or the U.S. ongoing occupation of Korea, it is stunning to recognize just how much these historical events continue not only to haunt people who directly experienced them but also to reproduce the traumatic affects of such historical legacies in ways often unbidden by latter generations. As Avery Gordon has noted, such a possibility of a collectively animated worldly memory is "articulated in extraordinary moments in which you—who never was there in that real place—can bump into a rememory that belongs to somebody else…or something else in the world is remembering you."[2] The question that I repeatedly find myself asking recently is *Why now?*

Similar to Said's own experience, my intense feeling of being 'out of place' has not vanished but has dogged me persistently. However, though this feeling has persisted, it no longer has such stabbing and sharply painful, nagging discomfort that demands a resolution. Rather, my journey has led me to realize that the state of being 'unhomed' presents an epistemological gift. This epistemological 'gift' is an unexpected one—a conditionality that makes possible a radical openness to the unsettling 'unhomedness' of others.

The future of Asian American theology is located at the nexus in which theology envisions a future that negotiates diverse and multiple

---

[2] Avery Gordon, *Ghostly Matters: Haunting and the Sociological Imagination* (Minneapolis: University of Minnesota Press, 1997), 166.

points of reference, dancing together contrapuntally. For some, the many and different notes within the ever expanding scope of Asian American theology may seem non-harmonious and counterproductive; but for many of us, it can only be, despite its many different and sometimes contradictory voices, polyvalent. In this way, Asian American theological thinking transforms non-coercively and generously with a utopian cast by recognizing the worldliness of all theological reflection.

Deploying Said's notion of contrapuntal reading and the musical strategy of fugue in understanding the complexity of Asian American experience and subject formation, I suggest, is useful because it accentuates a non-totalizing ethico-political imaginative vision of the world. With this notion of the fugue in the background, this essay sets forth diverse reference points that postcolonial Asian American theologians might further examine.

By deploying a contrapuntal method, this essay might be seen as a fugue, requiring an assemblage of at times contrasting and contradictory moves. In particular, the essay brings into relation the following three complex contrapuntal moves: a) it moves from sites of Asian-America, to Asia, back to Asian America—specifically drawing from Korean American experience; b) it moves from Asian America to its neglected but potent implicature in African America, Latino/a America's colonial struggles; and c) it explores a variety of viewpoints accented by the interplay of dynamics of race, gender, sexuality, and globalization. In so doing, I hope to display, insofar as one essay can do, the tapestry of thinking within which an Asian-American theology works.

Postcoloniality as a Form of Dissensual Practice:
The Postcolonial and the Decolonial

> …It is possible to define a certain dissensual practice of philosophy as an activity of de-classification that undermines all policing of domains and formulas. It does so not for the sole pleasure of deconstructing the master's discourse, but in order to think the lines according to which boundaries and passages are constructed, according to which they are conceivable and modifiable…. Engaging in critique of the instituted divisions, then, paves the way for renewing our interrogations into what we are able to think and to do.
> —Jacques Rancière, *Dissensus: On Politics and Aesthetics*

Postcolonialism is a discourse that emerged after the period of colonization. However, this is not to say that the rise of nation-states 'post' declarations of independence from colonization has led to decolonization. Conceivably, formal colonization has ended in many places; but the conditions of coloniality, its range and scope, are operative ever more efficiently today. In fact, one can argue that conditions of coloniality have become sophisticated and intricately woven into the very desires of those who were once colonized. The work of decolonization can no longer be expected to happen in any clear and precise manner so that a clear and final meta-revolutionary blow might give birth to a new epoch. Rather, decolonization or 'deimperialization' can only take place in a dialectical movement in which intersecting movements to decolonize occur simultaneously in multiple sites.

The presence of the United States in most parts of Asia in recent history cannot be examined in its totality here, but suffice to say that the presence of the United States in Asia has been determinative in many ways. Some of the consequences of this presence continue to haunt not only those in Asia but also in the United States—and not only Asian Americans. Because of this interwoven history, postcolonial discourse can become a strategic reading of Asian American experience in the United States and thus suggest ways that identity formations emerge within a complex global nexus of relations of power. Specifically, this is to suggest that Asian American identities are not formed in isolation and within the boundaries of the U.S. nation-state, but rather are formed continuously within the relational flow and flux of global dynamics. This involves constructed domains and formulas that are both physical and epistemological. In this, too, there is recognition that given boundaries and borders are constructed as well as 'naturalized' in colonial projects. I will be suggesting, too, that postcolonial critique, is, at its best, a form of what Rancière terms 'dissensual practice',[3] wielded by those who continue to envision a decolonial world. I am reading the 'post' in 'postcolonial' as necessitating a critique—a dissensus—that envisions a *de*colonial world. As dissensual practice, postcolonial critique interrogates the limits and boundaries of not only what we believe to be

---

[3] Jacques Ranciere, *Dissensus: On Politics and Aesthetics* (New York: Continuum, 2010).

'given' but also what we are sanctioned to imagine. In other words, not only does postcolonial critique examine the effects and affects of coloniality in the history of various peoples, but it also interrogates the always-already-assumed 'givenness' and 'rightness' of notions such as the following: democracy, human rights, capitalism, communism, globalization, development, love, salvation, rights and wrongs, virtues, and vices. Postcolonial critique seeks to decolonize these often-assumed goods, not through some search for the native but by dismantling metanarratives of identitarianism and of the on-going imperial reach that pervades the innermost reaches of our very desires, nostalgia and hopes. This all means that its goal is not to ferret out and pinpoint the exact location of colonial damage. Rather, one of postcolonial critique's ongoing interests is an examination of the intermingling effect and affect of past and present colonial practices by both the colonizers and the colonized. As this envisions decolonized worlds, it then also is as much about the future as it is about the past.

Asian American identities are thus not shaped solely by their relation to 'America' or by the singularity of 'Asia', but are constituted by what it means to be part of the imagined geo-political dynamics of Asian and American, Asia and the United States. In this regard, Asian American theological thinking must transgress the given boundaries and limits already erected by the past. Transgression means to cross over. It is a "…moving from one domain to another, the testing and challenging of limits, the mixing and intermingling of heterogeneities, cutting across expectations, providing unforeseen pleasures, discoveries, experience."[4] For Asian American theological reflections, this assumes a radical critique of the imperial metaphysical logic of the West—both ontological and epistemological—that colonized most of our own structure of thinking and knowing. As philosopher William Spanos, a noted critic of Edward Said's work writes, "If there is any single motif that subsumes the last thirty years' various oppositional discourses, whether philosophical, cultural, or sociopolitical, it is the indefinite but very real notion of some other reality that, try as the custodians of the truth might to annul 'it', always returns to haunt this global truth."[5] Dominant and

---

[4] Edward Said, *Musical Elaborations* (New York: Columbia University Press, 1991).

[5] William V. Spanos, *The Legacy of Edward Said* (Chicago: University of

dominating logics, which are imperialist, ontological and epistemological, cannot forever subdue the return of the repressed that gives shape to the world that is still to come.

To that end, Said's notions of fugue and contrapuntality are suggested as useful metaphors. 'Fugue' is a metaphor that helps us to understand not only the integrity of singularity but also that of plurality. In music, fugue/fuga is a polyphonic composition described as texture rather than form. It is a contrapuntal composition in which many voices enter then fade and re-enter and often overlap with one another. Contrapuntal productivity is an intellectual practice traversing interdependent linkages and histories, seeking a kind of ever shifting but still textured sociality. Fugue is a musical practice that can become a useful theological practice that suggests possibilities and conditions that might make singularity and plurality possible even as it recognizes interdependent histories that point toward textual sociality. Contrapuntality as reading against the grain blurs the line of center/periphery, East/West, and citizen/non-citizen by questioning assumed binaries so that one begins to recognize the depth of our 'worldliness'—the inevitable fact of hybrid nature of all cultures and identities. Postcolonial contrapuntal reading of U.S. history, then, sheds light on how race, imperialism, colonization, gender, and sexuality all work to form the ideal 'American' that often did not and does not include Asian Americans in the dominant white imaginary. Ironically this simultaneous exclusion and inclusion gives birth to ever newly-regenerated notions of who that idealized 'American' is to be, which often continues not to be extended to Asian Americans, or for that matter to many who are not white. Providing whites with a ready alibi is of course the myth of the Model Minority (myths of inclusivity.) It also has a way of providing a false sense of honorary whiteness for some Asian Americans, a false sense of acceptance into whiteness. Simply put, as much as I would like to think that the Model Minority notion is just a myth that is resisted and actively disavowed and opposed by Asian Americans, I find that there are Asian Americans who accept and believe in their exceptionality—that as model minorities they are exceptional from among other minorities in this country and much closer to the American ideal than other minorities. As Vijay Prashad has noted, "The immigrant seeks a form of vertical

---

Illinois Press, 2009), 225.

assimilation, to climb from the lowest, darkest echelon on the stepladder of tyranny into the bright whiteness....Asians and Latinos have all tried to barter their varied cultural worlds for the privileges of whiteness."[6] On the other hand, we cannot blithely ignore various extenuating and often complex ways in which multiple reference points are held and negotiated delicately and intentionally by Asian Americans in the formation of their very plural subjectivity. Rather than seek vertical integration, there are those who instead intentionally cultivate and nurture a horizontal assimilation.[7] Cultivation of horizontal violence would involve a working across and with multiple sites of racial/ethnic communities and others who are continually marginalized to form collaborative alliances and mutual understanding. Because of the intense, so-called interventionist presence of the United States in much of Asia, Asian and American formations are in most cases co-constitutive of each other through shared multiple reference points, simultaneously bringing about the shattering force of the new with what seems like dissonance. In this regard, it is not only unjust but also dangerous to continue to view Asian American formation as separate from the intersecting histories of Asia and the histories of U.S. intervention and presence throughout Asia. Said's notion of contrapuntality/fugue is a helpful methodological vision because it combines the complexity of an ever-shifting, differentiated singular/plural world on the one hand, with a pervasive sense of 'over-againstness', similar to Ranciere's dissensus practice, on the other.

Dissensual practice is cognizant of Spivak's 'axiomatics of imperialism' in which one's complicity in the economic and social structures of so-called interventionist/imperialist presence should not be neglected. Contrapuntal reading as one form of dissensus practice, then, opens up a space in which one's own epistemological foundations (often trained in assumptions of Western Enlightenment) can be transgressed. Postcolonial theory (and theology more specifically) must be attentive to the possibility and danger of becoming unmoored from the task of decolonization. Because the 'post' in the postcolonial often inadvertently connotes an 'aftermath' or an 'end' of a colonial era, it can result in misleading conclusions that the postcolonial era is free of any

---

[6] Vijay Prashad, *Everybody Was Kung Fu Fighting: Afro-Asian Connections and the Myth of Cultural Purity* (Boston: Beacon Press, 2001), x.
[7] Ibid.

lingering colonial consequences. It is thus paramount for postcolonial critique to employ a 'decolonial' tactic (or to use Malini Johar Schueller's notion, to become a 'resistance postcolonialism') in which dissensual practice is a crucial part of the on-going analyses of what seems to be a continually-morphing of former colonial practices into ever new and shifting global theories and practices of globalization.

We can then respond to Kandice Chuh's question: "What is specifically useful about postcolonial and postcoloniality as critical terms of Asian Americanist analysis?"[8] Modified with theology in mind, we might ask the question in this manner: What is useful about postcolonial and postcoloniality as critical terms for Asian American theological reflection? Any response to this latter question must address the fundamental form of dissensual practice that is at the heart of any postcolonial theological project—a project that is always already attuned to a contrapuntal reading of a textured world.

Postcoloniality Between Asia and Asian America

> There must be a dialectical process in any deimperialization movement, then what conditions need to be created in the United States to bring about an effective movement there?
> —Kuan-Hsing Chen, *Asia As Method*

What are the conditions of possibility for Asians in America? Most Asian American studies have thus far tended to focus on the Asian in American. While the need for historical recollections of Asians and their roles in the United States is crucial to the kinds of tasks that Gary Okihiro writes about in the opening epigraph of this essay, such historical reconstructions have tended to focus solely on the domestic parameters of the U.S. nation-state. This is not enough. The complexity marking conditions of possibility for the diverse lives of Asians in the United States in the past, present and the future must be examined and reconstructed with closer scrutiny of what happened/s in the United States and, at the same time, with the United States' involvement

---

[8] Kandice Chuh, *Imagine Otherwise: On Asian Americanist Critique* (Durham: Duke University Press, 2003), 117.

elsewhere. For example, our recent domestic policy on immigration cannot be fully understood without understanding the historical underpinning of not only our domestic record of anti-immigration violence but also U.S. involvement in countries around the world. Postcolonial theorist, Gayatri C. Spivak writes that "war is an alibi every imperialism has given...and a civilizing mission carried to the extreme."[9] U.S. involvement in Asia is numerous and devastating. Asian American experiences cannot be coherently or fully understood apart from the analysis of U.S. involvement in those countries. For example, Asian American scholar Jodi Kim notes how important it is to conceptualize Asian American critique and cultural politics in ways that "mark the contradictions and ambivalent entanglements of American empire and gendered racial formations as the context out of which the post-World War II Asian American subject emerges and constitutes itself as such."[10] Thus, speaking and articulating meanings for Asian American subject formation cannot be done apart from the deeper examination of their connections to Asians' experiences of U.S empire in Asia. Asian American experience therefore is directly linked to the ways that Asia has experienced the United States and vice versa. Whether it is in the Philippines, Korea, Japan or Vietnam, U.S involvement in those countries has left a mark on not just Asian and Asian American subjects but also on the dominant U.S. imaginary. This is not to say that Asia remains unchanged or innocent of imperial dynamics; analysis also implicates Asia with its own-to use Chen's term-'subimperial' projects. For example, Korea's own imperial desires are manifested in various parts of the globe where the economic power can be exploited by Korea itself. Globalized Korean transnational capitalist forces can be found at work exploiting both laborers and the natural resources of these places. Furthermore, as in the case of Korea, they are not only going 'elsewhere' (as is Mexico) to practice their subimperial desires. Reflecting U.S. imperial desires, Koreans are also now facing phenomenal growth in the numbers of non-Korean laborers working and living in Korea. Many were legally allowed to come into Korea to serve needs not being met by Koreans themselves. The cultural, political and social conditions [and

---

[9] Spivak, "Terror: A Speech After 9-11," *boundary 2* 31:2 (2004), 94.
[10] Jodi Kim, *Ends of Empire: Asian American Critique and the Cold War* (Minneapolis: University of Minnesota Press, 2010), 7.

suffering] with which these migrant workers and increasingly large populations of permanent Korean residents live are appalling to say the least. While economically exploited, these people face cultural political, social conditions of racism and xenophobia living among Koreans. Just as Asian American analysis of U.S. imperial designs is a complex endeavor, one that involves a simultaneous analysis of relations of power that spread around the world, any analysis of Asia must recognize that Asia, too, is a complex constellation of regional historical enmities and conflicts that must be addressed. Asia is not some 'pure' and 'innocent' bystander victimized by U.S. empire. While the victimization of Korea by the United States is a crucial dynamic, Asia also has been complicit with aiding and abetting U.S. imperial designs elsewhere. It is important to ask why this ongoing relationship between, say, Korea and the United States is an important site of analysis for examining influences that shape the conditions of possibility for Koreans in Korea as well as of Koreans in the United States. More nuance and deeper analysis needs to be offered to the response I share here briefly.

How the U.S. imaginary constructs its understanding of Korea and of Koreans in Korea has a direct impact on ways that Koreans in America are understood and treated. It is part of the racism borne by Koreans (and by other Asian Americans) that most U.S. citizens cannot differentiate between Korean Americans and Koreans. There have been more instances than I can recount here in which I am treated as if I am a foreigner and not an American citizen. Moreover, I am also viewed as a victimized foreigner who needs and continues to need U.S. benevolent rescue. This latter construct allows for a whole slew of racist stereotypes to continue to operate and recycle in the psyches of the dominant U.S. collective. To be sure, this ensures not only that the positionality of Koreans in Korea remains frozen in time and place, but it also requires constructs of Korean Americans in the dominant U.S. imaginary to remain stagnant. By challenging this singularity and instead seeking multiple reference points, Asian American scholars transform the way we understand Asia, Asian America, and the United States always in the nexus of relations of power.

Postcolonial Asian America: Its Relations to Afro-Asian and Asian-Latino/a colonial struggles

> Polyculturalism is a ferocious engagement with the political world of culture, a painful embrace of the skin and all its contradictions.
> —Vijay Prashad, *Everybody Was Kung Fu Fighting*

A recent work on understanding of race by Korean Americans is the work of Nadia Y. Kim. Her work shifts studies of transnational understandings of race away from the more typical American-centered framework of U.S. immigrants.[11] By focusing instead on the context of U.S. imperialism and its global activities (specifically in Korea), she argues that Korean Americans' understanding of race precedes by a long time their immigration to the United States. Korean Americans' subject formation, she argues, began in Korea, especially during and in the aftermath of the Korean War. Korean immigrants' understanding of race, then, was not newly constructed after they set foot in the United States. Instead, Kim insists, both America's and Korea's racial formations were well underway even prior to immigration or the presence of Koreans in the United States. To be sure, the work of racial identity formation began not only for Koreans' understanding of themselves and of white Americans, but also for their perception of Latinos and African Americans even before Koreans set foot in the U.S. Before they entered the cultural landscape of U.S. discrimination against Latinos/as and against African Americans in the context of Jim Crow, they imbibed modes of this discrimination from the relations of the military service people in Korea. Analysis of the extent of racial formation and learning of racialized identities in Korea during this time exceed the scope of this essay, but suffice it to note that the lasting consequences of this complex racial formation, prior to immigration, have had major consequences in the immigrant communities in the United States. This orients Asian American thinkers, including theologians, to a much more complex task: reading events at multiple sites where a diverse Asia meets a diverse 'America.' In the remainder of this section I refer to two such sites: the Bandung conference in mid-20th century Indonesia and the still-debated

---

[11] Nadia Y. Kim, *Imperial Citizens: Koreans and Race from Seoul to L.A.* (Stanford: Stanford University Press, 2010).

case of *Plessy v. Ferguson* in late 19th century United States. These cases and others can move us toward re-examining our learned reflexes when it comes to complicity in inter-racial, racialized identity formations.

Consider, first, the case of Bandung. In April 1954, the Indonesian Government proposed the convocation of an Asian-African conference. This Asian-African Conference, also known as the Bandung Conference, was held in Bandung, Indonesia, from April 18 through 24 in 1955. Twenty-nine Asian and African countries attended the conference. The spirit of unity of the Asian and African people as demonstrated at the conference—opposing imperialism and colonialism, the struggle for the defense of national independence and world peace, and the promotion of friendship among the peoples—is known as the 'Bandung Spirit'. The conference enhanced the unity and cooperation among the Asian and African countries, inspired the people in the colonies to struggle for national liberation, played a significant role in promoting the anti-imperialist and anti-colonialist struggle of the Asian and African people, and consolidated their unity. In his book, *The Color Curtain*, Richard Wright records his observations of the Bandung Conference. He notes that the document jointly written at the conference was the "last call of westernized Asians to the moral conscience of the west."[12]

The Asian-African Conference was held at a time when post-war movement for national liberation in Asia, Africa and Latin America was vigorously surging forward, and the forces of imperialism and colonialism were met with heavy blows. It was the first international conference held by Asian and African countries themselves without the participation of any Western colonial power. The Bandung conference was an attempt to forge cross-racial political alliances, analyze the tensions that can make coalitions difficult, and trace the way those alliances are co-opted with monotonous regularity. Later, at the Havana Conference of 1966, the three continents of South America, Asia, and Africa came together in a broad alliance to form the Tricontinental—a movement of coalition building, collaboration and mutual recognition in working counter to the powers of injustice.[13]

---

[12] Richard Wright, *The Color Curtain* (Jackson: University Press of Mississippi, 1956), 202.

[13] Cf. Vijay Prashad, *The Darker Nations: A People's History of the Third*

The second case of complex racial calculus of Asians and 'America' returns us to the U.S. context. There is a long history of Afro Asian writing among U.S. figures, from W.E.B. Du Bois' engagement with Asian politics to Paul Robeson's internationalism, in which he attempt to forge cultural links between oppressed peoples across a variety of national, racial and political contexts. While efforts were made by Asians and Africans to forge alliances, it is also true that Asians and Africans were often pitted against each other in the racial framework of the United States. There are numerous cases in recent years that the media has pointed to as racial conflicts between African Americans and Asians, specifically between Korean- and African-Americans. Without going further into these events, I want to highlight an important event as an example of how frequently the white racial logic has made it difficult—if not impossible—for Asians and Africans to forge alliances.

The historical case of *Plessy v. Ferguson* is often recited as familiar history. In 1892, Homer Plessy purchased a first class train ticket in New Orleans. Plessy was "a citizen of the United States and a resident of the state of Louisiana, of mixed descent, in the proportion of seven-eighths Caucasian and one-eighth African blood."[14] The reigning one-drop rule legally classified him as 'black.' However, according to certain accounts, a "mixture of colored blood was not discernable in him." After buying his ticket, he sat in a vacant seat in the 'whites only' section and then was removed and jailed. In 1896 the Supreme Court ruled against Plessy by holding the constitutionality of the 'equal but separate' doctrine. The vote was seven to one. The single dissenting voice was that of Justice John Marshall Harlan. Marshall Harlan argued against the segregation noting, "There is no caste here. Our constitution is color blind, and neither knows nor tolerates classes among citizens. In respect of civil rights, all citizens are equal before the law."[15] Interestingly there is a little known part of his opinion. He invokes a third racial category, one that speaks of neither black nor white. He observes

---

World (New York: The New Press, 2007).

[14] Sanda Mayzaw Lwin, "A Race So Different From Our Own": Segregation, Exclusion, and the Myth of Mobility," in *AfroAsian Encounters: Culture, History Politics* eds. Heike Raphael-Hernandez and Shannon Steen (New York: New York University Press, 2006), 19.

[15] Ibid., 19

that there exists a third group whose difference prohibited its members not only from becoming U.S. citizens but also from entering the very borders of the nation. He noted "there is a race so different from our own that we do not permit those persons belonging to it to become citizens of the United States. Persons belonging to it are with few exceptions, absolutely excluded from our country. I allude to the Chinese race."[16] Harlan invoked the Chinese race in his dissent to provide bodily proof that the Louisiana state is unjust to the 'citizens of the black race.' While his disagreement with the other seven who voted against Plessy is admirable, his logic was still within the white racist framework. By positioning one racial group over another, he manipulates the already-percolating racial divide by redrawing it as one between Asian and African American. The imagined body of the 'Chinaman' troubles the order of the color line in a way that is different from the way Plessy's body does. Thus, the Asian body is deployed as a buffer between whites and blacks.[17] In effect, Harlan was arguing *against* segregating Plessy by invoking the acceptability of segregating the Chinese. In crude form, Harlan was saying *"Look, Plessy isn't Chinese, so he shouldn't be subject to the logic of caste."*

Given this kind of historical deployment of racial categories within the United States in addition to the decolonial movements of anti-colonial and anti-racist spirit of the Bandung gathering, how might Asians in America negotiate their own and others' racial anxieties and also resist racialized bifurcations? How might Asians in America collaborate with other racialized communities toward decolonization? The accusation flung at many Koreans by other racialized groups is that Koreans are racists. As I have indicated, perhaps this has much to do with learned racism in the context of the U.S. imperial presence in Korea. Rather than 'racists', Nadia Kim describes Koreans as "racially prejudiced" in the same way she "would not describe Black Americans who reiterate anti-Korean or anti-Asian stereotypes to be racist but prejudiced."[18] Kim's observation stems from her argument that globalization is not just the spread of military and capital but also a flow

---

[16] Ibid., 20

[17] The Chinese Exclusion Acts 1882-1943 not only prohibited Chinese immigration but also denied naturalized citizenship to those already here.

[18] Kim, *Imperial Citizens: Koreans and Race from Seoul to L.A.*, 9.

of images and ideas. One avenue of this is that the U.S. media saturation affects not only Koreans in Korea but also Koreans in America as well as other Americans. She goes on to argue that U.S. imperialism relies on "one group of color to help subordinate another group of color in a lesser country, thereby creating multiple and complex lines of inequality."[19] For those seeking to decolonize and resist racialized bifurcations, it is crucial that we engage in dissensual practices of resistant postcolonialism-one that springs from sites of quotidian practices of the political. It is thus necessary for postcolonial Asian American theology to examine the intricate ways in which we are all implicated in sustaining destructive racial ideologies in service to imperial desires.

Postcoloniality as Interplay of Race, Gender, Sexuality and Globalization

> It is often said that colonial imperialism is at an end in this world. We would better say that the end is in sight; or rather in the vision of certain men [sic]. It has not yet really ended.
> —W.E.B. Dubois, *Crossing the World Color Line*

It must be stressed, in this final major section that the multiplicity of moves in a contrapuntal method of Asian American theology must attend to the interplay not only between race and empire, or between race and coloniality, but *also* among these *and* gender, sexuality, and globalization. I have already suggested as much in the previous sections. It is necessary to comment on these with some greater specificity. Again, we find the interaction of a postcolonial complexity with dissensual practice. The contrapuntal fugue that is Asian American theology, then, reaches yet greater complexity and intensity. In this final section, I can only point out some of the dynamics of this interplay as illustrative.

Take first the issue of gendered experience. The construction of genders along a binary division must be criticized and problematized not only because of various ways in which this feeds into other social misogynistic impulses, but also because it is a bondage to the ways that

---

[19] Ibid.

men come to understand their identity. While in the past sexism was justified based on essentialist and biological notions of what constituted gender, feminist scholars today are arguing for anti-essentialist views and argue that one is not "born a female but becomes one." I extend this argument further to say then that one is not "born a male but becomes one" and even further to say that one is not born as a "woman of color" but "becomes one."[20] To be sure, rigid gender boundaries have always been transgressed and it is the task of feminist theologians to recover those transgressive occasions. I want to argue that a sustained and thorough investigation of how gender is also raced must continue to generate a wider conversation between scholars from all different racial/ethnic backgrounds. Gender is also simultaneously a practice of racing.[21] Here, I want to say that different people experience their gendered bodies differently. For example heteronormativity is often extended to neither women nor men of color. Thus, racialized men of color are often de-masculinized or overtly feminized. A white women's experience of heteropatriarchy, for example, cannot be universalized but rather should be localized, just as one Asian American woman's gendered self is understood differently. Moreover, this is the same for the way that a white Euro-American male's understanding of 'masculinity' is quite different from an Asian male's experience. While biologists argue that there is no such thing as different 'races' within our human species, the experience of race is a concrete reality. Structural and systemic oppression based on notions of existing racial hierarchy and superiority is concretely present in our history and in our present reality. In the history of settler colonialism in the Unites States, white racism rooted in white supremacy gave birth to the colonization of this land and its peoples in addition to institutionalized slavery; this is attested to in the weight of our nation's history. In fact, white racism defined who *were* and who *were not* even considered to be *human*. White racism continued throughout U.S. history and even today is at the core of beliefs that build and re-build our national identity.[22]

---

[20] Cf. M. Jacqui Alexander and Chandra Talpade Mohanty, *Feminist Genealogies, Colonial Legacies, Democratic Futures* (New York: Routledge, 1996).

[21] For an excellent critique of coloniality, race, gender and sexuality, see Anne McClintock, *Imperial Leather: Race, Gender and Sexuality in the Colonial Contest* (New York: Routledge, 1995).

White racism and sexism worked simultaneously to marginalize particular peoples in routinized daily practices of humiliation and loss of dignity. Racism and sexism are intermingled and often work to sustain the dominant identity through its anchoring in certain essentialist metanarratives about its own identity in opposition to different identities.

While the black/white dyad in critical race theory is important and must be sustained, we also need to complexify such conversations even more by examining how white racism deploys race differently against different groups of people so that there is no uniform strategy against all racialized people. Instead, its insidious nature is precisely due to its diverse strategies of deploying racism against different peoples differently.[23] Ultimately, it is important to recognize that racism so saturates heteropatriarchy that even white women are not exempt from being racialized. If gender and race are problematic categories that need further and ongoing theorization and theologizing by feminists and womanists, there is also a vital need to re-examine how we construct and understand sexuality.

Gender/race dynamics are bound up with those of sexuality/race. If the ruses of gender and race as clear categories are deployed as scaffolding to shore up and hold together structures of domination, heteronormativity is yet another concept that links all these threads together. Sexuality defined as 'straight', or as the 'norm', works to sustain patriarchal power over women and other men who transgress rigid sexual demarcations. In a heteronormative dominative structure, those who are deemed as 'other' are often seen to be sexually transgressive, degenerative, deviant, and in need of discipline and regulation. Not only are other racialized and gendered people then constructed as non-heterosexual, so also are those of other religions constructed by heteropatriarchal ideology as sexually deviant. We might ask if there are any differences between being a practicing white lesbian Christian and, say, a practicing lesbian Sikh?[24] How does race and

---

[22] Cf. Bonnie Honig, *Democracy and the Foreigner* (Princeton: Princeton University Press, 2001).

[23] Cf. Gary Y. Okihiro, *Common Ground: Reimagining American History* (Princeton: Princeton University Press, 2001).

[24] For an excellent discussion on white supremacy, heteronormativity, racialization of religion and sexuality, see Jasbir Puar, *Terrorist Assemblages: homonationalism in queer times* (Durham: Duke University Press, 2007).

gender get deployed here? According to the 'straight' epistemology, all those who are not heterosexual are deviant and queer. But there is also a lingering and persistent tendency even within queer communities to deploy race and gender against other queers of color which needs further unpacking. Moreover, we also need to ask the question of how and in what ways those who identify with LGBTIQ communities also sometimes fail to examine their complicity in the global capitalist project. Another complicating dimension is the ever expanding and deepening work of globalization as yet another way that coloniality has put on a new face.

The forces of globalization lead us to consider still further complexities without leaving the gender/race, and sexuality/race dynamics. In an age of rapid globalization, it is not surprising to say that feminist theology must also include finding ways to create just and sustainable existence. Colonization, imperialism and neoliberalism have left an indelible mark upon many lives and nations. Race, gender and sexuality have been used and deployed to mark the bodies that have been excluded and even abandoned. Nevertheless, there is an additional dynamic. In the age of globalization, which has and is shifting the way we define global power in our time, we are learning to recognize the emergence of a kind of 'financialization'[25] of the globe—one in which a division between the masses of the global poor far outnumber those few global elites whose access to wealth is far-reaching. As massive devastation is worked upon vulnerable people and the creation so that a privileged few accumulate wealth and resources beyond their need, we are faced with an unprecedented crisis of hunger, forced migration, disease, and death and—out of this mix—defiance and violence.

Amid the contrapuntal play of moves, we uncover questions that press toward dissensual practice to envision, again, a decolonized world. How might we theologize in ways that take life as sacred—all life? How do we theologize so that our world can continue and flourish? What deconstructive and reconstructive theological moves must be made so that we begin to reimagine the divine and this creation as sacred, as living in abundance rather than rooted in competition and scarcity? In

---

[25] Cf. Gayatri Chakravorty Spivak, *A Critique of Postcolonial Reason: Toward A History of the Vanishing Present* (Cambridge: Harvard University Press, 1999).

the West, we have a saying that "might does not make right." Yet, tragically, this is the base of our impulse for waging war on others. We steal other peoples' resources, exploit their labor, colonize their lands and create vicious cycles through self-hatred and violence and through injection of drugs, junkified informational technology and selling knock-off weapons—all in the name of progress and democracy. The caveat here is not simply that the 'West' is fast becoming the only practitioner of such modes of being in the world, but also that other powerful global elites have joined this rank. Feminist theology cannot but give critical attention to the ways that the financialization of the globe is deepening the suffering of masses of people worldwide. Globalization as a new form of neoliberal agenda is yet another re-created face of colonial legacy.

These are some of the queries of a postcolonial dissensual practice, and they set the agenda of an Asian-American theology that would address the interplay of race, gender, sexuality and globalization.

Coda

> To be human is to be intended toward the other.
> —Gayatri Chakravorty Spivak, *Death of a Discipline*

> The new global person ... is one whose heart is as large as the world.... A heart as large as the world is a heart that sees the connections of our lives, wherever we are located on this planet Earth.... A heart large as the world is the heart that experiences the pain of the world, especially the pain of those who have suffered the most. It is a heart that embraces the pain of the other, even the forces that are antagonistic to one's interest, for it knows that the pain of the one is the pain of all.
> —Eleazar Fernandez, *Reimaging the Human*

In arguing for a postcolonial deconstructive move, as I have throughout this essay, I want to insist that even when identity (whether gendered, raced, or sexualized, and whether performed in Asia or in the United States *or* in those complex places of intercontinental meeting) is provisional, one must engage in a persistent auto-critique in order to avoid over-determined authorization of identity and claims to authenticity. For example, the question of *who are the 'authentic inhabitants of margins'?* challenges 'womanist' or us to criticize ourselves persistently in order to avoid the ruse of monolithic, homogenous and totalizing notions of who or what we mean when we use the term 'Asian American' or 'feminist', queer. Instability of all rigid identitarianism must give way to identity as always positional and provisional in time and space. How, then, do we give narration to our experience/s without reifying certain essentialist stereotypes, or without reifying a particular narrative as the metanarrative? How do we speak about all the plurality, ambiguity, multiplicity and provincial ways that identity is understood, without allowing one's particular speaking and theorizing to feed into a particular imaginary, be it a white imaginary, that of a particular feminist imaginary, or for that matter even an Asian American queer feminist imaginary? We must be mindful of just how interdependent our lives are even when we live in 'worlds' apart from one another. We cannot in all honesty speak of the 'West' or the 'East' precisely because geopolitical histories cannot be so easily sliced and diced. While unique and specific peoples and national formations exist, there are also historical parallels and global links between different formations due to the ways that those formations are gendered, raced, or colonized.

Postcolonial contrapuntal reading of U.S. history sheds light on how race, imperialism, colonization, gender, sexuality all work to form the ideal of the 'heteropatriarchal American' that does not include anyone who transgresses the given, clear boundaries in the dominant white imaginary. How do we begin to theologize the ways in which we must right all the wrongs? Perhaps we must heed the words of people such as Gayatri Chakravorty Spivak (an atheist) when she notes that "one needs some sort of 'licensed lunacy' from some transcendental Other to develop the sort of ruthless commitment that can undermine the sense that one is better than those who are being helped..."[26] To avoid what Spivak decries as 'licensed lunacy', a continuous and sustained effort must be generated to move away from unilateral global feminist theologies and toward the building of coalitions and solidarities across differences—even those that seem insurmountable to some. By doing so, we will generate a worldview that embraces heterogeneity, multiplicity, and differences among and within ourselves and moves toward the

---

[26] Gayatri Chakravorty Spivak, *Other Asias* (Boston: Blackwell, 2008), 57.

recognition that all life is worthy of dignity and respect.²⁷ Indeed, we must train our imagination to dare to dream such fantastic possibilities as practices of postcolonial dissensual practice, always and already emphasizing the call for the decolonial in the postcolonial.

---

²⁷ For an excellent theological work that critiques the "logic of One" and offers a theology of multiplicity, see Laurel Schneider, *Beyond Monotheism: A Theology of Multiplicity* (New York: Routledge, 2008).

Chapter 6.

Elegies of Social Life:
The Wounded Asian American

James Kyung-Jin Lee

In his now classic meditation on pastoral care, *The Wounded Healer,* Henri Nouwen reaches into an even more iconic, ancient Talmudic legend to recast the role of the Messiah in the work of social transformation.[1] There is, Nouwen recounts, the story of Rabbi Yoshua ben Levi asking the prophet Elijah when the Messiah will come. "Go and ask him yourself," Elijah replies. The rabbi, astonished, asks where he is, and Elijah tells him that he is sitting at the gates of the city. When Rabbi Yoshua wonders how he will recognize the Messiah, Elijah describes him: "He is sitting among the poor covered with wounds. The others unbind all their wounds at the same time and then bind them up again. But he unbinds one at a time and binds it up again, saying to himself, 'Perhaps I shall be needed: if so, I must always be ready so as not to delay for a moment'."[2] Nouwen uses this image of the Messiah as a wounded healer to offer an image of pastoral care in which one's own sense of woundedness becomes the basis for recognizing the woundedness in others. It is this simple idea, woundedness as a more common bond between persons than any other form of sociality, that undergirds

---

[1] Henri Nouwen, *The Wounded Healer: Ministry in a Contemporary Society* (New York: Doubleday, 1979).
[2] Robert C. Dykstra, ed., *Images of Pastoral Care: Classic Readings* (St. Louis: Chalice, 2005), 76.

much of what it means to provide pastoral care to others in religious contexts, and in more secular parlance, to provide some measure of healing beyond therapeutic cure. You might imagine these pastoral and therapeutic encounters as intimate, face-to-face explorations of the soul and psyche, envisioning a chaplain's ear inches away from the raspy whisper of a patient lying on a hospital bed, or a counselor sitting side-by-side with a client who cannot face the world by herself. You might even recall, if you are so inclined, to reach back into that vision of the Messiah unbinding or binding his own wounds at the gates of the city, or of the story of Jesus inviting Thomas to touch the wounds on his hands and feet, visible evidence of his torture.

Keep all of these images in mind for another story. This one probably never happened, but still remains terribly true. It was first uttered in 1957, but few people listened then; over the next half century it has been told and taught to thousands of people, mostly college students, by hundreds of people, mostly college professors of English and Asian American Studies. This story picks up after another has ended. Ichiro Yamada, just returned to his hometown of Seattle after spending four years away—"two in camp and two in prison"—visits the University of Washington where he had been an engineering student before World War II forced him, his family, and hundreds of thousands of other Japanese Americans along the U.S. West Coast into camps (places ostensibly for their own protection, but which would invariably wound them all in ways immeasurable). Two years into his time "in camp," Ichiro makes the fateful decision that a few thousand other Nisei, U.S. born and second generation Japanese Americans, made when compelled to reply, "No-No," in response to two "loyalty" questions—whether they would willingly serve in the U.S. Armed Forces and whether they would forswear allegiance to the Japanese emperor. John Okada narrates in what would be his only published but now canonized novel *No-No Boy* (1957), that for this Ichiro was sent even farther away than his initial experience of internment, away even from the camps in which most Japanese Americans were confined; no-no boys were either sent directly to federal prison or spent the war years at the Segregation Center at Tule Lake, California. But this physical isolation from the main body of his community pales in relation to his return. In the eyes of those with whom he had grown up, Ichiro is seen as little more than an emasculated traitor, repugnant perhaps even more in the Japanese American community than he is in the national imagination that forced young men like him to make such impossible choices. He is, in the eyes of most in his community, socially dead. During his visit to the University Ichiro meets his former teacher, Professor Brown, whose overfriendliness does not disguise his desire to end the reunion prematurely. Although he acknowledges the injustice of the internment even before Ichiro does, Professor Brown quickly stands up and offers an insincere invitation to visit again. "It was seeing without meeting," Ichiro thinks to himself, "talking without hearing, smiling without feeling."[3] One need not doubt that Professor Brown has the best of intentions when he meets his former student, but no amount of goodwill can attend to the pain that Ichiro continues to experience, now exacerbated all the more; his pain, while acknowledged, is hardly reckoned with, so that the scene closes with Ichiro feeling "empty and quietly sad and hungry."[4] Professor Brown cannot look Ichiro in the eye, nor does he set up conditions under which Ichiro might feel authorized to reciprocate and participate in such communion.

Then our true story begins. While eating a hamburger, Ichiro encounters the "pleasant, thoughtful old face of Kenji, who was also twenty-five."[5] Meal completed, Ichiro, the no-no boy, walks with Kenji, a veteran, to his car. Kenji walks very slowly, and in a moment Ichiro discovers why: most of Kenji's right leg is gone. Ichiro asks Kenji about his wound, and Kenji responds, "Not having [my leg] doesn't hurt. But it hurts where it ought to be."[6] What follows is one of the most extraordinary exchanges between two men in Asian American literature. Kenji says, "It's not important how I lost the leg. What's important are the eleven inches," referring to what is left of his amputated leg; "I've got eleven inches to go, and you've got fifty years, maybe sixty. Which would you rather have?"[7] Kenji tells Ichiro that the amputations will continue until there is nothing left of his leg and, indeed, even this treatment will not prevent his premature death. Ichiro initially opts for Kenji's truncated future over his own anticipated long life of social death, but as the two unbind their wounds and show them to one another

---

[3] John Okada, *No-No Boy* (Seattle: University of Washington Press, 1976), 57.
[4] Ibid., 57.
[5] Ibid., 58.
[6] Ibid., 61.
[7] Ibid., 61.

it becomes clear that the purpose of the dialogue is less to determine a hierarchy of pain and more to confront the other's loss without qualification. Neither can take away what the other suffers; all that Kenji can say is that "mine is bigger than yours in a way and, then again, yours is bigger than mine,"[8] as each man makes a promise that he will see the other again.

Formally, this exchange establishes the characterological chiasmus bridged between the two men: Kenji's injury and the ongoing diseases that will kill him prematurely corporealize Ichiro's condition, able-bodied but suffering a social death exemplified by his complete alienation from his community. Okada uses a similar rhetorical device in another coupling, Ichiro's mother and the woman, Emi. Ichiro's mother is described as having "the awkward, skinny body of thirteen-year old...which had developed no further,"[9] and Emi, who in a Freudian fantasy becomes for Ichiro a surrogate maternal figure and lover, as "slender, with heavy breasts. . .[whose] long legs were strong and shapely like a white woman's."[10] In this latter case, Okada's focus on the different bodies the two women inhabit seems to underscore the relative legitimacy of their respective "fantasies": while Ichiro's mom is largely viewed as insane for her fervent belief that Japan has won the war, Emi's deep patriotism to American ideals better masks its similar baselessness, because like her appearance, her rhetoric ("this is a big country with a big heart") is easier to take.[11] But chiasmic renderings invite readers to look for deep connections as much as they highlight differences, and in these two couplings what we discern is not so much that one man is more pained than another (Kenji vs. Ichiro) or that one woman is more mad than the other (Emi vs. Ichiro's mother), but that all of these are expressions of woundedness that stem from the very same traumatic experience of the internment.

No other historical moment in Asian American history is more discussed and researched than the internment, perhaps because it is the signal event that gives the lie to the deep nationalist desire to "belong" to which so many of us aspire. There is something mundanely tragic in the

---

[8] Ibid., 65.
[9] Ibid., 10-11.
[10] Ibid., 83.
[11] Ibid., 96.

experience of the internment, at once inconceivable and more imaginable than, say, the horrific experiences of outright war, violence, and genocide that has been suffered by so many people of Asian descent (including Japanese Americans). The internment almost immediately invites ironic reflection, even from—perhaps especially from—those who were not sent away to these desert and swampy camps. Chester Himes, for example, begins *If He Hollers Let Him Go* (1945), the novel for which he is most well known, with a slightly wistful but certainly sardonic image of a young Riki Oyana singing "God Bless America" as he and his parents are sent off to the Santa Anita Racetrack-turned-Assembly Center, in preparation for their years in camp.[12] Perhaps Robert, Himes's African American narrator, can speak to this with special valence, given the specificities of his own embodied experience as a person racialized as black in the face of others racialized as white, or as Robert himself puts it so succinctly at the end of the first chapter, "the white folks sure brought their white to work with them that morning."[13] Himes doesn't dwell on little Ricky, but this light nod to Japanese American racialization even as the young boy sings his allegiance, is Himes's way of seeing in that moment a recognition of what Vijay Prashad calls the "horizontal assimilation," which U.S. people of color have learned as they watch other non-white groups suffer the innumerable expressions of white supremacy.[14] What is striking about the internment is the extent to which the betrayal felt by the Japanese American community was also so very ordinary in interrupting the collective, embodied experience of this community. "This embodied agency," Darius Rejali writes in a very different context, "confers intelligibility on our experiences. Ordinarily we do not notice this embodied universe in which we live, we *do* notice it when the structures and rhythms are interrupted, that is, in the course of ordinary betrayals. When ordinary betrayals occur, when habits that are second nature cease to make sense of our world, we experience our finitude."[15] The "ordinary betrayal" that is the experience of the

---

[12] Chester Himes, *If He Hollers Let Him Go* (New York: Thunder's Mouth, 1986), 3.

[13] Ibid., 15.

[14] Vijay Prashad, *Everybody Was Kung Fu Fighting: Afro-Asian Solidarities and the Myth of Cultural Purity* (Boston: Beacon, 2002).

[15] Darius Rejali, "Ordinary Betrayals: Conceptualizing Refugees Who Have Been Tortured in the Global Village," *Human Rights Review* 1/4 (2000): 9.

Internment interrupted in an instant an entire social narrative, and the reason the experience was so devastating, so traumatic, was its ordinariness. As documentarian Emiko Omori narrates in *Rabbit in the Moon* (1999), her film about the Internment, "The problem isn't that [the internment] was so bad. The problem is that it wasn't bad enough."[16]

This sense that the experience of the Internment wasn't "bad enough" to illuminate anything more than a diversion from a community's narrative arc toward greater belonging and assimilation is precisely what consigns the characters of *No-No Boy* to a mode that Arthur Frank calls "narrative wreckage," an inability to live with and in the story one has previously told of oneself, and the utter incapacity of that story to represent adequately the experience of this embodied existence. Here we might see correspondence with Rejali's notion of ordinary betrayal, except that it is not finitude as such that is the source of the betrayal or wreckage but the particular experience of finitude, not one of completeness or *telos*, but one of chaos, of in many ways the loss of narrative's capacity to mean. Why one's narrative no longer anchors is articulated in elegant simplicity by Frank: "The conventional expectation of any narrative, held alike by listeners and storytellers, is for a past that leads into a present that sets in place a foreseeable future. The illness story is wrecked because its present is not what the past was supposed to lead up to, and the future is scarcely thinkable."[17] The internment put the lie to the progressive temporality of Japanese American social and political "health." Bereft of this narrative of health so sought after, even as the community was placed behind barbed wire, something that Raymond Williams calls a "structure of feeling" emerged, "affective

---

[16] *Rabbit in the Moon* (1999). There remains an easy and often facile comparison between the experience of Japanese American internment and the Holocaust in which Japanese American suffering is diminished or summarily dismissed in the face of the atrocity of the attempted genocide of Jews and others by the Nazis. I continue to hear objections from students and others from the use of the term "concentration camp" to apply to the internment experience, as this American version—the logic goes—can never approach the horrors of the death camps in Eastern Europe. Not unrelated, this kind of analogical disavowal occurs also to blunt the experience of suffering by U.S. people of color in relation to the pain of people in the developing world.

[17] Arthur Frank, *The Wounded Storyteller: Body, Illness and Ethics* (Chicago: University of Chicago Press, 1995), 55.

elements of consciousness and relationships" that moved beyond the known verbal sociology of the community.[18] Indeed, not only did Japanese Americans experience the narrative wreckage of incarceration that made their social narrative no longer one of health but of illness, they also embodied the very essence of the socially ill: Japanese Americans became for the United States a pathogen that necessitated their quarantine, as politicians and military policy makers developed their social epidemiology. The experience of Japanese Americans of illness and as illness disrupted any utopian dream of acceptance. But what it also opened up was a narrative or what Avery Gordon calls a "sociological imagination" in which a new modality might emerge.[19] Thereafter, a new narrative was required, one that placed contingency, exigency, and non-continuity as primary modes of living. As Frank puts it, "In the beginning is an interruption. Disease interrupts a life, and illness then means living with perpetual interruption."[20]

Both Kenji and Ichiro know all too well what it is to live lives of perpetual interruption in *No-No Boy*, as both of them are marked as ill, albeit in different ways. Kenji drives a brand new Oldsmobile, material reward for his "sacrifice" on behalf of his country, but he must return again and again to the hospital to amputate more of what is left of his gangrenous leg, which he knows will kill him within two years. He was a good soldier and a "good patient" when he first lost his leg, but as his illness persists Kenji forecloses his narrative of good citizenship: "It wasn't worth it."[21] Conversely, and in an important way correspondingly, an otherwise physically healthy Ichiro becomes disease in the eyes of

---

[18] Raymond Williams, *Marxism and Literature* (Oxford: Oxford University Press, 1977), 198.

[19] "This sociological imagination does not just describe or rationally explain or tell us what to do. It also does not treat social construction—the making and making up of the social world and of us—as a professional curiosity or as the already available final answer to our most pressing questions. This other sociological imagination conjures, with all the affective command the word conveys, and it does so because it has greatly expanded impression of the empirical that includes haunted people and houses and societies and their worldly and sometimes otherwordly contacts." From Avery F. Gordon, *Ghostly Matters: Haunting and the Sociological Imagination* (Minneapolis: University of Minnesota Press, 1997), 204.

[20] Ibid., 56.

[21] Okada, *No-No Boy*, 60.

Japanese American veterans. When a flamboyant and bombastic veteran named Bull, who dons a gaudy pale blue skirt and ostentatiously shows off his white girlfriend, bumps into Ichiro in a bar, he "wiggled out into the open with exaggerated motions and began to brush himself furiously. 'Goddammit,' he says aloud, 'brand-new suit. Damn near got it all cruddy.'"[22] We can easily align Bull's assignment of Ichiro's "crud" with Mary Douglas's notion of "dirt" as "matter out of place."[23] Here, Ichiro's cruddiness is not simply his polluted status within a community that assigns veterans the role of "pure." A few lines earlier Bull calls out to Kenji by referring to his condition: "For crissake, if it ain't Peg-leg." Although meant in jest, in a kind of deliberate insensitivity designed to shore up a masculinist homosocial bond, Bull demonstrates just how subjected ill bodies are in a world that demands health. It is impossible for Kenji or Ichiro to live lives without interruption; their respective visible conditions (Peg-leg, crud) compel them to answer constantly the implicit question posed by those who consider themselves without injury, illness, or unhealthy: What is wrong with you?

If you hear the implication of blame, then you would be reminded of Susan Sontag's reflections on the cultural and social luggage brought to our modern understandings of illness. In *AIDS and Its Metaphor (1988)*, the sequel to her groundbreaking *Illness as Metaphor* (1979), Sontag references the disease on which she focuses much of her attention in the earlier essay: "Because of countless metaphoric flourishes that have made cancer synonymous with evil, having cancer has been experienced by many as shameful, therefore something to conceal, and also unjust, a betrayal by one's body. Why me?"[24] It is not much of a stretch to determine that these two questions—What is wrong with you? and Why me? —are intimately connected. This simultaneous identification of the wounded condition as one that invites both shame/blame and (ordinary) betrayal, rests in large part on the imperatives of what Arthur Frank calls the "restitution narrative" that pervades how we narrate our individual and collective lives. "Contemporary culture," Frank writes, "treats health as the normal condition that people ought to

---

[22] Ibid., 74.

[23] Mary Douglas, *Purity and Danger* (London: Ark Paperbacks, 1966).

[24] Susan Sontag, *Illness as Metaphor and AIDS and its Metaphors* (New York: Doubleday, 1989), 112.

have restored. Thus the ill person's own desire for restitution is compounded by the expectation that other people want to hear restitution stories. The plot of the restitution [narrative] has the basic storyline: 'Yesterday I was healthy, today I'm sick, but tomorrow I'll be healthy again'."[25] This desire for restitution cannot tolerate a condition in which restoration to full idealized health is no longer an option, as in the case of cancer or AIDS, or in the case of Kenji's disability or Ichiro's diminished social status. At the social level, ill, wounded bodies are made marginal, sent away, their "out-of-placeness" rendering them invisible so that healthy bodies can maintain the fantasy that they are normative, not contingent. Sontag's quote reminds us that such terrified repression of the inevitable (not potential) illness and woundedness of all bodies—what is wrong with you?—takes on moralistic tones, imposed by the healthy and internalized by the ill and wounded. At the level of the self, the ill, wounded body, the restitution narrative is the primary means through which alienation occurs in its most fundamental, existential mode: "The body that turns in upon itself is split from the self that looks forward to the body's restitution. The temporarily broken-down body becomes 'it' to be cured. Thus the self is *dissociated* from the body."[26]

So powerful and compelling is the restitution narrative, so embedded it is in determining the very fabric of our social being, that even when it is made clear to us that restitution is nothing more than a narrative fiction to which we ascribe the status of eternal truth, it still—if we let it—overwhelmingly regulates our behavior and our way of viewing the world. Both Ichiro and Kenji yearn for that utopia in which they are restored to a sense of health and wholeness. "Surely it must be around here someplace, someplace in America," Ichiro says, but wonders, "Or is it just that it's not for me?"[27] Kenji also thinks this utopia is somewhere else, that place where Japanese Americans can marry "anyone but a Jap." And who doesn't want to believe in the inevitability of health? Who in our liberal society, correspondingly, does not want to imagine a triumphant future shorn of its racist past? I was reminded powerfully of this imperative demanding health's inevitability while writing this piece, when a bout of illness interrupted me. In June

---

[25] Frank, *The Wounded Storyteller: Body, Illness and Ethics*, 77.
[26] Ibid., 85.
[27] Okada, *No-No Boy*, 159.

2010, I began experiencing what I eventually relayed to my doctor as an inability to draw a full breath, which hindered first my ability to go for my morning run, and later even made it difficult for me to sit or lie still without feeling agitated and breathless. It worried my wife and me enough that I went to see my doctor, who at first thought it a mild case of bronchitis, but later was concerned enough to refer me to a pulmonary specialist.

What struck me about my response to my illness (which was temporary this time around) was how wedded I was to putting on the public persona of a healthy person. I went to my office every day: I would greet colleagues and then shut my door and gasp. I dropped off and picked up my daughter from her pre-school with nary a word about what I was experiencing physically, not to mention the gnawing fear that I might be suffering the effects of my two decades as a smoker. Even in writing that last sentence, I found it difficult to put into writing the word "cancer," so devastating is its very articulation because as Sontag wrote in 1979, few other illness carry such tremendous cultural weight. Sontag railed against the metaphoric usage of the word in everyday social and political parlance, but perhaps even uttering "cancer" is unnerving because there is a recognition that cancer puts the lie to the restitution narrative's consistency and permanence, instead highlighting how the contingency of health is more normative than not. That I was confronted with the possibility that I could possibly be suffering from lung cancer, which again turned out not to be the case, made me redouble my efforts to perform as a fully healthy person; I knew that should my fears come to pass, I would experience a social response that has as its implicit questions: What is wrong with you? Why don't you deserve to get cancer? I knew this would be the response of many even before I reread Sontag's essays, because this was the conversation I had with myself: you, Jim, deserve this fate, this cancer. I felt on the verge of being out-of-place in my community and began to experience in a way that I never had before, of my body (the one that hoped for full restoration of health) turning against the one that was ill.

My capacity now to write the word cancer as a potential illness that I might inhabit, as well as my ability now to write about my experience of disorientation, of myself turning against myself, indicates that I have left my very brief visit to a view of the world that Frank describes as the "chaos narrative," which isn't a narrative at all per se, but instead "is always beyond speech, and thus it is what is always *lacking* in speech."[28] Frank adds, "Those who are truly *living* the chaos cannot tell in words. To turn the chaos into a verbal story is to have some reflective grasp on it."[29] Even though I knew better, my experience in chaos brought me to verbal breakdown; silence became my way of living through my short time there. When I was able to say aloud that I might have cancer, particularly to my wife, I understood that I was no longer living in chaos. I was also no longer in the world in which restitution was my narrative. The experience of being in chaos compelled me to reimagine my relationship to my body in a semantically simple but existentially dramatic shift: rather than contemplating "having" an illness, I began to see myself as "being ill." That is, whatever I might have "had"—cancer, chronic bronchitis, or some other ailment—was not some extrinsic alien invader that violated the sanctity of my body, and whose subsequent relationship with me would therefore always be one of antipathy and hostility against what made me ill turning my body against itself. Rather, to "be" or to "become ill" meant that illness made up a part of who I imagined myself to be, became intrinsic to my sense of identity.

This includes my sense of Asian American identity. Here, illness as a mode of woundedness is something that cannot simply be overcome by homeopathy, pharmaceuticals, or other methods of cure, nor is the sole hoped-for outcome the restoration of health. Nor is illness or woundedness something that can be, at any point, disaggregated from other forms of socially determined identity, of which Asian American identity is one, albeit a crucial one. Instead, to embrace woundedness as intrinsic to Asian American identity exposes the restitution narrative of idealized health for what it truly is, which by extension Asian American Studies scholars and activists have been saying for decades about the corresponding narrative of the model minority: a tyrannical expectation whose demand for physical (and social) perfection relegates all persons to failure within both society and themselves. Our colleagues in disability studies have been saying this for decades; there is a necessity to "reverse the hegemony of the normal,"[30] and those of us ensconced in

---

[28] Frank, *The Wounded Storyteller: Body, Illness and Ethics*, 101.

[29] Ibid., 98.

[30] Lennard J. Davis, ed., *The Disability Studies Reader*, Second edition (New York: Routledge, 2006), 15.

ethnic and feminist studies would surely not disagree with this call to undo the hegemony of normative bodies with regard to race, gender, orientation, class, or otherwise. Yet curiously, there remains something deeply unfathomable even after we have dispensed with the oppressive normativity of the model minority or healthy body in developing a "new ethics of the body [that begins with woundedness] rather than end with it."[31] This is not only rhetorical sleight-of-hand or analogy: indeed, it is possible that part of Asian American Studies's profound inability to move "beyond" the model minority has in large part to do with our unacknowledged, passionate attachments to the fantasy of health. To begin with, woundedness demands a constant acknowledgement that finitude, the end of health, is not only a possibility, but an inevitability. To begin in woundedness rather than end with it means admitting that just as race and gender can render someone silent and invisible, so does illness perhaps more than anything else, lend itself to a solipsism that compels a body to turn radically against itself. In this light, woundedness—in all its various forms, of which I emphasize illness—brings into focus the very contours of one's identity precisely because it foregrounds the contingency of all identity.

Perhaps the most dramatic rendition of how woundedness can be profoundly revelatory to Asian American identity and bodily ethics takes place in the work of those engaged in the contemporary medical profession. These narratives are most dramatic, even melodramatically so, because physicians, surgeons, and other health professionals have built a medical lexicon and semiotic specifically designed to turn bodies against themselves in the name of curing the wounded body. More than others who encounter ill, wounded, and damaged people, doctors turn the spaces in which the wounded reside—hospitals, for example—into other worlds. Medical sociologist Charles Bosk relates the story of a Dr. Smith who explains how he manages to go to work day after day at a pediatric hospital. "What you have to do is this, Bosk," Dr. Smith explains. "When you get up in the morning, pretend your car is a spaceship. Tell yourself you are going to visit another planet. You say, 'On that planet terrible things happen, but they don't happen on my planet. They only happen on that planet I take my spaceship to every morning.'"[32] The fantastic action

---

[31] Ibid., 237.

[32] Cited in Arthur Frank, *The Renewal of Generosity: Illness, Medicine, and*

of dissociating oneself from the very people one is purportedly called to care for is inculcated early on in medical school, as Dr. Pauline Chen, a transplant surgeon, writes in her memoir on mortality, *Final Exam*.[33] In what is more than anything a narrative of unlearning the protocols of medical practice that obfuscate real human suffering from the clinical encounter, Chen recounts the moment that the edifice and artifice of medical cover crashes around her when she is about to extract organs from the body of a young Asian American women killed in a car accident. At that moment of recognition, of the proximity between her body and this dead woman's, any ritual of procedure that Chen uses to objectify herself and dissociate from the experience is rendered powerless in the transformative encounter: a young woman's confrontation of her own finitude in the wake of another's death. "For a moment I saw a reflection of my own life and I felt as if I were pulling apart my own flesh."[34] Of the many encounters with patients, their families and friends, it is this one encounter that inexorably changes Chen to engage those in hospital beds—and beyond—in less clinical, more affective ways. It is this acknowledgment of her inevitable mortal body that enables Chen to move beyond a monadic mode of existence toward a dyadic, communicative one in which her very body—while still presently "healthy"—is no longer closed off from but a member of, the world of ill, dying people too. It is certainly not coincidental that this revelation takes place when Chen encounters another Asian American woman; illness, woundedness, and death are not extrinsic to but intimately connected to, one's race, gender, and other markers of social identity.

What can emerge from this realization of one's intrinsic relation to woundedness, as intimate as one's relationship to one's race or gender or sexuality, is what Frank calls "pedagogy of suffering." In this pedagogy, there is no utopian moment of unadulterated bliss; mourning is part of the line of thought. But unlike the psychoanalytic overdetermination of mourning and/as melancholy, mourning here is not simply for one's self or for the lost loved object, but includes the ability to mourn for others.[35] This capacity to mourn for others, derived from one's

---

How to Live (Chicago: University of Chicago Press, 2004), 22.

[33] Pauline W. Chen, *Final Exam: A Surgeon's Reflections on Mortality* (New York: Vintage, 2007).

[34] Ibid., 201.

reimagined relationship to one's body as communicative toward other (wounded) bodies, does not romanticize or idealize illness as a condition that is fully transcendent—almost no one wishes to be ill, and almost everyone yearns to be healthy for as long as possible—but the consequence of not becoming a communicative body in dyadic relationship with other bodies, of remaining monadic to one's self and toward others, is as Dr. Smith in his unwittingly eloquent way puts it, to live a life in which one travels to another planet every day. The pedagogy of suffering is the chiasmic relationship between (at least) two bodies borne of a shared acknowledgment of one's and the other's woundedness, one that puts the lie to any story of hope made synonymous with triumph. And indeed, it is on this pedagogy that something akin to social justice might emerge, not as mitigation of known social forms and inequalities, but instead as the constant attentiveness to structures of feeling that emerge from one's vigilance to woundedness, a "sensuous knowledge, of a historical materialism, characterized constitutively by the tangle of the subjective and objective, experience and belief, feeling and thought, the immediate and the general, the personal and the social."[36] It is a pedagogy that might lead to an ethic of social justice that moves beyond and between discrete identities and the politics of difference, because it recognizes that even the bonds of normative identification are tenuous and provisional, even and especially the seemingly most stable turned into instances of utter vulnerability. At the last instance, such fragility is all that might be available and one that must be relentlessly cultivated.

In *No-No Boy*, Ichiro's temporary lover, Emi, voices a fantasy of monadic relationship to woundedness. As Ichiro wonders aloud how he will live in his condition of total alienation and social death, Emi invites him to live on another planet, to live in a fantastic world in which the damage of the Internment did not take place: "Next time you're alone, *pretend* that you're back in school. *Make believe* you're singing 'The Star-Spangled Banner' and see the color guard march out on stage, and say the pledge of allegiance with all the other boys and girls. You'll get that feeling flooding into your chest and making you want to shout with glory. It might even make you feel like crying. *That's how you've got to*

---

[35] Frank, *The Renewal of Generosity: Illness, Medicine, and How to Live*, 136.

[36] Gordon, *Ghostly Matters*, 200.

feel, so big that the bigness seems to want to bust out, and then you'll understand why it is that your mistake was no bigger than the mistake your country made."[37] In the narrative of restitution only fantasy can bring the wounded person back into the communal fold, and the fantasy is not an option but an imperative: that's how you've *got to feel*. And it is precisely the terror of this imperative that makes this world unlivable for Ichiro and, eventually, for Emi as well, when she is no longer "voluptuous," young and healthy. Eventually, all of us will realize that behind the veil of triumph—of which health is the one that we cling to as our deepest fantasy—is the narrative that has the arc and feel of tragedy, the downward slope of the finitude of any social identity that left unattended is the signal mark of despair.

By the end of *No-No Boy*, Kenji is dead as is Ichiro's mother. The latter dies of and in despair, unable to replace the narrative of Japanese victory with something that provide meaning to her pathetic, racialized reality. Kenji dies as a tragic figure too, as one who saw before his end the poverty of the narrative with which his government and his community tried unsuccessfully to supply him. We don't read this in the novel, but Okada leaves Emi headed into that future as well, a future in which her narrative crashes. Still, that initial encounter between Ichiro and Kenji, during which the two men show each other their wounds and bind them up together—in effect, becoming communicative healers, wounded Asian American storytellers for one another—offers an incomplete, partial model of healing for the Japanese American community in the aftermath of World War II. By the end of the novel Freddie, another no-no boy, is killed, but the boorish veteran Bull doesn't celebrate. Instead he wails, "like a baby in loud, gasping, beseeching howls."[38] In that moment Bull inexplicably mourns the death of Freddie, the person that didn't belong in the Japanese American fantasy of restitution, and in doing so mourns his own woundedness, the damage done to him by years in camp. This capacity to mourn for others, to engage in a pedagogy of suffering in which a veteran cries for a no-no boy and another no-no boy puts a hand on a hulking veteran's shoulder in a gesture of generosity—both acts of wounded people showing and binding up each other's wounds—this is where Ichiro and perhaps Okada

---

[37] Okada, *No-No Boy,* 96. Emphasis added.
[38] Ibid., 250.

himself senses "a glimmer of hope."[39] If one's woundedness is, like Ichiro's and like mine during my days of chaos, one of profound alienation, isolation, and loneliness, then developing a pedagogy of suffering to bear witness to suffering that is shared—a new social ethic of giving voice to that suffering—can expand the capacity to know how society and its dimensions of power can be reorganized. Such bearing witness to woundedness as society's and indeed humanity's core undoes what we imagine to be the regulatory impulses that keep social order in check, just as illness and pain destroy any narrative of health and restoration. To embrace woundedness as a pedagogy of suffering invites greater possibility for the work of social justice by compelling us to always keep in mind the equally important work of empathy and listening. Such work is important not because the capacity to see another's wound as wound, something that corresponds with my own, is a definitive, concrete thing with a guaranteed outcome for solidarity, but rather that this is all the frail connection that we have. It points to a potential transformation— borne of knowing the depths of the passion of woundedness—that "acknowledges, indeed it demands, that change cannot occur without the encounter, with the *something you have to try for yourself*."[40] Indeed, it is after she experiences her own sense of mortality and grief in her encounter with the dead Asian American woman that Dr. Pauline Chen begins to write stories. It is in the testimony to one's intrinsic and inevitable woundedness and suffering that cannot be reduced to terms of alleviation that may bring out the impulse to make social meaning in that woundedness, which may indeed redefine the very notion of social perfection.

---

[39] Ibid., 261.
[40] Gordon, *Ghostly Matters*, 203.

Chapter 7.

Collaborative Dissonance: Gender and Theology in Asian Pacific America

Nami Kim

Gender as an analytic category has added complexity to the discussions in theology in Asian Pacific America primarily through the efforts of feminist theologians of Asian descent. Gender has been deployed to look at the ways in which human beings' identities, experiences, and relationships are constructed as well as to examine theological notions, assumptions, and agendas that have been considered "universal." The pioneering work of feminist theologians of Asian descent has also strongly criticized patriarchal social and religious institutions, naming gender oppression as evil and denouncing it in conjunction with other intersecting forms of oppression.[1] In light of landmark feminist interventions in doing theology in Asian Pacific America, one may wonder if gender is still relevant to theology in Asian Pacific America. Is it passé to talk about gender in theology in the twenty-first century? Or, does gender still matter in theology in Asian Pacific America? If it still matters, to what extent and in what ways does it matter?

---

[1] See Nami Kim and W. Anne Joh, "Gender and Sexuality in Asian and Pacific American Religious/Theological Studies," in *Asian & Oceanic American Religious Cultures Encyclopedia*, ed. Fumitaka Matsuoka and Jane Iwamura (ABC-CLIO, forthcoming).

This article reasserts that gender does indeed still matter in theology in Asian Pacific America, for much work needs to be done to confront the interplay of everyday unequal gender dynamics experienced at home, at work, and in various religious institutions and structural issues such as sexism and (hetero)patriarchy that persist in Asian Pacific America. Gender still matters in doing theology in Asian Pacific America not only because it, as an analytic category, continues to reveal the gendered nature of the theological subject inscribed in patriarchal theological discourse in the guise of universality; but also because it helps us question the relationships of power by challenging what has been taken for granted as "natural" and/or "divinely sanctioned" systems. Taking gender into account in theology is not simply adding gender as *an* issue (read "a women's issue") in theological reflection, thereby concerning women only. It is, rather, broadening, expanding, and transforming the conceptual framework, scope, and agenda of theology as well as critically examining the unspoken theological assumptions, presuppositions, categories, and concepts. It also means an ongoing, unrelenting critique of gender oppression that is interlocked with other forms of oppression prevalent across Asian Pacific America, reminding us that a theological project can never be value-neutral. Deploying gender at the intersections with race, ethnicity, class, sexuality, (neo)-coloniality, and ablebodiedness, among others,—and noting its interactions—is also important because gender can be and has been used to either essentialize one's theological and theoretical work, or to depoliticize it to denote the "scholarly seriousness" of one's work, by claiming that gender fits "within the scientific terminology of social science and thus dissociates itself from the (supposedly strident) politics of feminism."[2]

I begin with a discussion of the emergence of feminist theology in Asian Pacific America that has broken new ground by critically engaging gender as an analytic category and its attendant issues. Then I briefly explain why the term "theology in Asian Pacific America" is preferred to the usage of "Asian American theology," as it is not a self-evident description but a loaded phrase that requires unpacking. Finally, I identify four sites where "collaborative dissonance" may occur in doing

---

[2] Joan W. Scott, "Gender: A Useful Category of Historical Analysis," *The American Historical Review* 91/5 (Dec. 1986): 1056.

theology in twenty-first-century Asian Pacific America, each of which affirms the ongoing necessity to engage gender in theological projects in Asian Pacific America.

Feminist Theology in Asian Pacific America: Emergence and Continuance

What is called Asian American theology, a major theological articulation in Asian Pacific America, emerged during a time when various marginalized groups began to actively engage Christian theological discussions and movements in the late 1960s and early 1970s. Since then, Asian American theology as a contextual theological discourse has grown into the present corpus of work by three generations of theologians, reflecting the plurality and heterogeneity of the experiences and realities of the people who constitute a group called Asian American. In *Introducing Asian American Theologies*, Jonathan Y. Tan discusses both the first and the second generations of Asian American theologians, and Andrew Sung Park identifies the two stages in Asian American theology in *Liberation Theologies in the United States*.[3] Although an emerging third generation or third stage in Asian American theology is not included in their classification, the two generations or two stages of work in Asian American theology attest that "a single, uniform, and normative Asian American theology is neither feasible nor desirable in the context of multiple heterogeneous, hybridized, and contested identities."[4]

During its first stage, Asian American theology did not challenge its own gender insensitivity and patriarchal social and religious institutions that sanction gender hierarchy, whether in a leadership role in ministry or in theological/biblical teachings and interpretations. Neither did it consider gender justice as an integral part of theological undertaking. Although Asian American theology was already a gendered

---

[3] Jonathan Y. Tan, *Introducing Asian American Theologies* (Maryknoll, N.Y.: Orbis Books, 2008); Andrew Sung Park, "Asian American Theology," in *Liberation Theologies in the United States: An Introduction*, eds. Stacey M. Floyd-Thomas and Anthony B. Pinn (New York: New York University Press, 2010).

[4] Tan, *Introducing Asian American Theologies*, 164.

discourse, with primarily Asian North American male voices and perspectives in the center of its theological inquiry, these first-stage theologians were often not cognizant of the ways in which gender dynamics work in theology. During this first stage, Asian American theology emphasized the experiences of Asian Americans (read Asian American men) by calling attention to their racial and cultural marginalization in the United States and by challenging the dominant Western theological enterprise. In other words, it was Asian American men's experiences and realities of racial discrimination, and social and political marginalization that became the main locus of theological discussion in the majority of earlier Asian American theological work. During the same time period, Asian liberation theology emerged in Asia, including Minjung and Dalit theology, and constructed a liberationist theological discourse in light of the experiences of struggling "Asians" (read Asian men) in postcolonial nation-states in Asia.

In the meantime, the analysis of women's experiences and women's search for liberation accelerated. Feminist scholars in religion, particularly feminist Christian theologians, the majority of whom were based in North America and Europe, began to produce a significant volume of work criticizing the generic human experience and the universalized notion of human, which, in fact, meant man/men (read propertied heterosexual white men). Feminist theologians from the margins, however, began to challenge mainstream feminism and feminist theology for their unproblematized use of the category of woman/women (read upper-middle-class white heterosexual women), women's experiences, and gender-only analysis that left out other modalities of social relations and experiences. Included among these feminist theologians from the margins were feminist theologians of Asian descent, whose work can be classified under the second stage or second generation of Asian American theology. As Tan notes, one of the notable developments found among the second-generation of Asian American theologians is the "emergence of Asian American feminist theologians, who were absent among the ranks of the first-generation theologians."[5] In a similar vein, Park captures the characteristics of both stages:

---

[5] Ibid., 102.

Whereas the Asian American theologians of the first stage were critical of external social structures but paid little attention to the negative aspects of their own ethnic communities, the Asian American theologians of the second stage have reflected on intracommunal oppression and repression, including the issue of internal ethnocentrism, racism, and gender relations.[6]

The concern for gender has signaled new directions, approaches, and impacts in the field of theology in Asian Pacific America. Feminist theologians of Asian descent have paid close attention to the different historical and cultural contexts in which social categories, including gender, are produced, thereby criticizing the use of gender as an unchanging universal concept. Thus, feminist theologians of Asian descent have deployed gender contextually and at the intersections with other categories of analysis. While critically interrogating dominant androcentric Western theological discourse, feminist theologians of Asian descent have also leveled their criticism at sexism and patriarchy within Asian Pacific America, including religious institutions that maintain hierarchical gender relations and patriarchal power structures. The commitment of feminist theologians of Asian descent to bring sexual and gender justice to the faith communities and to the wider Asian Pacific America, as well as to the larger society, is noteworthy. To put it differently, what has made their feminist theological work significant is not simply their use of gender as an analytic category; it is also their unwavering criticism and denouncement of various structures of oppresssion in relation to gender, such as patriarchy, sexism, colonialism, orientalism, neocolonialism, militarism, racism, androcentrism, homophobia, and gendered violence. One of the most recent works to capture this significance of feminist theology in Asian Pacific America is an anthology entitled *Off the Menu: Asian and Asian North American Women's Religion and Theology*. Published in 2007, it is a collection of interdisciplinary, multiethnic, antiracist, anticolonial, transnational, and multigenerational work by feminist scholars, teachers and activists of Asian descent in religious/theological studies, including the third generation of Asian American theologians.[7]

---

[6] Park, "Asian American Theology," 116.
[7] *Off the Menu: Asian and Asian North American Women's Religion and*

The goal of feminist theologians of Asian descent has been not the inclusion of their voices into the mainstream but the transformation of the theological enterprise itself by placing the experiences of women of Asian descent at the center of theological inquiry. This is not a simple task because their experiences are neither identical nor without complexity. Therefore, this task will require ongoing, vigorous work, especially when the struggles of women of Asian descent seem to intensify with the unceasing, if not worsening, social, political, economic, and religious struggles facing Asian Pacific America in the twenty-first century.

Theology in Asian Pacific America

The interdisciplinary field of theology in Asian Pacific America is neither monolithic nor homogeneous, as it reflects the multiple and heterogeneous experiences of its constituents. Theology is contextual, and there is not an exception for the theological projects stemming from the context of Asian Pacific America, including feminist theology that is also wide ranging. The context for theology in Asian Pacific America includes the historical Asian (im)migrations to this country and the displacements of people from Asia and the ongoing U.S. neocolonialism and militarism that continue to affect the lives of people within and outside the borders of the United States. As Jodi Kim shows in her book *Ends of Empire*, the post-1965 immigration of Asians to the United States as well as the displacement experienced by Asians (for example, "refugee migrants" including "orphans"), have to do with various wars in which the United States engaged, such as the Korean War and the Vietnam War.[8] Setsu Shigematsu and Keith L. Camacho also pointedly state that "Asian and Pacific Islander displacements, dispossessions, and migrations to America have been punctuated by U.S. wars in Asia and

---

Theology, ed. Rita Nakashima Brock, Jung Ha Kim, Kwok Pui-lan, and Seung Ai Yang (Louisville, Kentucky: Westminster John Knox Press, 2007). Also see Kim and Joh, "Gender and Sexuality in Asian and Pacific American Religious/Theological Studies."

[8] Jodi Kim, *Ends of Empire: Asian American Critique and the Cold War* (Minneapolis: University of Minnesota Press, 2010).

the Pacific, and thus U.S. war waging has become an integral, if not naturalized, part of the grammar of these (im)migration narratives."[9] Shigematsu and Camacho convincingly argue that "to circumscribe our understanding of 'America' to the continental United States – as previous paradigms have tended to emphasize – is myopic in terms of the reach of American empire," because the United States "defined its national interests not along the borders of the continental United States but in Asia and the Pacific."[10] Further, such circumscription "runs the risk of miscalculating the formative role that U.S. militarization plays in shaping the historical displacements and migrations of the populations we now refer to as Asian America and Pacific Islander."[11] Scholars of Asian American politics have also argued that a "critical transnational perspective" needs to be adopted "to recalibrate the movement [of Asian peoples] away from [their] domestic roots – and toward the legacy of U.S. involvement in the Asian Pacific."[12] Viewing the "American" only as one part of "place" for Asian American politics, Lisa Lowe writes, "'Becoming a national citizen' cannot be the exclusive narrative of emancipation for the Asian American subject. Rather, the current social formation entails a subject less narrated by the modern discourse of citizenship and more narrated by the histories of wars in Asia, immigration, and the dynamics of the current Global economy."[13]

Based on this understanding of historical and current relationships between the United States and Asia and the Pacific, I use the term "theology in Asian Pacific America" rather than "Asian Amer-

---

[9] Setsu Shigematsu and Keith L. Camacho, "Militarized Currents, Decolonizing Futures," in *Militarized Currents: Toward a Decolonized Future in Asia and the Pacific*, eds. Setsu Shigematsu and Keith L. Camacho (Minneapolis: University of Minnesota Press, 2010), xxvi.

[10] Ibid., xxv.

[11] Ibid., xxv–xxvi.

[12] Christian Collet and Ikumi Koakutsu, "Does Transnational Living Preclude Pan-Ethnic Thinking? An Exploration of Asian American Identities," in *The Transnational Politics of Asian Americans*, ed. Christian Collet and Pei-te Lien (Philadelphia: Temple University Press, 2009), 169.

[13] Lisa Lowe, *Immigrant Acts: On Asian American Cultural Politics* (Durham, North Carolina: Duke University Press, 1996), 33. Quoted in Christian Collet and Pei-te Lien, "The Transnational Politics of Asian Americans: Controversies, Questions, Convergence," in *The Transnational Politics of Asian Americans*, 8.

ican theology." Using the phrase "theology in Asian Pacific America" allows us to avoid reinscribing the unproblematized construction of theological discourse either based on the reified notion of "Asianness" or on the uncritical claim of being "American." Kwok Pui-lan echoes this reasoning in *Off the Menu* when she argues for the need to employ new conceptual frameworks to analyze the "Asia Pacific" in light of globalization and transnationalism. Kwok suggests that a transnational analysis will help us see that "Asian" and "America" should not be viewed as two discrete entities, but, rather, the two should be seen as "constantly influencing each other within the broader regional formation of the Asia Pacific."[14] Also, Kwok reminds that Asians and Asian North Americans are "strategically located in the interstices" of extensive transnational networks, "whether they work in the Silicon Valley or in the financial districts of Seoul, Hong Kong, or Tokyo."[15]

Hence, the use of the phrase "theology in Asian Pacific America" is to foreground the context that requires a critical transnational framework in attending to theology in Asian Pacific America. Such use is not to suggest that the phrase encompasses *all* theological articulations arising from across Asia and North America. Nor does using a transnational framework in theology in Asian Pacific America presume an unrestricted, free movement of capital, technology, information, cultural resources, or human beings. Rather, doing so takes into account the unequal global power structures, because today's global world, as Espiritu rightly puts it in her book *Home Bound*, is "not just some glorious hybrid, complex mixity" but is "systematically divided."[16] Such a transnational framework will also be helpful because it challenges "methodological nationalism." As Nina Glick Schiller explains, methodological nationalism refers to a theoretical framework that equates society with the nation-state by adopting national borders as the "natural unit of study."[17] Preferring to use the phrase "theology in Asia Pacific

---

[14] Kwok Pui-lan, "Fishing the Asia Pacific: Transnationalism and Feminist Theology," in *Off the Menu*, 9.

[15] Ibid., 10.

[16] Yen Le Espiritu, *Home Bound: Filipino American Lives across Cultures, Communities, and Countries* (Berkeley: University of California Press, 2003), 4.

[17] Nina Glick Schiller, "Transnational Social Fields and Imperialism: Bringing a Theory of Power to Transnational Studies," *Anthropological Theory* 5/4 (2005): 440.

America" is an effort to avoid "methodological nationalism" in doing theology, which will help us understand different gendered racial formations within the United States. For instance, Nadia Y. Kim, in her study of the transnational process about racialization, argues that the United States racializes many of its immigrants "both before and after arrival."[18] Identifying U.S. imperialism in Asia since World War II as one of the key sources of racialization of Asian ethnics, she contends that the United States "racially 'Americanizes' other countries by way of its 'White-Black order.'"[19] Understanding the role of U.S. imperialism in forming (im)migrants' transnational understandings of race and their related identities helps us see gendered racial formations across Asian Pacific America.[20]

Collaborative Dissonance

In what ways and to what extent does gender still matter in theology in Asian Pacific America? How could theology in Asian Pacific America further broaden its parameters to bring gender justice to Asian Pacific America? As a way to respond to these questions, I identify four sites where "collaborative dissonance" is called for concerning gender in theology in Asian Pacific America.

Roger Kamien explains in his book *Music: An Appreciation* that a dissonance in music refers to "an unstable tone combination... dissonant chords are 'active'; traditionally they have been considered harsh and have expressed pain, grief, and conflict."[21] If "collaborative" implies the twofold meaning of "working together" and "working subversively against,"[22] "dissonance" signifies "unstable" approaches to

---

[18] Nadia Y. Kim, *Imperial Citizens: Koreans and Race from Seoul to LA* (Stanford, California: Stanford University Press, 2008), 12.

[19] Ibid., 3-6.

[20] Kim also demonstrates how U.S. "imperialist racial formations" takes place in South Korea, while South Korea "exports" its nationalism to the Koreans in the United States.

[21] Roger Kamien, *Music: An Appreciation*, 4th brief ed. (New York: McGraw Hill, 2002), 43.

[22] Kandice Chuh, *Imagine Otherwise: On Asian Americanist Critique* (Durham, N.C.: Duke University Press, 2003), 28.

gender issues, within which reside both limitations and potentialities to bring changes to the existing paradigms. These approaches are considered unstable in the sense that they are changeable, on the edge, and even explosive due to constructive tensions emerging from within. Like dissonant chords, such approaches are also "active" in that the tensions within them are constantly present, testing their own limitations and calling new potentialities forward.

As Fumitaka Matsuoka observes, theology is "a thoroughly historical discipline that does its work in the midst of communities and their traditions. It is the discourse by which the arguments of diverse perspectives are voiced in community."[23] Hence, calling for collaborative dissonance with regard to gender in theology in Asian Pacific America demonstrates the constructiveness of difference and the multiplicity in the (re)production of theological knowledge. To put it differently, calling for collaborative dissonance is neither to seek consensus nor to resolve conflicts in theological work for the sake of harmony, but, rather, it is to highlight the sites where different theological approaches and perspectives emerge, even at the cost of discomfort, conflict, pain, or resentment. In so doing, theology's gendered effects, which are multiple, including the destructive effects on the lives of heterosexual women and men and lesbians, gays, bisexuals, and transgender persons in Asian Pacific America, can also be acknowledged, and thereby challenged. Collaborative dissonance taking place in various sites of contestation will eventually contribute to enriching the diverse communities across Asian Pacific America, without silencing different views and approaches. It will simultaneously subvert the dominant theological discourse that does not account for the plural and diverse experiences of people in these communities. Challenges and problems confronting twenty-first-century Asian Pacific America in relation to gender are both larger structural issues across Asian Pacific America and internal conflicts stemming from within, matters that require working together and at the same time working subversively against. Hence, the sites where collaborative dissonance occurs are contested sites of struggle and transformation, where different theological approaches and perspectives, like dissonant chords, may emerge, both expressing and generating tensions, discomfort, and

---

[23] Fumitaka Matsuoka, *Out of Silence: Emerging Themes in Asian American Churches* (Cleveland: United Church Press, 1995), 4.

pain. And it is the hopes for working together to end injustice or working subversively against injustice that affect communities in Asian Pacific America on multiple levels and to various degrees.

Site One: U.S. Imperialism, "Other" Religion(s), and Women

One aspect of the context within which theology in Asian Pacific America is being articulated is transnational, and its transnationality cannot be discussed without critically examining the ongoing U.S. imperialist interventions in Asia and the Pacific. Current wars in Afghanistan and Iraq are not exceptions but are part of a continuing U.S. imperialist project to build a series of "future super-colonies."[24] The gloomy speculations over potentially imminent wars in regions like Iran and North Korea are not the news of bygone eras. The U.S. imperialist project has been and still is closely interrelated with its racist policy against people of color within the country's own borders, and, as Jaideep Singh tells us, "religion" in North America has become a "particularly powerful method of classifying the 'enemy' or 'other' in national life in recent years, impacting primarily non-Christian people of color."[25] Theology in Asian Pacific America, then, needs to respond to this context by examining the ways in which religion is invoked or utilized for imperialist political interests. All of this becomes more complicated when "other" religions are portrayed, not only by the mainstream media but also by some feminists, as inherently patriarchal, more oppressive, and less tolerant. For instance, along with the demonization of Islam, the narrative of Islamic states as the enemies of feminists and women was supported by many feminists.[26] Such framing of Islam through the

---

[24] Carole Boyce Davies, "Con-di-fi-cation," in *Still Brave: The Evolution of Black Women's Studies*, eds. Stanlie M. James, Frances Smith Foster, and Beverly Guy-Sheftall (New York: The Feminist Press at the City University of New York, 2010), 404.

[25] Jaideep Singh, "The Racialization of Minoritized Religious Identity: Constructing Sacred Sites at the Intersection of White and Christian Supremacy," in *Revealing the Sacred in Asian and Pacific America*, eds. Jane Naomi Iwamura and Paul Spickard (New York: Routledge, 2003), 88.

[26] See Inderpal Grewal, *Transnational America: Feminisms, Diasporas, Neoliberalisms* (Durham, N.C.: Duke University Press, 2005).

(mis)appropriation of feminist rhetoric by the key players of the current U.S.-led wars in Afghanistan and Iraq created the ground for launching America's so-called War on Terror.[27] In this political climate, defining "Islamic countries" as a primary "mission field" and targeting Muslims in North America as objects of evangelization by some Christian churches and organizations across Asian Pacific America require a serious response from theologians in Asian Pacific America.[28]

The site where U.S. imperialism, "other" religion(s), and women are intertwined becomes a contested location for theology in Asian Pacific America, as different theological perspectives may bring disparate arguments that are more likely to generate a cacophony than engender harmony. Developing a framework for a theological approach that resists attempts to become complicit with U.S. imperialist interests through the denouncement of colonialist and orientalist discourse of "saving other women" from their religion(s) constitutes one of the responses to this site. Such a framework critically interrogates Christian complicity in maintaining an imperialist agenda as well as the Christian dominance that is often overlooked in the larger U.S. social and political landscape. It is also a framework that critically examines how a discursive construction of religion, including that of "secular" feminists, as an ahistorical and/or essentialized entity, affects the ways in which women's oppression is framed and discussed. It remains to be seen what other approaches will emerge in this contested site.

Site Two: Religious Diversity and Gender Oppression

The multiplicity and heterogeneity of religion/culture are other characteristics of the context for theology in Asian Pacific America,

---

[27] See Gargi Bhattacharyya, *Dangerous Brown Men: Exploiting Sex, Violence and Feminism in the War on Terror* (London and New York: Zed Books, 2008).

[28] For instance, in August 2009, colorful flyers were handed out by a group of women and men of Asian descent in busy shopping mall complexes located in a metropolitan city in the U.S. South. The flyers showed a picture of a woman wearing a veil, along with the passage written in Korean, Chinese, and English that Christians should pray for their "unsaved" Muslim sisters and brothers during the month of Ramadan.

since Asian (im)migrants have brought with them various religious traditions, including "Confucianized Christianity."[29] However, there has been a lack of theological reflection on religious diversity and/or difference in spite of some Christian theological efforts to engage in conversations and dialogues with those whose faith can be categorized as part of "other" religions. Given the religious/cultural heterogeneity and multifaith traditions in Asian Pacific America, theologians of Asian descent would agree that theology in Asian Pacific America should take up the challenge of engaging different religious traditions, although the ways in which they engage may vary drastically. For instance, in an issue of the *Journal of Feminist Studies in Religion,* Kwok Pui-lan and Rachel Bundang discuss some of the areas in which women, through the grassroots movement and organization Pacific, Asian, North American Asian Women in Theology and Ministry (PANAAWTM), should work in the near future, stating that "PANAAWTM theology will need to develop paradigms for theology and religious studies that affirm our multicultural and multireligious contexts."[30]

Critical engagements of diverse religious/cultural traditions in Asian Pacific America, however, have not been an easy task. As Kwok and Bundang explain, a failure to appreciate our religious and cultural resources due to the legacy of Western colonialism has rendered theologians of Asian descent unable to engage those resources in theology. Even when religious and cultural resources became available, they were part of a racist and/or orientalist approach or a "nativist approach that tends to create a homogeneous national culture, often based on the reification of one religious tradition, interpreted androcentrically."[31] Kwok and Bundang suggest that feminist theologians should interrogate "not only Western Christianity but also constructions of gender and power in Asian religions and in Asian North America."[32] Therefore, engaging diverse religious traditions in theology

---

[29] Nam-Soon Kang, "Confucian Familism and Its Social/Religious Embodiment in Christianity: Reconsidering the Family Discourse from a Feminist Perspective," *Asian Journal of Theology* 18/1 (2004): 168-189.

[30] Kwok Pui-lan and Rachel A. R. Bundang, "PANAAWTM Lives!" *Journal of Feminist Studies in Religion* 21/2 (2005): 153. See also "The Future of PANAAWTM Theology" at http://www.panaawtm.org; and *Revealing the Sacred in Asian and Pacific America.*

[31] Kwok and Bundang, "PANAAWTM Lives!" 153.

in Asian Pacific America will require the development of new frameworks that not only critically examine orientalist and colonialist constructions of "other" religions but that also unrelentingly interrogate the gender dynamics and androcentric teachings and interpretations found in those traditions. Such frameworks for engaging religious diversity should not overlook the unequal power dynamics between hegemonic Christianity and "other" religious traditions.

Specifically, new frameworks for interreligious engagements are greatly needed in addressing issues related to gender oppression, because gender oppression cuts across ethnoreligious communities in Asian Pacific America in multiple and multifaceted ways. For instance, the persistence of sexual and physical violence/abuse against women and girls, and the complicity of religion in ethnoreligious communities, leaves devastated many women and girls – those directly and indirectly affected by violence. This communal problem of violence and the lack of communal response to it, especially from religious institutions, require continuous, collective intervention and investment, because violence threatens the health and life of women and girls on a daily basis, putting at risk the stabilization of the community as a whole. Preventing violence is an important communal health issue, one that demands concerted efforts in the arenas of organized religion's advocacy, research and teaching, and public policy. Fighting to end violence against women and girls can be most effectively accomplished when all ethnoreligious communities are actively involved in the eradication of violence, because this issue cannot be solved in isolation. Hence, developing new frameworks for interreligious dialogues and practices in theology in Asian Pacific America is urgent. These new frameworks should enable critical examination of how victims are affected by the violence of patriarchal religious teachings, practices, and interpretations of the sacred texts that have been used to justify violence. The new frameworks are also expected to advocate for and promote interreligious and interfaith solidarity work related to ending violence against women and girls anywhere in the community, including at home, at work, and in religious institutions as well as other social and political institutions.

As many feminist theologians of Asian descent and other scholars of racial/ethnic minority have cautioned, however, efforts to

---

[32] Ibid., 154.

deal with violence within ethnoreligious communities need to be done in a manner that does not "reinscribe and reproduce the racist and colonialist constructions of racial/ethnic minority groups and religious traditions other than Christianity as 'inherently patriarchal,' 'more violent,' 'more homophobic,'..."[33] One of the ways that new frameworks for interreligious engagements can help dismantle such constructions of racial/ethnic minority groups, as well as those of religious traditions, is to provide "a more nuanced analysis of patriarchy not as a fixed hierarchical gender relation but as a set of negotiated social relations in which gender and class are inextricably implicated,"[34] as Sheba Mariam George notes. This kind of analysis will further demonstrate how patriarchal relations are "negotiated, mediated, contested, and/or reproduced" in different ethnoreligious communities, which will, in turn, help various communities in Asian Pacific America understand and teach alternative behavior for (im)migrant men of Asian descent who have wielded violence against the women and girls in their communities as a way of compensating for any status losses they experienced during the transnational (im)migration process.[35] Such efforts, to be sure, will not bear fruit without our challenging the prescribed gender roles and relations within our ethnoreligious communities. Therefore, alternatives for male perpetrators should be carefully considered and expressed so as to not make worse the effects of gender oppression in the lives of heterosexual women, children, and sexual minorities. Also, ongoing critical analyses and discussions are needed to challenge the shifting dynamics of patriarchy that skillfully adapt themselves to the existing social milieu, even when these dynamics include appropriating a feminist critique of traditional masculinity and femininity. This intersection of religious diversity and gender oppression is another contested site where dissonance is anticipated, yet there continues to be hope for working together to end sexual and gender oppression in the communities of Asian Pacific America.

---

[33] See Kim and Joh, "Gender and Sexuality in Asian and Pacific American Religious/Theological Studies."

[34] Sheba Mariam George, *When Women Come First: Gender and Class in Transnational Migration* (Berkeley: University of California Press, 2005), quoted in Kim and Joh.

[35] Kim and Joh.

Site Three: Family, the Binary Sex/Gender System, and Heterosexism

Feminist theologians have long argued that unequal gender relations have been preserved by theological justifications of the heterosexual family, where the man is the head of the house while the woman and children are subordinate to him. In spite of feminist theological efforts to bring forth gender consciousness and gender justice, socially prescribed gender roles and identities and hierarchical gender relationships continue to be taught and practiced on a daily basis in Asian Pacific America. For instance, the rhetorical device of the "normal" family preserves socially accepted gender roles and relationships. This strategy works well in various communities across Asian Pacific America, given the strong emphasis on keeping the family intact in the face of increasing dissolution of the family unit due to "Western" individualism and "liberal" sexual mores, which are believed to be antithetical to the community-oriented "Asian" traditions and practices. Prevalent racial discrimination and prejudice in the larger society have also played a role in preserving the notion of the "normal" family in Asian Pacific America. Yet, heavy emphasis on the "normal" family has underscored the mainstream view of family, as it is maintained by the prescribed binary gender roles and gender functions reserved for men and women accordingly. The notion of the "normal" family further controls women's sexuality and reproduction, often dividing women into opposing categories, such as virgin versus sexually loose, chaste versus unchaste, motherhood versus childlessness. Thus, women of Asian descent who do not fit into or who refuse to adhere to these categories are rendered outsiders who have been "co-opted" by a "promiscuous" Western culture. Included among them are lesbians, bisexuals, transgender people, teenage mothers, and even feminists. The idea prevalent in various ethnoreligious communities that homosexuality is a "Western" byproduct supports this dichotomization of women. The family that is grounded in the binary sex/gender system and heteronormativity becomes a contested site in theology in Asian Pacific America. The family is a major social institution, whose influence and effects cannot be underestimated in theology in Asian Pacific America.

Without a doubt, gender, as a conceptual framework that is based on the binary system of masculinity and femininity, has challenged and broadened theological endeavor in Asian Pacific America, when the work did not engage gender as a category of analysis. Although gender is understood as a socially constructed notion that is historically and culturally variable, it often refers to the binary system of masculinity and femininity based on biological "sex." Theology has been critical of gender essentialism due to feminist intervention, but it still tends to accept the binary sex/gender system within which two fixed gender identities – man and woman – are taken for granted, which, in turn, normatizes the heterosexual experience and/or conceptual frameworks based on such experience.[36] Hence, gender as an accepted, rigid, two-sex/gender system needs to be further problematized. Moving beyond the binary sex/gender framework is crucial, and it requires reconsidering gender as multiple, since the critique of binary gender has often been a critique of superiority and inferiority inscribed into the two-gender system, but not the binary itself. The hierarchical gender system privileges masculinity as well as heterosexuality. And cultural devaluation of femininity and homosexuality solidifies the maintenance of the hierarchical gender system.[37] In other words, gender binary understood as gender inequality not only legitimizes gendered division of labor but also normatizes heterosexual desire.[38] Gender cannot be conflated with sexuality, yet it is important to understand gender and sexuality as mutually constitutive. It is, then, necessary to understand the relation between gender and heterosexuality in order to comprehend the persistence of gender inequality, for heterosexuality requires a binary sex system, according to which one's gender identity is supposed to follow.[39]

---

[36] For the critique of heterosexual ideology, see Marcella Althaus-Reid, "From Liberation Theology to Indecent Theology," in *Latin American Liberation Theology: The Next Generation*, ed. Ivan Petrella (Maryknoll, N.Y.: Orbis, 2005).

[37] See Kristen Schilt and Laurel Westbrook, "Doing Gender, Doing Heteronormativity: 'Gender Normals,' Transgender People, and the Social Maintenance of Heterosexuality," *Gender & Society* 23/4 (August 2009): 440-64.

[38] Kim and Joh, "Gender and Sexuality in Asian and Pacific American Religious/Theological Studies."

[39] Schilt and Westbrook, "Doing Gender, Doing Heteronormativity," 443.

Gender analysis in theology needs to further press our ethnoreligious communities to face the issue of human sexuality. Theology in Asian Pacific America has not fully examined how "normal" sexuality has been historically constructed. The ways in which heterosexuality is normatized in theological work need to be questioned and critically examined, especially how the family and various social units are conceptualized and organized. Hence, gender analysis requires theology in Asian Pacific America to be concerned not just with how dominant norms and practices of gender and sexuality function but also with how the prevailing narratives and forms of heteropatriarchal order can be deconstructed and demystified. Such analyses should accompany the critique of conservative patriarchal theology and religious institutions by examining how organizing concepts and underlying assumptions embedded in theological and biblical interpretations reinscribe heteronormativity. This work also requires theology to envision new practices, relations, structures, and narratives of social ordering that are not based on heteropatriarchal domination and subjugation. This entails redefining sexuality, including what Celine Parreney Shimizu calls "race positive sexuality" and "perverse sexuality" that have often been classified as non-normative sexual identities/acts and practices that "do not demand morality, chastity, and modesty that discipline women."[40] In this way, theology in Asian Pacific America can move beyond simply "accepting gay Christians in worship" or incorporating "non-heterosexual lives into heterosexual ideologies"[41] or addressing homosexuality only in connection to HIV/AIDS crisis. In other words, what theology in Asian Pacific America hopes to witness in this contested site is not the inclusion of anyone in a "normative" system, but rather, the transformation of the whole ideology and structure of the two-sex/gender system as well as heteronormativity. However, discord rather than accord is highly likely to occupy this site, at least, for a while.

---

[40] Celine Parreney Shimizu, *The Hypersexuality of Race: Performing Asian/American Women on Screen and Scene* (Durham, N.C.: Duke University Press, 2007), 144-45, esp. 229; Kim and Joh, "Gender and Sexuality in Asian and Pacific American Religious/Theological Studies."

[41] Althaus-Reid, "From Liberation Theology to Indecent Theology," 28.

Site Four: Minority Nationalism and Gendered/Sexual Regulation

Theology in Asian Pacific America works within a context that is fragmented by various boundaries, such as religion, ethnicity, gender, sexuality, age, ablebodiedness, language, and socioeconomic status. Though heterogeneous, this context is divided by hierarchical differences and stratifications. As Espiritu points out, recent immigration has "further diversified Asian Americans among cultural, generational, economic and political lines – all of which have compounded the difficulties of forging pan-Asian identities and institutions."[42] According to data released by the Asian Pacific American Legal Center of Southern California in 2009, age, religiosity, and English proficiency are the three major determining factors in voting on Proposition 8 across Asian Pacific America.[43] Acknowledging the complexities as well as internal conflicts present across Asian Pacific America needs to be one of the ongoing tasks of theology in Asian Pacific America. For instance, the intersections of patriarchy, middle-class upward mobility, and heteronormativity cut across different ethnoreligious communities, such as Korean Buddhists, Chinese evangelical Christians, Indian Hindus, Vietnamese Buddhists, and Filipino Catholics, generating schisms and estrangements within the community. At the same time, contestations and resistance against the normatization of heteropatriarchy as the foundation of social relations have also emerged within the very same communities. Examples can be seen in the activism of LGBTQ communities and their allies in Asian Pacific America, actions which are often viewed by the status quo both within ethnoreligious communities and the larger society as being divisive in maintaining the harmony of the community.

---

[42] Yen Le Espiritu, "Asian American Panethnicity: Challenges and Possibilities," in *Trajectory of Civic and Political Engagement: A Public Policy Report*, ed. Paul M. Ong (Los Angeles: LEAP Asian Pacific American Public Policy Institute, 2008), 120.

[43] Asian Pacific American Legal Center of Southern California, Press Release, January 22, 2009; Many Asian American Pacific Islander scholars and activists voice that passage of proposition 8 requires a more comprehensive analysis. See Kim and Joh, "Gender and Sexuality in Asian and Pacific American Religious/Theological Studies."

One of the areas where struggles over ethnicity, gender relations, sexual regulation, and religious identity occur is a site that Gayatri Gopinath calls minority nationalism, where collaborative dissonance may take place in theology in Asian Pacific America. While a rich body of feminist literature, racial/ethnic studies, and postcolonial research has analyzed nationalism as a racialized, gendered, and sexualized social system, there has not been much attention paid to how minority nationalism within different ethnoreligious communities is at the intersections of ethnicity, gender, sexuality, class, and religious identity.

For example, discussing the ongoing confrontation between queer Indians and Indian Hindu nationalists in New York City, Gopinath shows how minority nationalism maintains gender and sexual normativity.[44] According to Gopinath, the Federation of Indian Associations (FIA), a group made up of Indian businessmen, denied both the South Asian Lesbian and Gay Association (SALGA) and the Sakhi for South Asian women (an anti–domestic violence women's group) the right to march in the India Day Parade that the FIA sponsored. The FIA claimed they denied participation on the grounds that the groups were "antinational," constructing "India" as "Hindu, patriarchal, middle-class, and free of homosexuals."[45] As Gopinath explains, the FIA's later inclusion of Sakhi but continuing denial of SALGA to march illustrates the ways in which the categories of woman and lesbian are constructed as mutually exclusive in hegemonic nationalist discourses as they are reproduced in diaspora.[46] As the context for theology in Asian Pacific America becomes more fragmented and diversified, it will continue to be necessary to take a close look at how ethnic identity, socioeconomic status, gender and sexual regulation, and religion intersect with minority nationalism to produce certain disciplinary regulations and practices within transnational ethnoreligious communities.

---

[44] Gayatri Gopinath, "Nostalgia, Desire, and Diaspora," *Positions: East Asia Cultures Critique* 5/2 (Fall 1997): 467-489.

[45] Ibid., 471.

[46] Ibid., 471-72.

Conclusion

Dissonance can create anxiety, uncomfortable feelings, pain, and grief. Making gender matter in theology in Asian Pacific America can be disturbing, upsetting, annoying, and even frightening, as it creates dissonance, rather than consonance. Collaborative dissonance, however, is necessary for theology in Asian Pacific America precisely because it disrupts seemingly stable, agreeable, and comfortable conditions of everyday life. To put it differently, collaborative dissonance is a constructive action to take where struggles, contestations, and resistance against domination and subjugation are occurring. Gender, as an analytic category, is an important note creating this collaborative dissonance, and as such it still matters in doing theology in Asian Pacific America in the twenty-first century.

Chapter 8.

A Three-Part Sinfonia: Queer Asian Reflections on the Trinity

Patrick S. Cheng

Growing up in a first-generation Chinese American immigrant household in the San Francisco Bay Area, I experienced many interesting cultural rituals, not the least of which were weekly piano lessons. My parents made sure that my piano teacher came to our house week after week, like clockwork, for well over a decade – from elementary school through high school. While my classmates were playing after-school sports, going out on dates, or getting drunk at parties, I was sitting at home, dutifully practicing my Mozart or Chopin.

Although there were some aspects of piano lessons that I thoroughly disliked (for example, annual student recitals), there were other aspects that I did like, including playing J.S. Bach's inventions and sinfonias.[1] These two- and three-part contrapuntal compositions were originally keyboard exercises that Bach wrote for his students. I was fascinated from an early age by the intricate and distinct melody lines that sang out in different registers, yet all came together (surprisingly!) to form a single, unified piece.

---

[1] J.S. Bach wrote a series of two-part inventions, BWV 772-786, and three-part sinfonias, BWV 787-801. These works are commonly known as Bach's two-part and three-part inventions.

Today, as an openly gay Asian American Christian, I can't help but think that my love for Bach's inventions and sinfonias during my teenage years was a subconscious attempt to weave together the various aspects of my identity, which included my sexuality, race, and spirituality. Like the individual melodies in a Bach three-part sinfonia, these three aspects of my identity were simultaneously present in different registers of my life. The challenge, however, was – and remains – bringing these three aspects of my life together into a unified whole, just as Bach did with his three-part sinfonias.

In this essay, I will reflect upon my experiences as an openly gay Asian American Christian. In particular, I will argue that classical Christian trinitarian theology – like a Bach three-part sinfonia – can help queer Asian American Christians to understand better the complex interplay among the distinct "melodies" of sexuality, race, and spirituality that exist in our lives. Specifically, I will argue that the three classical trinitarian concepts of (1) *vestigia trinitatis* (vestiges of the Trinity), (2) *mia ousia, treis hypostaseis* (one substance, three persons), and (3) *perichoresis* (mutual interpenetration) are all ways in which queer Asian American Christians can better understand ourselves and our relationship to God.

Queer Asian Christians

During the last twenty years, many lesbian, gay, bisexual, and transgender ("LGBT" or "queer") Asian Americans have come out and written about living as double minorities – that is, individuals who are both queer and Asian – in North America.[2] One common theme in these writings is a strong sense of metaphorical homelessness. That is, queer

---

[2] See, for example, Quang Bao and Hanya Yanagihara, eds., *Take Out: Queer Writing from Asian Pacific America* (New York: Asian American Writers' Workshop, 2000); Song Cho, ed., *Rice: Explorations into Gay Asian Culture and Politics* (Toronto: Queer Press, 1998); David L. Eng and Alice Y. Hom, eds., *Q&A: Queer in Asian America* (Philadelphia: Temple University Press, 1998); Russell Leong, ed., *Asian American Sexualities: Dimensions of the Gay and Lesbian Experience* (New York: Routledge, 1996); and Sharon Lim-Hing, ed., *The Very Inside: An Anthology of Writing by Asian and Pacific Islander Lesbian and Bisexual Women* (Toronto: Sister Vision, 1994).

Asian Americans are never quite "home" in either the LGBT community or the Asian American community. Although we may have one foot in each world, we are never fully part of either.

For example, queer Asian Americans never quite feel at home in the predominantly white, middle-class LGBT community because of our experiences of racism. This often takes the form of either being fetishized on the one hand or completely ignored on the other. Nor do queer Asian Americans ever feel quite at home in the predominantly straight Asian American community because of our experiences of homophobia. This is particularly true in East Asian cultures with Confucian roots that place a heavy emphasis on "family values" and the importance of preserving the ancestral lineage through reproduction.

As Eric Wat, a gay Asian American writer, describes it, many queer Asian Americans are "run over at the intersection of racism and homophobia." That is, we are "forever left in the middle of the road, unacceptable to those at either side of the street."[3] Like Jesus, who "has no place to lay his head,"[4] queer Asian Americans (and also other queer people of color) often experience a profound sense of homelessness in terms of our identities. We are unable to lay our heads down in either the LGBT or the Asian American community.

This sense of metaphorical homelessness is magnified for queer Asian Americans who also happen to be Christians. For example, the experience of racism is intensified for queer Asian American Christians who worship in religious communities that are predominantly white. These communities are generally unaware and/or silent about the racism experienced by Asian Americans – who are still perceived as exotic foreigners and outsiders despite having been in the United States since the 1700s[5] – on a daily basis. Similarly, the experience of homophobia is intensified for queer Asian Christians who worship in evangelical and fundamentalist religious communities that use the Bible and church teachings to condemn LGBT people and same-sex relationships.

---

[3] Eric C. Wat, "Preserving the Paradox: Stories from a Gay-Loh," in Leong, *Asian American Sexualities*, 79.

[4] Luke 9:58 (NRSV).

[5] See Sucheng Chan, *Asian Americans: An Interpretive History* (Detroit, Michigan: Twayne, 1991), 25.

Finally, in addition to the above experiences of racism and homophobia, there is a third dimension of metaphorical homelessness for queer Asian American Christians. This third dimension takes the form of extreme secularism that is overtly hostile to organized religion, often seen in both the LGBT community and the Asian American community. In particular, there is frequently overt hostility expressed towards organized religion, particularly Christianity, within progressive and activist LGBT and Asian American circles.

In recent years, a number of queer Asian American Christians have written about their experiences of dealing with the three-pronged challenges of homophobia, racism, and extreme secularism. This includes individuals such as "Michael Kim," Eric Law, Jeanette Lee, Leng Lim, and myself.[6] Jeanette Lee, a self-identified biracial lesbian, writes that she is most alive when she is able to integrate her sexuality, race, and spirituality, which is a view that is shared by many queer Asian

---

[6] See, for example, Patrick S. Cheng, "Hybridity and the Decolonization of Asian American and Queer Theologies," *Postcolonial Theology Network*, entry posted October 17, 2009, http://www.facebook.com/topic.php?uid=23694574926&topic=11026 (accessed September 30, 2010); Patrick S. Cheng, "Multiplicity and Judges 19: Constructing a Queer Asian Pacific American Biblical Hermeneutic," *Semeia* 90/91 (2002): 119-33; Patrick S. Cheng, "Reclaiming Our Traditions, Rituals, and Spaces: Spirituality and the Queer Asian Pacific American Experience," *Spiritus* 6/2 (2006): 234-40; "Rethinking Sin and Grace for LGBT People Today," in *Sexuality and the Sacred: Sources for Theological Reflection*, eds. Marvin Ellison and Kelly Brown Douglas, 2nd ed. (Louisville, Kentucky: Westminster John Knox, 2010), 105-18; Patrick S. Cheng, "Roundtable Discussion: Same-Sex Marriage," *Journal of Feminist Studies in Religion* 20/2 (2004): 103-07; Michael Kim, "Out and About: Coming of Age in a Straight White World," in *Asian American X: An Intersection of 21st Century Asian American Voices*, eds. Arar Han and John Hsu (Ann Arbor, Michigan: The University of Michigan Press, 2004), 139-48 (written under a pseudonym); Eric H.F. Law, "A Spirituality of Creative Marginality," in *Que(e)rying Religion: A Critical Anthology*, eds. Gary David Comstock and Susan E. Henking (New York: Continuum, 1997), 343-36; Jeanette Mei Gim Lee, "Queerly a Good Friday," in *Restoried Selves: Autobiographies of Queer Asian/Pacific American Activists*, ed. Kevin K. Kumashiro (Binghamton, New York: Harrington Park, 2004), 81-86; Leng Leroy Lim, "'The Bible Tells Me to Hate Myself': The Crisis in Asian American Spiritual Leadership," *Semeia* 90/91 (2002): 315-22; Leng Leroy Lim, "Webs of Betrayal, Webs of Blessings," in Eng and Hom, *Q&A*, 323-34.

American Christians. According to Lee, her "most meaningful prayer/ activism" occurs when she can "address the intersections of race and sexuality" and thus bring all three parts of her identity together.[7]

There have also been a growing number of organizations across the United States that focus on issues relating to queer Asian American Christians, including Queer Asian Spirit in Cambridge, Massachusetts; the Network on Religion and Justice for API LGBT People in Berkeley, California ("NRJ"); as well as the Asian Pacific Islander Roundtable ("API Roundtable") project of the Center for Lesbian and Gay Studies in Religion and Ministry ("CLGS") at the Pacific School of Religion.[8]

Trinity and Asian Americans

As noted above, I believe that classical trinitarian theology can help queer Asian American Christians to understand better the complex interplay of sexuality, race, and spirituality in our lives. Before doing so, however, I want to explore how various Asian American theologians have written about the Trinity from their own particular social locations.

For example, Jung Young Lee, the late Korean-American theologian and professor at Drew University, wrote *The Trinity in Asian Perspective*, which explores the Trinity from an Asian American perspective. In the book, Lee proposes several creative models for understanding the Trinity. One such model is the "yin-yang" model of Asian cosmology based upon the Daoist circular symbol that contains both darkness and light. For Lee, this model consists of three parts: (1) *yin* (darkness), (2) *yang* (light), and (3) in-ness (i.e., the light within the darkness and the darkness within the light).

---

[7] See Lee, "Queerly a Good Friday," 82. Other individual who have taken on leadership roles with respect to queer Asian ministries in recent years include Sharon Hwang Colligan, Jonipher Kwong, Debbie Lee, Elizabeth Leung, and Boon Lin Ngeo.

[8] See, e.g., Queer Asian Spirit, http://www.queerasianspirit.org (accessed September 30, 2010); Network on Religion and Justice for API LGBT People, http://www.netrj.org (accessed September 30, 2010); Asian Pacific Islander Roundtable at the Center for Lesbian and Gay Studies in Religion and Ministry, http://www.clgs.org/programs/api_roundtable (accessed September 30, 2010).

Another model for the Trinity is what Lee calls interfaith "trilogue," which consists of two religions that are in dialogue with each other, and also a third element of inclusivity that is defined as a mutual commitment by each of the interfaith dialogue partners to live authentically within both traditions.[9] For Lee, these trinitarian models are important because they contain examples of "both-and" thinking, which transcends "either-or" thinking and is an important part of the Asian and Asian American experience.

Similarly, Peter Phan, a Vietnamese American theologian and Roman Catholic priest who is a professor at Georgetown University, has proposed a Vietnamese American trinitarian theology in *Christianity with an Asian Face*. Phan draws upon the Vietnamese *"triet ly tam tai"* world view, which is translated as the "three-element philosophy." This philosophy consists of three components that are deeply connected with each other: (1) heaven, (2) humanity, and (3) earth.

According to Phan, these three components are trinitarian because they are distinct but also deeply interdependent. Phan draws upon classical trinitarian concepts, including *perichoresis* (mutual indwelling or interpenetration) and *koinonia* (community or fellowship). For Phan, the three components of heaven, humanity, and earth are "united in a *perichoresis* or *koinonia* of life and activities" and "inscribed in the structure of reality itself."[10]

By contrast with Lee and Phan, Asian American feminist theologian Rita Nakashima Brock has criticized the use of classical trinitarian theology as inherently patriarchal. In *Journeys by Heart*, Brock argues that the "unholy trinity" of "father-son-holy ghost" must be liberated from patriarchy. This can only be done by a feminist christology that exposes "the brokenheartedness at the center of that trinity" and reinterprets Christian doctrine in "nonoppressive ways." For Brock, the classical trinitarian formulas are reflections of "patriarchal family relationships" in which all members are "possessions and extensions of the reigning authority figure," whereas true intimacy – whether

---

[9] Jung Young Lee, *The Trinity in Asian Perspective* (Nashville: Abingdon, 1996), 212-19.

[10] Peter C. Phan, *Christianity with an Asian Face* (Maryknoll, N.Y.: Orbis, 2003), 243-44.

inside or outside the Trinity – involves "interdependence" and not merely "fusion."[11]

Other Asian American feminist theologians, such as Kwok Pui-lan and Anne Joh, have reimagined classical trinitarian doctrines in light of their own social locations. Kwok, who is one of the strongest allies of LGBT Asian Christians in the theological academy, approvingly cites the work of Virginia Burrus, who argues that trinitarian doctrine should be used not so much to "find out truths about God," but rather to "trace the cultural shift in the conception of masculinity in late antiquity."[12]

Similarly, Joh argues that it might be possible to redeem the internal relationships of the Trinity from patriarchy if "the identity of the Father and the Son are almost completely fused." For Joh, this fusion would result in a radical way of understanding God. That is, God represents "radical inclusivity" insofar as God the Father has incorporated God the Son – as the "stranger/Other" or the "abject" one on the cross – into God's very own being.[13]

In the end, all of these Asian American theologians – as well as others[14] – draw upon their specific social locations to construct contextual trinitarian theologies that speak powerfully to their communities. As an openly gay Asian American systematic theologian, my writings have focused on reclaiming classical Christian doctrines in light of the LGBT

---

[11] Rita Nakashima Brock, *Journeys by Heart: A Christology of Erotic Power* (New York: Crossroad, 1988), xii-xiii.

[12] See Kwok Pui-lan, *Postcolonial Imagination and Feminist Theology* (Louisville, Kentucky: Westminster John Knox, 2005), 11. Some of Kwok's work relating to the intersections of sexuality and race include Kwok, "Asian and Asian American Churches," in *Homosexuality and Religion: An Encyclopedia*, ed. Jeffrey S. Siker (Westport, Connecticut: Greenwood, 2007), 59-62; Kwok, "Body and Pleasure in Postcoloniality," in *Dancing Theology in Fetish Boots: Essays in Honour of Marcella Althaus-Reid*, ed. Lisa Isherwood and Mark D. Jordan (London: SCM, 2010), 31-43; Kwok, *Postcolonial Imagination*, 100-21; and Kwok, "Touching the Taboo: On the Sexuality of Jesus," in Ellison and Douglas, *Sexuality and the Sacred*, 119-34.

[13] Wonhee Anne Joh, *Heart of the Cross: A Postcolonial Christology* (Louisville, Kentucky: Westminster John Knox Press, 2006), 89.

[14] For a more detailed discussion of trinitarian theology in the Asian and Asian American contexts with a focus on Jung Young Lee and Raimundo Panikkar, see Veli-Matti Kärkkäinen, *The Trinity: Global Perspectives* (Louisville, Kentucky: Westminster John Knox Press, 2007), 307-45.

and Asian American experience. I have found this focus to be especially important for LGBT Christians – whether or not Asian American – who have felt excluded by Christian theological discourse but who still wish to remain squarely within the Christian tradition. For example, I have written about rethinking the doctrines of sin and grace for LGBT people while still preserving classical notions of original sin.[15] Similarly, I have taken initial steps towards constructing a comprehensive systematic theology from the lens of LGBT experience and queer theory.[16]

While I am grateful for – and have benefited greatly from – the insights of feminist and other Asian American theologians with respect to their critique of the Trinity, my own project here is to reclaim classical Christian trinitarian discourse so that those of us who are queer and Asian American can reclaim our rightful place within the larger Body of Christ. As such, I believe that queer Asian American Christians can use trinitarian theology as a helpful resource for our own theological reflection, and it is to this task that I now turn.

Trinity and Queer Asian Christians

Like the Bach three-part sinfonia, classical trinitarian theology can help queer Asian American Christians reflect more deeply about ourselves and our relationship to God. In particular, three classical trinitarian concepts are especially helpful for this theological reflection: (1) *vestigia trinitatis* (vestiges of the Trinity), (2) *mia ousia, treis hypostaseis* (one substance, three persons), and (3) *perichoresis* (mutual interpenetration).

First, the concept of *vestigia trinitatis* – that is, vestiges or "footprints" of the Trinity are imprinted upon the human soul – can help queer Asian American Christians develop a better sense of self-love by affirming that we are in fact made in the image and likeness of God. Second, the concept of *mia ousia, treis hypostaseis* – that is, the Trinity is simultaneously one being in three persons – can help queer Asian American Christians embrace our wholeness and feel less fragmented in

---

[15] See Cheng, "Rethinking Sin and Grace for LGBT People Today."
[16] See Patrick S. Cheng, *Radical Love: An Introduction to Queer Theology* (New York: Seabury Books, 2011).

terms of our sexuality, race, and spirituality. Third, the concept of *perichoresis* – that is, the mutual indwelling and interpenetration of the three persons of the Trinity – can help queer Asian American Christians to affirm the fluidity of our sexual, racial, and spiritual identities and also give us hope that something new and wonderful is constantly emerging from the interplay of these categories.

1. Self-Love and *Vestigia Trinitatis*

One issue for many queer Asian American Christians is the lack of self-love. This is not surprising because it is difficult to love oneself when one is told repeatedly that she or he is not created in the image and likeness of God. This is particularly the case for many queer Asian American Christians who were raised in conservative ethnic religious communities. In my experience pastoring to the queer Asian American Christian community during the last decade, each Asian American ethnic group has a dominant religious community that is often the source of great pain for its LGBT members and their families: Presbyterian for Korean Americans, Baptist for Chinese Americans, Roman Catholic for Filipino and Vietnamese Americans, and Methodist for Japanese Americans.

Indeed, many Asian American churches were involved with the passage in November 2008 of California Proposition 8, the notorious amendment to the California state constitution that eliminated the right of same-sex couples to marry under civil law. In fact, one of the official sponsors of Proposition 8 was Hak-Shing William Tam, the secretary of a Chinese American evangelical Christian group, who claimed in a 2008 letter to supporters of Proposition 8 that same-sex marriages would lead to prostitution and pedophilia, even though such claims were not supported by empirical data or scientific evidence.[17]

It is not surprising that many queer Asian American Christians suffer from self-hate and self-loathing as a result of the lies about us that are spread by homophobic Asian American religious communities. Indeed, many of us have a hard time coming out to our families and friends because we fear that we will be labeled as heretics and expelled

---

[17] See Gerry Shih, "Same-Sex Marriage Case: Arguments at Court," *New York Times* (January 14, 2010), http://www.nytimes.com/2010/01/15/us/15sfbriefs.html (accessed September 30, 2010).

from our faith communities. According to "Michael Kim," a closeted gay Korean American Christian, coming out to the Korean American Christian community would be "quite literally, the ultimate failure – moral, social, and personal all at once."[18] Often times we voluntarily exclude ourselves from these communities because we do not believe that we are truly loved and made in the image and likeness of God.

I believe that the classical trinitarian concept of the *vestigia trinitatis* can help to counter the feelings of self-hate and self-loathing that many queer Asian American Christians experience and foster a greater sense of self-love. According to this concept, vestiges or "footprints" of the triune God are imprinted upon the human soul. This is because, according to the Book of Genesis, the human being is created in the image and likeness of God.[19] Indeed, the only reason the soul desires to return to God is because an image of its creator – here, the trinitarian God – has been imprinted upon it.

Augustine of Hippo explains the concept of the *vestigia trinitatis* in his great work on the Trinity, *De trinitate*. Specifically, Augustine argues that the three-fold nature of the Trinity is imprinted upon the tripartite structure of the human mind, which consists of one's own (1) memory (*memoria sui*), (2) understanding (*intelligentia sui*), and (3) will (*voluntas sui*). However, these functions of the mind are not three separate or distinct substances, but rather one unified substance of the mind. In other words, each function is integrated with itself and the two other functions: (1) the mind *remembers* that it has memory, understanding, and will; (2) the mind *understands* that it has memory, understanding, and will; and (3) the mind *wills* memory, understanding, and will.[20]

For queer Asian American Christians, the *vestigia trinitatis* is also imprinted upon our souls in a similar way. Specifically, vestiges or "footprints" of the Trinity can be found within our tripartite identities of being queer, Asian American, and Christian. Although each of these identities serves its own individual purpose, ultimately these sexual, racial, and spiritual identities are part of a single human being or soul.

---

[18] Kim, "Out and About," 147.

[19] See Gen. 1:27 (NRSV).

[20] See Catherine Mowry LaCugna, *God for Us: The Trinity and Christian Life* (New York: HarperOne, 1991), 93-96.

As such, like the Trinity, we are simultaneously one and three. Thus, we are called to love ourselves because we are truly made in the image and likeness of the one triune God.

In recent years, a number of unique spaces have emerged that allow queer Asian American Christians to love ourselves and recognize that we are indeed made in the image and likeness of God. One such space is the Queer Asian Spirit listserv, which is an email discussion group of queer people of Asian descent from all around the world who are interested in issues of spirituality and religion.[21] This listserv, which was started in January of 2000, has been a place where queer Asian American Christians – as well as our friends and allies from around the world – have been able to network and create a virtual community or fellowship.

Another space that allows queer Asian Christians to love ourselves is the Emerging Queer API Religion Scholars (EQARS) group, a monthly gathering of queer API religion and theology graduate students and scholars around the world that meets virtually by Skype to discuss our own writings and other matters of interest. The EQARS group – as well as the API Roundtable project of CLGS – is coordinated by Elizabeth Leung, who has been a leading voice and organizer of queer Asian Christians in recent years.

Groups like Queer Asian Spirit and EQARS have allowed many queer Asian American Christians to minister to each other, notwithstanding the physical and geographical distances that separate us. In the process of so doing, we help each other to recognize that the vestiges or "footprints" of the triune God – the *vestigia trinitatis* – have indeed been imprinted upon each of us with respect to the three-fold gifts of our sexuality, race, and spirituality.

---

[21] See the Queer Asian Spirit listserv, http://groups.google.com/group/queerasianspirit (accessed on September 30, 2010), and the Queer Asian Spirit website, http://www.queerasianspirit.org (accessed on September 30, 2010). With the advent of social networking, the Queer Asian Spirit group also has a presence on Facebook. See Queer Asian Spirit Facebook group, http://www.facebook.com/group.php?gid=110085042819 (accessed on September 30, 2010).

2. Wholeness and *Mia Ousia, Treis Hypostaseis*

Another issue for many queer Asian American Christians is a profound sense of fragmentation with respect to our sexuality, race, and spirituality. In other words, queer Asian American Christians often feel the need to compartmentalize one or more of our identities, in response to the particular social context in which we find ourselves at any given moment.

For example, when queer Asian American Christians are with the larger LGBT community, many of us are forced to downplay the Asian American and Christian aspects of ourselves. This is because we often experience the twin challenges of racism and extreme secularism within the LGBT community. With respect to racism, we are often ignored or fetishized as Asian Americans within the predominantly white LGBT community. With respect to extreme secularism, we often experience a great deal of hostility against organized religion and, in particular, Christianity within the LGBT community.

Similarly, when queer Asian American Christians are with the larger Asian American community, many of us are forced to downplay the queer and Christian aspects of ourselves. This is because we often experience the twin challenges of homophobia and extreme secularism within the Asian American community. On the one hand, many Asian American communities, especially those with strong religious ties, are virulently homophobic. On the other hand, many Asian American communities that are often the most accepting of LGBT people – for example, Asian American progressive or activist groups – can be quite hostile to organized religion in general and Christianity in particular.

Finally, when queer Asian American Christians are with Christian communities, many of us are forced to downplay the queer and Asian American aspects of ourselves. This is because we often experience the twin challenges of homophobia and racism within Christian communities. With respect to homophobia, it is no great surprise that many Christian communities are hostile towards LGBT people. However, many of these communities are also unaware of their racism and the specific cultural or pastoral care needs of Asian Americans.[22]

---

[22] For a discussion of issues relating to Asian Americans in the context of LGBT pastoral care, see David J. Kundtz and Bernard S. Schlager, *Ministry Among God's Queer Folk: LGBT Pastoral Care* (Cleveland: Pilgrim Press,

For example, Zondervan, the large evangelical Christian publishing house, published a Christian comic book in 2009 called "Deadly Viper" that perpetuated a number of offensive stereotypes about Asian Americans. Zondervan apologized and withdrew the publication, but only after many Asian American Christians had complained about it.[23]

Time and time again, I have been told by my queer Asian American Christian sisters and brothers that, at most, "two out of three" of their identities can be affirmed, but rarely all three. For example, one can be queer and Asian American at gatherings of queer Asian Americans (such as Gay Asian Pacific Islander Men of New York or Q-Wave) but generally not Christian. One can be Asian American and Christian at gatherings of our Asian American churches,[24] but generally not queer. And one can be queer and Christian at gatherings of queer Christians (such as the Metropolitan Community Churches), but generally not Asian American.[25] As a result, many queer Asian American Christians experience a profound sense of fragmentation.[26]

I believe that the classical trinitarian concept of *mia ousia, treis hypostaseis* (μια ουσια, τρεις υροστασεις in the Greek, or *una*

2007), 74-75. See also William Ming Liu, Derek Kenji Iwamoto, and Mark H. Chae, eds., *Culturally Responsive Counseling with Asian American Men* (New York: Routledge, 2010).

[23] See Sarah Pulliam Bailey, "Zondervan Issues Apology for Publishing 'Deadly Viper,'" *Christianity Today* (November 20, 2009), http://blog.christianitytoday.com/ctliveblog/archives/2009/11/zondervan_issue.html (accessed on September 30, 2010).

[24] See Viji Nakka-Cammauf and Timothy Tseng, eds., *Asian American Christianity Reader* (Castro Valley: Institute for the Study of Asian American Christianity, 2009); Tony Carnes and Fenggang Yang, *Asian American Religions: The Making and Remaking of Borders and Boundaries* (New York: New York University Press, 2004).

[25] There are exceptions, of course, to the general rule. For example, around a dozen queer Asians and allies met during the 2010 General Conference of the Metropolitan Community Churches in Acapulco, Mexico, and discussed our ministries to queer Asian Pacific Islanders in the United States and around the world.

[26] For a discussion of the experience of fragmentation for queer Asian Americans, see generally Cheng, "Multiplicity and Judges 19," 119-33. For the relationship between grace and wholeness in the lives of queer Asian American Christians, see Patrick S. Cheng, "Rethinking Sin and Grace for LGBT People Today," in Ellison and Douglas, *Sexuality and the Sacred*, 105-18.

substantia, tres personae in the Latin) – that is, "one substance, three persons" – can help to counter the experience of fragmentation in many queer Asian American Christians and foster a greater sense of wholeness. This concept, also known as the Cappadocian formula, was coined in the fourth-century C.E. by the great Cappadocians: Basil of Caesarea, Gregory of Nyssa, Gregory of Nazianzus, and Macrina the Younger.

According to the Cappadocian formula, God is both one and three. That is, the three persons of the trinitarian Godhead – the Unbegotten (Father), the Begotten (Son), and the Procession (Holy Spirit) – all share the same substance or common nature (*ousia*) and thus are *one* being. However, these three persons also have distinct identifying characteristics with respect to their origins and thus are also *three* persons (*hypostaseis*). This formula was adopted as the official position of the Christian Church with respect to describing the Trinity. Thus, the triune God is *mia ousia, treis hypostaseis*, or "one substance, three persons."[27]

Like the triune God, those of us who are queer Asian American Christians are also three and one. We are *three* because each of us brings her or his unique perspective with respect to sexuality, race, and spirituality. However, we are also *one* because each of us can relate to the shared experience of being a whole queer Asian American Christian person. This classical trinitarian understanding of ourselves based upon the Cappadocian formula of *mia ousia, treis hypostaseis* can help to counter feelings of fragmentation when we are isolated from other queer Asian American Christians.

In recent years, queer Asian American Christians have been able to gather together in a number of different spaces. These spaces are valuable from a pastoral perspective because they allow us to acknowledge the complexities of ourselves in threeness and oneness. For example, in January of 2010, NRJ and APIRT sponsored a West Coast weekend retreat, "Queer Spirit, API Roots," in Burlingame, California. Similarly, in April of 2010, Queer Asian Spirit and APIRT sponsored a day-long East Coast retreat, "Being in Wholeness," in New York City Chinatown. Both events, which were well attended with around twenty participants each, allowed queer Asian American Christians – as well as queer Asian Americans from other spiritual

---

[27] See LaCugna, *God for Us*, 66-68.

traditions – to see ourselves as whole beings with respect to our sexualities, races, and spiritualities.

Also, a number of LGBT Asian American organizations have created spaces in recent years that allow religion or spirituality to be discussed in a "safe" manner. For example, in August of 2009, the National Queer Asian Pacific Islander Association (NQAPIA) provided a space for an interfaith meditation session at its national meeting in Seattle, Washington. Other safe spiritual spaces include a workshop on queer Asian spirituality in December 2009 at the Asian Pacific Islander Coalition on HIV/AIDS (APICHA) in New York City, and a panel on queer Asian spirituality in April 2010 at Q-Wave, the lesbian, bisexual, and transgender Asian American Women's group in New York City. These spaces have been valuable for queer Asian American Christians because they have allowed us to see ourselves in terms of the trinitarian formula of *mia ousia, treis hypostaseis* or "one substance, three persons," and they have helped to heal the fragmentation that so many of us have experienced.

3. Fluidity and *Perichoresis*

A final issue for many queer Asian American Christians is the misconception that our dreams and destinies are sharply defined – and limited – by our sexual, racial, and spiritual identities. In other words, many of us feel that we are held hostage by these identities, and that we are forever trapped by our three-fold marginalized status as Asian Americans, as LGBT people, and (in many secular contexts) as Christians. This can lead to a sense of despair, hopelessness, and depression.

I believe that the classical trinitarian concept of *perichoresis* (περιχωρησις in the Greek or *circumincessio* in the Latin) can help to remind queer Asian American Christians of the ultimate fluidity of our sexual, racial, and spiritual identities. *Perichoresis* – defined as the mutual indwelling and mutual interpenetration of the three persons of the Trinity – was a term coined in the eighth century C.E. by the theologian John Damascene to express the intimate relationship between the three persons of the Trinity. In particular, *perichoresis* expresses the notion that each person of the Trinity is never an isolated entity to itself, but rather is always dependent upon the other two persons for its meaning.[28]

---

[28] See LaCugna, *God for Us*, 270-78.

Perichoresis also suggests that the three persons of the Trinity are engaged in a joyful, intertwined dance, since the word is derived from the Greek root word for dancing. As such, the term evokes a wonderful image of an eternal and ecstatic dance of love between the three persons of the Trinity. Just like the Bach three-part sinfonia, the dance between these persons is an intimate weaving together of three distinct strands of the Trinity that ultimately cannot be separated.

The ancient concept of *perichoresis* is remarkably consistent with the work of twentieth-century queer theorists like Michel Foucault and Judith Butler. These theorists have challenged fixed, static, or essentialist notions of sexuality, gender, and other identity categories.[29] Similarly, *perichoresis* challenges a fixed, static, or essentialist notion of each person of the Trinity. In other words, *perichoresis* is fundamentally queer, because it describes how the boundaries of each triune person are in a continual state of flux, constantly being interpenetrated by the other two persons.[30]

By extension, the concept of *perichoresis* also challenges any fixed or essentialist understandings of sexual, racial, and spiritual identities for queer Asian American Christians. That is, I cannot understand what it means to be queer outside of the context of being Asian American and Christian. Neither can I understand what it means to be Asian American outside of the context of being queer and Christian. Nor can I understand what it means to be Christian outside of the context of being queer and Asian American. For me, the blurred relationship among the three persons of the Trinity – as well as my

---

[29] See, for example, James Bernauer and Jeremy Carrette, eds., *Michel Foucault and Theology: The Politics of Religious Experience* (Aldershot, UK: Ashgate, 2004); Ellen T. Armour and Susan M. St. Ville, eds., *Bodily Citations: Religion and Judith Butler* (New York: Columbia University Press, 2006).

[30] For example, according to Foucault, prior to the late nineteenth century, there was no such thing as a fixed or essentialist category of the "homosexual." There were, of course, people throughout history who had sexual relations with persons of the same sex. However, there were no universal, pre-existing labels (for example, "homosexual" or "heterosexual") that *classified* a person primarily in terms of the sex of her or his preferred sexual partner(s). Rather, people were classified historically by what they did; that is, whether they played a penetrating (active) or penetrated (passive) role. See Riki Wilchins, *Queer Theory, Gender Theory: An Instant Primer* (Los Angeles: Alyson, 2004), 54-57.

sexual, racial, and spiritual identities – are similar to notions of intersectionality in critical race theory or hybridity in postcolonial theory.[31]

Thus, I believe that *perichoresis* can help queer Asian American Christians resist the notion that we are hopelessly trapped by our marginalized identities. Rather than feeling like we are inevitably limited by these identities, *perichoresis* allows us to appreciate the fact that our beautiful inner life is always evolving and changing. Indeed, as an openly gay Asian American Christian, I can map each of my distinct identities upon each of the three persons of the Trinity, and see how these identities constantly interact in a mutually interpenetrating dance.

For example, my racial identity as an Asian American corresponds to the first person of the Trinity (that is, God the Unbegotten, or the "Father"). As an Asian American, I feel connected to the racial, ethnic, and cultural heritage of my ancestors from East Asia. Although I grew up in the United States, I was raised in a first-generation immigrant household, and I will always feel connected to my Chinese American parents, my grandparents, and their ancestors.

My sexual identity as an openly gay person corresponds to the second person of the Trinity (that is, God the Begotten, or the "Son"). As a queer person, I am acutely aware of being an embodied and incarnational person, particularly with respect to my own sexuality and gender identity. For me, my queerness is an affirmation of the goodness of the incarnation, that is, the Word that became flesh.[32] As such, I feel deeply connected to other queer folk around the world.

Finally, my spiritual identity as a Christian corresponds to the third person of the Trinity (that is, God the Procession or the "Holy Spirit"). As a Christian, my religious identity allows me to be a living witness to the radical hope, faith, and love that will overcome death as well as all bodily – indeed, all humanly-constructed – categories at the eschatological horizon. This is what connects me to other people of faith around the world.

---

[31] See generally Cheng, "Hybridity and the Decolonization of Asian American and Queer Theologies." For an introduction to intersectionality, see Emily Grabham et al., eds., *Intersectionality and Beyond: Law, Power and the Politics of Location* (New York: Routledge-Cavendish, 2009). On hybridity, see Peter Burke, *Cultural Hybridity* (Cambridge, UK: Polity, 2009).

[32] See John 1:17 (NRSV).

Most importantly, however, *perichoresis* affirms that each of these three identities is intertwined with the other two identities in a unique way. Indeed, each queer Asian American Christian person brings a unique perspective based upon her or his three-fold mix of sexuality or gender identity (lesbian, gay, bisexual, transgender, queer, questioning, intersex), race (East Asian, South Asian, Southeast Asian, Pacific Islander), and spirituality (Metropolitan Community Churches, Roman Catholic, Anglican, Presbyterian, Baptist). And yet each person can also relate to the common, shared experience of being a queer Asian American Christian.

The interplay of these three identities is a reflection of the joyful dance of *perichoresis*, not only within myself, but also within other queer Asian American Christians, and even all of creation. In February of 2010, a large number of LGBT Asian Americans in New York City participated as the first openly queer contingent ever to march in the annual Chinatown Lunar New Year Parade. For me, the march was an amazing experience of *perichoresis*. I could feel all of my identities as a queer Asian American Christian – my ancestral roots, my embodied self, and my spirituality – come together and joyfully interact in ways that I had never experienced before.[33]

Conclusion

In sum, I believe that the classical doctrine of the Trinity– like Bach's three-part sinfonias – is a powerful way for understanding how God can heal the suffering and pain that often arises out of the queer Asian American Christian experience. The three classical trinitarian concepts of (1) *vestigia trinitatis* (vestiges of the Trinity), (2) *mia ousia, treis hypostaseis* (one substance, three persons), and (3) *perichoresis* (mutual interpenetration) can help queer Asian American Christians to achieve greater self-love, wholeness, and fluidity with respect to our sexual, racial, and spiritual identities.

Looking back on my childhood, I am glad that my parents made me take piano lessons for so many years. Although I no longer play the

---

[33] See the Lunar New Year for All website, http://asianprideproject.org/lunarnewyear/ (accessed on September 30, 2010).

piano on a daily basis, I am grateful that I grew up with an appreciation for how the distinct voices of a Bach three-part sinfonia are woven together and come together as a single piece. That appreciation has given me the language to come "out of silence" and to talk about my own identity as a queer Asian American Christian.[34] It has also given me a deeper understanding of how classical trinitarian theology can be highly relevant to queer Asian American Christians today.

---

[34] See generally Fumitaka Matsuoka, *Out of Silence: Emerging Themes in Asian American Churches* (Cleveland: United Church Press, 1995).

Part Three

Our Reportoire:
Perspectives from Various Disciplines

Chapter 9.

Composing Integrity:
An Approach to Moral Agency for Asian Americans

Sharon M. Tan

In the globalized, post industrial 21st century, many people live concurrently in different worlds and cultures. They have transnational life experiences and multicultural relationships. Because of the impact of these differing experiences, cultures, and relationships, they can hold simultaneously different and even conflicting values and norms as well as conflicting hermeneutics and interpretations of their experiences. Asian Americans[1] are a prime example of such persons: Asian Americans live simultaneously as Asians-in-America and Americans-of-Asian-ethnicity, and perhaps even with additional identities (if they also

---

[1] Asian Americans come from a wide variety of cultures and ethnicities: East Asians (Chinese, Japanese, and Korean); South Asians (Indian, Pakistani, and Sri Lankan); South-east Asians (Vietnamese, Hmong, Thai, Malaysian, Indonesian, Singaporean, Filipino, etc.). They adhere to a wide variety of religions (Buddhist, Hindu, Muslim, Daoist, Christian, Sikh, etc.) Many of these ethnic or religious groups experience strife with each other in their countries of origin. Thus, one might as well question combining these diverse peoples into a single category for purposes of this article. However, these diverse peoples are often treated as a single group "Asian Americans" in North American culture. This is a signature experience that is perhaps unique to life in this nation and which fundamentally forms the identity of Americans of Asian origin. Thus, I will treat "Asian Americans" as a group, discussing the attendant moral implications as an important theme in this chapter.

participate in other cultures). They often experience dissonance between their inner thoughts and interpretations (which may themselves conflict) and outer acculturation and accommodation to the dominant culture that may lead to moral confusion. This confusion, coupled with cultural powerlessness, can debilitate moral voice and agency or be rationalized into moral relativism and emotivism.[2]

Asian American theology ascribes this debilitation in large part to the marginalization of Asian Americans by race, ethnicity, and culture. Asian Americans live *in-between* cultures, not fully Asian, and not fully American. In his book *Out of Silence*, Fumitaka Matsuoka describes Asian Americans as "poised in uncertainty and ambiguity between two or more social constructs, reflecting in the soul the discords and harmonies, repulsions and attractions."[3]

Marginality, however, has a silver lining. Although the terms liminality and marginality have often been used interchangeably, Sang Hyun Lee proposes that liminality is marginality with a creative edge, or a marginality that is open to creative possibilities.[4] Likewise, in this essay, I will use the term liminal to suggest the creative, agentic and powerful dimension of marginality. The experience of marginality can provide a creative opportunity to develop a moral agency that attends and responds to the particularities of Asian Americans.[5] Asian Americans can create a sense of identity from their experiences of liminality by—and perhaps *only* by—cultivating their own integrity through moral imagination and moral action.

---

[2] In *After Virtue* (Notre Dame, 1981), Alisdair MacIntyre proposes that when there is no justification for the liberal individualist worldview, moral confusion prevails, and moral justifications degenerate into emotivism and relativism.

[3] Fumitaka Matsuoka, *Out of Silence* (Cleveland: United Church Press, 1995), 54.

[4] Sang Hyun Lee, *From a Liminal Place: An Asian American Theology* (Minneapolis: Fortress Press, 2010), 4.

[5] H. Richard Niebuhr, in *The Responsible Self* (New York: Harper & Row, 1963), 60, argues that the question that we should ask ourselves is not what is the goal or law of the situation, but first of all, "what is going on?" This marks a method for ethics that is contextual and is attentive to history and experience rather than abstract principles.

In this essay, I propose "complex integrity" as a creative and imaginative practice in which people author their personal moral narrative within their particular social and moral context and, in so authoring, take responsibility for their moral future. This involves discerning between the disparate values and perspectives one experiences, weaving these values and perspectives together to cultivate a moral identity, and acting to create a desired moral future. The practice of complex integrity fosters moral agency, or moral power, in two ways: first, it cultivates a wholeness and clarity of moral vision and character through prioritizing interpretations and discerning moral claims upon oneself, and second, it provides impetus for moral action toward social justice and reconciliation.

Asians in America live as strangers or visitors in a foreign land: they come out of the world that formed them or the world that formed their parents, and are deeply influenced by Asian cultures. As Americans of Asian ethnicity, they are viewed as minorities in the dominant culture, which in turn defines and shapes them as such. And eventually, for an immigrant or her or his family, there will at some point be a transition in identity from that of "Asian-in-America" to that of "American-of-Asian-ethnicity." This transition in identity has significant moral impact, because it entails an acceptance of the social and racial category by which the dominant society and culture views and classifies them, identification with other Asians not of the same ethnic, religious, cultural, or national background, and perhaps even identification with those groups with whom they were at enmity in their countries of origin. For example, Japanese and other Asians were on opposite sides of World War II, an event in the living memory and family history of Asians-in-America. For one to be classified as Asian American would be to identify with Japanese-Americans whose relatives conquered and tortured one's family members. Similarly, it would mean association of Indians, Sikhs, and Pakistanis with each other, groups with similar ethnic origins but widely divergent religious beliefs and a history of religious conflict. And it would mean identification among groups who differ in ethnicity, culture and religion, and have no common history—not even in colonization—simply because the dominant culture classifies them by origination in the vast continent of Asia.

Because Asian Americans live in-between cultures, there is no single theological, religious, or cultural meta-narrative that adequately interprets their lives in the 21st century. Multiple cultures and sources compete for priority in moral decision making. Such dilemmas lead many Asians living in Western cultures to a moral pragmatism and utilitarianism which can lead into moral relativism and moral disempowerment. In *The Remains of the Day*, novelist Kazuo Ishiguro tells of an English man so consumed by his desire to be a great and loyal butler that he does not recognize or question his employer's rising Nazi sympathies. Ishiguro, a Japanese-Briton, describes the butler as displaying both the profound moral passivity and emotional disconnectedness arising from the juxtaposition of conflicting moral norms.

This essay suggests that complex integrity is a practice and virtue that could guide one through the moral maze that Asian Americans and other persons experience. It is a form of doing ethics that is attentive to the particular contexts and stories that Asian Americans and others find themselves in, providing a vision of a moral future that follows with integrity from the past and present.

The Agency Gap in Asian American Theologies of Identity

The dissonance and ambiguity of split moral loyalties in the Asian American soul has several sources. The first is globalization, which brings into proximity and juxtaposes different cultures not only in a single lifetime but in a single day. The second is the moral and social location of Asian Americans in North American culture where they occupy positions of partial privilege and partial oppression.

Globalization and Asian American Experience

Globalization shapes the Asian American experience in three ways: in their experiences as middleman minorities, as model minorities, and in their experience of transnationalism. As these experiences have been described by others extensively, I treat them here in summary form.

Middleman minorities

Asian Americans are informed not only by their own experiences, but also by the experiences of their relatives and fellow nationals in the rest of the world. The Asian diaspora have often been cast in the role of "middleman minority" in the different societies in which they have settled. Middleman minority groups may have frequent economic success but they are politically impotent. They function as economic intermediaries between the culturally, politically or economically dominant and subordinate groups.[6] They do this by filling certain professional or specialty roles in the economy, usually prescribed by the dominant culture. The term was originally used for Jews in Europe, but expanded to include trading groups in Africa and Asia, as well as Asian and other small businesses in the United States.[7] Although they act as buffers, there is frequently a societal backlash against them, as is evident in anti-Semitism or anti-Chinese sentiment.[8]

Model minorities

In a variation of the middleman minority status, Asian Americans in the United States have also been categorized as model minorities.[9] This term refers to a societal group that is economically self-sufficient and relatively crime-free with values synchronistic with the dominant culture. Although apparently laudatory, this designation actually maintains and legitimizes institutional racism. It denigrates other races or cultures by implying that Asian Americans are the normative immigrant group; other groups that have not achieved economic success in the same way are therefore inferior. The appearance of economic success is often deceptive because it fails to note the higher percentage of Asian American household members participating in the labor market to offset lower per capita income. The term "model minority" in fact acts as a glass ceiling, veiling discrimination and other real problems.[10] It also carries the implication that Asian Americans are "innately foreign" and not assimilable.[11]

---

[6] Walter P. Zenner, *Minorities in the Middle: A Cross-Cultural Analysis* (Albany, New York: State University of New York Press, 1991), xii.

[7] Zenner, *Minorities in the Middle*, 5-8; Jonathan Tan, *Asian American Theologies* (Maryknoll, N.Y.: Orbis, 2008), 39.

[8] Zenner, *Minorities in the Middle*, 59.

[9] Tan, *Introducing Asian American Theologies*, 37.

[10] Ibid., 22-23.

[11] Zenner, *Minorities in the Middle*, 25-26; Rita Nakashima Brock, "Interstitial Integrity: Reflections toward an Asian American Woman's Theology," in Roger A. Badham, ed., *Introduction to Christian Theology: Contemporary North American* Perspectives 183-196 (Louisville, Kentucky:

Transnationalism

Immigration patterns in the 21st century entail multiple types of relationships between one's country of origin and one's resident country. New technology (for example cell phones, Skype, email, and Facebook) means that communication with extended family across continents is no longer solely the privilege of the upper classes. This has led to a hybridized and multidimensional transnational identity, one which is both rooted in the United States and connected with family in Asia.[12]

Asian American Identity and Agency

The moral and social experience of Asian Americans in the United States, formed by globalization and experienced as marginality, contributes to the nature of their moral agency. Yet, while marginality is the source of moral disempowerment, its creative twin liminality can be the source of moral agency.

Marginalization as Shaping Identity

The descriptions of Asian American identity and experience—middleman minority, model minority and transnationalism—coalesce in the notion of marginality. Middleman minorities are marginal because they function between the economically dominant and subordinate. Model minorities are marginal because they are tolerated as economically acceptable and self sufficient, but remain socially excluded. Transnational relationships lead to a sense of marginality when Asians maintain relationships and therefore social and moral obligations in different cultures and worlds, and obligations in one world prevent acculturation in the others.

Peter Phan calls these experiences "betwixt and between," or sites of intercultural encounters where premodernity, modernity and postmodernity intersect.[13] Marginalization has been also described as a form of oppression. Jung Young Lee characterizes the experience of Asian Americans as marginalization,[14] as does Inn Sook Lee with the

---

Westminster John Knox Press, 1998), 185.

[12] Tan, *Introducing Asian American Theologies*, 55-56.

[13] Peter Phan, *Christianity with an Asian Face: Asian American Theology in the Making* (Maryknoll, N.Y.: Orbis Books, 2003) ,10.

[14] Jung Young Lee, *Marginality: The Key to Multicultural* Theology

experience of Korean American women.[15] Matsuoka calls it a "deep spiritual pain" which arises from the

> unresolvable conflict between the impossibility of letting go of one's own ethnic, cultural, and ancestral belonging and at the same time realizing that the assertion of one's own particularity is perceived as deviance by the society at large.[16]

He continues:

> A liminal [or marginal] person is one who has internalized the norms of a particular group but is not completely recognized by the members of that group as being a legitimate member. As long as this relationship prevails, one's role in countless situations will be ill-defined, or defined in different ways by the individual and the group as a whole. Such liminality leads to uncertainty, ambivalence, and the fear of rejection and failure.[17]

But there is more. There is an added dimension to Asian American experience when an Asian living in the United States, either in the first generation or, often, in the transition to the second generation, starts to identify him or herself as "Asian American." Since this new identity as Asian American is racially defined, the transition is a form of *racialization*. In the transition to an American identity, one's ethnic and socio-political identity is transformed into a racial identity. In addition to the conflict between the cultures of the old world and the new world, the Asian American experience now also includes an identification with other Asians in North American society who are dissimilar in ethnicity.[18]

(Minneapolis: Fortress Press, 1995).

[15] Inn Sook Lee, *Passage to the Real Self: the Development of Self Integration for Asian American Women* (Lanham, Maryland: University Press of America, 2009).

[16] Matsuoka, *Out of Silence*, 59.

[17] Ibid., 61.

[18] For example, when my neighbor's house went up for sale, I wondered with my children who would move in. I wondered aloud if it would be a Chinese or South Indian family (similar to those I grew up with in Malaysia, in

The Asian-living-in-America now must negotiate both cultural identity as an American, and a racial identity as "Asian" and as a "person of color." Such a person could navigate the moral dimensions of both identities with complex integrity if they could accept the benefits and minimize the disadvantages of each identity without allowing one identity to dominate the other.

The racialization that Asian Americans experience is a further form of marginalization. If the Asian–living-in-America is marginalized by culture, religion, and/or national origin, the Asian American is marginalized by race. In other words, the adoption of Asian American identity by a person is an implicit recognition *and acceptance* of the way race shapes U.S. society. One with complex integrity would be able to author a moral identity that responds with responsibility and agency to this racialization.

Liminality as Shaping Moral Agency

Despite the perception that Asian Americans have some social power because of their lighter skin and model minority status, their experience of marginalization has impacted their moral agency by creating confusion and silencing their voices. The experience of marginality as oppressive has led Asian Americans to draw deeply from liberation theology.[19]

Liberation theologies tend to dichotomize the moral world between dominant and marginalized groups or between the oppressor and the oppressed. Within this dichotomous way of seeing the world, Asian Americans, depending on their national origin, socio-economic location and immigration experience, generally identify either with the dominant culture, or more often perhaps, with the marginalized.

This dichotomy between dominant and marginalized, oppressor and oppressed, does not adequately describe the Asian American

---

addition to Malays). My three-year-old corrected me very firmly, "we just want children, any skin." This illustrates the difference between my first generation Asian-in-America self and my second generation American-of-Asian ethnicity children due to the transition in identity–whilst I focused on the ethnicity and culture of the adults, my children assumed that the culture of the *children* would be one they all shared despite differing ethnicity.

[19] Lee, *Marginality*, 23-29; Matsuoka, *Out of Silence*, 111; Tan, *Introducing Asian American Theologies*, 121-142.

experience. The characterization of Asian American experience as "betwixt and between" not only describes a type of marginalization, *it also describes a situation of privilege*. In other words, Asian Americans are simultaneously both marginal and dominant.

Since dominant and minority or marginal status is relative, people and groups can be simultaneously dominant and marginal in different spheres.[20] As Asian Americans function as a middleman minority economic "buffer" between the dominant white culture and other less privileged cultures, they partake of both cultural characteristics, but belong wholly to neither. As Asian Americans inhabit the model minority designation, they suffer from discrimination because of their "minority" status, but also benefit from a certain racial and cultural tolerance because of the "model" status. In transnational contexts, although they are not white, they bear the privilege of being U.S. citizens.

This situation of partial marginalization and partial privilege has a specific shape and characteristic. Although it takes on different characteristics in different parts of the country and in different socio-economic spheres of life, generally, the partial privilege is racial and economic. For example, Asians are not as dark-skinned as some other groups, and Asian women (but less often Asian men, with a few exceptions) are sometimes portrayed in media as beautiful and sexually desirable. The partial economic privilege emerges from several factors: Asian immigration in the late 20th century was generally voluntary,[21] and screened by the U.S. government for those with specific skills.[22] The

---

[20] Martin Marger, *Race and Ethnic Relations: American and Global Perspectives* 4th ed. (Beverly, Mass.: Wadsworth Publishing Co., 1997), 52-53.

[21] Ogbu has categorized the minority groups in the United States as "voluntary" and involuntary. Voluntary minority groups are those who have immigrated into the United States, and see the United States as a land of opportunity, working toward economic goals that are not available in their home countries. They are more willing to assimilate and work to achieve economic success or success in school. Involuntary minorities are those that have been conquered and made a minority against their will, for example, African Americans and certain Hispanic Americans. They are more prone to resist identification with the dominant group and see success in school as a betrayal of their own culture in favor of the dominant culture. John Ogbu, *Minority Education and Caste* (New York: Academic Press, 1978).

[22] Vijay Prashad, *The Karma of Brown Folk* (Minneapolis: University of

large percentage of professional and educated elites, and extensive kinship networks produced relative economic success. There are significant exceptions, but the successes have been more noted than the failures. Except for U.S. citizenship, however, economic success has not come with political privilege[23] nor has it allowed cultural assimilation. In contrast, African Americans in certain parts of the country, for example, Atlanta, have more political power but not the racial privilege or economic success.

Recent scholarship in Asian American theology is moving beyond idealized notions of culture and identity toward recognizing more fluid, conflicted, and complex notions of identity.[24] Asian Americans realize they must negotiate between the cultures in which they simultaneously live.[25] Rita Nakashima Brock calls this "holy insecurity," that is, a complex cross-cultural identity with multilayered experience of dominance and subordination.[26]

Although marginalization has been a source of disempowerment, it can also be a source of moral empowerment. In fact, it is only out of a realization of our complex notions of identity, out of recognition that we have both partial power and partial oppression, that we can find liminality, the creative and powerful aspect to marginalization. Out of this liminality we can develop a moral agency that is particular to the Asian American experience. Our experience as Asian Americans differs from that of the dominant white culture and the other subordinate minority cultures. Thus, we must recognize that we have different interpretations and thus different *responsibilities* from both the dominant and other subordinate groups.[27]

Minnesota Press, 2000), 69-82.

[23] Greg Oswald, *Race and Ethnic Relations in Today's America* (London: Ashgate, 2001), 138-142.

[24] Tan, *Introducing Asian American Theologies*, 171.

[25] See Phan, *Christianity with an Asian Face*, 10-21; Lee, *Marginality*, 23-29.

[26] Brock, "Interstitial Integrity: Reflections toward an Asian American Woman's Theology," 183-19.

[27] H. Richard Niebuhr suggests that a moral agent acts in response to the world around him or her, in interpretation of action upon him or her, in anticipation of the responses to his or her responses, and in social solidarity with others. H. Richard Niebuhr, *The Responsible Self* (New York: Harper and Row,

Asian American moral agency must respond to both the experiences and interpretations of our partial power and of our partial oppression. In other words, we must be attentive to, responsive to and responsible for the fact of partial privilege. In particular, we have a responsibility to connect that partial privilege to our partial oppression.[28] This is the task of complex integrity: we have the responsibility to use our partial privilege to ameliorate the oppression of others. The particular pain of oppression we feel is a call to us to work for justice for others suffering similar and worse pain.

There are two aspects to fulfilling our responsibilities due to partial privilege. First, we have to develop *intercultural conscience;* that is, to do the intrapersonal work to prioritize the conflicting cultural and moral claims we experience and to respond appropriately, or *justly,* to the culturally divided and divisive claims on us. Second, we are to strive for wholeness between our inner and outer selves, between our character and our action. We must be able to harness our partial power to work toward justice and reconciliation for those more oppressed than ourselves. The practice through which this takes place is *complex integrity*.

Complex Integrity

Integrity is generally understood as involving honesty and wholeness of body, soul and spirit, or body and mind. It is personal character work that consists of discerning "right from wrong," clarifying one's convictions and morals, and then expressing them in moral action. The notion of integrity is relatively simple, if not easily achieved, in a monocultural setting where norms and values are fairly clear and unquestioned. A person of integrity is one who is honest and good with both internal and external consistency of principle, word and action.[29]

1963), 61-65.

[28] This responsibility reflects the biblical tradition connecting lament and prophecy. The biblical prophets connected their prophetic power and utterances with the particular griefs of their time and experience. For example, Jeremiah mourned the wickedness of Israel on behalf of God by acting it out (Jeremiah 7-9). The story of Hosea is especially poignant: his unfaithful wife is compared to unfaithful Israel, and his mourning and call to his wife to repent expresses God's mourning and call to Israel to repent.

The work toward integrity becomes more difficult when moral principles or expectations conflict, when the culture is not seamless, when the convictions and morals of a lifetime have come under question, or when there are varying answers to moral questions of character. Complex integrity describes a virtue that multicultural people living in multicultural societies need to cultivate to realize their moral agency and empower their moral selves. To understand its full implications, it may be helpful to contrast it with "simple integrity."

Simple integrity

Integrity, generally understood, has two parts: the notion of honesty and moral reflection and the notion of wholeness, which is consistency of belief and action. For example, Stephen Carter defines integrity as "a difficult process of discerning one's deepest understanding of right and wrong,... [that] then further requires action consistent with what one has learned."[30] This notion of integrity includes a (Kantian) duty to follow principle.[31] Integrity involves honesty and consistency; it is consonance between the inner self of belief and principle and the outer self of word and action. This is the understanding of integrity emphasized in much of the political and business literature on integrity.

As a search for the "*deepest* understanding of right and wrong," this understanding of integrity carries an implicit assumption that the determination of what is right and wrong is made with reference to the norms and values of a single culture or relatively consonant group of cultures. Asian Americans, however, do not live in such a monocultural or consonant world. For example, traditional spiritual beliefs and practices often conflict with Western medicine and technology.[32] In another example, Asian Christianity often differs from Western Christianity. If Asian Americans attend predominantly white or culturally white churches, their Asian expressions of spirituality or morality may not be supported. Conversely, if they attend predominantly

---

[29] See Mark Halfon, *Integrity: A Philosophical Inquiry* (Philadelphia: Temple University Press, 1989), 4-5.

[30] Stephen Carter, *Integrity* (New York: Basic Books, 1996), 10.

[31] Ibid., 20.

[32] See, for example, the account in Anne Fadiman, *The Spirit Catches You and You Fall Down* (Farrar, Straus and Giroux, 1998).

Asian churches, they may chafe at the hierarchical or traditional values and expectations. In another instance, because Asian character values of humility and self deference are not valued in North American culture and workplaces, Asians may have to assume Western values and character traits in order to succeed, which may in turn cause personal dissonance. Further, conflicts arise when unspoken values nevertheless profoundly shape family interactions. For example, is a first born son (or daughter, when there are no sons) who leaves the home to strike a life for himself in another city independent, ambitious and entrepreneurial for breaking with dying tradition and establishing a career and a new paradigm of relationships (North American values), or he or she *cowardly* and *selfish* for not shouldering the burden of caring for and relating to aging parents (Confucian values)?

In addition to honesty, consistency, and wholeness within the norms of the dominant culture, we must negotiate the dissonance between the different cultures that we are a part of and loyal to. Thus integrity requires a more complex understanding of wholeness, and has particular contexts and narratives. Since Asian Americans participate in a wide variety of experiences and cultures, what might be integrity will even vary from person to person.

Brock proposes an "interstitial integrity" that eloquently describes the experience of Asian Americans navigating multiple cultures. To live in interstitial integrity is to be able to live in the tension of multiple worlds, and to find meaning

> by refusing to disconnect from any of them, while not pledging allegiance to a singular one. It allows space for the multiple social locations of identity in a multicultural context. ... Interstitial integrity allows us to evaluate our behavior and exercise moral discrimination and self-evaluation. But because we live in the interstices, we must also engage in solidarity with others who also live in the interstices.[33]

Brock seems to suggest that Asian Americans possess this integrity by the simple virtue of living in different worlds. In other

---

[33] Brock, "Interstitial Integrity: Reflections toward an Asian American Woman's Theology," 191.

words, interstitial integrity is not a moral process or virtue, but a theological characteristic that describes identity and an ethical way of being. However, she does not propose a way of achieving the self-understanding and acceptance that she describes.

Complex integrity

Through "complex integrity" we can cultivate and develop the moral agency that we need to live in this multi-moral world. It is a virtue—a habit or practice that leads to human flourishing—that reconciles the different parts of our moral selves which are subject to different cultural loyalties and moral norms. Complex integrity imagines and creatively works toward a new and desired moral future rather than in adherence to a single tradition or interpretation of the past. Complex integrity is creative and personal: it need not be individualistic, but since it has to do with the character of the individual that is navigating the multiculturality of the globalized 21st century world, it is personal.

William James suggests that we can live into what we believe by acting accordingly and thereby making it "true."[34] This is the neo-pragmatic premise of complex integrity: we create our integrated identity by imagining it and acting into it. We must attend simultaneously to both the internal dispositions of character and the external moral actions that display that character. Complex integrity thus synchronizes questions of character and moral action. We love God *and* we love our neighbor as ourselves.[35] In fact, loving God and loving neighbor is each made possible only by the other.

The prerequisites to complex integrity are cognitive flexibility and epistemological humility. This reminds us that all theological and moral systems are humanly *constructed*—as are one's particular interpretations, understandings and loyalties—and thus subject to negotiation and prioritization. As in Gandhi's notion of nonviolence, we understand that Truth exists; but because we do not know it absolutely, we cannot force our idea of truth upon others.[36] Likewise, we cannot

---

[34] William James, "The Will to Believe," in *The Will to Believe and other essays in popular philosophy* (New York: Dover Publications, 1956).

[35] See discussion of virtue ethics in Maureen H. O'Connell, *Compassion: Loving Our Neighbor in an Age of Globalization* (Maryknoll, N.Y.: Orbis, 2009) 45-46.

force one cultural idea of truth onto our own divided selves, further subjecting our minds and hearts to violence and cultural imperialism. Rather, the principle of non-violence implies that we accept and even embrace our bi- or multi-cultural lives with their contrasting and even conflicting truths and norms.

Reconciliation as a moral template for complex integrity

There are many psychological templates for cultivating integrity. Many approaches to integrity are either psychological, professional, or business.[37] There are a few books that treat integrity from a philosophical point of view.[38] Most, however, do not address integrity in a way that is helpful in navigating the particular complexity of the Asian American's multicultural moral world.

Cox, La Caze, and Levine do address integrity in a more nuanced way in *Integrity and the Fragile Self*. They propose that integrity, as a virtue, is

> not a kind of wholeness, solidity of character or moral purity. It involves a capacity to respond to change in one's values or circumstances, a kind of continual remaking of the self, as well as a capacity to balance competing commitments and values and to take responsibility for one's work and thought.[39]

This reflection upon human experience, while recognizing the kinds of conflicts that Asian Americans might face, does not articulate a method for cultivating the capacity it suggests we need.

To cultivate an integrity that can develop moral agency and inspire moral action, I look to the notion of *reconciliation*. Complex integrity involves reconciling our different and even conflicting interpretations of our experiences, values and norms. I suggest

---

[36] Joan Bondurant, *Conquest of Violence: The Gandhian Philosophy of Conflict* (Berkeley: University of California Press), 20, 31-32.

[37] See, e.g., Henry Cloud, *Integrity: the Courage to Meet the Demands of Reality* (San Francisco: Harper, 2009).

[38] See Halfron, *Integrity: A Philosophical Inquiry*.

[39] Damian Cox, Marguerite La Caze, and Michael P. Levine, *Integrity and the Fragile Self* (London: Ashgate, 2003), 41.

reconciliation as a *moral* approach to integrity that can provide a way to understand and negotiate the conflicting moral norms and cultural loyalties Asian Americans face.

The basic processes in reconciliation are forgiveness, repentance, justice, and renewed community. Forgiveness and repentance heal broken relationships. Repentance ceases the wrongdoing that breaches the relationship, and seeks to make amends. Forgiveness ceases the cycles of revenge and violence that keep people apart. Rather than ignoring the real harms done by those in relationship to each other, both involve moral accounting and truth telling and are thus consonant with the notion of honesty. Justice and renewed community rebuild alienated relationships. Justice is foundational to the creation of a better, more whole relationship. The processes of renewed community work to implement the just order or relationship desired. Both are consonant with the notion of wholeness, as they both seek to recreate and institute a more peaceful and just relationship between the parties.

As processes, rather than end states, these are neither linear nor consecutive, but concurrent. The different processes interweave and interact and sometimes double back on themselves, slowly moving on all fronts in the direction of wholeness and reintegration. Thus reconciliation is not static, but characterizes a relationship by ongoing practices of forgiving, repenting, seeking justice, and community.

Forgiveness

As Asian Americans seeking complex integrity, forgiveness is the determination to face the moral conflicts and wounds that we encounter. In other words, to be truly integrated, we must acknowledge the harm that has been done to us. This includes the recognition of the impact of racism, imperialism, and oppression in our lives, and admitting our internalization of racism and imperialism, and our participation in structural racism, imperialism and oppression. For example, when Asians participate in societal discrimination against those of darker skin, we show that we have internalized racism. Or, when we try to gain access to power and privilege by distancing ourselves from other struggling groups, we participate in structural imperialism.

Honesty starts with the self. If one is dishonest with oneself, one cannot be honest with others. If one is dishonest with oneself, one cannot be whole, or integrated. Forgiveness is premised on this. Unlike the notion of condonation, which is to ignore or accept as right the wrong that has been committed, forgiveness requires complete honesty and moral accounting of the wrong, and then the openness to remaining in relationship with the wrong-doer.[40]

Forgiveness as a step toward integrity is the forgiveness of self, that is, complete honesty about the self and its strengths and flaws, and the acceptance of that self with its strengths and flaws. Too often we do not face the truth because are not willing to accept ourselves as we are, or because we do not want to change.

Forgiving ourselves first entails our recognition of the wrongs done to us and our complicity in internalizing those wrongs, and then acknowledging our part in perpetuating those wrongs. But forgiveness is not the end of the process of reconciliation. The corollary to forgiveness is repentance.

Repentance

After facing one's faults, in repentance one stops committing those wrongs against the self and rectifies them if possible. In other words, to be truly integrated one must be aware of the ways one has harmed, or continues to harm others, and must also be *committed to stopping that harm.*

In our context as Asian Americans seeking complex integrity, repentance is the determination not to be co-opted into a culture that is alienated from oneself and oppressive of others, and then acting to *reverse* the different forms of direct, internalized, and structural racism. In other words, it is the commitment not to "pass" within the dominant culture in order to benefit from a system that exploits others. It is also to recognize where we have internalized racism and domination, and been prejudiced against and oppressive of others –women, children, those darker skinned than we are, those less educationally or economically advantaged – and to cease our own prejudice, denial, and oppressive actions. It involves being committed to stopping the harm we cause by our participation in structural and internalized racism and acting on it. This leads us to the next aspect of reconciliation: justice.

---

[40] Donald Shriver, *An Ethic for Enemies* (Oxford University Press, 1995), 7.

Justice

Justice is the structure of right relations, or the conditions under which people have the incentives to engage in right relations. It is the overarching backdrop, and goal toward which reconciliation works. True reconciliation presupposes that injustice and all the relevant concerns of justice are being addressed.

Justice as part of complex integrity is the cultivation of right relationships among one's various inner selves and between the inner and outer selves. The classic Greek notion of justice is to give each his or her due. Thus, justice within the self could be to honor appropriately the different moral claims to which we are subject. To do ourselves justice as Asian Americans is to give our various alliances and loyalties their due, by honoring appropriately the different claims, norms, and cultural values in our lives, as both Asians and Americans. Linking this to the biblical language of *shalom*, to honor appropriately the different cultural claims upon one's life is to be whole, at peace with oneself.

Determining the "appropriateness" of the different claims, however, is perhaps the most subjective part of the whole process. How do we determine what is appropriate? Karen Lebacqz points out in her narrative theory of justice that whilst we do not know what justice is, we can recognize injustice when we see it. We strive for justice by countering injustice. Justice is the story of our fight against injustice. In fighting injustice, step by step, we will find our way towards a more just future.[41]

I suggest that thinking in terms of narrative justice is a promising way for Asian Americans to process the different cultural claims they are subject to. We do not know a theoretically "perfect" or "just" balance of cultures, and surely, that differs from one cultural mix and experience to another. But we can recognize when cultural claims are unjust. We counter those injustices as we encounter them, thus slowly progressing toward a more just future. When we recognize specific instances of oppression or injustice, either internally or in society, we resist them. In other words, in an ongoing interactive process of discerning and acting, we oppose *inappropriate* cultural claims as we encounter them, and thus

---

[41] Karen Lebacqz, *Justice in an Unjust World* (Minneapolis: Augsburg Press, 1987).

move toward an appropriate moral balance. For example, a person facing conflicting world views also faces conflicting claims to his or her priorities. Does an employer hire an undocumented alien, contravening the law, but also providing income and work to one in need? Narrative justice would answer the question by asking first what injustice would need to be countered, and what in fact one could do. One with complex integrity would take that answer and then consider it with the need to "give to Caesar what is Caesar's, and to God what is God's."

Renewing community

The last step in the template of reconciliation is to renew community, to rebuild the ongoing relationship between formerly estranged parties. Within the societal narrative framework, this is to reauthor a community's story to include narratives of all the society's members. In the personal work toward complex integrity, this step reunites the disparate parts of ourselves back into relationship with each other. We write a narrative for the future that incorporates the various subnarratives of our life, and then we live and act into that future.

This step, renewed relationship between the various parts of ourselves, first requires that we Asian Americans accept our biculturality. We stop striving for monoculturality either by clinging unquestioningly to our identity in the old world or by acculturating equally unquestioningly into the dominant society. It may mean accepting the fact that conflict in identity, with its attendant conflict in moral norms, is a normal and inevitable response to the fractured worlds we live in.

Complex integrity thus requires moral imagination. Moral imagination is to "see simultaneously what is and what might yet be for the best, to engage at the same time the most creative of human passions, and consequently to lure into action and to sustain commitment."[42] In moral imagination we imagine the moral future that we desire, and take steps toward it. It is in the steps we take toward our desired future that we weave our subnarratives together and unite the disparate parts of ourselves. The end result is moral agency—moral power—which is effective moral action flowing from moral character.

---

[42] James Mackey, *Religious Imagination* (Edinburgh: Edinburgh University Press, 1986), 23.

The Practice of Complex Integrity

Complex integrity as a virtue is acquired through practice. The practice of the process of complex integrity comes in two parts: reflecting on one's life from a moral perspective, and acting as a consequence of the moral reflection.

Moral reflection and narrative

Meta-narratives by which one measures consistency and loyalty, and thus integrity, are no longer found persuasive in a globalized postmodern world that conflicts, collides, juxtaposes, and blends cultures. In the absence of persuasive meta-narratives, many turn to the personal narrative to justify their choices and to interpret their experiences in light of the various traditions that claim them. Because the personal narrative is constructed from particularities of lived experience, it is also contextual, and takes us out of the abstract into the praxis of life.

Inn Sook Lee describes a process through which Asian American women (primarily Korean) move toward integrity, or the "real self." The steps in this process include conscientization, reflection or introspection, and integration.[43] The first stage, conscientization, happens when Asian American women become aware of the dissonances between their inner, authentic selves, and the cultural expectations of them, for example, to be submissive. I suggest that it is at this stage of conscientization, or awareness of moral and cultural inner conflict, that it becomes useful for Asian Americans to tell the narrative of their moral lives. This helps us articulate the moral dissonances and conflicts we face and determine the source of the moral conflicts.

I suspect that idea of a personal moral narrative may be particularly challenging for Asians, who are stereotypically uncomfortable with drawing attention themselves, and who are, also stereotypically, more comfortable operating in their collective or social roles. Speaking up exposes one to the risk of having our personal lives

---

[43] Inn Sook Lee, *Passage to the Real Self* (Lanham, Maryland: University Press of America, 2009), 163.

and our flaws exposed, and of being seen to be imperfect. In other words, it exposes us to shame. This shame is part of the silence which Matsuoka describes.

In the same way repentance is a morally and theologically appropriate response to guilt and/or remorse, complex integrity is a morally and theologically appropriate answer to the cultural shame that subjects some Asian Americans to lives of emotional and moral passivity and conformity. It takes courage and humility to admit subjecttivity, to be vulnerable and risk shame. To undertake personal moral narrative is a moral choice that promotes courage, honesty, self-awareness, and humility.

The link between narrative and integrity has antecedents in the story of Job. The Hebrew Bible terms Job a person of integrity, because he articulated his moral dilemma and confusion. Counter to the prevailing theologies of the time that his friends articulated, he claimed to be righteous, in spite of the disasters that befell him. God did not censure him, but rather describes him as one with integrity for speaking his truth even though it meant questioning the prevailing moral norms and theological explanations of his time. Likewise, Asian Americans, in articulating their moral dilemmas due to their bi- and multi-cultural experiences and interpretations, lament the brokenness of North American globalized society rather than passively accepting the dominance and triumph of its hegemonic cultural narrative. This truth-telling is a step toward complex integrity of the self and healing for society.

Appendix 1 is a set of instructions I developed to guide one in writing a personal moral narrative, which is a first step toward constructing an imagined moral future. The moral narrative invites reflection, analysis, and imagination, and prompts one toward moral action.

Moving into the Future: Agency

After the introspective work of inner reconciliation, we must look outward toward moral action. Complex integrity culminates in moral agency. Inn Sook Lee terms this integrity, the "final rite of passage in which Asian women ... embody their autonomous selves."[44]

Agency is the natural outcome of integrity, and integrity fosters agency. Integrity does not only reside in the intellect, within ourselves: we must express our convictions in our actions. Our actions and moral stances must support what we believe, what we accord to ourselves. We create wholeness and integrity by acting into it, by taking steps toward the moral future that we desire. We create—or co-create—the moral path we travel on. The image of a rock climber comes to mind: the rock climber hammers a stake into the rock surface and hangs her weight from the stake for dear life—all while hammering another stake into the rock. She transfers her weight to the next stake, and does the same again and again, thus creating her way as she goes.

Thus, after we have been introspectively honest with ourselves, determined the injustices in our lives and prioritized our moral obligations, integrity mandates that we turn outward. Justice at this point requires that we do what we can for whomever we can. Christian or biblical notions of justice include loving our neighbor as ourselves and doing to others as we would have them do to us.[45] In so far as we desire justice and reconciliation for and within ourselves, we must work toward justice and reconciliation for others. Cox, et al. also link the notion of integrity with the notion of commitment, which

> involves an agent's disposition to act in certain ways: a person is committed to a principle when they generally act in the light of it, even when this is difficult and uncomfortable; they are committed to a cause when they consistently act to advance it; to a project when they consistently act in pursuit of it and to a person when they consistently act in what they take to be the person's interests.[46]

There is no moral dissonance to the reciprocal "golden rule," which has parallels in Asian moral philosophies. Tu Weiming argues that the Confucian way rests on two principles: "Do not do unto others what we would not want others to do unto us…[and] In order to establish ourselves we must help others to establish themselves."[47] In addition, in

---

[44] Ibid., 163.
[45] Matthew 7:9-12, 22:37-39; Mark 12:31; Luke 6:27-31.
[46] Cox et al., *Integrity and the Fragile Self*, 83.
[47] Tu Weiming, "Joining East and West: A Confucian Perspective on

Confucian philosophy, the heart and the mind are signified by the same word *xin*. Virtue and action integrate; moral actions build one's character. For example, to develop *ren*, or the Confucian notion of humanity and benevolence, one desiring to promote oneself promotes others.[48] Both the notion of *junzi*, or best self, and *renren*, the person who loves sacrificially, focus on the cultivation of virtue and the love of others.[49] The completion of virtue is to help others.[50]

Likewise, we know what is perhaps the most quoted of Gandhi's sayings: "Be the change." This calls for acting (non-violently) on behalf of Truth, with which Gandhi equates justice and liberation. "Being the change" means acting in the way we want the world to become, which in turn requires the moral imagination to envision the moral future we want and the moral courage to work toward it—for our sake and for the sake of others.

Conclusion

To cultivate complex integrity as a habit or pattern of living is a way of developing moral agency, moral character that flows into moral action. Complex integrity as a virtue is ultimately a personal pattern of habits and actions that signify an honest and whole life. It is to come to terms with the cultural and moral dissonances that we face, prioritize between them, and to imagine a moral future that we act into.

I suggest that those with partial privilege, who live in a marginalized in-betweeness, have a responsibility to use the unique gift of wisdom gleaned from our liminal state and our partial privilege to speak out on behalf of those who are oppressed. To find the courage to do so, we imagine a moral narrative that leads us into a more just future, to live into that future by acting in solidarity with others who are oppressed. This is the moral call to Asian Americans: to work toward justice and reconciliation for all.

Human Rights," in *Harvard International Review* (1998): 44-49.

[48] May Sim, *Remastering Morals with Aristotle and Confucius* (Cambridge: Cambridge University Press, 2007), 27-29, citing Confucius' *Analects*, 6:30

[49] K. K. Yeo, *Musing with Confucius and Paul* (Eugene, Oregon: Cascade, 2008) 281-82.

[50] Ibid., 345-48, citing Analects 4:25 and 6:28.

Moral Autobiography or Narrative of Moral Life

Section A: Write an account of your life, including the following elements:
1. *Social location*: where you grew up, your family's socio-economic status, other social and economic information, e.g. "I grew up in L.A./Kenya/London/rural Wisconsin," "I was born into an upper-middle class family/I grew up on a farm/I was a missionary's kid" etc.
2. *Moral events and decisions you have made in your life*: things that you did or happened to you that influenced you morally, e.g. poverty, divorce, moving to Africa to be a missionary, alcoholism, vows of poverty or celibacy, end of life decisions for a parent/loved one, adoption or abortion, divorce, etc.
3. *Moral location*: what was the moral culture in which you grew up in, e.g. type of church, 60's Woodstock generation, particular traditional values (Amish, Confucian), philosophical traditions (transcendentalism), etc.
4. *Moral authorities*: What have been your particular moral authorities (e.g. your particular scriptural tradition, your particular church's teachings, your particular philosophical traditions, etc.)? Have they ever conflicted, and if so, how have you navigated those conflicts?

Section B: Reflect on your life so far, including the following elements:
5. *Issues of moral character*: How has your character been shaped by the moral events in your life? E.g. "my growing up poor, or gay, or black has led me to make a struggle for justice a priority;" "my divorce has made me a more humble person;" "I continue to be torn between career and family," "seeking success is important to me," etc. What habits have you acquired as a result of your moral past?
6. *Reflection on the trajectory of your life so far*: Does there seem to be an overarching moral direction to your life, or has it been confusing and fragmented? What are the conflicts and dissonances that you experience? Where have you felt silent, or powerless, or pain? What do you think might be needed for clarity and/or integrity?

Section C: Imagining your future and getting there
    7. *Imagining your moral future*: Where do you want to go in the future? What might consist of a good life for you, given your social and moral locations? What is realistic, and what is achievable? What are the barriers to your moral future, and how may they be overcome? What *can* you accomplish?
    8. *Moral action to realize your moral future:* How might you get to your imagined moral future? What are some major steps you need to take? Some minor steps? What do you need before doing something? What prevents you from the "Just Do It?"

Chapter 10.

Singing Bluegrass in a Mother Tongue: A Pedagogy for Asian North American Churches

Boyung Lee

> *We are sailing onward, sailing, sailing o'er the foam*
> *We are talking to the captain as the angry billows hum*
> *Soon, yes soon, we'll reach the harbor, and we're safely o'er the tide*
> *We are going onward to the other side.*
> —From *On the Sea of Life* by Sloan Angel

Bluegrass would appear to be an unusual metaphor for a discussion about Asian North American pedagogy.[1] It is not a genre of music by and about Asian North Americans, nor a popular one among them. Notwithstanding that, I use it in this essay to explore the characteristics of Asian North American pedagogy and its future. I first got to know about bluegrass music through my spouse who is from the mountains of Appalachia, the birthplace of bluegrass. Anyone who has visited the hills of Appalachia, especially central Appalachia, would be

---

[1] A major suggestion I make in this paper is that Asian North American church pedagogy should be intercultural in its approach to other racial and ethnic minority groups. A good example of embodied interculturality is bluegrass music. I thus frame discussion about pedagogy for Asian North American churches using bluegrass metaphors. Bluegrass music's ontogeny provides a backdrop for thinking out loud about intercultural pedagogy's merits.

moved by its beauty and, at the same time, shocked by its poverty-stricken life. According to ABC News, isolated pockets in central Appalachia have three times the national poverty rate and the shortest life span in the nation.[2] The poverty and life circumstances there are beyond the imagination of many people living in this country. But if one pays attention to music from the area, especially bluegrass gospel, one immediately notices that the music is upbeat; it's about hope for a better tomorrow in God's reign and realm. In the midst of uncertain and unpleasant circumstances, Appalachians sing about perseverance, and I find this a refreshing focus for Asian North American pedagogy. Bluegrass also provides great insights for Asian North American church's pedagogy because, first, bluegrass is a type of music created through a transformation of different soulful musical genres of at least two marginalized groups of people, namely, that of poor white Americans and that of African Americans; second, bluegrass music improvises using various instruments, each of which sometimes leads. Utilizing the origin, creation, and improvisational style of bluegrass music as metaphors, this essay explores the distinctive features of Asian North American church pedagogy. Then, after analyzing the history and practices of Asian North American communal pedagogy, I explore pedagogical strategies to regenerate and strengthen future generations of those who metaphorically sing bluegrass in their mother tongues.

The Characteristics of Asian North American Church's Pedagogy

Bluegrass was turning back to the great heritage of older tunes that our ancestors brought into the mountains before the American Revolution.[3]

---

[2] "A Hidden America: Children of the Mountains: Diane Sawyer Reports on America's Children Living in Poverty in Appalachia," 20/20, ABC News aired on February 19, 2009. Available at http://abcnews.go.com/-2020/story?id=6845770&page=1.

[3] Alan Lomax, "Bluegrass Background: Folk Music with Overdrive," *Esquire* 52 (Oct. 1959): 108. Quoted from Robert Cantwell, *Bluegrass Breakdown: The Making of the Old Southern Sound* (Urbana and Chicago: University of Illinois Press, 1984), 62.

Bluegrass has roots in Scottish, English, Welsh, and Irish traditional music. When the early immigrants from that region came to this continent, many of them settled in the hills of Appalachia whose topography eschewed easy transit. Living in isolation in the lonesome hollows of the Appalachians, they remembered Celtic melodies of their motherlands and fashioned their stories of hardship through them, thus producing a vigorous pioneer music of their own.[4]

Likewise, Asian North Americans also kept many of the cultural values that they or their ancestors brought from their motherlands to North America and developed their own unique pedagogy around faith communities: their pedagogy is holistic, communal and ontological in terms of nature and methodology.[5] A good education integrates the past, the present, and the future *together* and helps learners develop their own pedagogy. In many senses, Asian North American pedagogy church is structured to help its members uphold past experiences from their motherlands, incorporate them in their new life circumstances at a new place, and thus develop something new for the future. Such an approach to education is by nature holistic, and it is greatly influenced by the education of our motherlands.

Unlike religious education of the white mainline church where religious education is narrowly focused on Christian knowledge and identity formation in classroom contexts, Asian North American religious education practiced in churches has a much broader scope, and takes holistic approaches. In this sense it is kith and kin to education from Appalachia, where one's identify is forged through hardship, but

---

[4] Wayne Erbsen, *Rural Roots of Bluegrass: Songs, Stories and History* (Asheville, North Carolina: Native Ground Music, 2003), 13.

[5] According to my own research, the current faith education of motherlands, especially Korean religious education, has lost many of these characteristics. However, both Asian North American pedagogy and Asian North American women's pedagogy still hold many of these characteristics. See, Boyung Lee, "A Philosophical Anthropology of the Communal Person: A Postcolonial Feminist Critique of Confucian Communalism and Western Individualism in Korean Protestant Education," Ph.D. Dissertation, Boston College (2004), and Boyung Lee, "Re-Creating Our Mothers' Dishes: Asian and Asian North American Women's Pedagogy," in *Off the Menu: Asian and Asian North American Women's Theology and Religion*, ed. Jung Ha Kim, Seung Ai Yang, Rita Nakashima Brock, and Kwok Pui Lan (Louisville, Kentucky: Westminster John Knox Press, 2007), 293-308.

translated through music coupled with communal optimism about a new tomorrow. The church's theology was originally a musical catechesis that accentuated a new tomorrow despite the snarls of industry, the coalmine, or the economy. This entailed a sense of community that gave new oomph to incarnational theology. As John Wesley ventured, "Joy from heaven to earth come down" (see "Love Divine All Love's Excelling") was an ever-present reality. On a similar note, one immediately finds that Asian North American faith communities, especially Christian churches, provided more than Christian education to their members. The church was a community center where early Asian North Americans immigrants found a stable and relatively safe haven for their hard lives as well as a place of worship, evangelism, and religious instruction.[6] Many Asian North American churches offered English classes for the adults and motherland language classes for children. Church education has been the agent of acculturation and cultural retention. Even after one hundred years of immigration history, one can easily observe that most Korean churches offer Korean language classes for their children on Saturday mornings, as well as English, citizenship test preparation classes, and voting and census education for adults during the week. In other words, the scope of their religious education is beyond explicitly religious content taught in classrooms, and encompasses skills for life and identity formation for Asian North Americans as Christians, coupled with civil education. The wide range and scope of Asian North American pedagogy is very faithful to the meaning of education.

Asian North American pedagogy as holistic pedagogy is based on and utilizes a multidimensional concept of curriculum, one that is esteemed by several educational theorists. This arguably moves beyond my bluegrass metaphor, but imagine if you will, a banjo, mandolin and bass all playing variants of a melody simultaneously and each as the lead. Asian North American education pedagogically frames topics with various methodological emphases. Similarly, noted curriculum theorist Elliott W. Eisner, says that each school offers students three different curricula: the explicit curriculum, one that is the actual content,

---

[6] Wenh-In Ng, "Pacific-Asian North American Religious Education," in *Multicultural Religious Education*, ed. Barbara Wilkerson (Birmingham, Alabama: Religious Education Press, 1997), 193-194.

consciously and intentionally presented as the teachings of the school; the implicit curriculum, one that through its environment includes the way teachers teach and interact with students; and the null curriculum, those ideas and subjects in educational programs that are sidestepped. By leaving out options and alternatives, the school narrows students' perspectives and the range of their thoughts and actions. Thus the explicit curriculum, which is often regarded as the entire curriculum, is only one facet of teaching. In fact, Eisner points out that the implicit and the null curricula might have more influence over students than does the explicit curriculum.[7]

Indulge me in a digression by way of illustration: although Asian North Americans have been in the United States and Canada for over two hundred years, there are hardly any published materials including religious education text books and curricula explicitly written by North American authors from Asian North American perspectives. Several years ago, eight Asian North American religious educators from Canada and the United States wrote an anthology on Asian North American religious education – we are still looking for a publisher. Every publisher we have contacted has told us the project is important, but it does not have a market because Asian North Americans do not have one common language, as presumably do African Americans, who may primarily use English (French?), and Latino/a Americans, who may primarily use Spanish (Portuguese?). In sum, the mainline religious education leaders seem to hold onto an unsaid assumption that Asian North American experiences in religious education are pedagogically insightful solely for Asian North Americans, and thus despite our long presence here we still do not have many published resources, which is to say that we can only strum one instrument rather than cultivating ways to sing compellingly with banjo, washboard and whatever else. My point: Although there are not many opportunities for explicit curriculum resource development, Asian North Americans have been teaching themselves using implicit and null curricula as major resources, thereby transforming their daily life contexts and activities into holistic classroom and teaching moments. When written texts were available only for their neighbor's education or

---

[7] Elliott Eisner, *The Educational Imagination: On the Design and Evaluation of School Program* (New York: Macmillan Publishing Company, 1985), 97.

focused on other's experiences as if they were universal for Asian North Americans, Asian North Americans used their own lived-world experience – e.g., Asian religio-cultural and socio-political traditions, Asian myth, folktales, songs, poems, proverbs, and teachings from different Asian religions – for their own and their children's education.[8] For example, every year a local church located in the China Town of San Francisco hosts cultural nights for the wider community. The events are composed of Chinese dances, music, poetry, storytelling, etc., performed by young people who belong to Chinese language schools and Sunday schools in the area. Although many of the participants are not Christians, every year the church coordinates with the two groups to let the wider community know about their cultural heritages, and to teach their children, whether they are 1st or 5th generation Chinese in America, and thus convey Chinese cultural values and ways of communal living. Similar broad educational opportunities are provided year after year for Asian North Americans through this church's annual bazaar and festivals. For example, a participant in the annual bazaar of the Buena Vista United Methodist church, a Japanese and Pan-Asian congregation located in the San Francisco Bay Area, reports:

> It was unspoken that the *mochi* making was the symbolic act of promising to be with each other in the coming year as a church family, to welcome in the *oshogatsu* (New Year) in relationship with each other. As the various stages of *mochi* pounding took place, there would be stories shared about past years and how it had been long ago – without the machinery, purely by hand. Funny incidents would be recalled, and times of extraordinary happenings would be memories brought out and shared with pleasure and pride.[9]

---

[8] Kwok Pui Lan, *Introducing Asian Feminist Theology* (Cleveland, Ohio: Pilgrim Press, 2000), 38-50.

[9] Ellen Tanouye, "Festivals: Celebrating Community, Story, and Identity," in *People on the Way: Asian North Americans Discovering, Christ, Culture, and Community*, ed. David Ng (Valley Forge, Pennsylvania: Judson Press, 1996), 186.

In short, as Maria Harris, feminist Christian religious educator, ventures, everything that a church does – fellowship meetings, informal gatherings, small group meetings, and so on – should be understood as curricula,[10] and in this sense, Asian North Americans have developed much broader and deeper curricula for their own education. In other words, if White congregations' emphasis is that of the explicit curriculum; some congregations demarcate between theory and lived faith, Asian North American churches are attentive to faith education's implicit and null curricula. This segues to my bluegrass metaphor, for the gist of bluegrass music is to sing the Lord's music as though tomorrow is today.

Another distinctive feature of the pedagogy of Asian North American churches is also communal in both its purpose and process, and this also has kinship with bluegrass gospel, which emphasizes personal salvation but typically links God's saving history with collective transformation. Unlike individualism, which values each person's individuality and independence, the value of the individual in communal Asian societies depends on how well a person adopts communal norms and functions to promote social harmony. Attachments, relatedness, connectedness, unity, and dependency among people are much more important than are independence and individuality. *I'd Rather Live by the Side of the Road* comes to mind as a statement of faith, where personal mission is conjoined with the commonweal. Similarly, anyone who has paid attention to Korean linguistics can easily find that Koreans rarely use the I-ness words such as "I," "my," and "mine." They instead like to use the word *uri* meaning *we*. Almost everything is called "our [something]," instead of "my [something]." For example, when one refers to one's wife, one does not say "my wife"; rather one says, "*our* wife." We-ness language is a source of comfort for Koreans. They are uncomfortable with I-ness language.[11] This We-ness language use is also salient among Korean North Americans including 1.5 and second generations. For example, I noticed several 1.5 generation

---

[10] Maria Harris, *Fashion Me a People: Curriculum in the Church* (Louisville, Kentucky: Westminster/John Knox Press, 1989), 63.

[11] Sang Chin Choi and Soo Hyang Choi, "Cheong: The Socio-emotional Grammar of Koreans" (unpublished manuscript, Seoul: Chung Ang University, 1993).

Korean Americans, who used to be members of my young adult group, switched their I language to We language as soon as they changed their conversation from English to Korean. I asked them whether they noticed their own change, and most of them said, "No," because using We language while they speak in Korean is very natural.

Although the use of what I call We linguistics is a unique Korean practice, the importance of community is true for most Asian and Asian North American cultures.[12] In their family-centered communities, Asian and Asian North Americans venture that "our family" means all of the I's melted into one "we." Here, "we" does not mean the coexistence of "I" and "you" as independent individual units; rather it indicates that "you" and "you," and "you" and "I" are the same reality: "I and you exist not as separate units but as a unified one. At the moment when two individuals abandon their own perspective and put themselves in their partner's shoes, they become one, not a separate two."[13] A good example of such communal selfhood is found in Japanese linguistics. The English word "self" is usually translated by the Japanese word *jibun* and vice versa. However, unlike the English word for self, *jibun* connotes "one's share of the shared life space;"[14] that is, oneself is an inseparable part of our selves. When two Japanese people exchange greetings by asking how the other party is, the customary way of saying it is "How is *jibun*?" which literally means, "How is ourselves?"[15] In sum, persons in Asian and Asian North American communal societies can be fully understood only in connection with the larger social whole: "Others are included within the boundaries of the self."[16]

---

[12] According to Geert Hofsteade, who measured the extent of individualism and communalism in 66 countries, most Asian countries like Korea, China, Taiwan, Japan, and Singapore, are comparatively highly communal societies. Geert Hofstede, *Cultures and Organizations: Software of the Mind* (London: McGraw Hill, 1991).

[13] Soo-Won Lee, "The Cheong Space: A Zone of Non-Exchange in Korean Human Relationships," in *Psychology of the Korean People: Individualism and Collectivism*, ed. Gene Yoon and Sang-Chin Choi (Seoul: Donga Publishing Corporation, 1991), 92-94.

[14] Hazel R. Markus and Shinobu Kitayama, "Culture and the Self: Implications for Cognitions, Emotion, and Motivations," *Psychological Review* 98 (1991): 228.

[15] I thank the Rev. Mitsuho Okado, a Japanese D.Min graduate of Pacific School of Religion, for helping me understand the meaning of Jibun.

Therefore, in Asian and Asian North American pedagogy, it is critical that communal personhood is respected, and that members feel a sense of belonging. By being with each other they acknowledge a resource of life greater than their own individuality.[17] An outsider may say church bazaars and festivals that seem to be too much work for the modest profits raised are not economically smart plans. However, members of those small Asian North American congregations say it is their churches' cultural and communal identity that allows such projects to exist. Every year all generations of folks work together, because the fellowship and bonding through sharing and storytelling strengthen their relationships.[18]

This communal value seems to be one of the driving forces for Asian American college students who join campus evangelical groups. According to sociologist Rebecca Kim, one out of four Evangelical college students at New York City colleges and universities are Asian American; Asian Americans constitute 70 percent of the Harvard Radcliffe Christian Fellowship; Yale's Campus Crusade for Christ is 90 percent Asian, whereas twenty years ago it was 100 percent white; the Asian American membership at Stanford's InterVarsity Christian Fellowship increased by 84 percent from 1989 to 1999, compared to a 31 percent increase in its overall membership.[19] Regarding this phenomenon, Kim reports:

> In addition to Bible studies and worship gatherings, campus ministries offer multiple opportunities for social gatherings. They have pizza parties, special banquets, study sessions, trips to amusement parks, sports events, bonfires at the beach, and retreats into the mountains. In campus ministries, students can meet life-long friends and even find one's future spouse. As a staff member of IVCF explains, "This is not just a place of worship; it is

---

[16] Markus and Kitayama, "Culture and the Self," 224-253.

[17] Michael Yoshii, "The Buena Vista Church Bazaar: A Story within a Story," in *People on the Way*, 53.

[18] Tanouye, "Festivals," 186.

[19] Rebecca Kim, "Asian Americans for Jesus: Changing the Face of Campus Evangelicalism," SSRC (Feb 06, 2007), 1. Available online at http://religion.ssrc.org/reforum/Kim.pdf

a place of community where you develop deep bonds with people."[20]

In other words, whether they grew up as evangelical Christians at home or not, they find a community, a home away from home, in these evangelical campus ministries groups in which they share racial bonding, and similar communal cultural values.[21]

Another important feature of the pedagogy of Asian North Americans that is influenced by the cultural values of their motherlands is its ontological nature. In Asia, although formal education and written texts were mostly for elite men for a long time, both elite education and stealth pedagogy of the powerless aimed at the formation of people as its purpose. For example, Confucian education, which greatly shaped both elite and non-elite education of East Asia, aimed at raising moral agents who work for the achievement of universal harmony and moral societies.[22] To be a moral agent an educated man should attain benevolence, the highest virtue of Confucianism, through self-cultivation and study. In other words, the purpose of education is the formation of moral agents rather than the transmission of knowledge – at least in theory.

The ontological nature of the motherlands' education often continues through the Asian North American church's work, particularly in the first generation's efforts to maintain and instill Asian identity in their children. For now, let us set aside whether the way they do this is appropriate or not, which I will discuss later in the essay. Instead, let us focus on how Asian North American churches have done it through their education. First, as stated above where the holistic nature of Asian North American pedagogy was discussed, many Asian North American churches provide English-speaking ministries for the younger generation to retain them within the boundaries of Asian North American churches. Although the church provides English-speaking ministries to promote children's Christian faith formation, the first generation also attempts to

---

[20] Rebecca Kim, "Asian Americans for Jesus," 2.

[21] Rebecca Kim posits that for Asian Americans, campus ministries not only solve the problem of spiritual estrangement, but also shields students from marginalization as ethnic and racial minorities. Rebecca Kim, "Asian Americans for Jesus," 2-3.

[22] Confucius, *The Analects*, VII 26. Also Tu Wei-Ming, *Confucian Thought: Selfhood as Creative Transformation* (Albany: SUNY Press, 1985), 23.

play multiple roles through language and culture school programs. The church hopes to strengthen their children's tie with Asian culture and ethnic language.[23] The second model is a further development of the first. Some Asian North American churches financially support their congregation's 1.5 and 2nd second generations in starting their own ministries until they become fully independent churches. Most churches born out of such cooperative efforts become Pan Asian North American churches where Asian North Americans of different Asian national origin constitute membership.[24] Because 1.5 and second generations face different identity issues than those expected by their parents' generation, despite their completely English language based ministries, they wrestle with Asian identity issues as well as Christian faith formation. Borrowing from Derald Wing Sue and David Sue's now classic work on stages of bicultural identity development, members of Pan Asian North Americans are spread from the dissonance stage to the immersion and resistance stage, to the introspection stage, to the integrative and awareness stage.[25] In short, Asian North American faith education has been an important medium through which its members have developed, rejected, reclaimed, and integrated their Asian North American identity. Developing one's identity involves one's entire being and the world around one; so the pedagogy of Asian North Americans is clearly based on epistemological *and* ontological enterprise.

---

[23] Grace Sangok Kim, "Asian North American Youth: A Ministry of Self-Identity and Pastoral Care," in *People on the Way*, 224.

[24] Grace Sangok Kim, "Asian North American Youth," 224.

[25] Derald Wing Sue and David Sue, *Counseling the Culturally Different: Theory and Practice* (New York: Wiley, 1981), 93-117. Sue and Sue list 5 different stages of the bicultural identity formation process: the conformity stage, during which immigrant children and youth abandon their motherland's cultural practices to be like their white peers; the dissonance stage, when older teens are confronted with racism, which brings about confusion, and thus questions about accepted values of the mainstream societies; the immersion and resistance stage, during which people react or even reject Western cultural values, and seek out their Asian ancestral heritage with uncritical eyes; the introspection stage, when people notice both desirable and problematic elements in both the mainstream cultural values and their ancestral heritage, and yet do not know how to integrate them; and the integrative and awareness stage, when people finally are able to integrate both cultures, and form their own identity.

Ongoing Challenges that the Pedagogy of Asian North American Churches Faces

> *"It's exciting, you know, a lot of people thinks you work against each other, and in one sense of the word you probably do, because if the fiddler's playing a number and then the banjo comes in and he sells his chorus good, the fiddler knows he's up against it – he's going to have to get to work. And the mandolin, he follows to do his part as good as the banjo or better...."* [26]

Bill Monroe, the father of bluegrass – from whose band name, Bill Monroe and the Blue Grass Boys, the name bluegrass originated[27] – describes one of the key features of the music: improvisation. Although there is a main melody, players with different instruments improvise the melody as they are inspired by each other, by the audience and by occasions. Musicians of other genres typically divide their roles as lead instrumentalist or accompanist: one instrument carries the lead while the others provide accompaniment, or all instruments play the melody together. However, in bluegrass each musician takes her or his turn, playing the melody and improvising, while the others perform accompaniment. If we evaluate different musical genres on the basis of their accompaniment styles, bluegrass easily ranks as democratic and equality-based music.

Bluegrass music's improvisation and accompaniment style provide great insights for challenges faced by Asian North American pedagogy: Gaps between the first and following generations; hierarchical and patriarchal cultural practices; lack of concern for social justice issues, including racism and homophobia; and rather passive relationships with other racial/ethnic minority communities, etc. In my opinion, these challenges are rooted in Asian North American communal values that expect community members to sing the community's tune

---

[26] Bill Monroe, "My Life in Bluegrass," interview with Alice Foster, Newport Folk Festival Program, 1969, 17. Quoted from Cantwell, *Bluegrass Breakdown*, 165-167.

[27] James Rooney, "Bossman Bill Monroe," in *The Bluegrass Reader*, ed. Thomas Goldsmith (Urbana and Chicago: University of Illinois Press, 2004), 43-45.

rather than their own. The rhythm frequently is set by a leader to ensure communal harmony, which sometimes sacrifices the powerless and isolates cultural groups from society at large.

One of the serious and ongoing challenges Asian North American faith communities face is tension between first generation church leaders and 1.5 or second and subsequent generations.[28] Some members of the community, including pastors and religious educators, oversimplify the tension as a communication problem due to language barriers, however the matter is deeper and bigger. As discussed above, Asian communal cultural values require individuals to define themselves as part of the community and to subordinate personal goals to those of the community. Attachments, relatedness, connectedness, oneness, and dependency among people are much more important than independence or individual autonomy. Those who pursue only their own benefit are easily expelled from a community's psyche. In order to create harmony in community life each member is expected to suppress her or his own desires and emotions, and to give heed to others' desires and emotions. However, the values of harmony and community are based on a hierarchical view. The hierarchy of superior and inferior maintains the orderliness and harmony of relationship.[29] The superior partners have the rights and duties of educating the inferior partners, and the inferior partners have obligations but no rights. In these hierarchical relationships, the inferior ones are forced to sacrifice for the value of harmony. The superior, older generation is wiser and should be listened to, as they will guide the younger and not-yet wise generation.

First-generation Asian North Americans bring these cultural assumptions and try to impose them on their children and younger generations of church members, but the youths learn that autonomy and independence are virtues through their school education, so tension is inevitable. "Traditional values like respecting older and more senior adults often make it difficult for younger members to be heard, let alone be allowed to make suggestions and decisions on an equal footing."[30] Especially if the younger people are in the conformity stage of their

---

[28] Ng, "Pacific-Asian North American Religious Education," 204.

[29] Theresa Kelleher, "Confucianism," in *Women in World Religions*, ed. Arvind Sharma (Albany: SUNY Press, 1987), 138.

[30] Wenh-In Ng, "Pacific-Asian North American Religious Education," 204.

bicultural identity development, the tension between the groups will not easily be resolved.

The rapid growth of Asian North American evangelical groups on college campuses can be looked at from this cultural gap perspective. According to Rebecca Kim, for example, churched second generation Korean and Chinese Americans are not happy in their parents' churches. Many find the first generation led immigrant church to be patriarchal, hierarchical, divisive, dry, rigid, and disconnected to their cultural and spiritual needs. Thus, as soon as they leave home for college younger Asian North Americans seek out spaces and opportunities to "do their own thing": Campus ministries for Asian North American evangelicals are most often organized by the second generation to address their own issues in their own ways under their own leadership.[31]

To resolve this tension between generations Asian North American pedagogy needs to rethink and broaden its purpose of education. Although churches work hard to help the younger generation develop identity through education, it is oriented toward conformity to first generation Asian identity and cultural values. The contrast between their own and later generation's identification as Asians and Americans is regarded as the loss of Asia-ness by first generation Asian Americans. And as long as education is based on assumptions and expectations about conformity, the tension will never be resolved. There will be little common ground for genuine and open communications.

Another challenge that Asian North American churches face is the prevailing discrimination against women. Despite growing numbers of Asian North American women leaders in society and business, Asian North American churches have not kept up with women's issues. For example, in the United Methodist Church there are about 130 Korean American ordained clergy women, however the majority of them are serving non-Korean United Methodist churches. Among those who serve Korean United Methodist congregations, younger clergy women are serving as associate pastors, and senior members are serving small and struggling congregations that they started.[32] The lack of visibility of

---

[31] Rebecca Kim, "Asian Americans for Jesus," 3.

[32] An oral report given by Rev. Youngok Park, the President of The Korean United Methodist Clergy Women's Association at its 2007 Annual Meeting, Honolulu, Hawaii, August 8, 2007.

women clergy in Korean United Methodist churches is not due to their unwillingness to serve Korean American churches, but because of the churches' unwillingness to accept women as their spiritual leaders. The situation of lay women is not much different. Although it is improving, women are typically excluded from church leadership positions and decision-making bodies, so women are still exercising their leadership only in traditional women's areas. For example, many of the oldest Korean American churches from which many Korean American social leaders have come, are still waiting for the day the church elects a woman elder.

Discriminatory attitudes toward women are not limited to the first generation of Asian North American women. Every year hundreds of young Asian North American women visit plastic surgeons for hymen reconstruction before marriage.[33] As we often hear from media about Islamic society's honor culture in connection with women's virginity, one may assume that young women in plastic surgery clinics are mostly Islamic women. Surprisingly, however, many of them are Korean and Chinese descendants who grew up in the United States or Canada and are about to be married to fellow Asian North American young men. The patriarchical and hierarchical view of their culture of origin puts young women at the bottom of the ladder in the community. In such a culture a women's body is considered the property of male members of the household. Under this system, women's sexuality and chastity belong to her family, and women have to live under severe sexual suppression; losing one's virginity brings shame and humiliation to the the entire family, the back bone of the community.[34] Although such a view toward women's sexuality has greatly changed in motherlands, it is still shaping male and female relationships in Asian North America in the 21st century.

Asian North American church pedagogy has a huge task in front of it, for there is hardly any curriculum written for and by Asian North

---

[33] Lynn Sherr, "Like a Virgin, Young Women Undergo Surgery to 'Restore' Virginity," reported on 20/20, ABC News on June 20, 2003. Available at www.psurg.com/abcnews-2003-06-20.htm.

[34] Hyung Kyung Chung, "'Han-pu-ri': Doing theology from Korean women's perspective," in *We Dare to Dream: Doing Theology as Asian Women*, ed. Virginia Fabella and Sun Ai Lee Park (Hong Kong: Asian Women's Resource Center for Culture and Theology, 1988), 140.

Americans, especially in Asian languages, and there are no religious education resources written from a feminist perspective. Moreover, as younger generations' faith formation is more and more often shaped by campus evangelical movements, the future status of Asian North American women in faith communities based on a combination of Asian patriarchal values and evangelical theology, does not present a pleasant picture. Improving the role and status of women in Asian North American communities is a much bigger task than a faith community's religious education alone can address. It is an issue of clergy formation and lay leadership, and a task of Asian North American theological education. How do Asian North American theologians, especially theologians of non-evangelical traditions, connect better with local faith communities? What will be some of the entry points for feminist theology to impact Asian North American clergy formation? How can mainline approaches to campus ministries be connected to 1.5 and second generation Asian North Americans? These are some of the questions that many Asian North American theologians have wrestled with for a long while, and there seem not to be many clear answers yet. If these questions cannot be answered by theologians alone, with whom should we be partnered?

In sum, in Asian North American communities, a community member is expected to sing the community's tune rather than one's own. The rhythm frequently is set by a leader to ensure communal harmony, which sometimes sacrifices the powerless and isolates cultural groups from society at large. Maybe this is a time for us to learn our old song in a new way, much as bluegrass musicians play: every member takes turns leading the melody and improvising while others provide an accompaniment.

New and Yet Old Challenges That the Pedagogy of Asian North American Churches Faces

If in the old South, with its pervasive Irish and Scots-Irish settlement, there occurred on the folk level an energetic interchange and fusion of a black-and-white song, it is perhaps because between the two traditions there were strong musical affinities, reinforced by a social system that discriminated against both groups.[35]

Bluegrass has its roots in the ancient British folk music that was kept for centuries in the hills of Appalachia. However, the hillbilly music could become what is now known as bluegrass only when it was transformed by contact with African American folk traditions, jazz and blues. Poor white Americans of Appalachia and enslaved African Americans found mutual attractions in each other's music, pieces that expressed life's hardship and perseverance, and they influenced each other and developed their own distinctively unique music. Robert Cantwell, American Studies scholar, describes the contact and mutual influences as follows:[36]

> The African love of cross-rhythm found a home, albeit a narrow one, in off-beat accentuation, which was in the gait of Scots song and was a favorite device of Irish fiddlers; African gapped scales and modalities found an echo in those of the Gaelic tradition; folk singers from both parts of the world delight it, in different ways and in different degrees, in the high pitches, a declamatory style, vocal tension and ornament, and improvisation.

Through intercultural exchanges of music and life stories, both found home at each other's homes, and were transformed.

Asian North American church pedagogy cannot be just and compassionate pedagogy in the future unless it works with its neighbors and outgroup members both within and without. As a matter of fact, one of the downsides of Asian North American church's pedagogy being based on communal values, despite its holistic nature, is its lack of openness toward outsiders. One of the salient features of communal cultures is their clear distinction between ingroup and outgroup.[37] Those who have 'we' relations are considered members of the ingroup, and those who do not belong are members of outgroups. Once people are

---

[35] Cantwell, *Bluegrass Breakdown*, 120.
[36] Ibid.
[37] Kyung-Hwan Min and Hai-sook Kim, "Regional Conflict in Korea: A Pathological Case of Collectivism," in Yoon and Choi, Psyc*hology of the Korean People,* 330-349.

regarded as being within the boundary of 'we,' they incur instant closeness, assume social interdependence, and consequently give more favor to others inside the group."[38] Accordingly, the more networks people share, the smoother business flows. Although the primary purpose of these networks is to promote good social relations, since they are only ingroup-centered networks, these networks often cause conflicts between ingroup and outgroup members in a communal society. They put great emphasis on interpersonal harmony with ingroup members, but their attitudes toward outgroup members are businesslike or even antagonistic.[39] There are two types of outgroup members: within and without, namely, Asian North American sexual minorities, and other racial ethnic minority groups in North America. To be a just and compassionate pedagogy Asian North American religious education must be anti-homophobic and intercultural.

If generational tension and sexism are strongly implicit in the curriculum of holistic, communal and ontological Asian North American church's Pedagogy (explicit curriculum), homophobia is its strong null curriculum.[40] In most Asian North American cultures, sexuality is a taboo subject, one that cannot be discussed in public except in the context of procreation. For example, although Asian North Americans have inseparable ethnic and sexual identities within themselves, they are forced to separate the two publicly, and focus solely on their cultural Asianness.[41] Such invisibility of sexuality contributes to the creation of homophobia in heterosexual-centered Asian North American

---

[38] Gyuseog Han and Sug-man Choe, "Effects of Family, Region, and School Network Ties on Interpersonal Intentions and the Analysis of New Activities in Korea," in *Individualism and Collectivism: Theory, Method, and Applications*, ed. Uichol Kim, Harry C. Triandis, Cigdem Kagitcibasi, Sang-Chin Choi, and Gene Yoon (Thousand Oaks: Sage Publications, 1994), 213.

[39] Harry C. Triandis, *Collectivism vs. individualism: A reconceptualization.* Unpublished manuscript, University of Illinois, 75-76. Quoted from Seong-Yeul Han & Chang-Yil Ahn, "Collectivism and Individualism in Korea," in Yoon & Choi, *Psychology of the Korean People*, 302.

[40] Boyung Lee, "Teaching Justice and Living Peace: Body, Sexuality and Religious Education in Asian American Communities," *Religious Education* 101, no. 3 (Summer 2006): 402-419.

[41] Russell Leong, "Introduction: Home Bodies and Body Politics," in *Asian American Sexualities: Dimensions of the Gay and Lesbian Experience*, ed. Russell Leong (New York: Routledge Press, 1996) 3-5.

communities, and marginalizes sexual minorities. Like heterosexual Asian North Americans, sexual minorities are discriminated against due to their Asian race in a racially hierarchical society, including those of LGBTQ communities; however and unlike their counterparts, they face homophobia, too. Thus Asian North American sexual minorities are treated as the "other" by both the racial/ethnic Other and the sexual other.[42]

The separation of sexual identity and ethnic identity, according to Kwok Pui Lan, sometimes leads to greater tolerance for LGBT behaviors – as long as they are kept out of the public eyes.[43] However, if sexuality, especially homosexual identity, becomes a public topic, those who are involved, especially the family, feel shame because they have failed to live up to the norm of the community. As discussed above, in Asian North American cultures that emphasize communal harmony as one of the highest virtues; attachments, relatedness, connectedness, oneness, and interdependency are more important than independence and individuality. Since such values require everyone to be in need of one another, people are vulnerable when facing separation.[44] Therefore, by not bringing up the taboo subject of sexuality and by not making public a family member's homosexuality, Asian North American parents and families try hard to meet perceived social expectations. By being openly LGBTQ, which the community neither accepts nor approves, Asian North American sexual minorities immediately become outgroup members within their own community.

The majority of Asian North American faith communities have chosen either not to speak about it, or to condemn homosexuality within the community. Kwok Pui Lan ventures that the lack of interest and research on sexuality and homosexuality among Asian North American theologians and churches is due to the long-lived influence of 19th century mores and Western missionary theology: "Many of these churches were established by Western missionaries, steeped in the Victorian sexual codes and the cult of female domesticity."[45] Arguably,

---

[42] Leong, "Introduction," 3.

[43] Kwok Pui Lan, "Gay Activism in Asian and Asian-American Churches," *The Witness* 87: 28.

[44] Jae Un Kim, *The Koreans: Their Mind and Behavior* (Seoul: Kyobo Book Center, 1991), 115.

[45] Kwok Pui Lan, "Religion, Sexuality, and Asian and Asian American

when Asian cultural values and Victorian sexual codes met in Asian churches and Asian North American churches, it created a rigid atmosphere of sexuality, an attitude still strongly present in Asian North American churches. For example, in the United Methodist Church the largest ethnic group besides Caucasians is Korean (about 400 congregations). However, none of these churches participates in the Reconciling Ministries Network, "a national grassroots organization that exists to enable full participation of people of all sexual orientations and gender identities in the life of the United Methodist Church."[46] In fact, out of over 200 reconciling congregations and campus ministry groups, there are only two Asian American congregations, both of which are located in the San Francisco Bay Area.

Challenging homophobia needs to be an integral part of religious education in Asian North American communities. Without promoting sexual minority's full humanity and rights, there can be no justice for Asian North Americans. Often in Asian North American justice education, anti-sexism and homophobia are considered less important than the quest against racism. The stereotypical rhetoric is that, although women's and LGBTQ issues are important, they are not as urgent as racial justice, and thus the operative formula is *urgency vs. importance*. However, if we are serious about justice and peace these issues should be dealt with side by side, not one after the other. Again, without justice for the most marginalized people in the community, there is no complete justice.

One of the ways to deal with sexuality and homosexuality in Asian North American church education is to engage creative teaching materials. I find that using popular media is helpful because of its explicit use of sexual themes, and the distance that it provides in presenting topics around sexuality and homosexuality as other than personal and immediate community issues. Particularly, Margaret Cho's stand-up comedy show, *I'm the One That I Want,* is excellent for Asian-

---

Cultures: Embodying the Spirit in Our Communities," paper delivered at the Opening Panel of PANAAWTM (Pacific, Asian, and North American Asian Women in Theology and Ministry)'s 19th Annual Conference. Pacific School of Religion in Berkeley, California. March 18, 2004.

[46] Reconciling Ministries Network, Mission Statement. Available at www.rmnetwork.org/whoarewe.php.

American contexts. Cho, a Korean American woman, was a star in *All American Girl*, a sitcom that featured TV's first Asian American family. In her comedy, Cho addresses sexuality as a part of who she is, and she also talks about why her TV show lasted only one season (ABC 1994-1995): she was not "Asian enough" by ABC TV standards. Some popular media formats are already dealing with ethnic and sexual identity issues in more and more integrated ways, and may give entry points to Asian North American congregations willing to engage the topics without knowing how and where to start.

To contribute to the betterment of society in North America, Asian North American pedagogy needs to be an intercultural pedagogy. Especially, it needs to be a better neighbor of other racial ethnic minority communities. Rita Nakashima Brock, in a private conversation with me, said that the current mode of cultural discourse in theological and religious education assumes that there is one big circle with one center. Once the one main circle of the dominant culture is posited, each of the other groups forms a small circle around the dominant culture's circle. Most of the time small groups are only talking with the center, so they are not in conversation with any other small groups in their neighborhoods. The result is that small circles compete with each other to be the privileged dialogue partner of the dominant culture's center. Asian North American pedagogy has been the one of those competing circles.

Hyondok Choe, a Korean German philosopher, describes such a model as *multiculturality*.[47] For Choe, the concept of "multicultural" was introduced to recognize and explain the reality of contemporary society where several different cultures exist as a result of migration and colonization. Compared to a monocultural model in which the dominant group of a society does not recognize the rights of minority cultures or the dominant culture discriminates against those who do not belong to the mainstream, multiculturality appears to be a step forward. However, Choe argues that if we are really serious about the existence and rights of

---

[47] Hyundok Choe, "Introduction to Intercultural Philosophy: Its Concept and History," in *Communication and Solidarity in the Era of Globalization: In Quest of Intercultural Philosophy*, ed. Department of Philosophy of Chonnon National University (Gwangju, Korea: Chonnam National University Press, 2006), 5-27.

all, we need to explore ways to live together in peace and solidarity that accentuate the unique contributions of one and all, for "the concept of 'multicultural' society is helpless facing the situation of living in parallel (in ghettos, for example) and cannot develop a model for living together."[48]

The concept of multiculturality has been the dominant mode in Asian North American pedagogy, too. We have been busy lifting up our own voices, but have not paid much attention to creating new modes of communication with other voices, especially with other racial ethnic minority communities. As we continue to work for the betterment of the world out of our own history and experiences, we also need to be mindful of our neighbors. Asian North American pedagogy needs to ask whether our pedagogy brings the liberation of those who are the most marginalized among and beyond our community. When someone is suffering due to exclusion and oppression while we are pursuing justice for our own community alone, no one can take our work for world transformation seriously. Therefore, while each community must work out its own critical norm of pedagogy, it is important that we as Christian religious educators hold ourselves accountable to one another, and test our community's norm in public discourse and constant dialogue with other communities.[49] To test whether our pedagogy is creating *good neighborhood*, we must ask an important question posed by Nami Kim, a Korean American feminist theologian: Is our comfort is gained at the cost of somebody else's?[50] As those mountaineers of Appalachia and African Americans sang their own songs, yet learned from each other and created new songs, when we are able to sing together with our neighbors within and without and learn from each other, Asian North American pedagogy will be able to sing a new song for a new time.

---

[48] Choe, "Introduction to Intercultural Philosophy," 16.

[49] Kwok Pui Lan, *Discovering the Bible in the Non-Biblical World* (Maryknoll, N.Y.: Orbis Books, 1995), 19.

[50] Nami Kim, "My/Our Comfort Not at the Expense of Somebody Else's: Toward a Critical Global Feminist Theology," *Journal of Feminist Studies in Religion* 21, no. 2. (November, 2005): 75-94.

Conclusion

You ask what makes our kind of music successful. I'll tell you. It can be explained in just one word: sincerity. When a hillbilly sings a crazy song, he feels crazy when he sings, 'I Laid My Mother Away,' he sees her a-laying right there in the coffin. To sing like a hillbilly, you have to have lived like a hillbilly. You have to have smelt a lot of mule manure.
—Hank Williams [51]

In this chapter I tackle a vast task. Approaches to Asian North American church pedagogy are widely various, in number as massive as the size of the Asian continent. Moreover, the enormous tasks before Asian North American church pedagogy are as numerous as its approaches. However, if as Hank Williams said, we sing our song with sincerity, one day we will be able to sing our old and new songs with harmony and melody; or as Fumitaka Matsuoka sagaciously opines, "We need to seek a way of relating to each other that we do not yet have or that we have long forgotten: a way of speaking about mutual relatability, intelligibility, and interdependence that goes beyond our capacity to the binary, adversarial and oppositional discourse of human relationship."[52]

In bluegrass gospel all digressions are pathways to the reign of God, so indulge me one detour by way of Robert Kegan. Kegan, a constructive developmental psychologist and an educator, suggests that through an ongoing ("evolutionary" in Kegan's term) interaction with others and their physical/ cognitive/cultural environments, human beings develop an authentic sense of who they are, and construct their truth accordingly. Kegan suggests a three-way meaning-making process: confirmation, contradiction and continuity.[53] Confirmation is when a particular environment corresponds and supports the meaning-making system that people already have. When new experiences, events, and opinions conflict with these world-views, people are challenged to transform their current meaning-making system. Kegan calls this

---

[51] Quoted in Erbsen, *Rural Roots of Bluegrass*, 43.

[52] Fumitaka Matsuoka, *Color of Faith: Building Community in a Multiracial Society* (Cleveland, Ohio: United Church Press, 1998), 5.

[53] Roberts Kegan, *The Evolving Self: Problem and Process in Human Development* (Cambridge, Massachusetts: Harvard University Press, 1982), 113-132.

contradiction. When people face contradictory events and contexts, they either emotionally isolate themselves, thus maintaining their existing framework - a process which Kegan deems unhealthy, or else they incorporate new meaning through which they conjoin both "old" and "new" realities. Kegan refers to this process of incorporation as continuity.

Despite its problems, Asian North American church pedagogy needs to take pride in its own roots and not be afraid of challenge leading to new "wholes" and thus strumming continuous and unfolding future traditions. Between here and there we will sometimes be *On the Sea of Life*, and yet still sing our songs replete with hope for a new tomorrow, for. . . .

> *We are sailing onward, sailing, sailing o'er the foam*
> *We are talking to the captain as the angry billows hum*
> *Soon, yes soon, we'll reach the harbor and we're safely o'er the tide*
> *We are going onward to the other side.*

Chapter 11.

Informality, Illegality, and Improvisation: Theological Reflections on Money, Migration, and Ministry in Chinatown, NYC, and Beyond

Amos Yong

Fumitaka Matsuoka, the honoree of this chapter and the book within which it appears, has long been at the forefront of encouraging the North American church and its theological establishment to think about racism vis-à-vis the multidimensional complexities of globalization.[1] He has thus identified the need to "revisit our relationships in light of complex histories" in order to retain the credibility of Christian faith and of our faith communities in a racist, pluralist, and globalizing world.[2] Both the truth-telling of heretofore neglected or silenced voices and the reconciliation between those in the center with those on or outside the margins are needed for the church to effectively engage the public square. Such a prophetic posture is central to the peace witness of the ecclesial tradition, the Church of the Brethren, which has long informed Matsuoka's teaching and thinking.[3]

---

[1] Matsuoka's most poignant books are *Out of Silence: Emerging Themes in Asian American Churches* (Cleveland: United Church Press, 1995), and *The Color of Faith: Building Community in a Multiracial Society* (Cleveland: United Church Press, 1998).

[2] Fumitaka Matsuoka, "The Changing Terrain of 'Globalization' in ATS Conversations," *Theological Education* 35:2 (1999): 17-25, quotation from 22.

[3] E.g., as reflected in the following Matsuoka essays: "*Jesus Christ Our*

In this essay I want to heed Matsuoka's call by reflecting on the realities of Chinese undocumented immigrants to New York City (NYC) and through this begin raising questions for consideration about contemporary discussions in theology of mission and its interface with theology of economics. More precisely, I want to shift the terms of the discussion away from either development or liberation[4] (or other dualistically constructed categories like capitalism or socialism) in order to take a fresh look at the issues through the lens of the informal economy. My hunch is that an informal economic perspective will be suggestive for thinking creatively, liberatively, and normatively (i.e., theologically) about the interface between religious life and contemporary globalization. Toward these ends, four primary tasks are undertaken, corresponding with the four main sections of this essay, that of 1) situating the reflections concretely within the complex and largely silent recent history of Chinatown, NYC; 2) identifying the global and transnational economic structures and their religious links that constitute the backdrop of Chinatown; 3) critically mapping the informality of the Chinatown economy onto that of the apostolic experience of the earliest messianic believers; and 4) considering innovative and improvisational forms of ecclesial ministry and praxis for the church that is *in* but not constrained by the informal sphere. The goal throughout is to re-examine the relationship between race/ethnicity, religion, globalization, and economics by focusing on the informal economy. I will conclude with some broad reflections on a pneumatological theology of economics, mined from the discussion in section 3 on the apostolic narrative of the book of Acts; I will also return to one of the central themes of Matsuoka's lifework as it has been shaped by the Brethren and Mennonite traditions, the theme of the shalom – the peace, justice, and righteousness – of the coming reign of God.

Lord from a Missiological Perspective," in Richard A. Kauffman, ed., *A Disciple's Christology: Appraisals of Kraus's Jesus Christ Our Lord*, Occasional Papers 13 (Elkhart, Indiana: Institute of Mennonite Studies, 1989), 28-37; "Race and Peoplehood," *Brethren Life and Thought* 44:3 (1999): 33-46; and "Reflecting on Theological Education at Bethany Theological Seminary," *Brethren Life and Thought* 49:1-2 (2004): 108-16.

[4] Which is not to slight the import of either of these projects, explicated superbly in Thia Cooper, *Controversies in Political Theology* (London: SCM Press, 2007).

One caveat before proceeding. I come to this work as an Asian evangelical and pentecostal systematician rather than as a scholar of Asian American Christianity or of globalization, migration, or economics.[5] My interests thus are in registering more specifically Asian American perspectives in an Asian American evangelical theological conversation which has heretofore been dominated by and large by white or Caucasian methods, concerns, and contributions. Looking at the Asian American experience in Chinatown, NYC, will be a helpful springboard to engaging these theological matters. My intention in the following is therefore to open up previously unasked questions in evangelical missiology and theology related to globalization and the economy rather than to provide definitive responses to issues raised by consideration of NYC's Chinatown. Along the way I seek, from the perspective of the evangelical commitment to scripture, to invite a re-reading of the early Christian experience in order to tease out how such a fusion of apostolic and contemporary Asian American immigrant horizons might precipitate fresh trajectories for evangelical missiology and theology of economics.

Informality and Illegality in Chinatown, NYC

Kenneth Guest is an anthropologist at Baruch College's Weissman School of Arts and Sciences in New York. His *God in Chinatown* is an ethnographic exploration of the relationship between religion and the globalization and immigration processes between the region of Fuzhou, on the southeast coast of the People's Republic of China, and the ethnic Chinatown enclave of New York City.[6] The

---

[5] Which is not to say that I am oblivious to such scholarship – I have written briefly about recent developments in my "Asian American Religion: A Review Essay," *Nova Religio: The Journal of Alternative and Emergent Religions* 9:3 (2006): 92-107 – but only that this is a narrowly focused case study of a unique Asian American experience, undertaken for explicitly theological purposes related to the task of evangelical theology.

[6] Kenneth J. Guest, *God in Chinatown: Religion and Survival in New York's Evolving Immigrant Community* (New York and London: New York University Press, 2003). I rely mainly on Guest in this essay because my major interests are finally theological and he provides a useful springboard for reflecting in that mode on the Asian American immigration experience.

religious diversity among the Fuzhounese of New York City is refracted in Guest's study through a Buddhist temple, a Daoist temple, two Roman Catholic parishes, and two Protestant congregations. The latter receives more extensive coverage: the Church of Grace derives from the Chinese Christian tradition of John Sun's Home of Grace, and the New York House Church has connections with the Little Flock churches of Fuzhou. An important thesis the book argues is that religious matters are not subservient to a more "fundamental" socio-economic domain; rather they inform those domains from within, and in doing so, reflect realities both in Fuzhou and NYC.[7] Hence, religious beliefs and practices bridging multiple nationalities and ethnicities mediate the construction of alternative identities, in part in response to the perennial human quest for meaning, but also in response to the broader discourses of the ethnic enclave in dominant American society. Throughout, Guest combines theoretical analysis, ethnographic observation, and testimonial narrative to underscore how the Chinatown enclave provides a site for mobilization of social capital for immigrants in terms of connecting existing social networks, enabling the exchange of information and (financial) resources, and supporting the processes of legalization.

My focus in this essay is specifically on Fuzhounese illegal immigrants,[8] and their transnational quest to "realize America in their hearts."[9] Undocumented immigration from Fuzhou began in the mid-

---

[7] The centrality of religion for immigration is documented also with regard to the very different experiences of middle-class Taiwanese in Southern California by Carolyn Chen, *Getting Saved in America: Taiwanese Immigration and Religious Experience* (Princeton, New Jersey and Oxford: Princeton University Press, 2008).

[8] It is difficult to know for sure how many Fuzhounese live in NYC, given the undocumented status of many of them. In the early 2000s, Guest noted popular estimates of 60-70,000 in NYC, while also saying: "The 2000 Census has identified 700,000 Asian in New York City, just under 10 percent of the population. Chinese are the largest group with 361,000 residents, followed by 214,000 South Asians and 86,000 Koreans. In the 1990s Chinese ranked third only to immigrants from the Dominican Republic and the former Soviet Union among New York City's new arrivals" (*God in Chinatown*, 16-17).

[9] This is the title of Fumitaka Matsuoka and Eleazar S. Fernandez, eds., *Realizing the America of Our Hearts: Theological Voices of Asian Americans* (St. Louis: Chalice Press, 2003), which illuminates the longings and aspirations of Asian migrants to America.

1980s and continues to the present. Most undocumented Fuzhounese begin their trek as youth[10] and find their way to America usually through organized international smuggling syndicates. The going rates in the late 1980s had tripled by the early 2000s to over $60,000, with up to 20 percent due up front and the rest upon arrival.[11] Immigrants thus incur indebtedness to their families and relatives or, if the latter are unable to pay the bill, become indentured servants to the smugglers or their local brokers (at best) or are beaten, even maimed, as punishment (at worst).

Of course, Fuzhounese immigrants brave the journey to America in search of a better life. But upon arrival, they find a highly stratified ethnic enclave. Unless one has connections, one finds him- or herself defined by their region or city of origin, dialect, socio-economic class status of one's family "back home," or educational achievements. This stratification persists even within churches found in the enclave. The result is that most immigrant youth find themselves in the working class, with limited English skills, and owing large sums of money to their families of relatives in Fuzhou, or to the smugglers (known as snakeheads) or their brokers. As Guest thus notes, "Save for a limited number who successfully apply for political asylum, all remain undocumented, outside the mainstream, working in the informal economy."[12]

Many, if not most, struggle to survive working (and sleeping) in restaurants, garment shops, and other non-registered businesses. They work six days a week – and not atypically pick up hours on their "day off" for other "employers" – for more than 12 hours a day and are paid sometimes as low as $2.00 per hour. The majority are without medical insurance, child care, or any other benefits.[13] The most hard-working and entrepreneurial pay off their debts faster than others – and even after that many continue to remit funds to their families – and some even eventually make their way up the socio-economic ladder, gradually obtaining promotions to higher paying positions. As Guest puts it, on the one hand,

---

[10] Kenneth J. Guest, "Liminal Youth among Fuzhou Chinese Undocumented Workers," in Tony Carnes and Fenggang Yang, eds., *Asian American Religions: The Making and Remaking of Borders and Boundaries* (New York: New York University Press, 2004), 55-75.

[11] Guest, *God in Chinatown*, 28, 67.

[12] Ibid., 31.

[13] Ibid., 42.

"Fuzhounese immigrants, particularly undocumented immigrants, are extremely creative actors working to manipulate a system stacked with disadvantages.... At the same time, this isolated ethnic enclave is a trap for many Fuzhounese who, marginalized by language, culture, and class from both the mainstream U.S. economy and the Chinatown elites, have no way to escape."[14]

So why then do so many continue to make the journey illegally to America? No doubt, those who "make it" send reports and remit money back home regularly in ways that build up the hopes and dreams of those without other viable options.[15] The fact of the matter is that the opportunity to earn even US$2.00 an hour – usually for much more than forty hours a week – is more than what many can make if they stayed and worked in Fuzhou.[16] This is especially the case since rural Fuzhounese confront a depressed economy and then are at a disadvantage if they move to the city as legal employment is in many cases limited to city residents. Further, the expansion of the human smuggling network combined with the pull of the U.S. labor market make emigration more attractive, even without legal papers. Last but not least have been the executive orders entered that have been favorable to immigrants. Fuzhounese are undeterred by their lack of documentation since on at least two occasions in the last half generation, they have been the beneficiaries of changing immigration laws: the Immigration Reform and Control Act of 1986, under the presidency of Ronald Reagan, which granted amnesty to those who could demonstrate their arrival in America before 1982, and the presidential orders of George H. W. Bush in 1989 and 1990 which granted asylum to Chinese students in light of the Tian An Men Square massacre and China's population control policies. There is always the hope that another executive order will legalize their status and make it possible to attain the American dream.[17]

---

[14] Ibid., 43.

[15] For further discussion of this transnational dimension, see Kenneth J. Guest, "Transnational Religious Networks among New York's Fuzhou Immigrants," in Helen Rose Ebaugh and Janet Saltzman Chafetz, eds., *Religion across Borders: Transnational Immigrant Networks* (Walnut Creek, Calif.: AltaMira Press, 2002),149-63.

[16] Guest, *God in Chinatown*, 41.

[17] Ibid., 66-67.

Within the wider transnational and global context, however, people emigrate illegally for many other economic reasons that they may not be able to clearly articulate. What they feel most palpably is the high unemployment or under-employment realities of their home region; and what they hear about is the lure of employment and upward socio-economic mobility options in America, while seeing the "proof" of such in the comparatively affluent families who are on the receiving end of remittances sent home from relatives or family members working overseas. Yet global market demands and labor supplies are structured by trade agreements between nations, and by demographic shifts, especially aging populations of receiving countries versus growing populations of developing countries.[18] Further market-determined exchange rates that do not favor developing nations drive the unemployed or under-employed to look for work elsewhere, while structural adjustments imposed on developing nations usually involve a decline in their social welfare protections. Last but not least, transnational corporations increasingly monopolize economic production, leaving free enterprise to float perilously in the informal economy. These economic factors in the background lead us to probe more deeply into the nature of economic informality, a reality within which Fuzhounese immigrants to NYC in a significant sense live, move, and have their being.

The Informal Economy and Globalization

By definition, the informal economy exists outside the regulated and legislated (formalized) economy. An extremely heteronomous domain, a phenomenology of the informal economy, globally considered, would include at least the following kinds of economic agents and activities: street vendors, rickshaw/cart pullers, shared transportation, recyclers, petty traders/hawkers, small item producers, (very) small business owners (often at street corners rather than in their own rented or

---

[18] See Mary DeLorey, "International Migration: Social, Economic, and Humanitarian Considerations," in Donald Kerwin and Jill Marie Gerschutz, eds., *And You Welcomed Me: Migration and Catholic Social Teaching* (Lanham, Md.: Rowman & Littlefield, 2009), 31-53.

owned buildings), casual living arrangements, home-workers (garment and shoe makers, embroiderers, assemblers, etc.), piece-rate workers, sub- and sub-sub-contractors, off-site data processors, farm- and agricultural-workers, unregistered/undeclared workers, cooperative partners and partnerships, and part-time, temporary, and self-employed workers. As should be clear from this very brief enumeration, informal economic activity cuts across explicitly economic initiatives but in many cases also connects these with other social, communal, and cultural relationships and interactions.[19]

While there is some overlap between informal economic transactions and premodern economies, the former is now acknowledged to be a more or less permanent feature of the present global market economy.[20] Of course, informal economic activity is especially noticeable in regions (and nations) working to enter the global economy and during periods of economic crisis and recession in developed nations. But as we have now seen with regard to the Chinatown enclave in NYC, informal economic activity exists in the very heart of the western world as well. Hence it is clear there is enough continuity between the formal and informal economies, rather than a strict demarcation between them, that even in industrialized environments upwards of one-fourth of all economic activity occurs in the informal sector.[21] In fact, economists are suggesting that we move beyond any rigid conceptual dichotomy between the formal and informal economy.[22] The most active theoreticians working in this arena are seeking ways to formalize informal economic activities – i.e., find ways to capture informal economic transactions in the formal economy that benefit both

---

[19] A classic analysis of the informal economy is Hernando de Soto, *The Other Path: The Invisible Revolution in the Third World*, trans. June Abbott (New York: Harper and Row, 1989).

[20] See Alejandro Portes, Manuel Castells, and Lauren A. Benton, eds., *The Informal Economy: Studies in Advanced and Less Developed Countries* (Baltimore: The John Hopkins University Press, 1989).

[21] See "Women and Men in the Informal Economy: A Statistical Picture" (International Labour Organization, 2002), available at http://www.ilo.org/public/english/employment/gems/download/women.pdf (accessed 27 January 2009).

[22] See Basudeb Guha-Khasnobis, S. M. Ravi Kanbur, and Elinor Ostrom, eds., *Linking the Formal and Informal Economy: Concepts and Policies* (Oxford and New York: Oxford University Press, 2006).

sides, or to register the value of personal property owned by informal economic agents in ways that will enable their emergence in the formal economy without excessive liability – in order to unleash the potential of these assets as a means of engaging and even empowering those otherwise impoverished according to the standards of the global economy.[23] This would certainly be helpful for our Fuzhounese immigrants except for the fact that they would still have to deal with the challenges related to their lack of documentation.

How else, then, might the informal economy be understood? On the one hand, the existence of the informal sector "can be viewed as a constructed response on the part of civil society to unwanted state interference."[24] In the Fuzhounese case, there are, in addition to these economic considerations, immigration factors which motivate their avoidance of the state. On the other hand, it is also fair to say that the explosion of informality has occurred in reaction to the mercantilism and state, national, or even international bureaucracies that hinder effective formalization of economic activity at the grassroots. As instinctive responses of the masses to poverty, underdevelopment, and the inefficiencies of the legal-political system, the informal economy exhibits a good deal of energy, spirit, entrepreneurship, ingenuity, productivity, persistence, and just plain hard work. By its nature, then, the businesses of the informal economy are unregistered, its transactions not computed (nor computable) in gross national products, and its incomes untaxed (and often untaxable). Yet while the informal economy certainly includes semi-legal and even unlawful activity (involving undocumented immigrants, for example), it is probably more accurate to understand this global phenomenon in terms of extra-legality.[25] Herein also lie the

---

[23] E.g., Ahmed M. Soliman, *A Possible Way Out? Formalizing Housing Informality in Egyptian Cities* (Dallas: University Press of America, 2004).

[24] Alejandro Portes, "The Informal Economy and its Paradoxes," in Neil J. Smelser and Richard Swedberg, eds., *The Handbook of Economic Sociology* (Princeton, New Jersey: Princeton University Press, and New York: Russell Sage Foundation, 1994), 426-49; quote from 444.

[25] See de Soto, *The Other Path*, 13-14. As de Soto suggests elsewhere, whereas many see the informal economy as being on the underside of the world economic system, "In fact it is legality that is marginal; extralegality has become the norm. The poor have already taken control of vast quantities of real estate and production"; see Hernando de Soto, *The Mystery of Capital: Why*

challenges: extra-legal operations in the informal arena result in unprotected employment (workers are without benefits of any sort), impinge on the capacity of informals to grow, develop, and expand their trade (at least in the formal/legal sector), and leave them vulnerable to theft, violence, and extortion, not to mention unjust business practices within an unequal playing field (unequal for the Fuzhounese not only because of their illegal status but also because of their linguistic deficiencies).[26] In short, life in the informal economy is not ideal, and it is probably fair to say that informal economic agents do what they do in order to survive on the economic margins of society.

It is such a quest for survival that drives a significant part of the activity of the informal economy. Our discussion of transnational Fuzhounese migration from East Asia to NYC reflects this human search for hope, opportunity, and meaning, and this inevitably leads many to intersect with the religious institutions of Chinatown. Guest's discussion of religion in Chinatown, then, illuminates the role that churches, temples, and religious agents (i.e., fortune tellers) play vis-à-vis the illegality and informality of their parishioners. Focusing more specifically on the Christian churches in Guest's study – which by and large are limited to two once-related evangelical-type congregations – we can see how these have facilitated the strenuous adjustment processes involved in migration that involves half the world's population. Churches provide what Guest calls "safe harbors" with familiar customs, smells, sights, foods, and language.[27] Information exchange occurs, social networks are opened, socio-economic capital are mobilized, and financial, medical, and care resources are made available to vulnerable immigrants. Financial assistance most often occurs inter-personally between members and adherents as people with needs are brought into the orbit of the church, although in some instances compassion funds established by congregations are "used to assist members who are ill or unemployed or

---

Capitalism Triumphs in the West and Fails Everywhere Else (New York: Perseus, 2000), 30.

[26] For an early study of the blurred lines between lawful and unlawful interactions in the informal domain, see George Jenkins, "An Informal Political Economy," in Jeffrey Butler and A. A. Castagno, eds., *Boston University Papers on Africa: Transition in African Politics* (1967; reprint, New York: Frederick A. Praeger, 1968), 166-94.

[27] Guest, *God in Chinatown*, ch. 7.

stricken by other misfortune."[28] In some instances, church leaders or members also support immigrants through the legalization process.

But precisely because such churches are constituted by people who live in an undocumented domain of informality, they walk a fine line in their ministry. As evangelicals of the conservative (rather than progressive) sort, Fuzhounese Christians are in general disinclined to engage with the socio-political, economic, or structural issues that are pertinent to life in Chinatown. Thus sermons do not tackle the social challenges of smuggling, sweatshops, indentured servitude, prostitution, or gambling, and if these matters are mentioned in church newsletters, they "typically serve as background for testimonies of miraculous healing and exhortations to pray for comfort and relief."[29] Things may be gradually changing in some of Chinatown's churches, but even then, there are still challenges: the stratification of the wider community also exists within churches so that legal immigrants are not always sympathetic to the plight of the undocumented. After all, those who have survived the process of illegal immigration and "made it" – i.e., attained legalization –wonder why the next generation should get assistance that was unavailable before.

In short, religion in Chinatown also operates on the borders of legality and formality. And this is the case not only for immigrant destinations but also for their places of origins. Segments of Christianity in Fuzhou, for example, are illegal in the sense that they are unregistered with the government. In addition, there are also theological expressions that are unorthodox when measured according to the traditional teachings of the church. In a sense, then, Fuzhounese immigrants to NYC have simply moved from one domain and type of illegality to another.[30] And this is not an experience peculiar to the Fuzhounese diaspora.[31]

---

[28] Ibid., 198; on this same page, Guest also notes how one of the Buddhist temples in his study has a revolving loan fund that is available for repayment of smuggling debts in extreme situations.

[29] Ibid., 182.

[30] As Eleazar Fernandez suggests in his reflection on the Filipino American immigrant experience, the westward migration for Filipinos can be likened in some respects to the ancient Israelite search for liberation in Egypt since it is only after arriving in America the realization occurs that survival is much more difficult than initially realized, to the point that immigrants find themselves entrapped, unexpectedly, in what they thought was in the "promised land." See

The Early Church: Improvisation between Informality and Empire

My suggestion in this essay is that thinking with and through the informal economy might also shed new light on the interface between ecclesia and economics, especially about how the church functions at least in part through setting into motion an alternative set of economic practices. If the values and goals of the formal economy are based on competition, balancing the supply and demand market, the achievement of surplus/profit, and the principle of re-investment of such for the further generation of wealth, the minimal goal of the informal economy appears to be that of achieving subsistence and comfort. Without access to the formal sector, informals necessarily work in (non-formalized) subsidiary organizations and often find solidarity with one another as they seek common cause.

Elsewhere, I have argued, in dialogue with the latest findings of contemporary biblical scholarship, that the practices of the earliest followers of the Messiah can be seen as an ecclesial expression of informal economics.[32] Jesus' calling for a retrieval and implementation of the Jubilee ethics – i.e., his teachings regarding poverty and wealth,

---

Eleazar S. Fernandez, "Exodus-toward-Egypt: Filipino-Americans' Struggle to Realize the Promise Land in America," in Eleazar S. Fernandez and Fernando F. Segovia, eds., *A Dream Unfinished: Theological Reflections on America from the Margins* (Maryknoll: Orbis Books, 2001), 167-81.

[31] Thus, for example, in Latin America, pastoral agents of both Catholic and Protestant parishes, both those deeper in the region and those at the border, often provide assistance for emigrants who are without documentation. In other words, the intertwining of religion and non-documented immigration persists not just in North American destinations but at various nodes and along the various migrant paths across the global south. See, e.g., Jacqueline Maria Hagan, "The Church vs. the State: Borders, Migrants, and Human Rights," in Pierrette Hondagneu-Sotelo, ed., *Religion and Social Justice for Immigrants* (New Brunswick, New Jersey and London: Rutgers University Press, 2007), 93-101.

[32] See Yong, *In the Days of Caesar: Pentecostalism and Political Theology* (Grand Rapids: William B. Eerdmans Publishing Company, 2010), ch. 7.3. As an evangelical and pentecostal theologian, I have repeatedly returned to the experiences of the earliest Christians as recorded in the New Testament for resources to think through contemporary theological issues. This is not to say that there are no other valuable dialogue partners in the history of Christianity or even outside the Christian tradition. For our immediate purposes, however, I limit my scope to the early Christian experience of informality.

gift-giving, sharing, and mutuality[33] – were designed to overcome the disjunctions between the rich and the poor and to effectively empower new economic relations rather than support the prevailing economic status quo. His followers embodied, at least for a time, an egalitarian community which met the needs of its members through informal and reciprocal forms of provision. In the following, I want to briefly examine the economic aspects of the early messianic community, especially as unfolded in the book of Acts, in light of our discussion of religion and informality in Chinatown.[34]

We are told very specifically in Acts that "All who believed were together and had all things in common; they would sell their possessions and goods and distribute the proceeds to all, as any had need" (2:44-45).[35] Later, after the community had increased to over 5,000 men (not including women and children – Acts 4:4), it is noted:

> Now the whole group of those who believed were of one heart and soul, and no one claimed private ownership of any possessions, but everything they owned was held in common.... There was not a needy person among them, for as many as owned lands or houses sold them and brought the proceeds of what was sold. They laid it at the apostles' feet, and it was distributed to each as any had need (Acts 4:32, 34-35).

I suggest that from an evangelical theological perspective such a set of ecclesial economic practices was part and parcel of the outworking of the

---

[33] See Sharon H. Ringe, *Jesus, Liberation, and the Biblical Jubilee: Images for Ethics and Christology* (Philadelphia: Fortress Press, 1985); Michael Prior, *Jesus the Liberator: Nazareth Liberation Theology (Luke 4:16-30)*, The Biblical Seminar 26 (Sheffield: Sheffield Academic Press, 1995).

[34] Although I am not unaware of the issues regarding the historicity of Acts – succinctly discussed by Charles H. Talbert, *Reading Luke-Acts in its Mediterranean Milieu*, Supplements to Novum Testamentum 107 (Leiden and Boston : Brill, 2003) – my evangelical theological interests do not require adjudication of these matters; in effect, the questions for Asian American evangelicals in particular, and American evangelicals in general, is how the scriptural witness to the apostolic experience can speak to their contemporary lives.

[35] Unless otherwise indicated, all biblical quotations are from the New Revised Standard Version.

presence and activity of the Spirit of Jesus who the author of Acts tells us was poured out upon the world. This pneumatological economy unleashed the economic practices of mutuality and reciprocity taught by Jesus. Let me make some observations about this economic life of the Spirit seen in the early messianic community.

First, the lines between the formal and informal economies were blurred in the early Christian experience. Yes, there were those who owned, bought, and sold property according to the formal economic conventions of that time. On the other hand, there was also charitable giving, and distribution based on need, not merit (or labor). Further, there was communal "ownership" at least in the sense that none exercised their rights to private ownership. Most importantly, what we see here is not any intentional plan to establish a communal economy; rather the apostolic leaders simply responded to the massive migration from the rural areas: those who had heard about the gospel or about the signs and wonders accomplished among by the apostles were gathering "from the towns around Jerusalem" (Acts 5:16) and these needed to be fed, housed, and cared for.

This leads to our observation that by and large, the earliest Christian community consisted of migrants.[36] The early messianic communities were comprised not just of local migrants from the surrounding Judean countryside, but also of Hellenistic Jews and godfearers from the Jewish diaspora around the Mediterranean world. The original 3,000 who responded to Peter's sermon on the Day of Pentecost were those who had returned to Jerusalem for the Pentecost feast from the ends of the earth (Acts 2:5-11). While mostly Jews or proselytes to Judaism, these migrants were all at least bilingual, thus signifying their having been formed, perhaps deeply, by the various Mediterranean cultures. In part for this reason, miscommunication and misunderstanding eventually threatened to undermine the messianic community: some members of the diaspora who had returned home and

---

[36] I develop the ideas in the next few paragraphs elsewhere at greater length: "The Im/Migrant Spirit: De/Constructing a Pentecostal Theology of Migration," in Peter C. Phan and Elaine Padilla, eds., *Theology and Migration in World Christianity: Contextual Perspectives*, vol. 2: *Theology of Migration in the Abrahamic Religions*, Christianities of the World 2 (New York: Palgrave Macmillan, forthcoming).

stayed were neglected by locals who had taken the lead in food distribution and care (Acts 6:1-2). In short, internal divisions along migration lines ensued, and while the apostles were initially able to address the issues, they turned out to be unsustainable in the long run, at least in part because persecution broke out against the messianic community.

Such persecution highlights the third aspect of early Christian origins: its political character. The healing of a lame man at the Beautiful Gate was the first event that instigated a confrontation between the apostles and the local political leadership.[37] The local council decided to curtail the apostolic activities of preaching and healing: "let us warn them to speak no more to anyone in this name." In response to which the council leaders called the apostles in and "ordered them not to speak or teach at all in the name of Jesus" (Acts 4:17-18). Hence messianic proselytism in the name of Jesus was prohibited. But there was also an economic dimension to the initial encounter between the apostles and the lame man. He initially asked for alms, but Peter said: "I have no silver or gold, but what I have I give you; in the name of Jesus Christ of Nazareth, stand up and walk" (Acts 3:6). In a sense, this established the economic and political trajectory of the early messianic community: they would be constrained neither by the formal economy (they were, after all, already sharing all things) nor by the political legalities (thus their response to the council's circumscription: "Whether it is right in God's sight to listen to you rather than to God, you must judge; for we cannot keep from speaking about what we have seen and heard"; Acts 4:19-20).

Hence it was that the church operated on the borders of economic formality and political legality. With regard to the former, the focus of this essay, it might be said that the church developed its own theological or ecclesiological form of economics, one that bypassed the conventional economic structures of its time by empowering the weak in their midst in the name of Jesus and by mobilizing the generosity of the faithful. In this sense, the economics of the first Christians can be understood as anticipating contemporary economic life in the informal

---

[37] See also my *Who is the Holy Spirit: A Walk with the Apostles* (Brewster, Mass.: Paraclete Press, 2011), esp. chs. 8-15, wherein I provide brief exegetical reflections on Acts 3-6 in light of Jesus' teachings as recorded in the Gospel of Luke.

sector. Might analysis of the practices of the church from the perspective of the informal economy unveil how ecclesial solidarity as a way of life provides an alternative set of economic values to those of the formal economy?

To bring things back to the present, perhaps the practices of the earliest Christians can, against the backdrop of the Asian American experience in NYC's Chinatown, spur theological thinking about the kinds of economic arrangements that emphasize mutuality and sharing as well as local accountability and initiative which is applicable for contemporary globalization.[38] Rather than being dominated by the economy of exchange and its supply-and-demand transactions, can the church be guided by a pneumatological economy of grace – a set of economic relations and practices inspired by the Spirit of Jesus – that highlights charity (giving without anticipation of return), forgiveness (not only of sins but also of debts), and solidaristic fellowship (cultivated through interpersonal relations, common meals, and daily interactions) instead? If this is possible, might the explicitly theological economy of the earliest messianic believers empower our own rethinking about political economy vis-à-vis the informality and illegality of Chinatown, NYC, and other like environments in the twenty-first century?

Rethinking Money, Migration, and Ministry: Contemporary Globalization and Ecclesial Improvisation

I now want to re-engage the issues at the intersection of religion, globalization, and economics raised by Guest's work in light of the early Christian experience. The following basic theological considerations regarding economics, migration, and ministry may be pertinent not only in Chinatown but also in the transnational zones of the global economy.[39]

---

[38] Here I have been helped by the concrete discussions of Lee Hong Jung, "*Minjung* and Pentecostal Movements in Korea," in Allan Anderson and Walter J. Hollenweger, eds., *Pentecostals after a Century: Global Perspectives on a Movement in Transition* (Sheffield: Sheffield Academic Press, 1999), 138-60, esp. 158-59.

[39] From an American point of view, note that almost one out of every ten undocumented immigrants in the USA is from Asia – see Gemma Tulud Cruz, "Expanding the Boundaries, Turning Borders into Spaces," in Ogbu U. Kalu,

Perhaps the insights to be gained from the Acts narrative for a Christian theology of economics may be more relevant for our contemporary experience than initially anticipated.

To begin, I have highlighted how the earliest messianic believers were both *in* the world and yet not *of* it. Economically, we saw that they worked within conventional economic constraints but experimented with an alternative mode of mutual care and gratuitous provision. Similarly, both historically and today, Christian religious orders and congregations, come-outers, and restorationist house churches have also operated both formally and informally vis-à-vis the established economic systems of their times.[40] In these cases, the various forms of mutuality, reciprocity, sharing, and solidarity in ecclesial communities can be understood as providing a range of informal economic services within congregational and communal life both as an expression of their religious identity and as part of their Christian ministerial and evangelistic witness. World Christianity as a mass urban movement also involves dynamic national, international, and transnational populations that form new communities and networks in place of the family and clan relations that have been left behind, and it is within these new enclaves (churches, congregations, and communities) that people find both spiritual and material comfort, support, and aid.

Amidst the present forces of globalization, the largely impersonal features of the global market are tempered by ecclesially shaped relations that draw from, enrich, and network with local enterprises, communal associations and cooperatives, and kinship, extended household, and other domestic economic ventures. Whereas the global economy is driven by speculative finance, credit extensions, and

---

Edmund Kee-Fook Chia, and Peter Vethanayagamony, eds., *Mission after Christendom: Emergent Themes in Contemporary Mission* (Louisville, Ky.: Westminster John Knox Press, 2010), 71-83, at 72 – so our thinking about illegality and informality at Chinatown has wider implications for considering a theology of migration in global (not just vis-à-vis the East Asian) context.

[40] These can be teased out, for example, from some of the contemporary literature – e.g., Andrew Walker, *Restoring the Kingdom: The Radical Christianity of the House Church Movement* (London: Hodder and Stoughton, 1985), and Luke Wesley, *The Church in China: Persecuted, Pentecostal and Powerful* (Baguio City, Philippines: Asian Journal of Pentecostal Studies Books, 2004).

the flexibility of money as *the* medium of economic exchange, the church serves God rather than mammon. The church nurtures relationship while providing (especially voluntary) services and enabling a more discerning engagement with the needs of those who are otherwise struggling to survive on the margins of the neoliberal market regime. Fuzhounese immigrants, for example, are excluded from the formal economy precisely because of their undocumented status. As such, a theology of economics that is relevant to their situation must critically engage with the informal economy. In the informal domain, it is not what the church has on the books that matters, but how it empowers agents to survive and make meaning in life that counts.

In one respect, I urge that we go beyond what political economists define as the margins of the informal economy and include the sphere of reproduction and care.[41] The church that privileges the poor also prioritizes widows, orphans, children, the aged, the infirm, people with disabilities, and those otherwise vulnerable, so that the care of these groups of people is registered as most important from the standpoint of the economy of grace. For immigrants who are already vulnerable because of their undocumented status, losing spouses, getting sick, becoming disabled, or growing old multiplies the challenges that are confronted. In this framework, there is an even more urgent need for various forms of what we may call collective entrepreneurship to emerge. On the one hand this sustains vulnerable members who are on the margins if not the underside of history, while on the other hand it inspires creativity not only for survival's sake but also for the wider communal good. Churches and congregations in Chinatown and various heavily populated transnational zones already function in some of these ways. I am simply urging that we attend more intentionally to the biblical and theological issues so that we can be more truthful, practical, and relevant to the situations at hand.

The preceding reflections, however, should neither dull us into a false sense of accomplishment in the dialogue between religion and

---

[41] See Eva Feder Kittay and Ellen K. Feder, *The Subject of Care: Feminist Perspectives on Dependency* (Lanham, Md.: Rowman & Littlefield, 2002), and Eric Gregory, *Politics and the Order of Love: An Augustinian Ethic of Democratic Citizenship* (Chicago: University of Chicago Press, 2008), esp. ch. 3.

economics nor blind us to the challenges confronting the realities of life in the informal economy. Hence a number of clarifications are in order. First, note that such a consideration of the church from the perspective of the informal economy does not remove the church either from the world or from the global market.[42] This is neither a call for the overthrow of the neoliberal economy nor an advocacy of one or another form of socialism or communism, but rather a reminder about how the church, when going about its business of communal edification, will inevitably recommend an alternative set of economic values if not its own distinctive economic way of life. I am concerned that such recommendations be made in the footsteps of Christ by the power of the Spirit and resist being co-opted by the economic powers that be.

Second, especially in light of the work of the church in immigrant enclaves, I simply wish to highlight how conscientious ecclesial participation in the informal economy can serve as a protest against the self-interested greed, consumerist materialism, and rampant hedonism that are pervasive in the neoliberal market economy. Communal solidarity, private initiative directed toward the public good, and local and interpersonal relations, exchanges, and accountability – all of these should be advocated by the church because together, they combine to ameliorate the debilitating effects of the Fall in our economic lives. Yes, life in the ethnic enclave is indeed a struggle for survival; if the church cannot speak and embody the gospel in such economic domains, so much the worse for its witness. However, to the degree that the church can model the mutuality, reciprocity, and hospitality of the earliest followers of Jesus, to that same degree it can be subversive of the invisible hand that stratifies both the formal and informal economic domains.

---

[42] Sometimes, Mennonite intellectuals are more predisposed to withdrawing from the capitalist order and forming an alternative economics based on local community and advocating moral and environmental critiques of the current order from the Mennonite margins. I am sympathetic to the theological motivations behind such concerns but do not think that a withdrawal from the market is either feasible or the best way forward. See Jim Halteman, "Mennonites and Market Capitalism," in Calvin Redekop, Victor A. Krahn, and Samuel J. Steiner, eds., *Anabaptist/Mennonite Faith and Economics* (Lanham, Maryland: University Press of America, 1994), 321-31.

Finally, my assessment of the church as operating in effect within the informal sector is not intended to naively affirm all that transpires in that domain.[43] Obviously, the church should not legitimate the distribution of contraband (i.e., drugs, music, and other goods), condone tax evasion, bribery, kickbacks, and other forms of unlawful activity, or look askance at the delivery of illegal services (i.e., prostitution and slave-trafficking). The church also must not think that a functional informal sector is a means of pacifying the poor or that it alleviates the church's responsibility to speak prophetically to the world (that includes the state) regarding the enactment of economic justice. Last but not least, the church should not ignore the wider structural forces of globalization that drive undocumented migration and unjust and criminal economic activity.[44]

---

[43] This is the job of a more expansively considered theology of economics, such as those proposed by Douglas Meeks, *God the Economist: The Doctrine of God and Political Economy*, new ed. (Minneapolis: Fortress Press, 2000), and Kathryn Tanner, *Economy of Grace* (Minneapolis: Fortress Press, 2005). See also the concluding reflections below.

[44] One of these issues is precisely that pertaining to the economic inequities between the global south and the Euro-American West. On this note, I recommend both Nimi Wariboko, *God and Money: A Theology of Money in a Globalizing World* (Lanham, Md.: Rowman & Littlefield, 2008), and Philip Goodchild, *Theology of Money* (London: SCM, 2007), for the not faint-of-heart who are interested in rethinking the theological dimensions of the global economic system. What Wariboko calls the *Earth Dollar* (as opposed to dominant national currencies like the dollar, the euro, or the yen) works to level out the playing field economically between richer and poorer countries, tempering the violent shifts in the foreign exchange rates that exacerbate the economic conditions of the most impoverished and vulnerable regions of the world, and enabling the development of and entry into the global market of the latter without hindering the economic growth possibilities of the more established and affluent nations. Goodchild's major constructive proposal is to develop banks of evaluative credit which can provide religious and moral guidance for the assessment and investment of money in the market economy. My contribution to this discussion is primarily theological, reminding us of the equal importance of ecclesial practices which embody the values of the Spirit since apart from such concrete relations we will in due course lack models for effective mutuality and cease to be able to develop viable criteria for the evaluation of money itself.

These caveats raise the question of what the church should do to address the many injustices that are perpetuated within the informal economy. The fact is that the informal economy is dominated by the poor, who are exploited by both criminals (through illegal activities) and the more well-to-do (i.e., who put the poor to work in sweatshops), besides having to negotiate the challenges of otherwise unjust political, social, and economic systems. Desiring neither to idealize poverty nor sentimentalize or patronize the poor, I suggest that a pneumatological economy of grace according to Jesus' Jubilee paradigm enacted in the early church will be sensitive to global factors that impinge on unjust economies while focusing on local projects and initiatives, especially at the congregational and parish levels. In other words, Jesus' meeting the needs of the poor in various aspects invites the contemporary church to be alert to the multiple levels of poverty that afflict people today. Individual healing is therefore incomplete without the provision of basic material necessities, friendships, and spiritual care, access to social, educational, political, economic, medical, and civil resources, and attention to an environmentally and ecologically sustainable way of life. Solidarity with the poor thus requires formation of subsidiary organizations that include those outside ecclesial communities in order to identify and redress the causes of poverty at each level, and in order that feedback from lower levels can also trigger revision, reform, and reorganization at the higher levels. Socio-structural inequalities related to gender, race, class, and physical, intellectual, and other sensory-disabilities must be engaged both at the grassroots where such can be sensitive to the particular challenges involved, and at the political levels where more general and abstract policies can be formulated in order to forge a more just society.[45] In the latter domain, the church must be a prophetic voice that calls attention to the biblical vision of shalom but also provides instantiations of such shalomic practices in order to point toward a better way.

This last set of recommendations also reminds us that in addition to operating at or within this informal domain, the church remains active in the formal economy at many levels. The preceding proposals should not be taken to suggest that the church ceases formal operations as an economic agent. In fact, the church in its various local forms and even

---

[45] Andrew Hartropp, *What Is Economic Justice? Biblical and Secular Perspectives Contrasted* (Milton Keynes, UK: Paternoster, 2007), ch. 2.

global shape itself can and should be understood as corporations of various types, and should be subject to the different political, social, and legal strictures within that formal domain. To some degree, many of the church's contributions to political reform, social justice, and economic development projects should be properly formalized.

For instance, in dealing with the undocumented Fuzhounese to Chinatown, the issue of illegal immigration is one that requires further attention. Yet there are at least two domains of political activity that must be engaged on this matter: one regarding the structural factors that pertain to international free trade agreements which impact developing economies, and the other regarding the rights and responsibilities of sovereign nations to protect their borders. These are complicated matters which deserve extensive ecclesial and theological consideration.[46] Our spotlight in this essay on the more concrete local church's response to the presence of undocumented workers negotiating the informal economy does not mean that these other aspects intertwined with such situations are undeserving of sustained deliberation. So while appropriating the lens of the informal economy is helpful for inviting reflection on what is happening in the transnational zone that is Chinatown, NYC, we should also recognize that the church functions variously, and rightly, in the formal economic and political sectors as well.[47]

---

[46] A helpful ecclesial document in this regard is *Strangers No Longer: Together on the Journey of Hope – A Pastoral Letter Concerning Migration from the Catholic Bishops of Mexico and the United States* (2003), available online at http://www.usccb.org/mrs/stranger.shtml (last accessed 5 June 2010). Roman Catholic scholars have been at the forefront of articulating a theology of migration – e.g., Solange Lefebvre and Luiz Carlos Susin, eds., *Migration in a Global World*, Concilium 2008/5 (London: SCM Press,2008); Daniel G. Groody and Gioacchino Campese, eds., *A Promised Land, a Perilous Journey: Theological Perspectives on Migration* (Notre Dame: University of Notre Dame Press, 2008); Donald Kerwin and Jill Marie Gerschutz, eds., *And You Welcomed Me: Migration and Catholic Social Teaching* (Lanham, Md.: Rowman & Littlefield, 2009); and Gemma Tulud Cruz, *An Intercultural Theology of Migration: Pilgrims in the Wilderness*, Studies in Systematic Theology 5 (Leiden: Brill, 2010).

[47] And of course, there are many other factors besides the economic one that clamor for recognition in the emerging discussions about theology and migration. A perceptive and programmatic text in this regard is by the Lutheran theologian Dorottya Nagy, *Migration and Theology: The Case of Chinese Christian Communities in Hungary and Romania in the Globalisation-Context*,

Concluding Theological Musings:
The Spirit's Shalom in Pentecostal Key

The preceding has led us to see that the church's economic witness is not exhausted in its formal transactions. In fact, the distinctiveness of the church's economic witness occurs, I have suggested, in the diversity of its informal economic activities. From an evangelical theological perspective, these alternative ecclesiological economies can be seen as retrieving and channeling the pneumatological economy of grace unleashed on the Day of Pentecost. The many kinds of ecclesial economic activity can thus be seen as expressions of a pneumatologically-shaped version of local autonomy and participation which empowers an ecclesially-inspired form of creativity and initiative, and fosters an ecclesially-rich sense of appreciation for the diversity of the global Christian body politic.

Beyond this more general vision of the informal church, however, I suggest a more explicitly Lukan interpretation animated by the thesis that the many tongues of the Spirit are anticipations of the many gifts that are expressed in the economic sphere.[48] From out of this more pneumatological and charismatic framework arise a set of ecclesiological alternatives, nurtured within the informal sector, wherein all members are honored, especially the weak, so that all are available to come to the aid of those who are suffering, even as each potentially contributes her or his own peculiar gift for the edification of the whole. Empowered by the Spirit, these informal economic ways of life and activities may also function as prophetic parables that challenge the corruption, injustice, hedonism, and environmental degradation characteristic of neoliberal capitalism that sometimes runs unrestrained within a free market economy. In short, the Spirit not only provides for and edifies the needy through the generous dispensation of the gifts (charisms) of the body of Christ, but also enables a solidarity of life that resists the world's economy of domination.

The result will not be *the* shalom of the coming kingdom but will

---

Mission Studies 50 (Zoetermeer, The Netherlands: Uitgeverij Boekencentrum, 2009).

[48] This is the thesis of my monograph *In the Days of Caesar*, the economic aspects of which are explicated in ch. 7.

be intimations of the peace, justice, and righteousness that will be established on that day of the Lord. For the ancient prophets, the Hebrew shalom referred to the wholeness, completeness, security, friendship, well-being, and even salvation of the people both individually and collectively.[49] Herein will the sick find their healing, perhaps not necessarily in bodily cures but certainly in and through their integration in reconciling, caring, and welcoming communities. Herein also will the gospel find its penultimate fulfillment, perhaps not necessarily in affluence and material wealth, but certainly in and through the Spirit-inspired sufficiency of mutual, sharing, and generous communities of faith. In our global context of pluralism, immigration, transnationalism, and the neoliberal market economy, such a pneumatologically inaugurated *shalom*, initiated in part on the Day of Pentecost and perhaps unfolding variously in the church today even among congregations situated in the ethnic enclave of Chinatown, NYC, may be a harbinger of the peaceful and just community that human beings have long sought. Such a Spirit-inspired people of God, a true fellowship of the Spirit, will manifest the diversity of the ecclesial body together around the name of Jesus and this in turn has the potential to generate and dispense with authentic health, wealth, and shalom beyond the world's economy of exchange.[50]

---

[49] E.g., Malinda Berry, "Mission of God: Message of *Shalom*," in Dale Schrag and James Juhnke, ed., *Anabaptist Visions for the New Millennium* (Kitchener, Ont.: Pandora Press, and Scottdale, Penn., and Waterloo, Ont.: Herald Press, 2000), 167-73.

[50] Thanks to Eleazar Fernandez for inviting my participation in this festschrift, and to an anonymous reader for the *Journal of Race, Ethnicity, and Religion*, for help in improving this article. I also appreciate comments by my graduate assistant, Tim Lim, on an earlier draft of this paper.

Chapter 12.

Should the Pedal Point Always Bring Dissonance Back into Harmony? Interrogating *missio Dei* from an Asian American Perspective

J. Jayakiran Sebastian

> His tongue,
> his one underground worker perhaps,
> bound by a sentence
> pronounced in the West,
> occasionally broke out
> in a rash of yowls
> defying the watch-towers of death,
> police dogs:
> a river of wild statistics;
> or in riddles
> crafted for cell-mates
> aspiring to doctorates
> from the Universities
> of Texas, Bogota, Bombay,
> perspiring
> students of socio-linguistics.[1]

---

[1] Adil Jussawalla, "from *Missing Person*," in Arvind Krishna Mehrotra, ed., *The Oxford India Anthology of Twelve Modern Indian Poets* (Delhi: Oxford University Press, 1992), 135.

The concept of "missio Dei" has been a dominant missiological paradigm for several decades and has come to govern missiological thinking and theological self-understanding. In this sense it has functioned as a "pedal point" or underlying motif over against which all discussion of missiology has had to contend. This contribution questions this way of thinking and posits an understanding of mission as mission "to" God which opens up new and fresh ways of thinking, belief, and praxis, including the Asian and Asian American contexts. I have spelled out the implications of what such an understanding means in my contribution to a major initiative undertaken through a collaborative effort between the Center of Theological Inquiry at Princeton, New Jersey, and the United Theological College, Bangalore, India, the fruits of which were published in two volumes entitled, *News of Boundless Riches: Interrogating, Comparing, and Reconstructing Mission in a Global Era*.[2] In my article I asked:

> What are the contours of talking about the implications of a missiological understanding of *our* mission to God? For those of us who have a deep and abiding commitment to the exploration of theological issues and themes that we believe are crucial in the present context of pluralism and disparity, religious and economic, the question regarding our mission to God holds both promise and frustration. Promise, because we can now own responsibility for our actions and truly attempt to translate our commitment to both inter-religious understanding and missiological praxis in a world of competing claims and counter-claims regarding how the divine is conceived and understood; frustration, because such an endeavour is fraught with the possibility of motivations being misunderstood and propositions and

---

[2] Volume I, eds. Max L. Stackhouse and Lalsangkima Pachuau, and Volume II, eds. Lalsangkima Pachuau and Max L. Stackhouse (Delhi: ISPCK/UTC/CTI, 2007). My contribution is found in Volume I, as J. Jayakiran Sebastian, "Interrogating *missio Dei*: From the Mission of God toward Appreciating our Mission to God in India today," 26 – 44.

proposals being misattributed, with motives being implied.[3]

Interrogating 'Asian' and 'Asian American'

In the Preface to the two volumes, the present Director of the Center of Theological Inquiry, William Storrar, noted that:

> This is a unique two volume collection of essays on Christian mission in the era of globalization, looked at through the prism of India and the Gospel's encounter with the peoples, cultures and religions of Asia. It offers informed contextual insights from that great continent for all those around the world, who are engaged in the practice of cross-cultural mission and inter-religious dialogue. It also provides critical theological perspectives on mission that addresses such complex theoretical issues as post-colonialism in the global South, the end of Christendom in the global North, the missionary nature of other world religions, and the challenge of religious pluralism and peaceful co-existence in all parts of the globe.[4]

The project itself was a fine example of a sustained and serious effort to constructively and creatively work on missiological issues and themes collaboratively, something that ought to be emulated in many more fields of the theological and missiological enterprise, given the fact that many scholars in the West do not valorize work done predominantly in the so-called third world context, unless such work happens also to be published in the Western academic circles. This has consequences for thinking about Asian and Asian American theological initiatives, where very often the "Asianness" serves as an overarching label, without taking issues of the other side of the hyphen, the American, seriously enough.

---

[3] Sebastian, "Interrogating *missio Dei*," 42.
[4] In both Volumes I and II, vii.

This was brought home to me recently at the fourth Asian Theological Summer Institute, organized since 2007 under the guidance of Dean J. Paul Rajashekar at the Lutheran Theological Seminary at Philadelphia. This is an annual mentoring program for doctoral students of Asian heritage supported by the Henry Luce foundation and brings faculty mentors into intensive interaction with Asian and Asian American students from all over the country. During the time they are together, apart from benefiting from comments from mentors and peers, students from a variety of academic settings and disciplines bond over matters of mutual concern and interest. For me, coming from almost two decades of teaching in the Asian context and now teaching in the United States, certain cultural assumptions I have made about underlying "Asianness" have been called into question. As someone coming from India I can say that when two fellow Indians meet a normal conversation involves the recalling of names of people one knows and polite exchanges about whether the other perhaps also knew the same people. At the summer institute when I met two Asian American students whose ethnic background was from one of the Asian countries, I told them about the time I was a doctoral student in Hamburg, Germany, and how I had a classmate from that country, and asked politely whether they perhaps had heard of him. The immediate, frank response was, "There are millions of people in our country, and you are asking whether we know one of them!" This was indeed telling, and while this may be a simple example, it marked a cultural difference between being Asian and being Asian American that is important to note in any discourse of Asian American theology or missiology. For instance, drawing on the work of Jung Young Lee, Peter Phan summarizes that "[a]s Asian Americans, Asian immigrants are both Asian and American. To stress in-bothness means first of all affirming one's racial and cultural origins; for an Asian this means affirming 'yellowness,' like the dandelion. Being on the margin, however, prevents this affirmation of ethnicity from being exclusive, since the margin is where worlds merge. Thus to stress in-bothness means, secondly, affirming American-ness...."[5] The question remains as to the outcomes when worlds and worldviews merge. Just as there is no homogenous "Asian-ness" there is no common "American-

---

[5] Peter C. Phan, *Christianity with an Asian Face: American Theology in the Making* (Maryknoll, N.Y.: Orbis Books, 2003), 113.

ness," and the growing literature in the field of ethnic congregations in the Untied States bears ample witness to the complexity of this phenomenon.[6]

At the same time, one must not overdraw the line between Asian-ness and Asian American-ness, for as a perceptive commentator (writing about the East Asian context) remarks, American-ness is never far away in Asia. Noting that "[t]hroughout the region, U.S. institutional forms have been copied," he writes that the "power behind the culture of U.S. imperialism comes from its ability to insert itself into a geocolonial space as the imaginary figure of modernity, and as such, the natural object of identification from which the local people are to learn."[7] If this is the case and the immigrant imagination has already been shaped by American-ness even in their home countries, then the reality when seeking to set down roots in a new context is certainly multilayered and complex. As a review-blurb for a recent book, dealing with the realities encountered by ethnic congregations in the United States, I wrote:

> Immigrant communities have always faced a variety of challenges in the new cultural, economic, social, and religious contexts in which they find themselves. The quest to retain as well as redefine one's religious identity – personal, familial, and community-based – has never been easy and unproblematic. Ways of believing and belonging are constantly in the process of being negotiated. The collection of essays in this volume serves several important functions: it provides 'snapshots' of the Indian-American-Christian communities and offers glimpses of congregational life in process; it addresses issues of how identity is both problematized as well as navigated; it tackles inter- and

---

[6] One example that looks at both the Buddhist and Christian traditions and examples is Carolyn Chen, *Getting Saved in America: Taiwanese Immigration and Religious Experience* (Princeton: Princeton University Press, 2008). Chen writes: "Becoming religious is a way that immigrants address the practical problems that they face as new members of American society. But none of these problems are necessarily 'religious,' nor do they warrant religious solutions."(53)

[7] Kuan-Hsing Chen, *Asia as Method: Toward Deimperialization* (Durham and London: Duke University Press, 2010), 177.

intra-generational challenges; it raises issues of ecumenical importance, including questions of shared worship space and pastoral and worship leadership within the wider community. Long-held ways of what was considered to be normative; time-tested structures of leadership; cherished patterns of worship; and confessional centrality have all had to reckon with the impatient winds of change that are blowing all around, emerging not just from dominant societal and cultural norms from without, but also from the new-found freedoms that immigrant communities have to reckon with within. Fences can be built and windows boarded up, but the winds cannot be wished away. The process of coming to terms with the existence of these new realities can be painful and abrasive, and immigrant worshipping communities have had to find ways and means to prepare not only a whole new generation of leadership but also support the present leadership in the process of recognizing what this means in practice. It is in these processes that this book makes an important contribution and I warmly commend it not only for study, but also for reflection on what gifts immigrant communities bring to the multicultural mix that makes the religious pilgrim experience in the United States vibrant, exhilarating, and also challenging, especially at the crossroads of life.[8]

In terms of on the ground mission realities one should not forget that such communities have engaged in "mission from the rest to the West,"[9] and this too has implications for our consideration of the distinctive ways in which Asian and Asian American missiological

---

[8] Back cover of Anand Veeraraj and Rachel Fell McDermott, eds., *Pilgrims at the Crossroads: Asian Indian Christians at the North American Frontier* (Bangalore: Centre for Contemporary Christianity and Institute for the Study of Asian American Christianity, 2009).

[9] Title of an article by Peter Vethanayagamony, "Mission from the Rest to the West: The Changing Landscape of World Christianity and Christian Mission," in Ogbu U. Kalu, Peter Vethanayagamony, and Edmund Kee-Fook Chia, eds., *Mission After Christendom: Emergent Themes in Contemporary Mission* (Louisville, Kentucky: Westminster John Knox Press, 2010), 59-70.

discussions can lead to the interrogation of the assortment of ideas, events, partnerships, and even intrusions that happen under the banner of mission.

Interrogating *missio Dei*

At this point I want to thank Max L. Stackhouse[10] and Lalsangkima Pachuau, the editors of the two volumes on missiology mentioned earlier, for recognizing that one of the problems in the Western context is that of accessing and using material published in other contexts and giving me permission to reuse my article in other publications, thereby supporting my hope that the contributions made would not only reach a wider audience, but that at least some people would think about the politics of publishing and scholarship. I will draw on that article[11] to ask the question "should the pedal point always bring dissonance back into harmony?"

Faced as we are at the beginning of the twenty-first century with a plethora of mission theologies, combined with major efforts to think about the need and necessity of mission in a globalized context, the question regarding the relevance and understanding of the term "mission" is a pressing one. An entire issue of the *International Review of Mission* was devoted to the theme "Missio Dei Revisited Willingen 1952 – 2002."[12] The issue contains a wide range of articles that look at

---

[10] In his major essay, reflecting on the project as a whole, Stackhouse writes: "Today, as we live with the awareness of a new context, a globalizing one that disrupts and comprehends all local contexts and offers the fragile possibility of a global civil society that could become a very complex world civilization, our missiology must not cease, but take upon itself the quest for ways to structure this new fabric with an inclusive justice, one that brings the various offices and powers of life to their proper purpose and into interdependence with the wider fabric of life." Max L. Stackhouse, "'All Things to All People': Mission and Providence in a Global Era," in Pachuau and Stackhouse, eds., *News of Boundless Riches*, Vol. II, 250 – 275, here on pages 274 – 275.

[11] In this section since I am using a part of my article, I will not refer to it as such since it is already cited in footnote 1. Also, I have removed some of the elaborate footnotes that appear in the original article.

[12] *International Review of Mission*, Vol. XCII, No. 367 (October 2003).

the concept from historical and contextual perspectives. Writing from a contemporary Korean perspective, one of the authors points out that the concept has "broken down barriers, but it has also created new ones: barriers between conservatives and progressives, between evangelism and humanization, between saving souls and social involvement," and goes on to say that such barriers are only "gradually disappearing." This article raises two important questions as a conclusion; firstly, the relationship between *missio Dei* and money, and secondly the relationship between *missio Dei* and other religions.[13]

This paradigm, that of understanding mission as *missio Dei*, has dominated missiological thinking for the last fifty years at least,[14] and has been enormously influential and generated a rich assortment of theological, ecclesiological and missiological contributions.[15] However,

---

[13] Soo-il Chai, "Missio Dei – Its Development and Limitations in Korea," in *IRM* (October 2003), 548 – 549.

[14] David Bosch, in his magisterial *Transforming Mission: Paradigm Shifts in Theology of Mission* (Maryknoll, N.Y.: Orbis, 1991), explores the background of the emergence of this term, pointing out how the idea emerged at the Willingen Conference of the International Missionary Council in 1952 where the influence of Karl Barth "on missionary thinking reached a peak," and where the "classical doctrine on the *missio Dei* as God the Father sending the Son, and God the Father and the Son sending the Spirit was expanded to include yet another 'movement': Father, Son and Holy Spirit sending the church into the world" (390). Bosch goes on to explore how this term has had important implications for the *missiones ecclesiae* and indicates the processes by which nearly all Christian denominations have welcomed and used this term (389-93).

[15] See, for example, the contribution of Arthur F. Glasser, in *Announcing the Kingdom: The Story of God's Mission in the Bible* (Grand Rapids: Baker Academic, 2003), who interprets the goal of *missio Dei* as that of incorporating "people into the Kingdom of God and to involve them in his mission." He also deplores the "non-involvement in mission on the part of the church," because involvement is necessitated by the reality that "the Father is the Sender, Jesus Christ the One who is sent, and the Holy Spirit the Revealer ... " (245). This is to be read within the conviction of the writer that "at every level of the biblical evidence conversion demands commitment to conduct that is reflective of the coming Kingdom of God." He goes on to ask: "Is it not also true that persons who are not born again may on the day of judgment wish that they had never been born at all?" (358). The influential Indian Jesuit thinker, Michael Amaldoss, in his article, "The Trinity on Mission," in Frans Wijsen and Peter Nissen, eds., *'Mission is a Must': Intercultural Theology and the Mission of the Church* (Amsterdam: Rodopi, 2002), 99-106, writes that, "To contemplate the

for various reasons, not the least of which is connected to my engagement with the issues and themes raised by a pluralistic and postcolonial approach to the missiological questions of our time, I have increasingly become uneasy with the concept of *missio Dei*. It is not that I believe the concept has not made a significant contribution to our understanding of mission and missiology, but I have come to believe that we need to interrogate this concept and offer a theological critique of how this concept has played out in empirical terms in order to provoke and stimulate other possibly more productive and more relevant ways of thinking and acting in this religiously plural and culturally globalized world. My discontent resulted in the following proposal, made during an international consultation sponsored by the World Council of Churches. (The theme of the consultation itself is symptomatic of the wider concern with the issue of missiology and relevance, missiology and credibility.) At this meeting[16] I suggested that:

> [A] re-examination of the *missio Dei* paradigm is necessary, because what is needed today is a mission paradigm that affirms our mission *to* God. Having gone through the consequences of theological thinking regarding the mission *of* God, and having explored human responsibility in this task, a reversal of the direction in trying to take seriously the human experience of both variety and difference in God/divinity, and what this means for the question as to whether there can ever be an understanding of a *common* mission of humankind, becomes an urgent theological task.[17]

Trinity, our mission in the world is a freeing experience, so that we can carry on our own mission without aggression and anxiety, conscious that we are making a real contribution to the realization of God's plan for the world. We learn to be sensitive to what God is doing in the world and to coordinate our own mission with God's mission" (106).

[16] "Believing without Belonging: In Search of New Paradigms of Church and Mission in Secularized and Postmodern Contexts," Northelbian Centre for World Mission/ Christian Jensen Kolleg, Breklum, Germany, 26th June – 2nd July, 2002.

[17] This has been published as J. Jayakiran Sebastian, "Believing and Belonging: Secularism and Religion in India," *International Review of Mission*, Vol. 92, No. 365 (April 2003): 204-11, quotation on page 211.

Naturally such an affirmation provoked concern and a desire on the part of the participants to probe into the source of such discontent as well as a genuine bewilderment that such a mode of questioning had even been thought necessary. If the Indian theologian Arvind Nirmal was right in his famous assertion that God does not read or write theology and that "theology has nothing to do with God,"[18] can we transpose this theological point to the field of missiology and ask in what sense we can make the claim that mission is *of* God? If mission is not *of* God, then what mission are we talking about? We have not been afraid of coming to terms with the reality that mission as a human enterprise has been flawed and problematic[19] where it has been asserted that, "[a]long with gunboats, opium, slaves and treaties, the Christian Bible became a defining symbol of European expansion."[20] Have we then tried to cover up for the harsh realities of how mission was organized and how mission was experienced by talking about something we could claim had a divine origin?[21] If mission is both a divine and a human enterprise, then what?

---

[18] See the provocative questions and incisive probing in Arvind P. Nirmal, "Theological Research: Its Implications for the Nature and Scope of the Theological Task of the Church in India," in Gnana Robinson, ed., *For the Sake of the Gospel: Essays in Honour of Samuel Amirtham* (Madurai: T. T. S. Publications, 1980), 73-82.

[19] Reflecting on the biblical models of mission, Bosch writes that our missionary ministry "is never performed in unbroken continuity with the biblical witness; it remains, always, an altogether ambivalent and flawed enterprise. Still we may, with due humility, look back on the witness of Jesus and our first forebears in the faith and seek to emulate them." David J. Bosch, "Reflections on Biblical Models of Mission," in James M. Phillips, and Robert T. Coote, eds., *Towards the Twenty-first Century in Christian Mission: Essays in honor of Gerald H. Anderson* (Grand Rapids: Eerdmans, 1993), 190. The idea of mission as emulating Jesus is expressed by Lucien Legrand, when he writes: "Many are the paths of mission. Ultimately, they all follow the way of Jesus: emerging, going elsewhere (Mark 1:38), they return to Jerusalem (Mark 10:32; cf. Luke 9:51), and from there, by death and the Resurrection, lead to the glory and the oneness of God." In Lucien Legrand, *Unity and Plurality: Mission in the Bible*, trans. Robert R. Barr (Maryknoll, N.Y.: Orbis Books, 1990), 163.

[20] R. S. Sugirtharajah, *The Bible and the Third World: Precolonial, Colonial and Postcolonial Encounters* (Cambridge: Cambridge University Press, 2001), 1.

[21] Paul G. Hiebert, in his *Missiological Implications of Epistemological Shifts: Affirming Truth in a Modern/Postmodern World* (Harrisburg, PA: Trinity

Why use binaries? Can binaries become so intertwined that disentanglement is not only impossible, but also unnecessary? Why not talk about a theandric mission; theandric seen not as the result of binaries being intertwined, but as the very nature of the being of the divine?[22]

If "life is always *on the way* to narrative, but it does not arrive there until someone hears and tells this life as a story,"[23] then has the *missio Dei* concept reversed the direction and tried to shape a story out of its own understanding of the narrative, a narrative not woven on the way but offered ready-made one-size-fits-all to those on the way? The prophetic and provocative "Princeton Proposal for Christian Unity" notes that the "life of the church...calls for continuous critical sifting and reconstruction of human identity. Elements that constitute our differences must be questioned, judged, reconciled, and reconfigured within the unity of the body of Christ...."[24]

Press International, 1999), concludes by saying that "In mission, our central task is not to communicate a message but to introduce people to that person, Jesus Christ" (116). However, several questions remain: How do we "introduce" anyone? Can there be an introduction without interpretation? Why and how are we motivated to introduce someone to "people"?

[22] Slavoj Žižek, the 'wild man of theory' and provocative critic of culture writes in his *The Puppet and the Dwarf: The Perverse Core of Christianity* (Cambridge, Massachusetts: MIT Press, 2003), 138: "Insofar as the ultimate Other is God Himself, I should risk the claim that *it is the epochal achievement of Christianity to reduce its Otherness to Sameness*: God Himself is Man, 'one of us.'...The ultimate horizon of Christianity is thus not respect for the neighbor, for the abyss of its impenetrable Otherness; it is possible to go beyond – not of course, to penetrate the Other directly, to experience the Other as it is 'in itself,' but to become aware that there is no mystery, no hidden true content, behind the mask (deceptive surface) of the Other."

[23] Richard Kearney, *On Stories* (London: Routledge, 2002), 133. Italics in original.

[24] Carl E. Braaten and Robert W. Jenson, eds., *In One Body Through the Cross: The Princeton Proposal for Christian Unity* (Grand Rapids: Eerdmans, 2003), section 23, page 28. The document goes on to note that "our churchly identities lack the winnowing and transformative power of the gospel. Our missions in a particular place all too easily enter into complex collusions with divisions of class, culture, ethnicity, or status already present there. Rather than reconciling the divided, the gathering of men and women into churches may reinforce their divisions." Section 33, p. 34.

In one sense this concern was also the concern of the one who did more than anything else to put the concept of *missio Dei* at the forefront of ecumenical thinking – Georg F. Vicedom. It was dissatisfaction with the way in which mission had been justified on the basis of "missionary thought in the Bible," as being "possible and necessary among the nations," as "being derived from the church as a secondary assignment," or as part of the spreading of "'Christian culture.'" For Vicedom the *missio Dei* derives from the reality that "the Bible in its totality ascribes only one intention to God: to save [hu]mankind."[25] One is justified in asking whether Vicedom is right in ascribing the desire to save as being the only intention exhibited by God in the Biblical testimony. Nevertheless, what emerges is a sense of dissatisfaction with what passes for mission in his context and his desire to remind the church that "God Himself does mission work."[26] It is interesting that Vicedom concludes his work with a section on the "church of suffering" and writes that the "suffering of the congregation culminates in the redemption which is bestowed when Jesus Christ ushers in His Kingdom. With this God concludes His *missio*."[27] What happens when the *missio Dei* is trumpeted and reinforced by churches and structures which have

---

[25] Georg F. Vicedom, *The Mission of God: An Introduction to a Theology of Mission*, trans. Gilbert A. Thiele and Dennis Hilgendorf (Saint Louis: Concordia Publishing House, 1965), 4.

[26] Vicedom, *The Mission of God*, 51. This affirmation leads Vicedom to explicit and heavy Christological concentration when he writes: "The special *missio Dei* begins with Jesus Christ, for in Him God is both the Sender and the One who is sent, both the Revealer and the Revelation, both the Holy One who punishes and the One who redeems. Through His Son in the incarnation and enthronement God makes Himself the very content of the sending. ... The work of providing the content of the sending is completed in Jesus, and thus meaning and goal have been given to every sending. Beyond Jesus there is no further revelation of God. Even the Holy Ghost derives His message from the things of Jesus and in this way leads all men into all truth. Since Jesus died and rose for the salvation of men, any redemption apart from Him is impossible, even though men ever and again strive to classify Christ among many figures who try to indicate a way of salvation. Whoever places Christ's 'once-for-all-ness' in question also places the one God who has sent Him in question. ... Apart from this *missio Dei* in Jesus Christ there can be no further sendings today" (52 – 54).

[27] Vicedom, *The Mission of God*, 142.

moved a long way away from suffering, however cleverly suffering is defined?[28]

Darrell Guder, whose contribution to the two-volume missiology project is entitled "The *missio Dei:* A Mission Theology after Christendom,"[29] provides us with a fine summary laced with critical insights on recent thinking regarding this concept.[30] Among many other things, Guder points out how the understanding of *missio Dei*

- critiqued the previously existing mission models and helped the move from an ecclesio-centric model to a Trinitarian model in the mission enterprise

- has been the object of criticism by influential theologians, even from the Western tradition

---

[28] One must also note the suspicion that postmodern thinking has generated among some missiologists. Much of it is based on a stereotypical, narrow and caricatured understanding of the promise and attraction of postmodern thinking to those who see in its varieties stimulating new ways of orientation and thinking. An example of this suspicion is found in the book by Paul Avis, *A Church Drawing Near: Spirituality and Mission in a Post-Christian Culture* (London: T & T Clark, 2003), where he writes: "The mission of the Christian Church cannot collude with the acids of post-modernity. We used to use the expression 'the acids of modernity', but modernity now looks comparatively benign. Christian theology can recognize common ground and common interests with modernity, even in the absence of a common framework of beliefs and values...Above all, Christianity cannot baptize the post-modernistic dissolution of the self, of community and of reason...Post-modernity knows no accountability. Individual or group self-expression is self-authenticating. The rainbow of spiritualities invites no boundaries or bonds. But these constraints are indispensable, nevertheless." (94) It is ironic that modernity is upheld as some kind of benign bulwark against the permeating "acids"! In addition all talk about "constraints" is problematic, especially when seen from the point of view of those who have been constrained in various ways, not least theologically.

[29] Darrell L. Guder, "The *missio Dei*: A Mission Theology after Christendom," in Stackhouse and Pachuau, eds., *News of Boundless Riches*, Vol. I, 3 – 25.

[30] As a supplement to this, also see, Darrell L. Guder, "From Mission and Theology to Missional Theology," in *The Princeton Seminary Bulletin*, Vol. XXIV, No. 1, New Series (2003): 36 – 54.

- also provides for an understanding of the *missio hominum*

- generates a variety of responses in face of pluralism, diversity and hope

Of interest at this point is the Princeton doctoral dissertation by Ken Miyamoto. Miyamoto in his impressive work reminds us of several important points, including the assertion that the Trinitarian understanding of *missio Dei* quickly moved to an exploration of how this matters and has consequences when one affirms the reality of this world as the arena of God's activity and God's mission. It also offers a nuanced and critical reading of the emergence and use of this idea in the ecumenical movement and in the Asian setting.[31] Miyamoto has revised and summarized part of his thinking in his contribution to the noteworthy book edited by Lalsangkima Pachuau, *Ecumenical Missiology*.[32] Here he writes that "ecumenical Asian theologians have almost always used '*missio Dei*' with a world-centric connotation. They have appropriated this Western term as the symbol that provides a focus around which this-worldly holiness in the Asian churches is given a coherent expression."[33] Questions abound: How does one link "this-worldly holiness" and the commitment to justice and social transformation? The respected ethicist Gustafson offers us sharply pointed questions regarding our understanding of God's preferential option for the poor and oppressed:

---

[31] Ken Christoph Miyamoto, *God's Mission in Asia: A Comparative and Contextual Study of This-Worldly Holiness and the Theology of Missio Dei in M. M. Thomas and C. S. Song* (Ph. D. diss., Princeton Theological Seminary, 1999).

[32] Ken Christoph Miyamoto, "This-Worldly Holiness and the *Missio Dei* Concept in Asian Ecumenical Thinking," in Lalsangkima Pachuau, *Ecumenical Missiology: Contemporary Trends, Issues and Themes* (Bangalore: United Theological College, 2002), 99 – 128. The various articles in this book raise a variety of questions and probe a range of issues.

[33] Miyamoto, 118. Miyamoto goes on to point out that the understanding of the *missio Dei* "has not been limited to this function," and that several Asian theologians have used this concept to contribute creatively "to the emergence of contextual theology in Asia."

If God prefers the poor, why am I, my family, and countless others so fortunate? If God prefers the poor, is the destitution, the pain and suffering of those millions whose plight draws our compassion due only to the human fault – sin? Or is much of it the outcome of historical and natural conflicts and forces beyond the capacity of any individual human, or any government, or any nongovernmental organization to alleviate, not to mention eliminate? If God prefers the poor, is God impotent to fulfill that preference? Or is it up to Christians, and non-Christians who often better marshal their powers, to actualize God's preference for the poor?... It is clearly the Christian mission to prefer the poor and oppressed. But if that is a purpose of the Almighty, the Almighty is not Almighty.[34]

These poignant questions serve in raising more questions. Is *missio Dei* the only authentic way of valorizing mission? Must we regress into the infinite depths of the heart of God in order to find a source for mission? In other words, as Richebächer asks, is *missio Dei* the "basis of mission theology or a wrong path?"[35]

---

[34] James M. Gustafson, *An Examined Faith: The Grace of Self-Doubt* (Minneapolis: Fortress Press, 2004), 105.

[35] Wilhelm Richebächer, "*Missio Dei*: The Basis of Mission Theology or a Wrong Path?" in *IRM* (October 2003), 588 – 605. Richebächer concludes by pleading "for a more precisely defined formulation based on the original meaning and function, viz. that of *missio Dei Triunius*, for the sake of the invitation to believe and the dignity of all religions." (599) Jacques Matthey, in his article "God's Mission Today: Summary and Conclusions" (*IRM* (October 2003), 579 – 587), reflecting critically on the 50th anniversary of Willingen conference where the papers in the special issue of *IRM* were presented, asks whether one can "continue to use the *missio Dei,* or do we need a different paradigm?" He cautions us against trying to go "deeper into any analytical description of inner-trinitarian *processiones*", and asks: "Who are we to know the inner life of God? We could easily fall into the temptation of transferring to God our vision of the ideal community or society." He also reminds us that "If we were to lose the reference to *missio Dei*, we would again put the sole responsibility for mission on human shoulders and thereby risk, missiologically speaking, believing that salvation is gained by our own achievements." (582)

And So – What about Missiology and the Pedal Point in the Asian American Context?

This is not the time to quote from the constructive part of my article where I sketched out an understanding of *missio Dei* as *missio humanitatis qua itinerarium in deum*. Please note that I didn't forget to make a comment on the "Latin captivity of mission"! Rather this is the time to ask, given the questions that I have raised about *missio Dei*, what implications this has for Asian American theology and missiology in the present day context.

In the important and vibrant *A People's History of Christianity* published by Fortress Press, Minneapolis, an attempt has been made to answer a fundamental question: What will history look like if it is written from the perspective of those on the margins and fringes, "from below?" The General Editor writes:

> [T] his seven-volume series breaks new ground by looking at Christianity's past from the vantage point of a people's history. It is church history, yes, but church history with a difference: 'church,' we insist, is not to be understood first and foremost as the hierarchical-institutional-bureaucratic corporation; rather, above all it is the laity, the ordinary faithful, the people. Their religious lives, their pious practices, their self-understandings as Christians, and the way all of this grew and changed over the last two millennia – *this* is the unexplored territory in which we are here setting foot.[36]

This perspective is reiterated in the final volume dealing with global Christianity in the twentieth century where one of the contributors writes that "Christian history takes on a new vitality when historians embrace the multiple and ongoing stories of people all over the globe for whom Christianity is a living tradition. This kind of new history opens up the everyday realities of Christians that have been concealed by theological abstractions, all-to-neatly-framed timelines, typologies that

---

[36] Denis R. Janz, "Foreward" in Richard A. Horsley, ed., *Christian Origins – Volume 1: A People's History of Christianity* (Minneapolis: Fortress Press, 2005), xiii.

suggest stasis rather than dynamism and unquestioned assumptions about what elements of Christian history are significant enough to record."[37]

This approach has many implications for the way in which we understand mission in the Asian American context:

1. In missiological discourse we need to take seriously both parts of the hyphen, "Asian-ness" and "American-ness" and see where the pressure on the hyphen lies. How has the Asian American imagination been shaped by this pressure? What has been carried and how has it been packaged? What about the generational shifts as communities settle and grow in a new context but in a context where "home" functions as a sounding board for better or for worse, leading in several cases to conflict regarding real or imagined values, and in other cases to enrichment and dynamism?

2. The link between existing ecclesial paradigms and structures and Asian American ecclesiology and missiology needs deeper exploration. In the past several years there has been a significant move away from paternalism on the part of existing communions of churches and the diasporic communities they helped foster. Has this led to a mutual appreciation and understanding of the challenges that various partners in mission prioritize? Questions of gender justice, gay rights, the persistence of poverty, race equations, immigration reform, and eco-sensitivity are all issues that have the potential for collaboration as well as conflict. How have these been negotiated without shallow generalizations or uneasy compromises?

3. Increasing prosperity among diasporic communities has led them to make material and financial interventions in their countries of origin, supporting "mission" initiatives and

---

[37] Mary Farrell Bednarowski, "Multiplicity and Ambiguity," in Mary Farrell Bednarowski, ed., *Twentieth-Century Global Christianity – Volume 7: A People's History of Christianity* (Minneapolis: Fortress Press, 2008), 1 – 31, here on page 29.

functioning as catalysts of what they see as positive change. What is the ideology underlying such intervention? What is the role of the local agents in encouraging materialistic giving, and what is offered in exchange? How has this become part of the prosperity culture and to what extent does this foster dependence? How does one discern between various options, between individuals and the collective, between existing institutions and those that have sprung up to tap into such possibilities? What about the reality of corruption and nepotism at various levels and the easy link between materialism and blessing?

4. Given that modern communication methods and social networking tools are more and more the preferred means for the swift propagation of ideas, events, the spread of news as well as comments and interpretation of news items, astounding stories, feel-good snippets, scriptural verses, prayers and spiritual messages; how have the diasporic communities been able to discern wisely and judge appropriately between sensational and emotionally appealing versions of what mission should be (and is all about!) and more sober and reasoned analysis of what mission should look like in this globalized and interdependent world where hegemonic tendencies have not been quelled but are intensified?

These are only some of the issues that confront those of us concerned with the ongoing relevance and vitality of missiological engagement and praxis, not only at the level of theologians and missiologists, but at the level of congregations and communities. One should not forget that "[t]here is a growing recognition that Asian American theologies need to go beyond merely ethnocentric theologies that are narrowly confined to the needs of specific racial-ethnic Asian American communities, to theologies that would engage with, as well as challenge, the broader Christian world."[38] In the name of harmony and

---

[38] Jonathan Y. Tan, *Introducing Asian American Theologies* (Maryknoll, N.Y.: Orbis Books, 2008), 83.

resolution many paradigms, including that of the *missio Dei*, have functioned as 'pedal points' and tried to bring various voices playing above them into some form of uniformity and conformity. We should not hesitate to state that one possible way forward where Asian and Asian American theological and missiological interaction can make an impact in the academy, the church, and the wider community is through the sustained and informed interrogation of such paradigms. We need to question the pedal point of *missio Dei* in order that we may not only be faithful to our heritage but also prophetic and contextually relevant as we work together to shape and define our common future.

Chapter 13.

Discordant Notes:
Proselytism in an Age of Pluralism

J. Paul Rajashekar

The year 2010 marks the centenary of the World Missionary Conference held at Edinburgh. The conference symbolized a tremendous optimism for the evangelization of the world among Western churches and mission societies; the leaders of the conference were so confident in the success of Christian missionary endeavors that they came up with the slogan, "Evangelization of the world in our generation." It was the same fervor that led some to believe that the 20th Century would be a "Christian Century." This seminal conference gave birth to the formation of the modern ecumenical movement among Protestant Christians, eventually leading to the formation of the World Council of Churches. It must be remembered that the conference in 1910 was held during the heyday of modern Protestant missions implicitly or explicitly supported by the colonial powers that had ruled large parts of the world, especially in the Middle East, Asia, Africa and Latin America. The Edinburgh conference was held at a time when a "missiology of conquest," based on "Modernist" assumptions was a dominant element. The "unholy" alliance between colonization and Christian mission provided the background for the evangelization of the non-Christian world.[1]

---

[1] David J. Bosch, *Transforming Mission: Paradigm Shifts in Theology of Mission* (Maryknoll, Orbis, 1991). Stephen B. Beavens and Roger P. Schroeder, ed. *Constants in Context, A Theology of Mission for Today* (Maryknoll, N.Y.:

A century later it seems Western societies no longer exhibit the same degree of enthusiasm or missionary fervor that once dominated Christian thinking. It has become apparent that the old missiology of conquest has lost its credibility with a changing or changed perception of mission and evangelization of the world today. This is in part attributable to a tremendous resurgence of world religions and non-Western cultures on formerly colonized continents. Major religions of the world have shown significant vitality and have expanded their geographical reach. Asian religions are no longer confined to Asia and their presence in Western societies is becoming more pronounced. Interestingly, in recent decades, after the collapse of the colonial enterprise, Christianity too has registered significant demographic growth in the formerly colonized worlds of Asia, Africa and Latin America. The newly coined term "World Christianity" has garnered considerable attention in Christian churches recently.[2]

It is premature to determine the prospects for the future growth of Christianity in predominantly non-Christian societies, notwithstanding the demographic projections put forward by centers for the study of World Christianity.[3] This highly optimistic projection of the growth of Christianity in many parts of the world comes at a time when most Western Christian denominations are experiencing a steady erosion of membership and decline in church attendance.[4] The process of de-Christianization seems to be more accelerated in European societies than in North America. There are, of course, many sociological factors that have contributed to this erosion of Christianity in traditionally Christian societies, the most important factor being the emergence of a pluralistic consciousness. In the North American context today there is a greater awareness of the reality of religious pluralism and an increasing trend toward disaffiliation or non-affiliation with organized religion.[5] Further-

---

Orbis, 2004).

[2] David Jenkins, *The Next Christendom, The Coming of Global Christianity* (London: Oxford University Press, 2002).

[3] See latest statistics in *International Bulletin for Missionary Research*, 34:1 (January 2010).

[4] Eileen W. Lindner, ed. *Yearbook of American and Canadian Churches 2010* (New York: NCCUSA, 2010); Lovett H. Weems Jr., "No Shows: The Decline in Worship Attendance," *The Christian Century*, September 22, 2010.

[5] The Pew Forum on Religion and Public Life, *The US Religious Landscape*

more, religions of the world have gone global and have begun to extend their reach and influence beyond their home base, or countries and cultures of origin.

The "globalization" of religions in our time on the one hand has brought about greater recognition of religious diversity in most societies, on the other it has contributed to even greater tensions and conflicts. Globalization of Religions in effect has challenged every religious community to come to terms with the reality of religious pluralism. This reality is more acutely felt in Western societies. In North America, in a recent book titled, *American Grace: How Religion Divides and Unites Us*, the authors disclose that while most American citizens acknowledge or welcome religious diversity in their midst, there is a profound dislike towards those who are outside of "America's Judeo-Christian framework."[6] This dislike is directed not only toward Muslims but also toward Buddhists. The recent controversy surrounding the attempted Qur'an burning in Florida is an extreme example of emerging hostility toward non-Christian faiths existing alongside of a growing acceptance of religious diversity in the United States.

A similar form of hostility toward certain religious faiths has reared its ugly head in many parts of the world. Much of this hostility is directed against Christians and Muslims because of perceived fears of Christian-inspired world dominance by the "American empire" and Muslim fundamentalist-inspired terrorism directed against destabilizing societies around the world. Notwithstanding the political dimensions of this conflict, the underlying source of interreligious tensions lies in the fact that both Christianity and Islam, as convert-seeking religions, have been seen as predatory and unwilling to come to terms with religious plurality and diversity in the world. As the world's two largest religious communities, they have not only been at loggerheads with each other, but also together they have been perceived by other religious communities as a threat to religious identity and cultural survival. As a consequence, both Christianity and Islam have come under severe scrutiny: they must justify their proselytizing activities beyond merely citing their internal scriptural mandates, in the presence of other faiths

---

Survey, http://religions.pewforum.org/reports.

[6] Robert D. Putnam and David E. Campbell, *American Grace: How Religion Divides and Unites Us* (Simon Schuster, 2010).

and in response to other religious claims and commitments. Christians in particular have now been challenged to reexamine the legitimacy of *proselytism* or *evangelization* in the face of the globalization of religions. These issues have emerged as highly contested and explosive in many cultural contexts. How one reconciles the Christian desire for proselytism with the reality of religious pluralism has therefore become a crucial issue.

"Can We All Just Get Along?"

One may recall this memorable remark made by Rodney King, a victim of police brutality following the Los Angeles urban unrest of April 1992 that resulted in the death of 53 people and 1 billion dollars in damage. The phrase, "Can we all just get along?" has forever become synonymous with the riot.[7]

One could as well pose that question in our context of religious pluralism. Why do religious people target other people as objects of proselytization? Why must one interfere with the faith and beliefs of other people? Why don't we mind our own business and let others mind theirs? Can we not simply get along with one another without intruding into each other's religious and spiritual lives?

Exclusivist claims for the superiority of one's beliefs are not merely internal claims heard within the confines of one's religious community but are also heard by those outside of it. When those claims are translated into overt or covert forms of persuasion or proselytism they become problematic in the context of religious and social pluralism. The etiquette of pluralism, with its demands for politeness, toleration, civility and acceptance of the other, sees proselytism as an assault on someone else's identity and therefore socially disruptive. Whatever the internal scriptural, doctrinal or inner warrant there may be within a religious community, outwardly, religious communities tend to be a bit more circumspect, if not embarrassed about, their proselytizing activities. The idea of proselytism often brings about some theological discomfort among Christians, and therefore there is a tendency to soften or hide

---

[7] "The L.A. Riots: 15 Years After Rodney King," http://www.time.com/time/specials/2007/la_riot/article/0,28804,1614117_1614084,00.html.

what is being done under benign or non-threatening rubrics such as "sharing the faith," "reaching out in love," "witnessing" and the like. However carefully Christians may nuance the meaning of *mission, evangelism, witness* or *evangelization* in their theological self-understanding, these categories are often conflated with *proselytism* in public discourse. In the mind of the public, proselytism seems to have an unethical or improper ring to it. In religiously plural and culturally diverse contexts the ethics of proselytism invariably comes into collision with the etiquette of pluralism.

Attitudes toward proselytism are shaped by historical, theological, social, cultural and political considerations, and responses to it vary from context to context. Convert-seeking religions, especially Christianity and Islam the two dominant colonizing religions, have been subject to severe critique for their proselytizing activities by those who are threatened by such activities and by those who hold deep pluralistic convictions. Proselytism is related to issues of religious freedom and religious conversion. Change of *religious allegiance or conversion from one faith to another, whether voluntary or involuntary, whether involving a single individual or an entire community, can be unsettling in society. In* the 1970's when new religious movements burst into secularized Western societies there was a great deal of hue and cry, and accusations of "brainwashing" were leveled against such proselytizing new movements. In other contexts – especially in Asia, Central and Eastern Europe and Africa – conflicts have risen between indigenous religions and "foreign religions" promoting proselytizing programs. The fear that religious conversions may alter the demographic equation within a society and may destabilize established religious and communal identities has caused violent reactions in some contexts.

In recent years reaction against and controversy over proselytism, conversion, dissemination of religious views and missionary activities have become all too common:

> In the aftermath of the tragic tsunami in 2005, it was widely reported that a US-based Evangelical group was accused of proselytism when it transported 300 children from Banda Aceh to Jakarta, Indonesia, to be placed in a Protestant orphanage. This incident created uproar among Indonesian Muslims that Christian humanitarian efforts

were being used to proselytize Muslims in hard to reach areas. Indonesia's largest Muslim organization, the *Nadhlatul Ulama* (NU), called on the government to investigate the issue on the grounds that such initiatives could undermine the climate of religious harmony in the country.[8]

In India several Indian states have promulgated "Freedom of Religion" laws to restrict religious conversions by "allurement or fraudulent means" as disruptive to communal harmony. Hindu nationalists have been strident in reclaiming the cultural rights of Hindus to remain and practice their inherited faith without interference from the proselytizing activities of another religion. Critics of the bill fear that it could be misused to torture and imprison Christian missionaries on fabricated charges.[9] Proselytism is a politically charged issue in such post-colonial contexts, where the religion of the former colonizers is still feared.

The Russian Orthodox Patriarchate has criticized Roman Catholic and Protestant missionaries alike for invading the Orthodox "canonical territory." The critique is based on an understanding that certain churches have an ecclesiastical authority within a geographical domain of the people or nation, inside of which evangelization has been and continues to be the responsibility of the national church. The inseparable identity of church, culture and land in some Eastern Orthodox Churches makes proselytism by others an illegitimate activity. In 1997, at the urging of the Russian Orthodox Church, the Russian Duma passed the law of "Freedom of Conscience and Religious Organiza-

---

[8] http://www.asianews.it/index.php?art=2370&l=en.
[9] http://christianpersecutionindia.blogspot.com/2008/03/freedom-of-religion-bill-passed-in.html. For a scholarly discussion of the issues in the Indian context, see Sebastian C. H. Kim, *In Search of Identity, Debates on Religious Conversion in India* (London: Oxford University Press, 2003).

tions," proscribing religious propaganda for religious organizations that have been in existence in Russia for less than fifty years.[10] In a similar vein, the Pope and the Roman Catholic Church have expressed resentment toward Evangelical incursions into predominantly Catholic territories in Latin America.[11]

Most recently, the baptism of Magdi Allam, an Egyptian-born Italian journalist, into Catholicism by Pope Benedict XVI during the Easter vigil in 2008, infuriated many Muslims around the world. Supporters interpreted the Pope's action as the defense of religious freedom, evangelization and co-existence of religions. "We no longer stand alongside or in opposition to one another," Benedict XVI said in a homily reflecting on the meaning of the baptism; "Thus faith is a force for peace and reconciliation in the world: distances between people are overcome; in the Lord we have become close."[12] This message, coming as it did on the heels of the Pope's controversial remark about the religion of Prophet Mohammed as spreading faith by violence, created considerable controversy.[13]

These few examples will suffice to illustrate a renewed attention to the problem of proselytism in a religiously plural world.

---

[10] David Kerr, "Christian Understanding of Proselytism," *International Bulletin of Missionary Research* 23 (1999): 10.

[11] See Papal Encyclical, *Redemptoris Missio*. Paul E. Sigmund, ed., *Religious Freedom and Evangelization of Latin America: The Challenge of Religious Pluralism* (Wipf & Stock Publishers, 2009).

[12] http://www.vatican.va/holy_father/benedict_xvi/homilies/2008/documents/hf_ben-xvi_hom_20080322_veglia-pasquale_en.html.

[13] http://www.vatican.va/holy_father/benedict_xvi/speeches/2006/september/documents/hf_ben-xvi_spe_20060912_university-regensburg_en.html.

Meaning and Limits to Proselytism

Proselytism often evokes a strong reaction; the term no longer carries the positive meaning it did in its origins in the Jewish and Christian tradition. In its original Biblical meaning *proselytism* referred to Gentile converts to Judaism, or more precisely, a Gentile who had begun to observe Jewish law. Jesus' criticism of the treatment of Jewish proselytes (Mat. 23:15) indicates that their incorporation into Israel was a matter of controversy even in Jesus' time. Nonetheless, in the New Testament Jewish proselytes were among the first Christians (Acts 2:10; 6:5; 13:43). However, conversion in the New Testament did not imply a change in community so much as a call to new obedience to God in Jesus Christ. Conversion did not necessarily mean a breach in relationships whereby a person left one community to become a member of another. Those who are joined to Christ are not to cut themselves off from their own communities or families. On the contrary, they are to consider their baptism a beginning of a new mission of solidarity with Christ and others.[14] In that sense the post-biblical histories of both Judaism and Christianity suggest a continued acceptance of proselytism as a positive form of religious propagation.

Proselytism did not acquire a negative connotation until the time of the European Enlightenment, when the term came to be identified with intolerance. Against the backdrop of an era of religious strife in post-Reformation Europe, issues of personal liberty and tolerance gained prominence, and aggressive evangelism or religious pressure began to be viewed as disruptive of peace.[15] Enlightenment philosophers tended to equate proselytism with religious fanaticism. This negative meaning of proselytism has been carried over to the English language as a pejorative connotation, suggesting a coercive or manipulative activity that seeks to change the religious allegiance of another. It is sometimes used in a disparaging sense as referring to unworthy or fraudulent means employed to win over or persuade the *proselytizee* to the faith of the *proselytizer*. In the minds of many proselytizing is not ordinarily seen as a good thing, especially if it involves "evangelistic malpractice" such as

---

[14] Eugene P. Heideman, "Proselytism, Mission, and the Bible," *International Bulletin of Missionary Research* 20 (1996): 10-12.

[15] David Kerr, "Christian Understanding of Proselytism," 8.

intimidation, coercion, economic enticement, and similar practices.[16] But the difficulty here is that "intimidation, coercion, manipulation and enticement" are categories seldom defined or distinguished and are elusive to prove without psychologizing their meaning. *Proselytism* implies persuasion, but at what point instances of authentic persuasion become real or perceived intimidation or subtle coercion cannot be determined in the abstract.[17] There is a genuine temptation to view whatever claims one disapproves of, rejects or feels uncomfortable with, as proselytism.

The category of *proselytism* therefore implies a moral judgment. Those who disapprove of proselytizing activities tend to make a moral judgment about the intent and integrity of the proselytizer. Advocates of proselytism, too, are engaged in moral judgment about the religion of the *proselytizee* as wrong, deficient or unsatisfactory while seeing the rightness, fullness and propriety of the beliefs and values of the *proselytizer*.[18] There is an implied moral, theological or religious superiority of the proselytizer and conversely, the inferiority of the proselytizee.

What complicates a clear understanding of *proselytism* is as much a matter of perspective as it is of improper method. Changes in religious affiliation or membership can happen through spontaneous conversion or through external inducements. What constitutes sacred duty or obedience to the evangelistic mandate for one group appears as improper proselytizing to another. There is no rigorous legal distinction between *proselytism* and *evangelism,* therefore Christian missionaries accuse other denominations or evangelical groups of engaging in the former while the latter is what they themselves claim. Within Christian denominations proselytism often implies "sheep stealing," finding converts to one's confession among members of – "belonging to" – another Christian confession. The history of Christian missions past and present is replete with examples of such activities and accusations. The growth of certain "Mega Churches" in recent times is attributed to their

---

[16] Cecil M. Robeck Jr., "Mission and the Issue of Proselytism," *International Bulletin of Missionary Research* 20 (1996): 1.

[17] Paul J. Griffiths and Jean Bethke Elshtain, "Proselytizing for Tolerance," *First Things* 127 (Nov. 2002): 30-36.

[18] Ibid., 31.

drawing members away from other established churches through effective marketing, the use of glitzy mass media and a strong appeal to switch denominational affiliation.

Proselytism, Religious Freedom, and Human Rights

Proselytism, whether proper or improper, legitimate or illegitimate, does raise issues of religious freedom. A free exercise of one's religion can be an intrusion into the privacy or group identity of another. Proselytism thus raises serious questions about issues of human rights pertaining to religious freedom, understood both as *freedom of religion* and *freedom from religion*. The exercise of the freedom *of* religion includes the right to profess, practice and propagate, and the freedom *from* religion implies the right *not* to be coerced or persuaded into accepting religious beliefs and behavior. The 1948 *Universal Declaration of Human Rights* affirms "the right to freedom of thought, conscience and religion," adding that "this right includes the freedom to change [one's religion or belief]."[19]

Those who argue for legal restrictions on missionary activity, however, cite the 1966 *International Covenant on Civil and Political Rights*, which reaffirms the right of religious freedom by stating, "This right shall include freedom to have or to adopt a religion or belief of [one's] choice." At the same time, the covenant specifically prohibits coercion: "No one shall be subject to coercion which should impair his [sic] freedom to have or to adopt a religion or belief of his choice."[20] In subsequent international discussions on religion and human rights (especially in the 1981 *Declaration on the Elimination of All Forms of Intolerance and Discrimination Based on Religion or Belief*) there is no reference to the right to change or adopt a religion. It is simply stated that one has the right "to have a religion or whatever belief of one's choice,"

---

[19] Article 18. See, Johan van der Vyver, "Religious Freedom and Proselytism: Ethical, Political and Legal Aspects," *Ecumenical Review*, 50:4, 419-429.

[20] Brian Dickerson, "The United Nations and the Freedom of Religion." *International and Comparative Law Quarterly*, 1995, cited by David Kerr, "Christian Understanding of Proselytism," 12.

reiterating that this choice must not be impaired by any form of coercion.[21] In international law there seems to be a "shift from an emphasis on the freedom to change a religion, to an emphasis on the freedom to retain a religion."[22]

This brief discussion with reference to international law suggests an inherent tension that freedom to have or adopt a religion or belief necessarily entails the freedom to choose a religion or belief. The right to replace one's current religion or belief with another, or to adopt atheistic views, entails also the right to retain one's religion or belief. Thus the problem of proselytism is invariably a *clash between rights*. In religiously pluralistic societies it is not easy to find balance or determine which right should prevail in concrete situations.[23]

Proselytism becomes an even more difficult issue when one recognizes that religious communities have different understandings of conversion *into* and *out of* faith. The right to abandon and adopt another religion or the right to remain without a religion is not readily accepted in some religious communities. Apostasy and heresy are punishable offences in some religious communities, as in Islam, while conversion into the community is welcomed. Such beliefs and practices, it must be remembered, were once part of history of the church in Medieval Europe; heresy and theological dissent were repressed or received harshest sanctions, including torture and burning at the stake.

While *conversion* is central to Christian faith (also to Islam and Judaism), not all religious faiths have a similar understanding. In Hindu and Buddhist traditions conversion is inconceivable in the sense of an abrupt or radical change in beliefs, but is rather an evolutionary progression of beliefs that lead to self-realization. The Hindu objection to proselytism is summarized by a well-known Indian philosopher:

> Hinduism is wholly free from the strange obsession of some faiths that the acceptance of a particular religious

---

[21] For an excellent analysis of religion and human rights issues, see Nathan Lerner, *Religion, Beliefs and International Human Rights* (Maryknoll, N.Y.: Orbis, 2000).

[22] David Kerr, "Christian Understanding of Proselytism," 12.

[23] For an excellent analysis of religion and human rights issues, see Nathan Lerner, *Religion, Beliefs and International Human Rights* (Maryknoll, N.Y.: Orbis, 2000).

metaphysic is necessary for salvation, and non-acceptance thereof is a heinous sin meriting eternal punishment in hell. Here and there outbursts of sectarian fanaticism are found [in Hinduism]...but the main note of Hinduism is one of respect and good will for other creeds.[24]

In a similar vein Mahatma Gandhi opposed the Christian view of conversion and said, "I am against conversion, whether it is known as *shuddhi* by Hindus, *tabligh* by Mussalmans or proselytizing by Christians."[25] The evangelistic outreach by Indian Christians therefore has often come under deep suspicion by the dominant Hindu majority in India because the Christian faith is identified with the religion of the colonizer. Christian propagation of the gospel and conversion of Hindus are seen as unwarranted judgment and denigration of ancient Indian beliefs and values. Hindu resentment, sporadic violent reaction against Christian evangelistic activities, and laws that prohibit or restrict conversions to Christianity (or Islam) passed by certain Indian States in recent years are based on the assumption that religious faith is something inherited from one's ancestors, which cannot be rejected in favor of another.

In the Hindu world-view, and from the perspective of some Asian religions and philosophies, religion represents a tradition (Sanskrit, *sampradaya*) and therefore cannot be false. A religious tradition represents the collective experience of a people, therefore the idea of a single religion or an exclusive allegiance to one particular faith for humankind appears illogical. From this perspective religious belief is not a matter of individual choice or a personal affair but rather an assent to communally sanctioned values and commitments. Proselytism, therefore, is vehemently opposed in the interest of protecting communal or cultural identity. *Conversion* invariably implies a rejection of ancestral heritage and turning against it, so has acquired a negative or pejorative connotation Hindus often reject arguments that support proselytism on the basis of international human rights law because of their

---

[24] S. Radhakrishnan, *The Hindu View of Life* (New York: Macmillan, 1964), 28.

[25] M. K. Gandhi, cited in M. M. Thomas, *The Acknowledged Christ of the Indian Renaissance*, 2d ed. (Madras: Christian Literature Society, 1976), 209.

understanding that those laws operate on Western individualistic assumptions. Despite such rejections, the modern offshoots of Hindu traditions have indeed engaged in overt proselytism, as is demonstrated in the Hare Krishna movement. This suggests that religious traditions, notwithstanding their historical claims, can and do engage in proselytism in situations where they find themselves in the minority or for reasons of self-preservation.

Ecumenical Perspectives

In Christian ecumenical discussions *proselytism* has often surfaced as a subject of discussion. Soon after its formation, as early as 1954, the World Council of Churches (WCC) responded to intra-Christian proselytism and produced a study on *Christian Witness, Proselytism, and Religious Liberty*.[26] This was one of the first documents to draw the distinction between authentic Christian witness and proselytism. The early WCC discussions were primarily intra-Christian focused on issues of proselytism among Protestants and Roman Catholics. In subsequent discussions of proselytism both interreligious and intra-Christian dimensions were included.

The intra-Christian problem of proselytism ("sheep stealing") was addressed in ecumenical conversation between Protestant churches associated with the WCC and Roman Catholic and Orthodox communions. In later discussion the issue was with the evangelical "invasion" of traditionally Catholic or Orthodox territories. In a study document entitled, *Towards Responsible Relations in Mission*, a WCC working group employed the term "invasion" to describe the "pain that unilateral and insensitive mission activity has caused" by sects and new religious movements. The document affirmed that the "commitment to evangelism is inseparable from the commitment to the unity of the Christian body."[27] At the Fifth World conference on the Faith and Order of the WCC in 1993 in Santiago de Compostela, the issue of proselytism,

---

[26] World Council of Churches, *Ecumenical Review*, 9 (Oct. 1956): 48-56.

[27] For a detailed discussion on the subject, see Cecil M Robeck Jr., "Mission and The Issue of Proselytism," *International Bulletin of Missionary Research* (January 1996): 2-8.

including coercive and manipulative methods in the act of evangelism, was seen as a distortion of the "real though distorted *koinonia* that Christians already share."[28]

As regards interreligious proselytism, the WCC discussions have repeatedly affirmed that the Church has a mission and it cannot be otherwise, while remaining critical of coercive proselytism. The most vexing issue affecting ecumenical discussion, creating a divide between evangelicals and other Protestant communions, pertains to Christian proselytism among Jews. With the memory of the Holocaust still fresh in the minds of Christians there has been considerable hesitancy among some Protestants to engage in proselytizing Jews. There have been calls to proscribe such activity. However, those of evangelical orientation have been more insistent on obedience to the Great Commission by evangelization of "all" people. The missionary character of the church has never been questioned in Protestant ecumenical discussions, in spite of the emerging emphasis on interreligious dialogue in churches. There is a vigorous debate among many Christians about the place of proselytism/evangelism in relation to interreligious dialogue.

The Roman Catholic views, beginning with the Vatican II document *Ad Gentes* (1965) and the various Papal encyclicals (*Evangelii Nuntiandi*, 1975 and *Redemptoris Missio*, 1990), have never wavered in their affirmation of the "permanent validity of the Church's missionary mandate."[29] This missionary mandate is directed toward "non-Christians" (without definition). The Papal Encyclical, *Redemptoris Missio*, is critical of "proselytism by sects," while at the same time affirming the right to religious freedom and freedom of conscience. It defends the Church's right to convert people and claims that interreligious dialogue is "part of the Church's evangelizing mission." Interestingly, the Encyclical acknowledges that "followers of other religions can receive God's grace and be saved by Christ apart from ordinary means, which he has established does not thereby cancel the call

---

[28] Thomas F Best and Günther Gassmann, eds, *On The Way to Fuller Koinonia*, Faith and Order Paper no 166 (Geneva: WCC Publications, 1994), 256.

[29] For a detailed survey of Roman Catholic, Evangelical, Orthodox and Protestant Conciliar views on proselytism, see Joel Nichols, "Mission, Evangelism and Proselytism in Christianity: Mainline Conceptions as Documented in Church Documents," *Emory International Law Review*, 12: 563-656.

to faith and Baptism that God wills for all people."[30] The document does not address the implicit theological ambiguity of such statements.

It is evident from the preceding sketchy description of Protestant and Roman Catholic views on proselytism that there is clear consensus; any activity deemed coercive, unethical and manipulative or that violates the religious freedom of people is unacceptable. At the same time, Protestant and Roman Catholic (not to mention Evangelical) Christian views have consistently maintained the right to mission, evangelism and conversion as an inalienable right, central to the identity and claims of the Christian faith. In sum, ecumenical perspectives lift up the same tensions as found in international law regarding two competing freedoms, the freedom to practice one's faith and the freedom to change one's religion, and seek to maintain two competing theological commitments, that is, the right to witness/evangelize/mission and the right to practice and remain in one's religion.

Pluralistic Assumptions

As noted earlier, the emergence of a pluralistic consciousness among Western Christians has made many uneasy with proselytism because of its hegemonic assumptions. Proselytism, it has been argued, seeks homogeneity and resists the continued presence of the other. It wants to create "one world" based on the exclusive claim of *'one* prophet, *one* text and *one* church," as the Hindu critic Arun Shourie summarizes.[31] Pluralism celebrates diversity, individual autonomy and freedom, including the freedom to decide and choose one's beliefs without external persuasion and the promptings of a proselytizer. Pluralism values the religious privacy of the individual and prefers not to disrupt or disrespect established religious traditions and values or violate religious boundaries and exploit insecurities of people. By its very nature pluralism is bewildering, dizzying or unsettling to those who are religiously insecure or unsure, whose anxieties are provoked and challenged by the proselytizer.[32]

---

[30] Ibid., 587.
[31] Cited in Sebastian Kim, *In Search of Identity*, 143.
[32] For an insightful analysis of pluralistic assumptions, see Martin E. Marty,

On the other hand, pluralism in open societies invariably invites interreligious or intercultural encounter, engagement or jostling, therefore, in pluralistic societies it seems religious privacy is structurally impossible. Pluralism invariably evokes comparison between divergent beliefs and claims, and implicitly questions all absolute claims to belief and authority. In secular societies we are constantly subjected to all forms of persuasion, whether political or commercial, in everyday life. Pluralism, willy-nilly, undermines or questions our sense of religious autonomy and invites us to either associate or disassociate with competing worldviews, religious or otherwise. It radically challenges claims of religious exclusivism and demands consideration of alternative beliefs and values. Pluralism can indeed be bewildering in that it can either push one toward religious relativism or absolutism. It is not at all surprising, therefore, that pluralism paradoxically creates fundamentalism.

In a pluralistic age, which celebrates freedom and autonomy, pluralism itself can however, become an agent of proselytism, that is, it becomes a belief system or an ideology. Recognition of pluralism can be liberating to those caught in the tyranny of a religion or the captivity of a religious culture, but pluralism can also become a static or stagnant reality if it forecloses the possibly of conversion or change in religious beliefs. The claims of pluralism may very well serve as an antidote to hegemonic assumptions of proselytizing religions, but pluralism can itself become a hegemonic ideology, thus relegating religious beliefs and claims to remain in their respective ghettos or pushing them into cultural isolation or insulation. Absolute pluralism without the possibility of religious conversion to another faith, belief or ideology may well make our world rather stale and comatose.

Conclusion

The preceding analysis has explored the discord between proselytism and pluralism without resolving it. In an era of globalization

---

"Introduction: Proselytizers and Proselytizees on the Sharp Arête of Modernity," in *Sharing the Book, Religious Perspectives on the Rights and Wrongs of Proselytism*, eds. John Witte Jr. and Richard C. Martin (Maryknoll, N.Y.: Orbis, 1999), 1-14.

of religions the proselytizing impulse is no longer restricted to the convert seeking religions, instead all religious faiths have now exhibited a missionary impulse in response to the reality of pluralism. Our world of religious pluralism offers unprecedented choices in beliefs and values, so that proselytism becomes a necessary corollary of pluralism. Those with insecure identities may find proselytism a threat to religious or cultural self-preservation, but the etiquette of pluralism demands sensitivity to issues of religious identity and highlights the necessity of interreligious engagement as we address unethical or coercive aspects present in the proselytizing activities of religious faiths.

It is the very nature of pluralism to demand public accountability of faiths in the presence of the "other" in the religious market place. This accountability involves articulation of one's faith in relation to the other and not in the privacy of one's sanctuaries. Proselytism, evangelism and witness, call it what you will, is an unavoidable aspect of social and religious life. That said, whether "organized" or "strategized," proselytizing activities that target people or groups of people ("reaching the unreached") – whether undertaken by mission societies, churches, Mosques or Islamic centers – remain a legitimate issue for further discussion. Perhaps the era of "global mission," supported and sponsored by mission societies and agencies, has come to an end, and the overly optimistic claim of the Edinburgh Conference, "Evangelization of the world in our generation," will forever be an unfulfilled prophecy. The age of pluralism and the globalization of religions may have put the brakes on Christian assault of the religious and cultural space of others. Nonetheless, a more sober and critical assessment of the meaning of Christian mission and evangelism in a pluralistic age will continue to be on the Christian agenda as we commemorate the centenary of the Edinburgh conference of 1910.

Part Four

Orchestrating and Conspiring with Others: Conversations with Companions on the Journey

Chapter 14.

Requiem Mess:
The Bitter Medicine of Religious Change

James Treat

I first crossed paths with Fumitaka Matsuoka in 1992 when he returned to Pacific School of Religion as the academic dean. I was finishing up my doctoral dissertation at the time and serving as teaching assistant for Choan-Seng Song, the distinguished theologian and church leader from Taiwan. The following spring I began teaching Native American studies at UC Santa Cruz, two hours to the south. I nurtured my spirit by making regular pilgrimages back to Holy Hill, and in the fall of 1994 Fumitaka hired me to teach a course on Native Americans and Christianity. On two subsequent occasions I was invited to offer a condensed version of this course during the Cooperative Summer Session. So I have known Fumitaka as administrator, advocate, and friend; a collegial academic who understands that any authentic North American theology must account for the Native American experience.

What follows was written during my time in Berkeley, for an advanced seminar on Third World theologies. How should we evaluate theological propositions in light of cultural difference and colonial conflict? Having earlier concluded that biculturalism offers the best route to liberating conceptions of Native Christian faith, I finally acknowledged the limits of biculturalism and argued for the indigenization of Native Christianities as an organic, autonomous, open-ended process. My research and writing have continued to cross back and forth between domestic and transnational contexts, a cosmopolitan dialectic roused by kindred spirits such as Fumitaka Matsuoka and Choan-Seng Song. But be forewarned, dear reader: Native Americans were not Asia's second sons sent packing across the Bering land bridge, and we are not just another American minority group. There will be no simple solidarity between indigenous peoples and immigrants, subaltern or otherwise.

The Bitter Medicine of Religious Change

The Canadian film *Where the Spirit Lives*,[1] winner of the award for Best Feature-Length Film at the 1989 American Indian Film Festival, recounts the story of Ashtoh-Komi and her experiences in a missionary-run boarding school. Set in 1937, the fictionalized drama is based on actual events in the lives of Native children from the prairie provinces of Canada, and it faces squarely the complexities of the cultural, spiritual, and even physical genocide encountered by these children. The film also raises serious questions about the nature of the Christian faith and its place in a world indelibly marked by cultural pluralism.

As the film begins we observe Ashtoh-Komi, twelve years old and living among her Blackfoot people, playing with her brother and other children around their remote Rocky Mountain encampment. They are intrigued by the sight of an approaching seaplane, which lands on a nearby lake and taxis to the shore near them. After enticing several of the children into the plane by singing a frolicking Irish folk song and offering them pieces of brightly colored candy, the pilot locks the cabin door and proceeds to read aloud (in English) the government decree which states that they are required by law to receive a proper English education. The scene's obvious parallels to sixteenth-century Central America, where Spanish priests recited the *Requerimiento* to Indians before loosing the soldiers on them, are chilling.[2] Thus begins Ashtoh-

---

[1] *Where the Spirit Lives*, videotape, directed by Bruce Pittman (Amazing Spirit Productions, 1989).

[2] Wilcomb E. Washburn, ed., *The Indian and the White Man* (Garden City, New Jersey: Anchor Books, 1964), 307-309. A portion of the *Requerimiento* reads as follows: "One of these pontiffs, who succeeded that St. Peter as lord of

Komi's long and brutal journey into a foreign and unforgiving world, a world that would attempt to change her very spirit—or destroy her in the process.

The festival program encapsulates well what follows for Ashtoh-Komi and her friends: "Few incidents in the history of Canada's Native policies are as heinous as the one on which 'Where the Spirit Lives' is based: determined to instill in Native children a sense of white, Christian values, the government empowered agents to virtually abduct children from communities disregarding orders to send their young to English schools. Their ties to family and tradition cut, their language forbidden, Native children found themselves in remote schools where they were force-fed the bitter medicine of a Christian missionary education."[3] Bitter medicine indeed. During her time at the mission school Ashtoh-Komi finds that the other children are struggling against the same cultural bulldozer she faces. One friend experiences only confusion in trying to understand and establish her own identity, having been taken from her people as an infant and deprived of even their memory. Another girl suffers repeated sexual abuse at the hands of the dormitory matron until she finally escapes, only to be found several days later, having died from exposure. In one particularly disturbing scene, Ashtoh-Komi's idealistic young teacher is visiting with the school's headmaster/minister, who has taken up gardening as a way of coping with the remote, difficult life of the mission station. As the headmaster shows her some of his prize creations, the teacher is surprised at his obvious sense of accomplishment, commenting that the flowers look just like the profusion of plants growing wild on the prairie outside the mission grounds. Unperturbed by her naïveté, the headmaster replies that they may look alike but are actually quite different. He then calmly explains how he observes the utmost care for his plants as he digs them out of the

---

the world in dignity and seat which I have before mentioned, made donation of these isles and Terra-firma to the aforesaid king and queen and to their successors, our lords, with all that there are in these territories, *as is contained in certain writings which passed upon the subject as aforesaid, which you can see if you wish*...Wherefore, *as best we can* [i.e., spoken in Spanish and often without interpretation], we ask and require you that you consider what we have said to you, and that you take the time that shall be necessary to understand and deliberate upon it" (emphasis added).

[3] *American Indian Film Festival* program, 1989.

prairie sod, carefully cleans their roots so that not even a trace of dirt remains, and then plants them in the rich, clean soil of his garden plot. The teacher smiles politely, but as she realizes that the only distinction he is making is a moral one, the expression on her face changes from incredulity to fear.

I. Predicament: Discontinuity

Where the Spirit Lives highlights the complex issues involved in the meeting of two very different cultures and their accompanying religious traditions, issues that are complicated even further by the presence of an inequitable power relationship. It presents dual historical realities: an indigenous tribal culture clinging tenaciously to the vestiges of longstanding traditions and practices, and an invading Christian culture proceeding on the basis of a sadistic, even demonic, superiority complex. Both cultures find themselves not only facing each other but also confronted with the ideological predicament posed by their confluence, the predicament of cultural discontinuity.

While the film is a moving portrayal that all viewers can appreciate and be affected by, it is also especially painful in different ways for two particular audiences. For Natives, many of whom have firsthand experience with Indian residential schools (the last mission boarding schools in Canada were closed in 1988; some still exist in the United States), the film is a painful reminder of family, language, spirituality, and culture now forgotten or lost. For Christians, few of whom have firsthand knowledge of Indian missions, the film is indisputable evidence of yet another regrettable chapter in the history of the Western missionary enterprise. If Natives and Christians share one thing in their relationship to the events this film portrays, it is that these events constitute inescapable dimensions of their respective histories. Just as Natives must attempt to fashion individual and tribal identities out of the cultural remnants that have survived the centuries-long drive toward assimilation, so Christians must search for a basis for the proclamation of good news in the wake of so much news that has been irredeemably bad.

Christians often attempt to deal with the negative dimensions of their own history by drawing a distinction between the *ideals* of the gospel message as preached and practiced by Jesus and the *actions* of professing Christians as witnessed in history. "I'm not perfect, just forgiven," they proclaim. "Don't blame God for the mistakes of Christians." But such a superficial reading of the dilemma fails to satisfy all but the most thoroughly indoctrinated. The Seneca chief Red Jacket could draw on nearly two centuries of his people's experience with the Europeans when, in 1805, he responded to a British missionary's request for permission to establish evangelistic work among the Seneca. Red Jacket pointed out that his people already had a religion they were satisfied with, "which was given to our forefathers and has been handed down to us their children." Still, he was willing to consider the missionary's message, with one stipulation:

> We understand that your religion is written in a book... We only know what you tell us about it. How shall we know when to believe, being so often deceived by the white people? ...We are told that you have been preaching to the white people in this place. These people are our neighbors. We are acquainted with them. *We will wait a little while, and see what effect your preaching has upon them. If we find it does them good, makes them honest and less disposed to cheat Indians; we will then consider again of what you have said.*[4]

The presumed distinction between ideals and actions thus fails to adequately address the dilemma posed by the historical record. It is an artifice because the ideals of the gospel message are not so transparent as to allow their satisfactory separation from the actions of Christians who have acted "in good faith" and from within the faith. The message and the messenger certainly are not indistinguishable, but they also are not completely distinct. To paraphrase Red Jacket, the crimes of Christians implicate the Christian God.

This line of thought points to what is perhaps for Christians the most challenging aspect of *Where the Spirit Lives*, which succeeds as a cinematic portrayal because it combines the cold reality of a documentary with the warm humanity of a drama. Without departing from the generalized historical facts, it establishes a perspective that allows the viewer to experience the events portrayed in their immediacy.

---

[4] Washburn, *The Indian and the White Man*, 212-213 (emphasis added).

Transported to another time and place, and forced to observe unfolding events from the inside out, the viewer finds himself deprived of the luxurious objectivity that detached historical retrospect normally affords. What are otherwise mere historical events become living, breathing realities, and the questions these past realities raise become present—and necessarily open—questions today. These open questions encapsulate the predicament of discontinuity contained in the nexus of culture and religion: (1) The plurality of cultures (including the discontinuity between cultures) challenges the validity of cultural norms and the transmissibility of cultural values as well as the exclusivity of culturally bound religious understandings of revelation, cosmology, history, society, and morality. (2) The barbarity of Western culture in its treatment of non-Western peoples (and even of marginalized groups within its own culture) indicts Christian religious institutions, which have enjoyed a symbiotic relationship with Western culture throughout the process. Tissa Balasuriya comments on the consequences of this development for Christian theology:

> It was a handmaid of Western expansion, an unwitting ally in the exploitation of peoples of other continents, first by Europeans and later by North Americans. The symbiosis of the 'sacred duty' of civilizing, baptizing, and saving pagans and the North Atlantic quest for military, economic, political, and cultural domination was disastrous for Christianity itself. It not only made many aspects of Christian theology unacceptable to the rest of humankind, but it also dehumanized the content of Western theology and blinded its practitioners to the cultural implications of what they—and others—were creating.[5]

---

[5] Tissa Balasuriya, "Why Planetary Theology?" in *Third World Liberation Theologies: A Reader*, ed. Deane William Ferm (Maryknoll, N.Y.: Orbis Books, 1986), 326. Balasuriya's point is well taken, but he is mistaken when he describes traditional Christian theology as the "unwitting" ally of Western expansion and exploitation. Western theologians from Juan Gines Sepulveda to the Dutch Reformed theologians of apartheid have known full well the consequences of their willingness to sacralize colonial empires.

It should be noted, though it is sometimes forgotten or ignored, that Western Christians are themselves culturally discontinuous with the cultural milieu of Jesus and the early church. Harold Turner points out that the great Western colonial/missionary adventure that began in the sixteenth century resulted in the *second* wave of geographic expansion. "The first gathered up the Mediterranean world and spread out to include the continent of Europe."[6] The Roman numeral "I" in the subheading above is symbolic of the discontinuity that is inescapable for Western Christians; imperial Roman culture was as discontinuous with that of the Hebrews as is Western culture with that of tribal societies. Western Christians no more "own" Jesus than non-Western Christians do.

But despite this reality and the diligent efforts of many non-Western Christians, the Christian religion continues to be controlled by Western institutions and ideas. The discontinuity between Western and non-Western cultures has been and continues to be a major impediment to the meaningful incarnation of the gospel message among non-Western peoples. Christians have attempted to respond to the predicament of discontinuity in a variety of ways, and three general types of response can be identified: conversion, biculturalism, and indigenization. The significance of the Western missionary enterprise for Native children like Ashtoh-Komi has been described as "bitter medicine"; of course, medicine comes in a variety of forms. If cultural discontinuity can be thought of as a *condition*, then the *remedy* has appeared in three qualitatively different varieties: placebo (conversion), palliative (bi-culturalism), and prescription (indigenization).

---

[6] Harold W. Turner, "A Further Dimension for Missions: New Religious Movements in the Primal Societies," *International Review of Mission* 62 (1973): 321. He goes on to make an interesting observation: "After the initial spread into the Mediterranean world, Christianity has depended in each [advance] upon alliance with a culture more sophisticated than that of the peoples it was winning... It moved into Europe in association with a Christianized Graeco-Roman culture, and into the wider world of the primal societies in alliance with the successor Western European culture it had helped to mould" (322).

Two. Placebo: Conversion

In medical terminology, a placebo is a substance or treatment that lacks intrinsic remedial value but which nevertheless has the capacity to effect relief, and even healing, under certain circumstances. The successful application of a placebo depends entirely on the psychological dimension of the doctor-patient relationship; only the ability of the doctor to project the belief that a placebo will work, and the willingness of the patient to accept this belief as true, can produce positive results. Of course, there are many medical conditions which require a physical cure and for which a placebo will be ineffective. But in many cases the successful application of a placebo is evidence of the degree to which a medical condition is either imagined or remedied by stimulation of the human body's own internal defenses. With few exceptions, the call to conversion issued by Western missionaries has required this kind of trusting acceptance of their message on the part of non-Western peoples. Conceived without reference to the presence of cultural discontinuity, this understanding of conversion has functioned for non-Western peoples as a religious placebo.

African theologians Rosemary Edet and Bette Ekeya raise the question of the "growing cultural alienation" present within Christian churches, "because evangelization has not been that of cultural exchange but of cultural domination or assimilation."[7] In his encounter with the British missionary Red Jacket experienced firsthand this particular evangelistic orientation. The missionary, having been afforded the opportunity to address a number of principal chiefs and warriors of the League of the Iroquois (an unusual honor), informed them of his objective—and of their condition:

> I had a great desire to see you, and inquire into your state and welfare; for this purpose I have travelled a great distance...

---

[7] Rosemary Edet and Betty Ekeya, "Church Women of Africa: A Theological Community," in *With Passion and Compassion: Third World Women Doing Theology*, eds. Virginia Fabella and Mercy Amba Oduyoye (Maryknoll, N.Y.: Orbis Books, 1988), 3.

> I have come…to enlighten your minds, and to instruct you on how to worship the Great Spirit agreeably to his mind and will, and to preach to you the gospel of his son Jesus Christ. There is but one religion, and but one way to serve God, and if you do not embrace the right way, you cannot be happy hereafter. *You have never worshipped the Great Spirit in a manner acceptable to him; but have, all your lives, been in great errors and darkness.* To endeavor to remove these errors, and open your eyes, so that you might see clearly, is my business.[8]

The missionary's promise that the Boston Missionary Society would continue to send them "good and faithful ministers, to instruct you and strengthen you in religion," would seem to promote the kind of relationship leading to the "theological begging" Albert Widjaja sees as "one of the major outcomes of the Western missionary endeavor."[9]

Instead of addressing the predicament of cultural discontinuity and the issues thus raised, Western missionaries have usually conceptualized the terms of conversion in a way symbolized by the English word "two" in the subheading above. Conversion requires not only new beliefs and thoughts but a new *language* to express them with as well. In pressing for new patterns of communication, diet, dress, settlement, family structure, education, livelihood, artistic expression, economic relations, and political organization, missionaries have believed they will hasten the maturation of religious ideas and attitudes which they have assumed are inextricably embedded in "Christian civilization." Their understanding of conversion as an all-encompassing process, rather than as a sharply focused event, has led to the implicit goal of making non-Western peoples Western, of making Native Americans white. Despite their success at forcibly changing many outward patterns of behavior, however, they have been unable to penetrate that part of the human person "where the spirit lives." Conversion thus remains a religious placebo, dependent for success upon

---

[8] Washburn, *The Indian and the White Man*, 209-210 (emphasis added).
[9] Albert Widjaja, "Beggarly Theology: A Search for a Perspective toward Indigenous Theology," in *Third World Liberation Theologies: A Reader*, 368.

the cooperative belief by missionary and convert that it is the appropriate remedy for the condition of cultural discontinuity.

Tutcenen. Palliative: Biculturalism

Many non-Western peoples have converted (voluntarily) or been converted (coercively) to the Christian faith, though oftentimes not to the extent hoped for by Western missionaries. Most of these converts have chosen to retain or to recover many of their cultural and religious traditions while accepting other cultural and religious features of the Western world. They have elected to live in two cultures, to become bicultural. The Muscogee word *tutcenen* (three) in the subheading above symbolizes the nature of biculturalism for many Native Americans. By adopting the use of the English alphabet for their own language, Muscogee people have developed a form of communication that they did not possess before contact with the Western world. Though many Muscogees understand and use English, their indigenous language has not only survived but has actually been strengthened by the establishment of a written tradition.

But humans and human societies cannot remain forever in the tension found between two distinct cultural influences; every person and society is marked by an instinctive drive for a unified, internalized identity. Though it does possess remedial value, biculturalism is nothing more than a palliative, a temporary solution that can mitigate the effects of cultural discontinuity. It eases the pain induced by symptoms without curing the condition that causes them.

John Snow, Chief of the Wesley Band of the Stoney Indians and an ordained minister in the United Church of Canada, has recorded the history of his people's struggle for survival in the midst of Canadian society. Tribal self-government was finally returned to the Stoneys in 1969, and Snow explains how they responded to the opportunity for rebirth:

> The basic problem, we realized, was to rebuild the shattered Stoney tribal society. It was a must to rebuild our once proud society if we were to be successful in the new venture.

> Part of the solution to this was that the harsh realities of the twentieth century had to be faced squarely by our people...
>
> But, although we had to accept the dominant economy, technology, and legal system surrounding us, we did not have to accept all its cultural assumptions. The Stoney Indians' culture, language, and religion have been threatened ever since the white man arrived on this Great Island. With his excessive dependence on technology, restrictive legislation, greedy individualism, and smug certainty that he knows all the answers—even in religion—he has been a real and constant threat to our cooperative communal outlook, our respect for nature, and our value system. With the coming of self-government and a measure of self-determination, we did not have to accept this.
>
> *In other words, we came to understand that it was not an either-or choice: acculturation to the dominant society or clinging to our old ways in a world where they could no longer offer us and our children a good life. We came to understand that there was a third way—the way of biculturalism. We came to understand that we could still follow Stoney tribal custom but, at the same time, adjust to a technological age on our own terms. Our hope was (and still is) to retain the best in the Stoney culture and to take the best in the dominant culture.*[10]

Biculturalism is thus a process, the selective construction of a society out of the building blocks found in two distinct cultures, two cultures which both contain elements useful in dealing with present realities. Allan Boesak takes this position when he says he believes that, in addition to the biblical revelation, "both our traditional [African]

---

[10] John Snow, *These Mountains Are Our Sacred Places* (Toronto, Ontario: Samuel-Stevens, 1977), 123 (emphasis added).

religion and our traditional thinking have a liberating and humanizing word to say to our situation."[11]

The logo for a new Native American ministries program at a Baptist seminary illustrates the way biculturalism has functioned for many Christian Indians: a medicine wheel and a cross are superimposed, sharing only a common central point. This drawing was the winning entry in a competition searching for a design "which best symbolizes the Christian faith in American Indian cultural forms,"[12] that is to say, an indigenized Indian Christianity. The winning entry, therefore, does not actually satisfy the basic criteria of the competition; this drawing symbolizes biculturalism, not indigenization. Both the medicine wheel (symbol of traditional Indian religions) and the cross (symbol of the Christian religion) have been retained intact. Neither has changed; the two symbols are merely superimposed. Herein lies the tension contained in biculturalism, and until the two symbols can be synthesized the tension will remain. Biculturalism may be an indefinite but not a permanent condition; it is a transitional stage in the evolution of a single, unified identity. Biculturalism thus remains a religious palliative, useful as a treatment for the symptoms of cultural discontinuity but not as a cure for the condition.

---

[11] Allan Boesak, "Liberation Theology in South Africa," in *Third World Liberation Theologies: A Reader*, 271. Unfortunately, Boesak contradicts himself later when he asserts that the word of God is "the word that speaks to our total human condition and offers salvation that is total, complete. For us today this means that, although the Bible is not a handbook for politics or economics, *it nonetheless reveals all we need to know about God's will for the whole of human existence, including the spiritual, political, economic, and social well-being.*" Allan Boesak, "Black and Reformed: Contradiction or Challenge?" in *Third World Liberation Theologies: A Reader*, 275 (emphasis added). If God has already spoken comprehensively and finally through the Bible, then the "liberating and humanizing word" of African traditional religion would seem to be superfluous at best.

[12] *Central Baptist Theological Seminary Voice*, February 1989, 7.

IV. Prescription: Indigenization

In recent years both Western missionaries and non-Western converts have admitted the presence of cultural discontinuity and have called for the indigenization of Christian faith. As Manas Buthelezi has observed, this new approach has assumed the proportions of "an occupational pet-project of missionaries who have suddenly become aware of the fact that they have to change the content of their leadership role during the passing of the 'missionary era' if they want to have a place in the postcolonial dispensation at all."[13] Indigenization has thus become the prescription for the condition of cultural discontinuity. It is seen as the remedy that will bring together two cultures and allow for a more authentic expression of religious identity.

Non-Western Christians are divided on the question of whether the process of indigenization must be induced or whether it has a life of its own. Mercy Amba Oduyoye suggests that indigenization requires a conscious decision on the part of the theologian: "To contribute more effectively to the religious development of people, African Christian theologians have *a duty to theologize from this context and incorporate the authentic African idiom into Christian theology.*"[14] Kosuke Koyama, on the other hand, argues, "It is wrong to say that we must produce an indigenous theology. It is not necessary to produce one. It is there!"[15]

---

[13] Manas Buthelezi, "Toward Indigenous Theology in South Africa," in *Third World Liberation Theologies: A Reader*, 208. Later he suggests a reason for their enthusiasm: "There is a sense in which one can say that when the missionaries seem to be presumptuous in suggesting 'indigenous theology' to the African, they are, strictly speaking, looking for a solution to problems that stem from their own psychological 'hang-ups.' The missionaries have therefore to play a leading role in the formulation of indigenous theology in order to make sure that it solves their own problems as well. The suggestion here is that when the Africans seem to be encouraged to produce indigenous theology, they are just being used—as they have always been—to solve the psychological problems of the missionaries" (Buthelezi, 211).

[14] Oduyoye, "The Value of African Religious Beliefs and Practices for Christian Theology," in *Third World Liberation Theologies: A Reader*, 247. This statement is curious since earlier she asks, "Is syncretism not in fact a positive and unavoidable process?" (Oduyoye, 245).

[15] Kosuke Koyama, "Aristotelian Pepper and Buddhist Salt," in *Third World Liberation Theologies: A Reader*, 291.

Perhaps both are right; the best approach to indigenization may be to recognize what has already taken place and to encourage that even more be accomplished.

The Cherokee word "ᏅᏯ" (four) in the subheading above symbolizes the process of indigenization among Native Americans. The inventor of the Cherokee syllabary was Sequoyah, who as a young man had noticed the power that literacy gave to whites. Without an education or the knowledge of English, Sequoyah created a written language consisting of eighty-five characters, and within a few years of its official adoption in 1822 the majority of his people could read and write. Sequoyah had taken the *idea* of literacy and, using letters he had seen in Hebrew, Greek, and English texts as well as his own invented forms, created a means of expression appropriate for his own language.

The process of indigenization implies the continuation of religious change with the objective of resolving the condition of cultural discontinuity. Unless it is to be a false or superficial indigenization, it implies syncretism. Anthropologists and other scholars have observed the great variety of cultural and religious revivals that have occurred among non-Western peoples during the colonial/missionary era, calling these revivals revitalization movements. Harold Turner has looked specifically at the religious dimension of these movements and suggests the following working definition for them: "A historically new religious phenomenon arising in the encounter of a primal society and its religion with one or more of the higher cultures and their major religions, and involving some substantial departure from the classical religious traditions of all the cultures concerned, in order to find renewal through a different religious system."[16] Though at times it may seem that indigenization is a practical, workable remedy for the condition of cultural discontinuity, it is this question of orthodoxy that presents the most serious complication. Any syncretistic religious movement that makes "substantial departure" from two "classical religious traditions" will likely find itself scorned by both. The Native American (or Peyote) Church, for example, incorporates elements of both Christian and indigenous belief and ritual in a pan-tribal religious movement. Yet

---

[16] Harold W. Turner, "A New Field in the History of Religions," *Religion: A Journal of Religion and Religions* 1, no. 1 (Spring 1971): 17.

today both traditional and Christian Indians continue to oppose the movement because of its doctrinal and liturgical deviations.

While many Christians accept the idea of indigenization as sound evangelistic strategy, its actual implementation is subject to intense scrutiny and criticism. Because the Christian religion does not possess a "core" that exists independent of cultural expression, at least not one that can be meaningfully expressed and understood by human beings, there are no culturally neutral criteria with which to evaluate the orthodoxy of indigenized Christian faith. Indigenization involves not only form but also content; it is an open-ended and uncontrollable process. Though indigenization is the correct prescription for the condition of cultural discontinuity, it is a remedy whose side effects cannot be fully known before its use.

V/Five/*Cvkepen*/ᏓᎰᏯ. Persistence and Permanence

Two decades after his encounter with the British missionary, Red Jacket was asked why he was so opposed to missionaries.

> They do us no good. If they are useful to the white people and do them good, why do they not keep them at home? They are surely bad enough to need the labor of everyone who can make them better. [The missionaries] know we do not understand their religion. We cannot read their book—they tell us different stories about what it contains, and we believe they make the book talk to suit themselves. The Great Spirit will not punish us for what we do not understand, and the light which they give us makes the straight and plain path, trod by our fathers, dark and dreary... We are few and weak, but may for a long time be happy if we hold fast to our country, and the religion of our fathers.[17]

---

[17] William L. Stone, *The Life and Times of Sa-Go-Ye-Wat-Ha, or Red Jacket* (Albany, NY: J. Munsell, 1866), 397-398.

Red Jacket's reply raises two open questions mentioned earlier as encapsulating the predicament of discontinuity contained in the nexus of culture and religion: (1) the plurality of cultures and the discontinuity between them, and (2) the barbarity of Western Christianity in its treatment of non-Western peoples. While the first challenges the assumed exclusivity of the Christian faith, the second questions the validity of its very existence.

Perhaps Rubem Alves is correct in saying that "we live amid the ruins of our religious expectations."[18] Conversion, as Western missionaries have conceived it, has met with some success, but many observers have noted that the missionary enterprise among Native Americans yielded "overall Christian results among the least impressive in modern mission history." The response "seems to have moved from earlier cooperation, through a long period of indifference and passivity, to the more recent vocal opposition and political activism that reassert Indian identity and the renewal of Indian culture within a plural society."[19] Biculturalism as it is expressed by Christian Indians has brought much-needed stability and health to individuals and communities, but it is a temporary solution that only postpones the deeper questions of identity and culture. The need for cultural and religious synthesis is addressed by the call for indigenization, but the very nature of the syncretistic process is such that it cannot be anticipated, organized, or carried out without jeopardizing its success and authenticity.

What we are left with, then, are more questions than answers concerning the ambiguous role of Christian faith in the midst of cultural discontinuity. The missionary enterprise lies in abject failure, having succeeded in converting vast numbers of people but only through the widespread destruction of human culture, human creativity, and even human life.

At the conclusion of *Where the Spirit Lives*, Ashtoh-Komi discovers that her parents and extended family are still alive in their home village. Earlier the school headmaster lies to her, saying that they have died in a smallpox epidemic; his strategy is to make her

---

[18] Rubem Alves, "From Paradise to the Desert: Autobiographical Musings," in *Third World Liberation Theologies: A Reader*, 98.

[19] Harold W. Turner, "Old and New Religions among North American Indians," *Missiology: An International Review* 1, no. 2 (April 1973): 54, 57.

"adjustment" to the life of mission school more permanent, and for a time it appears to have worked. Ashtoh-Komi learns to read and to write, and soon she is participating in chapel services, singing hymns and reciting bible verses. On the verge of being adopted by a white dowager, however, she finally discovers the truth about her family. Early the next morning she and her brother escape, and in the final scene her young teacher chases after them on the open prairie. Ashtoh-Komi is alarmed by the teacher's approach, but it soon becomes clear that she is sympathetic to their flight. Looking for some redeeming feature in this history, I found myself hoping that the teacher had come to offer her assistance in their long journey home, or perhaps to tell them that she had decided to fight for the release of the other children and for an end to the government and church policies that permitted the school to exist. But as she catches her breath, the teacher says only, "I have come to ask for your forgiveness." In searching for a basis for the proclamation of good news in the wake of so much news that has been irredeemably bad, perhaps this aspect of Christian faith is the most troublesome: the concern for culpability before the practice of charity. In light of Kosuke Koyama's probing question, "To what kind of spiritual and theological heritage am I heir?" this pitiful begging of forgiveness may be the best that Western Christians can aspire to. [20]

---

[20] Koyama, in *Third World Theologies: A Reader*, 288.

Chapter 15.

A *Bembe* for Chino Cubanos

Miguel A. De La Torre

Prior to the Cuban Revolution of 1959, years before dispossession and displacement, my parents rented an apartment in a six-story building off *Calle Zanja* (Zanja Street) on the border of *el barrio chino* (Chinatown). Cuba's Chinatown consisted of several blocks lined with Chinese restaurants, cultural centers, and businesses, considered at the time the largest Chinatown in all of Latin America. Today *el barrio chino* is a shadow of its pre-Revolutionary days. A large portion of Chinatown's inhabitants migrated to the United States shortly after the Revolution, leaving la Habana's *barrio chino* with about 400 native-born Chinese and approximately 2,000 descendants. When the Revolution nationalized their small businesses, many fled to Miami, New York, and Union City, New Jersey, seeking new opportunities – specifically in providing Cuban style Chinese cuisine, thus adding *restaurantes chino cubano* to the U.S. immigrant lexicon.

Shortly after the Revolution, my parents, along with their one-year-old child, joined the thousands who made the trek into exile. They traded the warmth of the Caribbean for the chill (climatically and socially) of New York City. We lived in the old tenement slums a few blocks from Hell's Kitchen. My earliest memories are of a rat and roach infested studio apartment with a communal bathroom down the public hallway shared by other tenants on the floor. Both my parents worked several jobs to make ends meet. But in spite of our poverty, every

Sunday we went out for dinner as a family. We would walk to *un restaurante chino cubano* that was located on 8th Avenue and 57th Street, a few blocks from Columbus Circle. (Today a fast food restaurant occupies the premises.) There we would enjoy *sopa china* (Chinese soup), special fried rice, and a side order of *plátanos maduros* (fried plantains). The menus were, of course, in Spanish. Imagine my surprise as I grew into adolescence and finally met other Chinese people living in New York City who couldn't speak Spanish. In my childlike worldview, to be Chinese was also to be Cuban.

This sentiment is shared by many *chino cubanos*. Take for example the testimony of Frances Bu, born in Cuba in 1956, who also migrated to New York City. "I hate to say that, but race is an American hang-up... It would bug the heck out of [us] to have somebody ask [us], 'What race are you?' Yet they've got to know what your race is. And in Cuba, everybody was Cuban... I never felt any different. I actually didn't realize that I wasn't Cuban. I always thought of myself as Cuban."[1]

And yet while *chino cubanos* were as Cuban as I, a concept I accepted in my pre-adolescent years, I still had to be taught how to "see" *chino cubanos* differently, as being less than what it means to be Cuban. Because they were neither white, black, nor *mulatto*, they failed to neatly fit the well-established Cuban racial categories that I was taught growing up. Nevertheless, our social network of light-skinned Cuban compatriots living throughout the five boroughs of New York during the sixties and seventies taught me how to gaze upon those Cubans who fell short of the Hispanic version of the white ideal. Asian physical features (as well as black skin pigmentation) were translated as being less than perfect, if not inferior.

As a Latino, specifically a Cuban, I am well aware of the web of oppression in which I am situated. Although discriminated against by Euroamerican social structures because I am Hispanic, I must admit that those same structures privilege me because I am light-skinned and male. Ironically, while all Hispanics find themselves in an oppressive Eurocentric social structure, still, internal forms of oppression are created depending on who falls closer to the Hispanic version of the white ideal. Within systems of oppression, the oppressions of others are usually

---

[1] Cynthia Ai-fen Lee, "Our Histories in Conversation" in *Tomie Arai: Double Happiness* (New York: Bronx Museum of the Arts, 1998), 46.

developed to benefit those who remain "honorable whites" because they lack African, Native, or Asian features. Due to the overall system of white supremacy, additional oppression of group members by those with lighter skin-pigmentation develops among Latina/os

How then, is the existing oppression against Asians constructed within the Hispanic community? Sandra Louk is a Miami owner of a *restaurante chino cubano* (along with her parents and brother). During an interview with the Spanish version of the *Miami Herald* Louk captures the disconnect felt by many *chino cubanos*: "I have never been able to feel as part of a group, neither with the Chinese, nor with the Americans, nor with the Cubans. But I identify more with the Cuban-Americans, although they see me as a Cuban Chinese."[2] Japanese American scholar, Fumitaka Matsuoka, asks how ethnicity informs the meaning of life for Asian Americans, what it means to live in the balance between two cultures or generations.[3] But what I want to ask is what does it mean to live in three or more cultures - not just Asian and American, but also Latina/o? How does ethnicity inform the meaning of life for Cuban Asian Americans? While Matsuoka attempts to understand people of Asian ancestries in the United States, I wonder how we can understand those people if they first stopped in a Latin American country (specifically Cuba) prior to their journey to the United States? Not only are they part of Asian and North American culture, they are also Hispanics.

In his attempt to create community amidst the memories of historical injuries, Matsuoka reminds us that "past oppression and injustice inflicted by the nation are also remembered mythically and in narrative form."[4] Concentrating on U.S. Executive Order 9066, which incarcerated Japanese Americans during the Second World War, he

---

[2] Minuca Villaverde, "Feliz Año del Jabalí," *El Nuevo Herald* (January 29, 1995).

[3] Fumitaka Matsuoka, "Churches and Seminaries in China: Personal Reflection," in *With Faith We Can Move Mountains: Reflections of GTU Asia Pacific Bridges Consultation in China, 1995*, ed. Judith A. Berling (Berkeley: Asia Pacific Bridges, 1996), 2.

[4] Fumitaka Matsuoka, "Creating Community Amidst the Memories of Historical Injuries," in *Realizing the America of Our Hearts*, eds. Fumitaka Matsuoka and Eleazar S. Fernandez (St. Louis, Missouri: Chalice Press, 2003), 37

explores "how collective memories and experiences of injustice, betrayal, and pain...help groups form their own identities and shaped their own perspectives for the understanding and interpretation of [his] society."[5] But what about historical injuries that occurred in other nations, specifically Latin American nations—in my case Cuba? Or what about the injuries that continues to occur within the U.S., not just those inflicted by Euroamericans, but by fellow Hispanics? Are these injustices also remembered; and if so, how? It would be presumptuous of me as a non-Asian, to attempt to describe or interpret Asian-Hispanic culture and society. But what I can do is recover how my Hispanic culture historically and presently privileged me at the expense of Asian Hispanics in order to uncover my complicity with internal Latina/o structures of oppression. By exposing the Latino/a complicity with Eurocentric structures that oppress others, I hope to advance a discourse concerning Asian Hispanics that seldom takes place.

Matsuoka asks, "How did we come to be as we presently are?"[6] Although he asks this question from a North American perspective, for purposes of this chapter we will ask the question from a Cuban perspective. And like him, we will look at how the experiences of Asians within Cuban culture can give rise to common narratives that can be woven into the larger mosaic of the Asian experience within the dominant Euroamerican experience. In honor of Fumitaka Matsuoka's retirement from the faculty of the Pacific School of Religion in Berkeley, California, it is my hope to engage in a conversation with Matsuoka, a dance if you will, to uncover the intra-structures of Hispanic oppression.

In effect I will be participating in a *bembe* with Matsuoka. *Bembes* are Afro-Cuban dance rituals that invite the *orishas* (quasi-deities of the Cuban religion Santería) to possess the dancers so that mere mortals can hear a word from the Divine. *Bembes* are intimate fluid dances where gods and human become one so that deeper wisdom can be obtained. Like any dancer, we are constantly navigating through a crowded floor. In our case, exploring the oppression of our Cuban Asian

---

[5] Ibid.

[6] Fumitaka Matsuoka, "Reformation of Identities and Values within Asian North American Communities," in *A Dream Unfinished: Theological Reflections on America from the Margins*, ed. Eleazar S. Fernandez and Fernando F. Segovia (Maryknoll, N.Y.: Orbis Books, 2001), 119.

roots requires us to dance around the meaning of identity and its intersection with race, ethnicity, and nationhood. To explore the Cuban Asian perspective is to ask what it means to be Cuban. I am convinced that the Hispanic Asian *comunidad* (community) has a word rooted in the Divine to share – a word that is not limited to Asian Cubans. To that end, this chapter will attempt to explore the web of intra-Hispanic oppressive structures (primarily Cuban), giving special attention to Hispanic Asians (specifically Chinese).[7]

Missing from the racial-ethnic discourse in both Latino/a and U.S. studies are the voices and experiences of Hispanic Asians. While *chino cubanos* are children of two cultural groups - Asian and Hispanic - they are ignored by both "parents" as part of, yet disconnected from, two ethnic groups, as expressed by restaurateur Sandra Louk. Few if any Asian Americans explore their Latino roots; and even less Hispanics have seriously considered their Asian roots.[8] Although the Asian Latino/a voice is not difficult to find, unlike Black or Native Hispanic conversations, few studies pay attention to the particular Asian Hispanic discourse. Even so, as Fabiana Chiu-Rinaldi reminds us, "Asian Latinos represent a unique link between two of the largest immigrant groups in the United States."[9] Therefore, this chapter will explore how the Chinese came to Cuba and the oppression they faced, along with their migration to the United States and how these Cuban Asians continue to find themselves oppressed by a Eurocentric dominant culture and a Latino/a disenfranchised community.

Cuba, it has been said, is a *mestizaje*, a mixture of cultures, people, races, and ethnicities. We are an *ajiaco* brewing on the Caribbean stove. *Ajiaco* is a native dish, a renewable Cuban stew consisting of different indigenous roots that symbolizes who we are as a people.

---

[7] The author recognizes the multiple and diverse voices existing among Hispanics from different nations of origins and the varied Asian people who settled in particular Latin American countries. Nevertheless, the focus of this chapter will be on the Chinese who first migrated to Cuba, and then to the United States.

[8] An exception is Rudy Busto who has written on the intersection of the Hispanic and the Asian community.

[9] Evelyn Hu-DeHart, "Asian Latinos" in *The Oxford Encyclopedia of Latinos and Latinas in the United States, Vo. 1.* eds. Suzanne Oboler and Deena J. González (New York: Oxford University Press, 2005), 125.

According to Cuban ethnographer Fernando Ortiz, the first to use the *ajiaco* metaphor to capture the Cuban experience, native Indians provided the *maíz, papa, malanga, boniato, yuca,* and *ají*. The Spaniards added *calabaza* and *nabo*, while the Chinese added Oriental spices. Africans, contributing *ñame* and their culinary foretaste, urged a meaning from this froth beyond mere clever cooking. In effect, we eat and are nourished by the combination of all of our diverse roots.[10]

Fernando Ortiz used the term *ajiaco* within the context of a Cuba composed of immigrants who, unlike those in the United States, reached the island on the way to somewhere else. His usage of *ajiaco* did not indicate his belief that Cuban culture achieved complete integration; rather, the *ajiaco* is still simmering, not yet reaching a full synthesis.[11] I have used this term to refer to the distinctive nexus of our people's roots; specifically our Native, African, Spaniard, Asian and Anglo roots; rather than accenting the immigrant's identity. While I portray the *ajiaco* metaphor as positive, Ortiz included a racist element in his ethnology. This is evident when he described the negative aspects of the *ajiaco*. He wrote:

> The white race influenced the Cuban underworld through European vices, modified and aggravated under certain aspects by the social factor of the children of the ambient. The black race provided its superstitions, its sensualism, its impulsiveness, in short, its African psyche. The yellow race brought the addiction of opium, its homosexual vices and other refined corruptions of its secular civilization.[12]

Furthermore, Ortiz advocated that immigration occur solely from Northern Europe in order to "sow among us the germs of energy, progress, life." For him, to continue accepting other races only increased criminality on the island of Cuba.[13]

---

[10] For a more detailed exploration of the *ajiaco* paradigm, see my earlier work *La Lucha for Cuba: Religion and Politics on the Streets of Miami* (Berkeley: University of California Press, 2003), specifically the first chapter.

[11] Fernando Ortiz, "Los factores humanos de la cubanidad," in *La Habana: Revista Bimestre Cubana* (XLV, 1940), 165-169.

[12] Fernando Ortiz, *Los negros brujos: Apuntes para un estudio de etnología criminal* (Miami: New House Publishers, [1906b] 1973), 19.

Ajiaco symbolizes our *cubanidad's* (Cuban community's) attempt to find harmony among our diverse roots. But *cubanidad* is more than just a Cuban community. For Ortiz, *cubanidad* is a "condition of the soul, a complexity of sentiments, ideas and attitudes."[14] Unlike the North American melting pot paradigm that insists that immigrants who arrive upon U.S. shores are somehow placed into a pot where they "melt down" into a new culture - that nevertheless remains Eurocentric in nature - an *ajiaco* retains the unique flavors of its diverse roots while enriching the other elements. While none of the inhabitants representing the "ingredients" originated from the Island, all repopulated the space called Cuba as displaced people.

The Asian roots added to our *ajiaco* occurred when Chinese laborers were brought to the island to work as indentured servants, an alternative to African slavery. As landowners moved away from a slave labor pool, a need to procure new domesticated workers arose. The opening of China to European penetration in the 1840s created a potential new source of labor as Asians were loaded at Maceo for the deadly journey eastward. As early as 1806 the first laborers arrived in the Caribbean (Trinidad). By 1847 the first 206 Chinese were brought to Cuba, a number that increased to 140,000 during the next two decades, surging in 1939 to more than 300,000. Although by treaty Chinese laborers were not to be regarded as slaves, the distinction between slave and indentured servant lay in semantics. The increase of Chinese laborers to Cuba (and other Latin American countries) was probably due to their exclusion from the United States after 1882. It is interesting to note that some became citizens of the Latin American country in which they happened to settle in order to facilitate their entrance into the United States, not as Chinese, but as Cubans, Mexicans, Peruvians, etc.

Coolies were technically "free," however their conditions were as horrific, if not worse than slavery. Although the word "Coolies" has been used as a racial slur, I use it here to refer to the Chinese laborers as this word best captures their social location of oppression. The word Coolie is composed of two Chinese characters, *coo* and *lie*. *Coo* is

---

[13] Fernando Ortiz, "La inmigración desde el punto de vista criminológico," *Derecho Sociogía 1* (May 1906a): 55-57.

[14] Fernando Ortiz, "La cubanidad y los negros," *Estudio Afrocubanos 3* (1939), 3.

defined as "suffering with pain;" *lie* means "laborer." Hence the Coolie is the "laborer who suffers with pain," adequately describing his/her condition in Cuba. Their painful suffering began before they even arrived on the Island to labor. Many died during their long voyage to Cuba, ironically on the same slave ships previously used to transport Africans. Similar to the slave ships that originally brought Africans, an iron grating kept Chinese separated from the quarterdeck, and cannons were positioned to dominate the decks in the event they rebelled. In some instances almost half the human cargo perished in transport. In a very real sense, just as a Middle Passage existed where many Africans died upon the slave ships transporting them, and were discarded in the Atlantic Ocean; so too was a Pacific Middle Passage created. One of the first shipments of Coolies that was procured by Waldrop and Company sailed from Amoy on February 7, 1853 with 803 Chinese and arrived in La Habana with 480. In 1859 the Spanish frigate *Gravina* embarked with 352 Chinese and arrived with only 82.[15]

For those who survived the journey, working conditions on the Cuban plantation were unbearable. Chinese laborers usually arrived in Cuba with an eight-year labor contract. Although they were supposedly free laborers, within the Cuban imagination they were a new form of slave labor. The Cuban landlord on his way to the *barracoon* to contract field hands would more than likely say, "I'm going to buy a *chino*;" rather than, "I'm going to hire a *chino*." Because these Chinese "laborers" lacked economic value after eight years (when their work contract expired), they tended to be treated worse than slaves. Suicide for many became an alluring welcome. From 1850 to 1860 Cuba had the highest suicide rates in the world, 340 per million, of which 92.5 percent were committed by Chinese. When compared to Spain's fifteen per million, the desperation Chinese faced in Cuba becomes apparent.[16]

---

[15] Duvon Clough Corbitt, *A Study of the Chinese in Cuba, 1847-1947* (Wilmore, Kentucky: Asbury College, 1971), 16, 54. For a description of the suffering and humiliation caused by the brutal treatment of Chinese laborers, see Ch'ên Lanpin, *Chinese Emigration: The Cuba Commission Report of the Commission sent by China to Ascertain the Condition of Chinese Coolies in Cuba,* trans. A. MacPherson and A. Huber (Shanghai: The Imperial Maritime Customs Press, 1876); and Rebecca Scott, *Slave Emancipation in Cuba: The Transition to Free Labor, 1860-1899* (Princeton: Princeton University Press, 1985).

If Chinese laborers disobeyed their "superiors," they were "corrected" with over twelve lashes and/or the stocks. They were usually paid four to ten *pesos* per month, although substantial portions of their wages were extracted under a host of pretenses. Technically, they were provided with clothes, food, medical treatment and slave quarters. At the end of their contract the laborers theoretically could become tenant farmers or pay for return passage to their native land. Few lived long enough to exercise either choice. An estimated 75 percent died during their eight years of servitude.[17] The end result of this "free wage" system was so similar to slavery that until the abolition of African slavery, both systems could operate side-by-side. Since both systems were synonymous, the use of indentured servants did help facilitate the transition from slavery to a wage system.[18]

The procurement of Chinese laborers was at times similar to the procurement of Africans. According to a January 1859 report by the Spanish Consul at Amoy to the First Secretary of State in Madrid:

> Of each hundred Chinamen that have embarked for Havana recently, I can assure Your Excellency that ninety were hunted like wild beasts and carried on board the vessels..., or they were seduced by deceitful promises and were deceived about the Country to which they were being transported and the kind of work for which they were being recruited. This criminal conduct quickly spread alarm throughout these extensive coasts, increasing the complaints of mothers who asked for husbands and sons that had been carried off by force.[19]

---

[16] Jesús Guanche, "Procesos etnoculturales de Cuba," in *La Habana: Editorial Letras Cubanas* (1983), 319-320.

[17] Gonzalo de Quesada, *The Chinese and Cuban Independence* (Leipzig: Breitkopf & Hartel, 1925), 4-6.

[18] Corbitt, *A Study of the Chinese in Cuba, 1847-1947*, 1-5, 68. Also see Franklin W. Knight, *Slave Society in Cuba During the Nineteenth Century* (Madison: University of Wisconsin Press, 1970), 116-20; James J. O'Kelly, *The Mambi-Land, or Adventures of a Herald Correspondent in Cuba* (Philadelphia: Lippincott, 1874), 60-71, 271-90; and Hugh Thomas, *Cuba: The Pursuit of Freedom* (New York: Harper & Row, 1971), 186-88.

[19] Guanche, *Procesos etnoculturales de Cuba,* 28.

In many cases, the plantation overseers of Asians were former black slaves who were held in supreme contempt by the Chinese. Because most Chinese laborers were literate, they saw black Cubans as their intellectual inferiors due to widespread illiteracy in the former slave population. In some cases they revolted against the blacks that they accused of harsh treatment, and it was not uncommon for such revolts to lead to the overseer's death.[20]

Cuban structures of white supremacy constructed the Chinese laborer as similar to African slaves. Their worth was so insignificant that it gave rise to the popular saying, *"Vale más un muerto que un chino,"* a corpse is worth more than a Chinaman. Like Africans, few Chinese women were transported to Cuba. Market demands dictated the need for young men to work the sugar fields, not women. According to an 1861 Cuban census, there were 34,834 Chinese in Cuba of which 57 were women. By 1871, out of 40,261 Chinese in Cuba only 66 were women.[21] Additionally, social and legal regulations forbade Asian intermarriage with African or white Cubans, although cohabitation surely ensued.[22] The lack of available marriageable women gave rise to a homosexual construction of Chinese sexual identity. The consequence of white and black women rejecting Chinese men contributed to the cultural assumption that they had succumbed to "unspeakable vices," a euphemism for sodomy.[23] Cuban ethnologist Fernando Ortiz credits the Chinese for introducing homosexuality (as well as opium) to Cuba.[24] Cuban historian Hugh Thomas summarizes the situation by noting that: "The Spaniards accused the Chinese as they had once the Arawak Indians; they were thieves, rebels, suicides and *homosexuals* – the last scarcely fair, even if true, since the traders in Chinamen introduced almost no women."[25]

---

[20] Ibid., 63, 78, 113.

[21] Thomas, *Cuba: The Pursuit of Freedom*, 188.

[22] Corbitt, *A Study of the Chinese in Cuba, 1847-1947*, 114-115. Also see Guanche, *Procesos etnoculturales de Cuba*, 319-320.

[23] Verena Martinez-Alier, *Marriage, Class and Color in Nineteenth Century Cuba: A Study of Racial Attitudes and Sexual Values in a Slave Society* (London: Cambridge University Press, 1974), 79.

[24] Fernando Ortiz, "La inmigración desde el punto de vista criminológico," in *Derecho Sociogía*, 19.

This sinophobia has continued to modern time, even effecting Cuban social policies. Early in Castro's regime China exported to the island a shipment of "socialist" condoms; however, Cubans refused to use them claiming they were "too small," thus contributing to both the myth of the Chinese's small penis and to a national rise in pregnancy.[26] Unfortunately, such biases took on international proportions. Carlos Franqui, Castro's friend and biographer, believes that the intensity of the Sino-Cuban feud early in the Castro regime was due to Cuban historical attitudes toward the Chinese.[27]

Exploring the historical injuries to the Asian community leaves me wondering if the white Spanish roots of my Cuban *ajiaco* can find reconciliation with the Asian roots. While in Nanjing, China, Matsuoka, who is Japanese, spoke of what he had discovered; "the inescapable burden I carry of horrible historical injury my Japanese ancestors imposed upon the people of Nanjing some decades back." The elderly woman he was addressing responded with loving words of comfort and forgiveness. Matsuoka stated that in her response he had "a glimpse of faith by which we together gain our humanity, seeing the power and glory and holiness beneath the world's lost face."[28] The hope of this particular Caribbean Latino is to also share the inescapable burden, yet easily forgotten horrible historical injury that occurred in my homeland, imposed upon Asians some centuries back by my Spanish ancestors. Only then can I, along with the Cuban people, hope to glimpse the faith that can bind the diverse roots of our *ajiaco* together.

Besides the impact of historical injuries, Matsuoka insists that the diasporic experience, being in a "state of dislocation and dispossession," is equally important in influencing and informing Asian American theology.[29] If this is true, how much more of a contribution does the Hispanic Asian experience of being twice exiled have on the

---

[25] Thomas, *Cuba: The Pursuit of Freedom*, 188. Italics added.

[26] Carlos Franqui, *Family Portrait with Fidel: A Memoir*, trans. Alfred MacAdam (New York: Random House, 1984), 146

[27] Carlos Moore, *Castro, the Blacks, and Africa* (Los Angeles: Center for Afro-American Studies, University of California, 1988), 264.

[28] Matsuoka, "Churches and Seminaries in China: Personal Reflection," 47.

[29] Matsuoka, "Asian American Theology," in *Handbook of U.S. Theologies of Liberation*, ed. Miguel A. De La Torre (St. Louis: Missouri: Chalice Press, 2004), 218, 221.

discourse? The "double-consciousness" popularized by W.E.B. DuBois speaks to a triple-consciousness experience of knowing what it means to be Asian in a Hispanic culture, Hispanic in an Asian culture, and Asian Hispanic in a North Euroamerican culture – not fully accepted by either, yet having an epistemological advantage of being able to know all three. When in 2000 the U.S. Census Bureau first allowed individuals to select more than one category, Hispanics (who do not belong to a singular racial category) began to also identify themselves as white, black, Asian, etc. Of the approximately 35.3 million who first self-identified as Hispanics, almost 120,000 also checked the Asian box. Yet of people who first identified themselves as Asian, 249,000 also checked the Hispanic box.[30] Among these Hispanics who claimed an Asian identity were *cubano chinos*.[31] This raises questions about group belonging among Asian Latina/os.

Take the example of Emily Lo, a *china cubana* whose mother was born in La Habana to a Chinese father and non-Chinese mother. She recounts that when she took standardized tests at the U.S. high school she attended, she would at times fill in the bubble for Hispanic and at other times fill in the bubble for Asian, wondering if she could lay claim to either one. "Secretly," she wrote, "I disliked Chinese food, struggled with chopsticks, and was a bit frightened of my four uncles who spoke broken English. I would meet my younger cousins, born in China and attending school in New York's Chinatown, and we would stare at each other like we came from entirely different worlds." When she approached her grandma one day to ask if she was more Cuban or Chinese, her Grandma answered without any hesitation, "*Tú eres americana*." You are an American.[32] Matsuoka reminds us that, "Ethnic boundaries are difficult to draw. There is no way for the various groups to prevent or regulate individual crossings. Ethnicity is always fluid,

---

[30] Sarah J. Rangel-Sanchez, "Asians" in *Hispanic American Religious Cultures, Vol. I: A-M*, ed. Miguel A. De La Torre (Santa Barbara, California: ABC CLIO, 2009), 38.

[31] Evelyn Hu-DeHart, "Asian Latinos," in *The Oxford Encyclopedia of Latinos and Latinas in the United States, Vol. I*, ed. Suzanne Oboler and Deena J. González (New York: Oxford University Press, 2005), 125.

[32] Emily Lo, "A Cuban-Chinese *Familia*," in *Cuba: Idea of a Nation Displaced*, ed. Andrea O'Reilly Herrar (Albany, New York: State University of New York Press, 2007), 218.

dynamic, and evolving. Racial and ethnic identities derive their meaning from social and historical circumstances and they can vary over time."[33]

According to Emily Lo, "We had studied immigration in school, but our textbooks never considered families like mine, families that were of blended heritage before they ever set foot in America. We celebrated hyphenated ethnicities all the time in our diversity-conscious curriculums, but adding one more, like Cuban *and* Chinese Americans didn't fit any mold."[34] Matsuoka calls for a reorientation in theology that "utilizes, recognizes, and reclaims [the] resources of people wherever they are. This is a call to reclaim one's own heritage as Asian [and I would add Cuban and American]...and the marks of God's presence in one's own history, society and culture."[35] Emily Lo, along with multiples of *chino cubanos,* forces a new discourse concerning Cuban or Asian identity – a discourse which moves away from a narrow national paradigm of predominately "white" Cubans in *el exilio* (the exile) or Chinese-Americans (and their ancestors) who came directly from China. The *chino cubano* narratives move us toward greater complexities at the intersection of race, ethnicity, and nation(s). The question before us is if we *cubanos,* who have historically been privileged within our own marginalized U.S. Hispanic community, will continue to ignore the voices of *chino cubanos* except when it comes to *restaurantes chino cubano.* Surely *chino cubanos* have contributed more to our identity than mere culinary skills.

---

[33] Matsuoka, "Churches and Seminaries in China: A Personal Reflection," in *With Faith We Can Move Mountains: Reflections of GTU Asia Pacific Bridges Consultation in China, 1995*, 47.

[34] Lo, "A Cuban-Chinese *Familia,*" *Cuba: Idea of a Nation Displaced*, 217.

[35] Fumitaka Matsuoka, "Jesus Christ Our Lord from a Missiological Perspective" in *A Disciple's Christology: Appraisals of Kraus's Jesus Christ Our Lord*, ed. Richard A. Kauffman (Elkhart, Indiana: Institute of Mennonite Studies, 1989), 32-33.

Chapter 16.

Suffering We Know: The Hermeneutic of *Han* and the Dilemma of African American (Religious) Experience

Anthony B. Pinn

African American theologians typically consider engagement with other communities as a means by which to affirm—in light of the web-like nature of oppression—their particular theological read of experience. That is to say, there is an assumption of existential similarity (shared modalities of oppression and a need for liberation) leading to a set of common theological proclamations. Yet, what I propose here is a different type of engagement—the use of Asian American theological categories as a hermeneutic brought to bear on African American theological source materials. In this way engagement between African American and Asian American theological discourses is more fundamental, less pre-set, and more fluid in nature than is often the case.

For the purposes of this essay, I make use of an Asian American theological formulation of marginality and *han*, and I bring these together as a way to read one of the more troubling assessments of the absurdity and inevitability of embodied suffering—Nella Larsen's novel *Quicksand*.[1] While a variety of texts could have been picked for inclusion here, I discuss *Quicksand* in that it graphically represents a

---

[1] Nella Larsen, *Quicksand and Passing* (New Brunswick: Rutgers University Press, 1986), 1-135.

genre of cultural production ignored because of its stinging challenge to black and womanist theologies regarding the nature of oppression and the meaning of liberation. Furthermore, *han* as a central Asian American theological category allows for creative engagement of this text in ways that maintain its complexities.

Fiction Qua Theology

Cultural expression is tied to the "religious" in significant and repeating ways. Nathan Scott's early work in the area of "Literature and Religion" speaks to the manner in which the religious as "ultimate concern" is played out in significant ways through literary expression. There is something religious in the work of poets and novelists in that their prose speaks "testimony about the human condition…" and seeks to arrange and interrogate experience in complexity and significance.[2] In fact, as Anthony Yu notes, in many historical cases a community's literary tradition grows "in intimate—indeed, often intertwining—relation to religious thought, practice, institutions, and symbolism."[3] Hence, it is reasonable for scholars to work from the posture that one informs the other, and both relate to similar motivations. In short, the arts—in this case literature—tell something of the nature and meaning of the religious—its 'language', shape, content and concerns—and should not be missed by students of religion. This, of course, is not without problems: language is a tricky matter, and prose can paint vivid depictions of life that challenge the order theology seeks to speak into being.

Following this line of reasoning, some in the study of African American religion have mined African American literary tradition(s) for insights into the nature of black life and the mechanics of the struggle for liberation they assume defines this life. Materials are privileged and highlighted to the extent they promote a fundamental (and assumed

---

[2]Nathan Scott, "Religious Symbolism in Contemporary Literature," in *Religious Symbolism*, ed. F. Ernest Johnson (Port Washington: Kennikat Press, 1969), 160.

[3]Anthony C. Yu, "Literature and Religion," *Comparative Journeys: Essays on Literature and Religion East and West,* ed. Anthony C. Yu (New York: Columbia University Press, 2009), 1.

successful) wrestling against injustice—particularly in ways that affirm faith in a God committed to the advancement of those who suffer. White supremacy is read as a problematic handled through the tenacity of African American mechanisms of creativity and determination in spite of the absurdity of life arrangements. Hence, African American literature is presented within both black and womanist theologies as a running example of struggle against injustice in ways that affirm a traditional ethics of divinely sanctioned social change. Literature does this in several ways: (1) it outlines the nature of suffering and promotes strategies for change; (2) it offers critique of oppressions *as* a strategy for change; (3) it provides a posture toward the world in some way—either implicit or explicit—consistent with the basic parameters of activist Christianity; and, (4) it promotes the integrity of individual and collective black life as the core of liberation and as consistent with the best of the black (Christian) tradition. In other words, African American literary materials, drawn from the shared experience of struggle for life meaning, contain what Riggins Earl might call "foundational religio-ethical meanings constructs" through which ontological value is established and epistemologically spread. [4]

This scheme has both determined how literature is read and also what literature is read. Often missing from this list of utilized materials is Larsen's *Quicksand*, and I suspect this oversight has something to do with the troubling nature of enduring suffering found in Larsen's novel.

Larsen published *Quicksand* in 1928. This, as some readers may know, was a pivotal time in the history of the United States. The "Great Migration" of African Americans was in full swing, and African Americans undertaking this journey found in northern cities a continuation of the economic despair and marginalization that marked the geography they had fled. The ramifications of embodied 'blackness' combined with issues of gender-bias and class, plagued and deformed life options for African Americans across the landscape of southern Jim and Jane Crow and their socio-political equals in the North. Yet, within this context of struggle, African Americans were creating religious markers of identity that spoke against the traumas of their existential

---

[4] Riggins R. Earl, Jr., *Dark Symbols, Obscure Signs: God, Self, and Community in the Slave Mind*, Second Edition (Knoxville: The University of Tennessee Press, 2003), xxvi.

condition. They were creating cultural modalities that expressed a different and more robust aesthetic of black life. Hence, despite hardships and uncertainties, this was also a period of transformation—a shift in ontological and epistemological markers of me(an)ing; or, what Alain Locke named in 1925 the birth of the "New Negro." For Locke the cultural articulations of African Americans during the turn of the century suggested the emergence of a difference—people of African descent with complexity, capable of articulated new worlds of thought, action, and meaning. "With this renewed self-respect and self-dependence," writes Locke, "the life of the Negro community is bound to enter a new dynamic phase, the buoyancy from within compensating for whatever pressure there may be of conditions from without. The migrant masses, shifting from countryside to city, hurdle several generations of experience at a leap, but more important, the same thing happens spiritually in the life-attitudes and self-expression of the Young Negro, in his poetry, his art, his education and his new outlook, with the additional advantage, of course, of the poise and greater certainty of knowing what it is all about."[5]

Authors recorded the nature and meaning of African American life with all its points of promise and discomfort. Along these lines, "The Negro today," Locke reflects, "wishes to be known for what he is, even in his faults and shortcomings, and scorns a craven and precarious survival at the price of seeming to be what he is not. He resents being spoken of as a social ward or minor, even by his own, and to being regarded a chronic patient for the sociological clinic, the sick man of American Democracy."[6] Consistent with this assessment, Larsen promoted the reconstitution of the self as already always marginalized and configured. Movement, not the stability of a fixed identity and clear geography of life meaning, is the guiding epistemological trope.

Quicksand is marked by a presentation of the protagonist as a complex and embodied being, whose life is complex and tragic.[7] This

---

[5] Alain Locke, "The New Negro," in *The New Negro*, ed. Alain Locke (New York: Atheneum, 1986), 4-5.
[6] Ibid., 11.
[7] This recasting involved an effort to move beyond the apologetics of early writings in which African Americans were discussed as one dimensional and acceptable within the social structures of a "whitened" world.

intentionally moves beyond the apologetics of early writings whereby an effort was made to present African Americans as one dimensional and acceptable within the social structures of a "whitened" world. This process of articulating African American life amounts, from my perspective, to the smashing of idols noted by Locke as part of the emergence of the "New Negro." Creating comfort with African Americans (either within the community of African Americans or outside that community) was not the point of this new work. Instead, it sought to present the tragic without nihilism, forcing recognition of the troubled nature of life and in this way expressing the full humanity of African Americans, whose lives are rich, thick, and nuanced. And more to the point of this essay, this "New Negro" does not necessarily operate based on theological assumptions and precepts that might dull the senses and challenge reason for dominance. Religion and its theological framing are no longer assumed to provide the resolution to existential trauma.[8]

I believe it is this last point that has troubled students of African American religion, particularly those with a somewhat narrow perception of the content and workings of history as teleological in nature. Helga Crane, the protagonist of *Quicksand*, personifies a type of realism comfortably situated within the workings of modernity.[9] Breaking the "idol" of supernaturalism tied to expression of socio-racial and erotic embodiment, Larsen promoted the reconstitution of the self.

Helga Crane's Story in Brief

Mindful of this framing, the novel begins with Helga Crane restless, discontent with life within the structures of Naxos—a school formed for African Americans along the Booker T. Washington philosophy and model—because it seeks to limit the range of black life and forge African Americans who fit within the strictures of raced-based society. Struggles with the limits of identity formation for African Americans, and the added eroticization she encounters as a mulatto, are

---

[8] Locke, "The New Negro," 11.
[9] Thadious M. Davis, *Nella Larsen Novelist of the Harlem Renaissance: A Woman's Life Unveiled* (Baton Rouge: Louisiana State University Press, 1986), 3.

expressed through her movement across geography. Helga leaves. Yet, struggles with the limits of identity formation and the added eroticization she encounters as a mulatto are present in each place she goes: Harlem, Copenhagen, back to Harlem, and finally Alabama. The movement is graphic, but the actual time—the moment in time and space—constituted during and by this movement is rather vague.

Helga journeys in light of, and in reaction to, various cultural mappings, while sustaining little alteration to her self-awareness. Yet, it is during her second sojourn in Harlem that she succumbs to the promises of energetic Christianity, and it is in Alabama she hopes to live out these promises within the context of church practice and family stability. What she encounters consistently, however, is suffering and pain, isolation, and the compromise of her body and psyche. In response to her physical misery and existential trauma Helga makes a proclamation. "The cruel, unrelieved suffering had beaten down her protective wall of artificial faith in the infinite wisdom, in the mercy, of God," writes Larsen, "for had she not called in her agony on Him? And He had not heard. Why? Because, she knew now, He wasn't there. Didn't exist. Into that yawning gap of unspeakable brutality had gone, too, her belief in the miracle and wonder of life."[10]

Helga's life up to the point of her conversion in a small storefront church in Harlem, involved existential arrangements based on what she preserved as reason and logic applied to the historical circumstances of lived life. However, as Larsen seems to argue, the 'religious' dulls identity formation, and refocuses wellbeing and purpose away from the physicality of our existence. Even when Helga, as the above quotation marks, recognizes that the lynchpin of religiosity—God—is mythical, a trope without realness, the power of religion to shape and confine life-meaning remains intact. The novel ends with Helga tied to her troubled existential arrangements, pregnant again, ethically frustrated, and confined to the geography of her conservative Christian community. There is no teleology here; no push toward liberation so important in African American liberation theologies.

---

[10] Larsen, *Quicksand and Passing*, 130.

How Black and Womanist Theologies Might Explain Helga Crane

It is likely that black and womanist theologians would first read *Quicksand* as a signifying of (and shift with respect to) the nature and meaning of race. They, I imagine, would call into question the racial paradigm and the white supremacist sensibilities undergirding Helga Crane's struggle for identity outside the exotic and reified notions of racial dominance in place within her world. The story is replete with instances of racialization as negation, and it chronicles these instances against a struggle for difference as beneficial—here in terms of the liminal space of light skin and European 'blood.' After receiving a note from her (white) uncle, Peter Nilssen, in which he explains the poor reaction of his wife in meeting Helga and offers her a bit of money and advice to visit family in Copenhagen, she thinks to herself: "She didn't, in spite of her racial markings, belong to these dark segregated people. She was different. She felt it. It wasn't merely a matter of color. It was something broader, deeper, that made folk kin."[11] Yes, there are racial tensions and a mocking of racial distinction within the story. But it isn't necessarily the case that Larsen did this in a manner consistent with what now defines the ideological leanings of black theological discourse. Whereas black theology understands race (blackness, ontological blackness) as a marker for pride and sign of divine favor, Larsen's perspective is a bit more paradoxical. "In taking a bemused stance toward matters of race," writes Thadious Davis, "Larsen reflected an ironic vision of life, a willingness to dissent from acceptable racial discourse, and a complicated understanding of the arbitrariness of racial definitions."[12]

Womanist scholars, no doubt, would pick-up on the implications of gender and sexism for women of 'color.' The mode by which Helga Crane is 'other-ed,' they might argue, is not simply a function of race. More appropriately understood, it is the consequence of a complex arrangement of race, gender, and class. To the extent there is something autobiographical about *Quicksand*, Davis's point serves to support this

---

[11] Ibid., 55.

[12] Thadious M. Davis, *Nella Larsen Novelist of the Harlem Renaissance: A Woman's Life Unveiled* (Baton Rouge: Louisiana State University Press, 1986), 12.

triadic read: "Larsen's movement from nurse to librarian to writer demonstrates her personal search for class position, meaningful work, social prestige, and full self-expression as an African-American female."[13] "Her movement," Davis continues, "reconstituted through the lens of time, reflects the dual efforts of a woman constructing herself during the moment of the larger social construction of an African-American middle class and of a woman engendering herself during a period of confluence of race, gender, and art."[14] Axel Olsen's commentary in Copenhagen accompanying his proposal of marriage speaks to this dilemma—a configuration of race, gender, and class meant to stultify and reduce: "You know, Helga, you are a contradiction… You have the warm impulsive nature of the women of Africa, but, my lovely, you have, I fear, the soul of a prostitute. You sell yourself to the highest buyer. I should of course be happy that it is I. And I am."[15] Helga's response speaks, at least momentarily, to an assertion of self over against objectification that both black and womanist theological discourses might embrace. "But you see, Herr Olsen," Helga counters, "I'm not for sale. Not to you. Not to any white man. I don't at all care to be owned. Even by you."[16] Albeit an important statement on Helga's part, it does not entail "speaking truth to power" consistent with the grand design of black and womanist theological discourses. This is not the worst of it, not the most rigorous or 'damning' challenge to the basic structure of these discourses.

Helga Crane offers a theodical challenge, noted earlier, that black and womanist theologians might find a useful critique of white supremacist manipulations of the "religious" for the purposes of a discriminatory theology. When confronting her personal pain—seen in Helga's ongoing torment and angst associated with continued pregnancies, the dislike of her neighbors and church family, and in spite of prayer—Larsen concludes:

> With the obscuring curtain of religion rent, she was able to look about her and see with shocked eyes this thing

---

[13] Davis, *Nella Larsen Novelist of the Harlem Renaissance*, 456.
[14] Ibid., 456-457.
[15] Ibid., 87.
[16] Larsen, *Quicksand and Passing*, 87.

> that she had done to herself. She couldn't, she thought ironically, even blame God for it, now that she knew that He didn't exist. No. No more than she could pray to Him for the death of her husband, the Reverend Mr. Pleasant Green. The white man's God. And His great love for all people regardless of race! What idiotic nonsense she had allowed herself to believe.[17]

The "white man's God"…this idol has long been a target of theological critique within African American communities. And it appears that Larsen provides a literary equivalent. But is this really the nature of Larsen's commentary? African American theological critique of this fictive force is meant to promote struggle towards liberation and make possible proper connection to the true God, who fights alongside the oppressed for their liberation. The unmasking of this idol is, then, a theological breakthrough promoting a greater sense of self and greater potential for transformation. Yet, Helga's situation does not improve. Hers remains an existential quagmire—a struggle over freedom. In this regard, Larsen's theological insight fails to accomplish the aims of black and womanist theological critique.

Helga Crane's perspective does not line up with the liberation/transformation schematics of such deep importance to black and womanist liberation theologies. And this is a key reason why Larsen's work has received such limited attention within black and womanist theological circles. Yet this begs a question. Is there benefit in looking beyond black and womanist theologies for assistance with a re-thinking of materials such as Larsen's *Quicksand* that trouble staid theological depictions of suffering and redemption? I answer in the affirmative, but qualify my positive response: the benefit is available to use only when such troubling texts are approached using an alternate hermeneutic, one better equipped to appreciate the paradoxes marking much of African American life. I propose *han* as this alternate hermeneutic.

---

[17] Ibid., 130.

A Hermeneutic of *Han*

I am not the first African American theologian to engage Asian American conceptual frameworks. For example, Karen Baker-Fletcher, in *Dancing with God*, tackles the nature and meaning of sin in conversation with the paradigm of *han*.[18] Drawing on Andrew Park's writings, Baker-Fletcher uses *han* to capture both the 'content' and scope of disconnection and trauma particularly as related to a womanist sensitivity to "the relationship the presence of God in creation and the violation of creation" as connoting "sin."[19] Accordingly, through *han* one gathers a sense of how the oppressed—the "sinned against"—encounter the world, as well as the content of their predicament.[20] The oppressed experience misery, a troubling of deep ontological and material meaning, that produces a gross response. "The victims of various types of wrongdoing," writes Andrew Park, "express the ineffable experience of deep bitterness and helplessness. Such an experience of pain is called *han* in the Far East. *Han* can be defined as the critical wound of the heart generated by unjust psychosomatic repression, as well as by social, political, economic, and cultural oppression."[21] By means of *han*, the perspective of the oppressed is prioritized, and the world is viewed from their position. Pain experienced, hence, is the point of departure for understanding and action. The challenge of *han*, from my perspective, is this: It marks out the anger of the oppressed, the internalized tension and external trauma of their painful predicaments. It is the graphics of misery. *Han* cannot be easily distilled or isolated and removed, in that it influences all dimensions of one's existence: "It shows through the interpersonal social, cultural, and religious aspects of life. Like repression, *han* is submerged in the unconscious, forcing us to bury our oppressed feelings. *Han*, however, controls our ways of thought, emotion, and behavior."[22] It is both a significant marker of creativity and the shape and content of misery. Difficult to target in simple ways, *han*

---

[18] Karen Baker-Fletcher, *Dancing with God: The Trinity from a Womanist Perspective* (St. Louis: Chalice Press, 2006).
[19] Ibid., 92.
[20] Ibid., 95.
[21] Andrew Sung Park, *The Wounded Heart of God: The Asian Concept of Han and the Christian Doctrine of Sin* (Nashville: Abingdon Press, 1993), 10.
[22] Ibid., 17, 80-81.

can connote and signal contraction and paradox. Mindful of the above, one can argue that *Quicksand* ends with Helga acknowledging and responding to her *han*.²³

Helga Crane's *Han*

The inclination of black and womanist theologies might be to pull apart the various dimensions of Helga's misery—racism, sexism, and so on—but according to Jae Hoon Lee, "certain meanings of *han* can be found only by making it whole, instead of fragmenting it." Required, then, is a process of "synthesis," a holding together.²⁴ In this way *han* as hermeneutic interprets Helga Crane's story as a matter of internal and external struggle, a complex decoding of paradoxical feelings and desires, all couched in material and psychic developments. Rejection of God might be viewed as Helga surrendering a dimension of her *han*, "conscious *han*." It is a recognition that her misery is multi-dimensional, a result of oppression but also a result of *han* (e.g., anger and resentment) more elaborately configured.²⁵ This is "a removal of *han*-causing elements," but such a move is incomplete in that *han* is also unconscious.²⁶ Furthermore, it is the double nature of *han*—external and internal—that accounts for recognition of Crane's predicament as an insufficient means by which to confront the predicament: she remains within a context of oppression. Put differently, addressing the external markers of oppression is insufficient to address fully the nature and meaning of *han*. Or, as Jae Hoon Lee remarks, drawing on psychological paradigms, "The idea that the complex is the product of only external oppression and is removable by devoting oneself to the cause of social justice, does not account for the inner nature of the complex."²⁷

---

²³Jae Hoon Lee, *The Exploration of the Inner Wounds–Han* (Atlanta: Scholars Press, 1994), 2, 5.

²⁴Ibid., 7.

²⁵For a discussion of *han* with the life experiences of women, see Grace Ji-Sun Kim, The *Grace of Sophia: A Korean North American Women's Christology* (Cleveland: The Pilgrim Press, 2002), chapters 3, 7.

²⁶Park, *The Wounded Heart of God*, 174.

²⁷Jae Hoon Lee, *The Exploration of the Inner Wounds—Han* (Atlanta: Scholars Press, 1994), 150.

Helga Crane is not simply rejecting Christianity as a tool of oppression; rather, she is speaking out of and to *han* in a way that acknowledges external and internal causes and consequences of her misery. She is expanding her understanding.[28] (What we have here is more than recognition of 'internalized racism' for instance.)

Helga begins the process of "working through the reality of such painful events" but the story ends before this is accomplished.[29] Helga mines the self, and the end of the novel points to the beginning of the process. In other words, "recognizing the reality of the painful *han* and determining the diversion of *han*-energy are the avenues by which one transcends the unconscious level of *han*."[30] The expression of Helga's frustration, the acknowledgement of her role in the fostering of her predicament, is not a moment of defeat but rather the marking out of recovery as possibility to the extent the negative energy of *han* is released and can be used.[31] Perhaps Helga's situation, the ongoing connection to people and world, is an act of "*dan*" whereby the push for revenge is subsumed. In this regard, it is possible that Helga undergoes a transformation whereby "masochistic uses of aggression and sentimental love" are challenged by the practice of "aggression creatively."[32] (*Han*, nonetheless, remains—although transformed.) Such is not a call for a denial of socio-cultural change; rather, it is to put this change within perspective. Think of this in light of the following, first a definition of *dan* and then a stating of Helga's status: "On the personal level, 'dan' is the practice of 'self denial' through which one can remove the temptation of the 'easy life, circles of petite bourgeois dreams, and secular swamps without depth.'"[33]

And now, the last words of the novel:

> She must rest. Get strong. Sleep. Then, afterwards, she could work out some arrangement. So she dozed and

---

[28] Lee, *The Exploration of the Inner Wounds*, 149-150
[29] Park, *The Wounded Heart of God*, 174-175.
[30] Ibid., 175.
[31] Lee, *The Exploration of the Inner Wounds*, 127.
[32] Ibid., 160.
[33] Dong-hwan Moon, "Korean Minjung theology," quoted in Jae Hoon Lee, *The Exploration of the Inner Wounds – Han,* 153.

dreamed in snatches of sleeping and waking, letting time run on. Away.

AND HARDLY had she left her bed and become able to walk again without pain, hardly had the children returned from the homes of the neighbors, when she began to have her fifth child.

Helga Crane remains within her context of suffering, but with a much milder desire for revenge. There is no reconstitution of the self as victorious over injustice; and no reconstitution of right religion as the marker of ongoing change, and so on. The faith of black (Christian) religion is held in check by the absurdity of experience, and logic/reason only intensify this situation.

Without doubt, the issue of theodicy would surface for black and womanist theologians, particularly in light of Helga's dismissal of the God concept in light of human misery. And the response for black and womanist theologians might involve some version of redemptive suffering.[34] But not so for Helga Crane. Helga's re-envisioning God as robust trope, turns from theodicy to a mode of anthropodicy in that the idea of God's involvement in human suffering is secondary to human production of misery: "And this, Helga decided, was what ailed the whole Negro race in America, this fatuous belief in the white man's God, this childlike trust in full compensation for all woes and privations in 'kingdom come.'"[35] There is a suggestion here, lifted out through the hermeneutic of *han*, that resolution for Helga is not found in a traditional overcoming of existential conditions. Such an outcome is "good," but alone it is insufficient in that the material (socio-political and economic situation) is connected to the inner realities that make us who we are.

Questions still abound, and circumstances remain challenging. "How, then," Helga asks, "was she to escape from the oppression, the degradation, that her life had become? It was so difficult. It was terribly difficult."[36] Such a proclamation is a challenge to the typical sensibilities

---

[34]Anthony B. Pinn, *Why, Lord? Suffering and Evil in Black Theology* (New York: Continuum Press, 1995); Anthony B. Pinn, *Moral Evil and Redemptive Suffering* (Gainesville: University Press of Florida, 2002).

[35]Larsen, *Quicksand and Passing*, 133.

of black and womanist theologies, but the manner in which the challenge echoes *han* might shed light on its importance.

---

[36]Ibid., 134.

Conclusion

Postlude

Worlds Made a Part

David Kyuman Kim

A Matter of Memory

Let us be honest about our myths. There is an animating Orientalist myth in American racial discourse that maintains that Asian Americans have a preoccupation with "Asia," and, more specifically, with their so-called nations of origin—Korea, China, the Philippines, India, Japan, and so on. Surely, the folklore in question is in part self-perpetuated by Asian Americans. Nevertheless, it also reflects the lingering demands of assimilation in the white supremacist racial and ethnic hierarchy of America, even as the material and lived effects of globalization have become "normal." In light of these prevailing conditions, I want to consider how the dynamics of Asian American racialization torques under paradoxical forces. On the one hand, Asian American racialization responds to the demand to assimilate to cosmopolitan ideals of cultural pluralism; on the other hand, there is a countervailing pull for Asian Americans to dissimulate their desires for "Asia."

In order to understand the lived effects of these competing forces on Asian Americans, let us turn to the crucial work of memory, religion, and race. How might we think through the complex relationship amongst these three ways of being human in the world? Religion and race constitute memory in terrifically complicated ways. We know that race is not simply a structural affair. In everyday life, race is also a deeply embedding concern of the spirit. Taking the psychic and spiritual life of race and memory into consideration raises challenging questions: How do we develop an account of the interplay between the challenge of memory and the Asian American religious imagination? Furthermore, what roles do cultural and religious memory play in Asian American social and cultural criticism and subjectivity? With these questions in mind, I want to underscore the constructive uses of memory—specifically, forms of memory that speak to the folklore about Asian Americans I mentioned at the beginning, known more generally as nostalgia. How might cultural critics invert and repurpose the work of memory in light of the Orientalist logic that presumes an ineluctable Asian American nostalgia *for* "Asia"? What critiques are available that can identify the constructive uses of nostalgia and memory, such as anti-imperialist analyses that problematize cosmopolitan notions such as cultural pluralism as an unalloyed good? And how might these modes of cultural criticism begin to highlight some of the existential challenges of living through the tumult of constituting new racial discourses? Luckily we have a grand example of this sort of complex and highly sophisticated cultural criticism in the work of Fumitaka Matsuoka, the visionary theologian of the Asian American diaspora.

It is fair to ask: why turn to "nostalgia?" After all, aren't there other terrains of memory-work that leave Asian Americans less prone to the follies of sentimentalist Orientalism? Consider the etymology. "Nostalgia" comes from the Greek *nostos* ("home") and *algia* ("longing"). Nostalgia is at once a by-product of large-scale global forces, such as capitalism, the so-called "world religions," and political ideologies like democracy. Conversely, nostalgia is also a means and a mechanism of articulating intimate matters of the psychic life, most especially personal memory. Nostalgia provides a way of finding connections between these two spheres of human experience, which is to say, between the material, structural (i.e., the political and social), and cultural conditions of the world, on the one hand, and the interior life of the individual psyche, on the other. As critical theorists such as Adorno, Lukács, Foucault, and Butler have taught us, there is a tyranny to the circulation and constitution of memory. The realization of "authentic memory"—a rather capacious category that includes everything from authorized national histories to theological doctrines and ideological mandates—is an aspiration. Memory can be a hothouse for the growth and enforcement of cultures of significance and meaning. Intensifying the stakes, my core claim here is that a memory of integrity can serve as an achievement.

In thinking through the constructive uses of nostalgia, let me begin with a distinction laid out by Svetlana Boym in her incisive book *The Future of Nostalgia*—an analytic distinction between two types of nostalgia, namely, restorative nostalgia and reflective nostalgia.[1] Boym's typology of nostalgia helps to uncover the vicissitudes of the career of memory in modernity, in particular the constitution of history with regard to national and cultural identity. Note that this relationship often comes into sharper and unexpected focus, somewhat paradoxically, when nostalgia crops up as a resource for withstanding presiding forces of modernity and modernization such as market- and capital-driven globalization, otherwise known as neoliberalism. Let's unpack this complex circuit of experience by circling back to Boym's typology of nostalgia. "Restorative nostalgia" reflects the kind of sentimentalism, dogmatism, and absolutism often associated with nationalism and ethnocentrism. The longing and memory of this kind of nostalgia is "restorative" in so far as a focus on a fixed object is at play, such as "The Old South," "the homeland," or the idea of "America" as a cultural and political icon. As the stuff of cultural, social, *and* psychic identity, restorative nostalgia holds out a *telos* of a "transhistorical reconstruction of a lost home."[2] This is the stuff of national myths and narratives, "official" histories, and the allergic reaction to self-criticism that is, if not unique to, at least symptomatic of ideology. "Reflective nostalgia," on the other hand, concerns a much less fixed constellation of ideas. If restorative nostalgia seeks to reconstruct and restore "nostos/home" itself, then reflective nostalgia fixes on "algia," which is to say it finds its expression and meaning in longing, yearning, and desire—a longing, argues Boym, that "delays the homecoming—wistfully, ironically, desperately." Whereas restorative nostalgia is tied to "clear," material, cultural, and political aims that are construed as "truth and tradition" (home or homeland as nation-state, for example), reflective nostalgia, Boym contends, "dwells on the ambivalences of human longing and belonging. Reflective nostalgia does not shy away from the contradictions of modernity."[3] Surely among the most vexing of these

---

[1] Svetlana Boym, *The Future of Nostalgia* (New York: Basic Books, 2001).
[2] Ibid, xviii.
[3] Ibid.

contradictions of modernity is the simultaneous increase in human freedom *and* oppression.⁴

Restorative nostalgia depicts and deploys the memory of "home cultures" as qualitatively better than one's present social location and historical conditions. The ethic *and* ethos of restorative nostalgia is conservative by definition and design, developed with a lexicon of returns: restore, preserve, resurrect, and reconstruct *the* nation, *the* culture, *the* religion, *the* way of life.⁵ This is not to say that these nations, cultures, religions, and ways of life have actually ever existed in time and space. It is important to note the ways in which migration, mobility, alienation, and the like shape conservative and conserving frames of reference for "home." The metaphorical figures of restorative nostalgia are the archivist, the apparatchik, and the nationalist.

It is clear from Boym's critique and analysis that we will find constructive uses not in nostalgia's restorative form but rather in reflective nostalgia or what I will also call "critical nostalgia." Bearing this in mind, the metaphorical figure I want to focus on as representative of reflective or critical nostalgia is *the exilic writer*, especially in the mode of cultural critic and theologian of diaspora—both of whom, I maintain, seek out constructive ways to tap into cultural and social memory—itself an often ambivalently delineated though effectively influential means of establishing social existence.

Nostalgia, so Boym argues, is a "historical emotion," more specifically, an emotion—or really a set of emotions that speak to a condition not only of loss and detachment (from culture, history, tradition, and the like) but also of mourning. In this sense, nostalgia is expressive of another psychic state, namely, melancholy or, as Freud called it, "melancholia."⁶ In referring to loss, detachment, and mourning, I am situating and identifying nostalgia (and melancholy) with the

---

⁴ I discuss this paradox of modernity in David Kyuman Kim, *Melancholic Freedom: Agency and the Spirit of Politics* (New York: Oxford University Press, 2007), 86-88.

⁵ David Chidester, "Transatlantic Religion," in *Authentic Fakes: Religion and American Popular Culture* (Berkeley: University of California Press, 2005), 150-171.

⁶ Sigmund Freud, "Mourning and Melancholia," in Sigmund Freud, *The Standard Edition of The Complete Psychological Works of Sigmund Freud*, trans. and ed. James Strachey (London: Hogarth Press, 1957), 14:243-60.

memory conditions of modernity, especially the conditions that shape our sense of history and our relationship to space, time, and values. If the ethos of modernity and modernism incants progress and universalism, the critical ethos of nostalgia runs cross-grain with modernity and modernism, and is, I would argue, in conflict with one of the reigning inheritors of globalizing modernity, namely, cosmopolitanism. Why? Because uncritical nostalgia maintains a lingering preoccupation with that which modernity and modernism want to supersede and leave behind: the local, the particular, and specific and affective attachments.[7] Cosmopolitanism insists on a banal pluralism (this is a condition Kant lays out in his account of the conditions for the possibility for cosmopolitanism as a means of achieving "perpetual peace").[8] To this point, Boym writes:

> Modern nostalgia is a mourning for the impossibility of mythical return, for the loss of an enchanted world with clear borders and values; it could be a secular expression of a spiritual longing, a nostalgia for an absolute, a home that is both physical and spiritual, the edenic unity of time and space before entry into history. The nostalgic is looking for a spiritual addressee. Encountering silence, he [sic] looks for memorable signs, desperately misreading them.[9]

On this score, those engaged in restorative nostalgia are seeking to establish material conditions to resolve their mourning, such as a regressive lament over the absence of a sovereign nation-state. In contrast, the critical nostalgic is more apt (if not more happy) to dwell

---

[7] I take up this version of the secularization thesis in the chapter 1 of *Melancholic Freedom*, 3-22.

[8] Immanuel Kant, "Perpetual Peace," in *Political Writings*, ed. H. S. Reiss (Cambridge: Cambridge University Press, 1991 [1970]), 93-130. See also in the same volume, Kant's essay "Idea with a Universal History with a Cosmopolitan Purpose," 41-53. For an advocatory account of modern cosmopolitanism, see Kwame Anthony Appiah, *Cosmopolitanism: Ethics in a World of Strangers* (New York: W. W. Norton, 2006).

[9] Boym, *Future of Nostalgia*, 8.

and exist *in* the ambiguity and ambivalence of living without a persistent and compulsive need to reconstruct a mythic home.¹⁰

Critical nostalgia is by its nature shaded by *ambivalence*. It is an ambivalence that goes to the central role of longing and desire in nostalgia and is framed by questions such as: "If I get my object of desire ('home'), will it remain something I long for? If not, then do I really want it? Do I want to make it 'real'? Would 'getting it'—would getting *there* (again 'home')—take away the allure, the enchantment of the very idea of home?"

Indeed, as I write these words, the exhilarating revolutions unfolding in Tunisia, Yemen, Jordan, and Egypt have heightened a renewed sense of what is at stake in aspirations for reclaiming home and homeland.¹¹ After decades of living under repressive regimes, everyday people across north Africa and the Middle East are insisting, largely

---

¹⁰ This was certainly true in the Zionist debates around the turn of the 20th century. Consider the tact taken by Ahad Ha'am, one of the most powerful critics of the Zionist project that sought the establishment of "the nation of Palestine," what we now know as Israel. Ha'am argued that the creation of a political state—organized around an actual, physical/geographical space—would ultimately subvert and corrupt the spiritual bond among Jews around the world and across history. In other words, Ha'am maintained the conviction that the quality and character that constitute what it means to be "a Jew" and to be a diasporic people would become too world-bound, too prone to the corruption that comes with political institutions and practices. Surely, Ha'am's project relied on a utopian allure that most materialists would and did find wanting and politically naive. Nonetheless, his critique raises an interesting set of challenges to the *typos* of "nation" or even the notion of "a people" that follows from a Herderian nationalism grounded in practices such as a notion of a common language ("*Volkspracht*") as the foundation for national identity. Ahad Ha'am, *Selected Essays of Ahad Ha'am*, trans. Leon Simon (Philadelphia: Jewish Publication Society of America, 1936); see especially "Imitation and Assimilation," "Priest and Prophet," "Flesh and Spirit," and "The Spiritual Revival." For a sympathetic reading of Herder, see Charles Taylor, "Language and human nature," in his *Human Agency and Language: Philosophical Papers 1* (Cambridge: Cambridge University Press, 1985), 215-247.

¹¹ Pundits and social scientists alike seem to have settled on calling what is still unfolding in north Africa as "the Arab spring." The romance of this turn of phrase has its appeals, but it also seems to detract from the huge political, cultural, and social shifts rendered by the revolutions enacted and those still taking place.

through peaceful means, on their humanity and integrity—which is to say, making public their claims and insistence of themselves as "a people." Among the array of needs and forms of suffering that have inspired the aspiration for democracy in Egypt and other nations throughout the region is the desire to re-claim nation, heritage, and self-determination—all fortified and stoked by memories hard won.

Nostalgia is useful as a descriptive/analytic category as well as a normative one. As a descriptive/analytic concept, nostalgia can reflect the confusions produced in the wake of empire. Think here of the post-colonial mind. Or consider another example: the pervasive (mis)characterization of religion as imperial. How have the so-called "world religions" functioned as circuits of memory that shape racial identities in accordance with cosmopolitan idea(l)s. On the one hand, each of the "world religions" (Christianity, Islam, Judaism, Hinduism, and so on) achieved their global statuses by instilling in their respective proponents ambitions of expansion, growth, and, frankly, some form of ideological domination. This is as true of Constantine as it was of George W. Bush. The effectiveness of these crusades of spiritual global expansion relied, and continue to rely, not only on institutional and governmental agendas but also on campaigns to shape the heart and mind, which is to say, to establish, with varying degrees of success, ideological uniformity and conformity among their adherents.[12]

On the other hand, there have been religious figures and movements—for example, pacifist Hindus (Gandhi) or Christians (King), or anti-imperial Tibetan Buddhists (the Dalai Lama)—who have been committed to fighting domination through prophetic calls to political action and mobilization. Consider, as well, the political theologian Johann Baptist Metz's notion of "dangerous memory" (the passion of Christ is a dangerous memory to the forces of domination and oppression) or Gershom Scholem's deployment of the idea of the Jewish covenant with God as a promise of emancipation, freedom and justice.[13]

---

[12] While I am wary of an approach that would equate "religion" with "ideology," it remains that there are ideological features to the institutionalization of religions that seek measures of uniformity — in practice and intent –– among its adherents and practitioners. While it may be the case that conformity is a particularly effective mechanism for social and psychological control, it does not follow that all religions or all religious believers and practitioners are uncritical participants in their respective traditions.

Both are examples of nostalgia, of dangerous memory as a source of hope that fuels resistance. Abraham Joshua Heschel comes readily to mind as exemplary of this practice of prophetic witness. In a different vein, Fumitaka Matsuoka has consistently registered and given voice to the dangerous memory of the racialized diasporas of Asian America.[14]

Critical Nostalgia and the Spiritual Exile

In a normative mode, nostalgia finds expression in both Jewish and Christian theology, in particular in the form of messianic and/or eschatological expectations. This is what animates the remembrance of divine acts, such as examples and expectations of compassion—remembrances that vivify a vision of a coming or a return ("the messiah") that will bring justice to an unjust world. The analogy I am drawing here is with the discourse about racialization and ethnic identity found in analyses of Asian American life that romanticizes—and I mean this in the gooiest terms possible—aspirations of returning "home," where the home in question is one of the genealogical nation-states of Asia. Nonetheless, I am suggesting there are constructive uses to thinking about nostalgia; namely, it allows critical reflection about the confusion, ambivalence, and ambiguity rendered by empire. Indeed, I would argue that the memoryscape of critical nostalgia offers a constructive alternative to the somewhat tired discourses of "two worlds" and the increasingly generic notion of "hybridity."

To my mind, of considerably greater interest than the dialectical end-points of "home" and "abroad" or "empire and colony" are the in-between states that emerge through attempts to articulate and consider the power of memory and forgetting. In other words, from a phenomenological standpoint, the value of analyzing nostalgia is that it allows deliberate consideration of the experience of memory itself in

---

[13] Johann Baptist Metz, *Faith in History and Society*, trans. David Smith (New York: Seabury Press, 1980), 111; Gershom Scholem, "On Jonah and the Concept of Justice," *Critical Inquiry* 25:2 (1999): 353-361; Abraham Joshua Heschel, *The Prophets* (New York: Harper & Row, 1962).

[14] In addition to the deeply illuminating *Out of Silence*, see also Fumitaka Matsuoka, *The Color of Faith: Building Community in a Multiracial Society* (Cleveland: United Church Press, 1998).

everyday life. Nostalgia is a concept that peers into the time and space of life itself in ways that doesn't leave life standing "as is" but unsettles and destabilizes through claims about and for "the ordinary."[15] Nostalgia is not, I am contending, simply another way of speaking of the doubleness or duality of the self or of a people or of home or life itself. Instead, nostalgia reflects the ambiguity of the everyday—not the split between worlds but rather the fragmented, fragmentary nature of ordinary life. The critical and constructive work of nostalgia can help to render lost worlds a part of a whole not yet realized, a part of a history yet to come.

Fanon teaches us that modernity makes and reproduces itself through myriad disciplinary techniques that shape, delimit, and define the parameters of "the everyday."[16] In calling nostalgia a form of critical memory, I am arguing that the constitution and construction of nostalgia-work can be a form of critical reflection on the meaning of the past and the present, as well as a means of enabling visions of possible futures. Stated otherwise, one reason to take the phenomenon of nostalgia seriously is that it offers a glimpse into the operation of memory in modernity, and in so doing provides a picture of what makes up the everyday, the ordinary. I agree with Stanley Cavell's characterization of the relationship between memory, identity, and the ordinary/everyday: critical reflection on the everyday (or what Cavell calls, in his enticingly expansive manner, "philosophy" and "the ordinary") tends to generate a disappointment with the world as lived, by which he means the social world where we live and interact with others.[17]

The archetype that perhaps best exemplifies the problems and virtues of nostalgia is "the exile," the figure who experiences estrangement and longing in arguably the most exquisitely fraught mode. Boym identifies exilic figures like Nabakov and Brodsky as exemplars of the parlance of nostalgia; and I would include many if not all post-colonial writers, essayists, and artists, such as Edwidge Danticat, V. S.

---

[15] To my mind, one of the most fruitful and productive inquiries into the critical work of discerning "the ordinary" is found in the corpus of Stanley Cavell and his project of Emersonian perfectionism. See, e.g., Stanley Cavell, *In Quest of the Ordinary: Lines of Skepticism and Romanticism* (Chicago: University of Chicago Press, 1989).

[16] Frantz Fanon, *Wretched of the Earth*, trans. Richard Philcox (New York: Grove Press, 1965).

[17] Ibid., 3-26.

Naipul, André Aciman, Carlos Bulosan, Frantz Fanon, Theresa Cha, and Edward Said. In honoring the legacy of Fumitaka Matsuoka, it is appropriate to refine the archetype in question and focus on a figure of cultural criticism and critical race theology that has been so crucial for Asian American religious life, namely, *the spiritual exile*. Indeed, figures in exile are often the ones who "benefit" most from, or rather *with* nostalgia. After all, the exilic has a special place in most discourses about the pressing significance of place, space, and memory, especially in consideration of the physical, psychic, and emotional displacement that results from diaspora and other consequences of geo-politics. Among the most striking features of Matsuoka's work has been his role as a persistent prophetic witness to the spiritual exile of Asian American religious communities for whom he has been an indefatigable source of insight *and* foresight for over three decades.

No doubt, Matsuoka is a theologian of prodigious talents. But what are the qualities that make him such an engaging and important theological presence—one who was indispensable in giving shape and voice to the development of Asian American religious studies and theology at the end of the twentieth and through the turn of the twenty-first century? Evident at all levels are the synthetic power of his writing and his talents for building institutions. We know the books that have given voice to communities of faith and color. Think also of Matsuoka's leadership as dean of the Pacific School of Religion. Let us make note of his vision in creating the PANA Institute for Leadership Development and the Study of Pacific and Asian North American Religion. Behold his crucial support of the Asian Pacific Religions Research Initiative for over a decade. These achievements notwithstanding, I write in homage to my friend Fumitaka Matsuoka in gratitude for his prodigious work as a prophetic witness to the Asian American diaspora. In his deeply enacted care and compassion for the life and fate of Asian Americans of faith, Matsuoka has been a marvelous exemplar of the spiritual exile as cultural critic. Despite his humility in regard to these remarkable achievements, I am honor bound to acknowledge his role as one of the grand theologians of the Asian American religious diaspora. With this in mind, I want to consider the following questions: What does it mean to claim that you are a child of a diaspora who is also a spiritual exile? What responsibilities do we have as children of diasporas?

Narratives and stories of nostalgia—in both restorative and reflective forms—are expressions of myth. Nationalists who are dead-set at establishing material, political, and social re-instantiations of collective identity—for example, the ideological formations of "Israel" or a united "Korea"—operate, in my view, with an unhealthy dose of mythic utopianism. They have an ideal state in mind—where the multiple meanings of "ideal state" as political, psychological, and physical conditions are operational.[18] Paradoxically, the establishment of a political state, for example, cannot fully satisfy the restorative longing for home. After all, the ideal is what animates this form of nostalgia, and political institutions and the like are inherently non-ideal entities.

Reflective or critical nostalgia keeps the experience and expectations of home, loss, and detachment in mind, but not with the idea of realizing or instantiating home. The difference in horizons of expectations between restorative and reflective nostalgics is evident in the grammar of eschatology or end-time. The restorative nostalgic thinks the kingdom of God can be and will be rendered in the terms and conditions of ordinary time and space.[19] The reflective nostalgic accepts that the kingdom is always before us but not within reach. The grammar of memory, of critical nostalgia as it were, finds its expression not necessarily in the future tense ("The kingdom will come") but rather in the future perfect ("The kingdom will have come when...").

By "spiritual exile" I am referring to a figure whose psychic state of mind and mode of being in the world critically engages held-beliefs of a given people on history, immanence, transcendence, the divine, and the sacred. The spiritual exile embodies the struggle within a state of nostalgia and melancholy, acutely experienced as a form of cultural and spiritual nihilism.[20] It is this melancholy and nostalgia that is at once the end product of nihilism and also the expression of agency that defines the psychic condition of the spiritual exile. The spiritual exile inhabits an existential despair that can broadly confront crises of nihilism and can

---

[18] For a provocative examination of myth and the political, see Roland Boer, *Political Myth: On the Use and Abuse of Biblical Themes* (Durham: Duke University Press, 2009).

[19] Boym, *The Future of Nostalgia*, 9.

[20] For a nuanced consideration of coping with cultural nihilism, see Jonathan Lear's *Radical Hope: Ethics in the Face of Cultural Devastation* (Cambridge: Cambridge University Press, 2006).

engage survival strategies that, at once, inflect a melancholy that mourns the loss of the past, as well as a nostalgia that aspires to keep hold of and preserve history while resisting submission to the regnant knowledge regimes of the present. Fredric Jameson calls such regimes "organizational fictions"—which is to say that they are utopic narratives that structure and "make sense of" the text as well as experience.[21] To this end, I am suggesting that the critical nostalgia found in Matsuoka's work speaks to the strenuous efforts that are retrieving yet holding onto the worlds that have been lost and may or may not be recoverable through the fragments of memories, stories told, and geo-political legacies that often obscure more than they reveal.[22]

In a sense, what I am suggesting is that nostalgia is the "upbeat" voice of hope that accompanies the "black sun" (to invoke Julia Kristeva's dark metaphor) of melancholia. Whereas the melancholic, as a theorist like Kristeva describes her/him, lives "an abyssal suffering that does not succeed in signifying itself and, having lost meaning, loses life," the critical nostalgic, by contrast, is constantly seeking out glimpses of possibility.[23] Neither the nostalgic nor the melancholic functions with a subjectivity of wholeness; again, the psyche is distilled through fragments of memory and glimpses of possible futures. For all the loss that the melancholic endures, the critical nostalgic seeks out comparable forms of counter-memory to light up that black sun.

Kristeva is helpful here insofar as she identifies a link between melancholy and experiences of "symbolic breakdown," that is, when language loses its capacity to express linguistic, existential, and psychic meaning for the self. Language becomes empty and yet there remains the primary resource to articulate and express one's psyche. Take note of Kristeva's account of this breakdown:

> The spectacular collapse of meaning with depressive persons—and, at the limit, the meaning of life—allows us to assume that they experience difficulty

---

[21] Fredric Jameson, *The Political Unconscious: Narrative as a Socially Symbolic Act* (Ithaca: Cornell University Press, 1981).

[22] Cf. Cavell, *In Quest of the Ordinary*, 153-180.

[23] Julia Kristeva, *Black Sun: Depression and Melancholia* (New York: Columbia University Press, 1989), 189.

> integrating the universal signifying sequence that is language. In the best cases, speaking beings and their language are like one: is not speech our "second nature?" In contrast, the speech of the depressed is to them like an alien skin; melancholy persons are foreigners in their maternal tongue. They have lost the meaning—the value—of their mother tongue for want of losing the mother. The dead language they speak, which foreshadows their suicide, conceals a Thing buried alive.[24]

It is crucial to note that the critical nostalgia that Matsuoka has written about does not reflect an incapacitating despair. In this regard, the distinction from melancholy is clear. Instead, Matsuoka has written with care about the losses that Asian American communities of faith—in particular, Japanese Americans—have endured, not in terms of a nihilistic end-state but rather as a condition that indicates new possibilities of being in the world. *This* capacity for prophetic witness that does not capitulate to despair is what suggests Matsuoka as a poet of spiritual exile and of critical nostalgia. Matsuoka's poetic sensibility readily names "the pain and promise of pluralism," in which "the matter of Asian American self-identify is more accurately understood through our ability to cope with an often inhospitable society and to locate our own sense of dignity and worth within it. Such strife inevitably leads us toward a quest for a fair and just order in society."[25] Matsuoka's critical race theology of communities of color refuses to take on the organizational fictions of white Christian supremacy; which is to say that he resists a unifying coherence to the disparate elements of memory that simultaneously engender a critical nostalgia and constitute the possibility of agency. His theological work represents an instance of finding possibility from impossibility and foreclosure, as well as discerning a mode of agency that emerges from remembrance.[26]

---

[24] Ibid, 53.

[25] Fumitaka Matsuoka, *Out of Silence: Emerging Themes in Asian American Churches* (Eugene, Oregon: Wipf & Stock, 1995), 56-58.

[26] Judith Butler, *The Psychic Life of Power* (Stanford: Stanford University Press, 1997), 132-150.

As I indicated earlier, Matsuoka does not deploy utopian fictions, such as one finds in appeals to neo-Platonic returns to "the One" or other edenic visions that would explain away loss, exile, estrangement, and melancholy. To do as much would be to assume that wholeness, reconciliation, and truth are inherently desirable and emancipatory. If there is anything that postcolonial writers have taught us, it is that these visions of emancipation from imperial regimes are pipe dreams, flights of fancy from the deeply sedimented and embedded effects of the imperium. Expunging myths of unity and plenitude means resisting the temptations of disabling utopian notions of life without empire, without the history of colonialism. In concert with this effort, critical nostalgia seeks out new forms of agency. A spiritual exile like Matsuoka reveals agency in the nostalgic remembrance and embrace of things past, and in the subsequent contemplation of their persistence in the present, and in the foreshadowing of an enabling future. These difficult lessons are evident in what Matsuoka finds to be "the price Japanese Americans have paid for the preservation of their dignity... [that has proven to be] both painful and immeasurable, passed on to succeeding generations."[27] The theological excellence of Matsuoka's spiritual exile speaks to the work of the artist and the poet.[28] The critical distance he has to the "lost worlds" of "Japan" and even "the U.S." allows him an ironic space to reflect on the past, present and future. It is a stance through which he simultaneously engages and disengages with his material contexts of new languages and worlds.

Worlds Made a Part

As I suggested earlier, there are modes and forms of expression that are endemic to the experience of nostalgia. While not writing poetry as such, from his earliest essays up to his most recent work, I would argue that Matsuoka has written with a distinct poetic sensibility. When

---

[27] Matsuoka, *Out of Silence*, 25.
[28] Cavell identifies a similar path of disappointment, collapse of meaning, and self-transformation and transfiguration in Emerson and other perfectionist thinkers and artists. See, e.g., Stanley Cavell, *Philosophy the Day After Tomorrow* (Cambridge: Belknap/Harvard University Press, 2005), 7-27, 83-132.

effective, the poetic is a deeply illuminating index of the ordinary. It can offer insight into the everyday by offering highly distilled accounts of human experience. By way of conclusion, let me highlight Matsuoka's poetic sensibility and his role as bearing prophetic witness for spiritual exiles by drawing on a central strand of Angus Fletcher's recent poetic theory, specifically, his notion of "the middle voice." Fletcher argues that in contrast to languages such as ancient Greek and modern French, English language and grammar lack what he calls "the middle voice": a form of grammar that indicates a "back and forth between an inner self and the world out there." The middle voice refers to modes of perception that involve an exchange (the dialectic of gift-giving is an apt metaphor), as in the back and forth between persons. Fletcher writes, "Such mental activity is both inside and outside at the same moment, while we perceivers stand between."[29] The middle voice expresses perceptions that are neither active nor passive. It finds its expression in verbs such as "ponder," "sense," "move," "dwell," "loose and lose," "hold" and "attach and detach."[30] We can hear this middle voice of motion and emotion in the poetry of critical nostalgia, such as found in the work of the great Iranian poet Forough Farrokhazad. Consider Farrokhazad's poem "The Gift":

> I speak from the deep end of night
> Of end of darkness I speak.
> I speak of deep night ending.
>
> O kind friend, if you visit my house,
> bring me a lamp, cut me a window,
> so I can gaze at the swarming alley of the fortunate.[31]

Or hear Matsuoka's deeply compassionate account of the "promise in pain" prominent among Asian American Christians:

---

[29] Angus Fletcher, *A New Theory of Poetry: Democracy, the Environment, and the Future of Imagination* (Cambridge: Harvard University Press, 2004), 105.

[30] Ibid.

[31] Forough Farrokhzad, *Sin: Selected Poems of Forough Farrokhzad.* Translated by Sholeh Wolpé (Little Rock, Arkansas: University of Arkansas Press, 2007), 57.

> [T]he fluid and complex nature of Asian American Christians' search for an identity [is] often fraught with unresolved pain. What this indicates is the fundamentally ambiguous and yet dynamic ordering of life.... The order of life in this fashion, moreover, is likely to be expressed in terms of a shift in value orientation. Hospitality for the stranger, empathy for the disenfranchised, and courage to face the future, even amidst an overwhelmingly adverse condition, are far more significant than correct doctrine and consistency in logic. It is, in fact, the experience and acceptance of an ambiguous and dynamic state of life that allows a person the transformation of values and worldviews.[32]

To my mind, the grammar of the middle voice—which is to say, the grammar of being neither fully agent nor object but somewhere in-between, immersed and enmeshed between the two—is found in the expressive practice of nostalgia and memory. Nostalgia is the middle voice between history and the aesthetic—a memorial terrain between two different modes of narrative, if you will. In effect, all three (the historical, the aesthetic/poetic, and the nostalgic) aspire to a measure of fidelity to lived experience. It sounds banal to characterize this as a mode of "description," but if what is at stake is a struggle to understand the ordinary and the everyday effects of living under an imperial regime or the struggles of withstanding the penetrating effects of race and religion, then the challenge lies in figuring out how to depict and understand, and to give an account of lives lived.

Let me be clear: my argument is not a paean to the empirical by any stretch. Remember: these are claims about memory, about nostalgia––the artifacts of experience. Therefore, substantial consideration must be given to the supraempirical, that is, dispatches of the *interior* life—specifically, the expressions of the interior life that relate to but are distinct from the manifold of the social.[33] Furthermore, I want to avoid

---

[32] Matsuoka, *Out of Silence*, 77.

[33] Ricoeur's attempt to move from the "what" of memory (i.e., memory as an object of cognition and/or perception) to the "who" of memory (i.e., the self

any slip into sentimentalism or misty-eyed wistfulness. In the critical form I am putting forward, nostalgia can reflect a discipline and a rigor. One might call it a discipline of remembrance.

Matsuoka has consistently asked Foucauldian questions of the spiritual exile about the relationship between subjectivity and the ethical—hence, the questions I posed earlier about the responsibilities each of us has as children of one diaspora or another. Consider Foucault's questions about subjectivity and knowledge: "How have certain kinds of interdictions become the price required for attaining certain kinds of knowledge [*savoir*] about oneself? What must one know [*connaître*] about oneself in order to be willing to accept such renunciation?"[34] Along these lines, Matsuoka has queried into his own identification with a broader Japanese history, family legacies, and his self-understanding as a Japanese-American Christian born of this heritage. What official histories has he been subjected to? How can one distinguish between these ideological narratives and the hidden histories of the oppressed, of one's ancestors? In his inflection of the middle voice, Matsuoka has tried to determine how to understand history and his own role as a spiritual exile apart from the authorial interdictions of the history told by the victors: Japan, the U.S., the Church, specifically in darkness of the internment of Japanese Americans. "What I have witnessed in Japanese Americans," writes Matsuoka, "and particularly their Christian churches is that the motivation for recovery of 'sacred conventions' is rooted deeply and foundationally in their experiences of the historical injuries caused by the incarceration into concentration camps during World War II. The motivation for Japanese Americans… derives mainly from painful experiences that remind them what it means to have an alternative vision of society, an alternative value, a 'second language.'"[35] This is reminiscent of Theresa Hak Kyung Cha's classic

---

who remembers) requires understanding the "how" of memory (i.e., the means and ways memory works for the self). Paul Ricoeur, *Memory, History, Forgetting*. Translated by Kathleen Blamey and David Pellauer (Chicago: University of Chicago Press, 2004), 3-4.

[34] Michel Foucault, "Introduction," in *Ethics, Subjectivity, and Truth*, ed. Paul Rabinow (New York: Free Press, 1997), xxiv.

[35] Fumitaka Matsuoka, "Creating Community Amidst the Memories of Historic Injuries," in *Realizing the America of our Hearts: Theological Voices of Asian Americans*, ed. Fumitaka Matsuoka and Eleazar S. Fernandez (St. Louis:

Dictée, when she reflects in her own poetic terms on the Japanese colonial rule over Korea:

> Why resurrect it all now. From the Past. History, the old wound. The past emotions all over again. To confess to relive the same folly. To name it now so as not to repeat history in oblivion. To extract each fragment by each fragment from the word from the image another word another image the reply that will not repeat history in oblivion.[36]

A confession: I must say that I do not think that untold histories—-the "minor" discourses in history—are unambiguously good things to know. It is a postmodern conceit that learning about and uncovering untold pasts are inherently or necessarily redemptive or even emancipatory. This can be true and may in fact be the appropriate incentive to engage in uncovering what Edward Said calls "oppositional knowledge." Nonetheless, I am foregrounding nostalgia here as an acknowledgment of how genuinely difficult it is to come to terms with the unsettling past, a forgotten and suppressed history. Matsuoka's theology is hardly salutary in this regard. As Matsuoka powerfully argues, "past oppression and injustice inflicted by the nation are also remembered mythically and in narrative form....The memories persist with such power because it is a sign of allegiance to share these painful memories among [Japanese Americans]."[37] Matsuoka has vigilantly reminded us that once recovered there is no guarantee that redemption will come with the release of what Walter Benjamin calls the "oppressed past."[38] Uncovering the truth, saving history from oblivion, may not be enough to stave off melancholy nor to right past wrongs. This is a torturous lesson taught by the Truth and Reconciliation Commission in South Africa. Cha confronts us by

---

Chalice Press, 2003), 29-40.

[36] Theresa Hak Kyung Cha, *Dictée* (Berkeley: Third Woman Press, 1995), 33.

[37] Matsuoka, "Creating Community Amidst the Memories of Historic Injuries," 37.

[38] Walter Benjamin, "Theses on the Philosophy of History," in *Illuminations: Essays and Reflections*, ed. Hannah Arendt (New York: Schocken Books, 1969).

asking whether wholeness is truly redemptive. This is to ask if relenting to what Cioran calls the "temptation to exist" amounts to assenting to a totalizing historical memory that one knows occludes oppressions, violence, and suffering.[39]

And yet the hope is that a different future might be rendered through the articulation of a lost past. This is the opening that critical nostalgia seeks. Indeed, this is what suggests critical nostalgia as engendering, at minimum, episodic qualities of agency. Certainly, melancholy persists precisely because one cannot be assured that this will be the case. For the melancholic, the past cannot be mourned for fear that it will be lost. To mourn is to let go of an object of love, as Freud wrote of mourning and melancholia.[40] For the nostalgic, a future deeply saturated by the past is what renders hope.[41]

As a theologian of critical nostalgia, as a spiritual exile who is at the same time a cultural critic, Matsuoka has always sought to interrogate a condition in which the self can mediate between the causes of melancholy and the catharsis of reflective nostalgia and aesthetic production. As he argues in his classic *Out of Silence,*

> The capacity to live the life of ambiguity, or the "courage to be," is not merely the capacity to endure the status quo, however. It is, instead, the freedom to live in a world of pain without being complacent about and acquiescing to its own ordering power. It is the freedom to shatter the complacency of the existing order without even a blueprint for what the world beyond it looks like. Such a freedom, by nature, transcends the existing situation or conceptual ideal. It breaks into the world from beyond. It exists in the realm of faith. And it takes a certain social, cultural, ethnic, or class location in which one exists, a place of the "holy insecurity," a

---

[39] E. M. Cioran, *The Temptation to Exist*, trans. Richard Howard (Chicago: University of Chicago Press, 1998).

[40] Freud, "Mourning and Melancholia."

[41] Arjun Appadurai, "Hope and Democracy," *Public Culture* 19:1 (2007): 29-34.

fringe, to become receptive to such a freedom, a promise given in the good news.[42]

Matsuoka's virtuous insistence here indicates that to translate the experience of loss—to render into words the experiences of loss and remembrance—is a survival imperative for the spiritual exile. This sentiment is akin to Kristeva's argument that "[t]he artist consumed by melancholia is...the most relentless in his[/her] struggle against the symbolic abdication that blankets him[/her]."[43] The nostalgic agency Matsuoka has enacted over the last three decades is an agonistic struggle with what Wole Soyinka calls the "burden of memory and the muse of forgiveness."[44] The suffering of memory is painful and yet defines who one is. The past as memory, and forgetting as history—minor or suppressed—is constitutive even in our lack of awareness.

What refuge is there for the critical nostalgia that Matsuoka has so fruitfully engaged? As Ricoeur argues, texts can be forms of meaningful action insofar as they serve as expressions of the psychic life.[45] Matsuoka makes the case this way:

> The experience of "rage, resentment, and fear" is an opportunity that could lead to a new cognition, new epistemologies, and new ways of knowing and naming reality. The movement from pain and suffering caused by racism to a new vision of humanity requires painful lessons in memory and accountability. It requires a yearning, a passion, and a determination to know what has occurred, and at the same time, a will to move beyond bondage to past experience into a vision of a new and alternate ordering of human relationships.

---

[42] Matsuoka, *Out of Silence*, 79.
[43] Kristeva, *Black Sun*, 9.
[44] Wole Soyinka, *The Burden of Memory, the Muse of Forgiveness* (New York: Oxford University Press, 1999).
[45] Paul Ricouer, *From Text to Action: Essays in Hermeneutics II* (Evanston: Northwestern University Press, 1997), 144.

Through his writing and the communities that he has helped to build and sustain, Matsuoka has been able to convey the *agon* of psychic, cultural, and spiritual exile while also demonstrating how the production of texts and the collaborative work of sustaining communities are achievements and acts of defiance against despair.

As with the case of the nihilism that Kristeva finds in the work of Dostoevsky, I have come to conclude that the solemnity of forgiveness transfigures melancholy.[46] Matsuoka finds an expansive compassion in the darkness of the Japanese American internment. He writes, "If the experiences of historical injuries suffered by Japanese Americans point to their willingness to go beyond their inclination to dwell in the pain of the past and to reach out for strengthening a web of all people in the U.S. society, this society has not been able to value their generosity. This is the challenge that awaits America in truly becoming the America of all our hearts."[47] Similarly, Kristeva argues, the connection between such forgiveness and the meaning of critical nostalgia is "between suffering and acting out....[A]esthetic activity constitutes forgiveness."[48] Matsuoka's theological engagements represent the expressive compassion of the poet, the musician, the spiritual exile. To wit, the critical knowledge rendered through the middle voice *can* (though not necessarily does) come from nostalgia; critical nostalgia mediates and bridges the internal life, the psychic life, on the one hand, and the social world, on the other. The mediation of these two poles (What do we call them? "History and subjectivity"? "Experience and the psyche"?) constitutes a demanding challenge for many of our greatest cultural critics. Certainly, this is what Said labored to convey throughout his career. He wrote from an inheritance of the humanist tradition that begins with Vico's insight and provocation that history is the creation of the human mind and spirit. The main challenge to the critic, according to Said, is to work out of the bind that poststructuralists like Foucault established so convincingly—call it the free will problem of history: How do we find freedom and agency under conditions in which we are, at once, products of history and also agents who have animating wills and lives?

---

[46] Kristeva, *Black Sun*, 173-218.
[47] Matsuoka, "Creating Community Amidst the Memories of Historic Injuries," in *Realizing the America of Our Hearts*, 39.
[48] Kristeva, *Black Sun*, 190.

Nostalgia helps to negotiate this conundrum. It keeps us speaking in the middle voice of memory—of displacement and dwelling, of dispossession and self-possession—as we come to grips with the flux of time and space, and of history and place. A critical grammar of nostalgia can help make determinations about how to best apply the cache of memories that have an engaging hold on the imagination—home, language, culture, "my people". It evokes the question Said famously asked in his essay "Traveling Theory": "What is critical consciousness at bottom if not an unstoppable predilection for alternatives?"[49] In the end, the resource and resourcefulness of a nostalgic mind—in the risks that it undertakes to retrieve and retell history, as well as to engage in rigorous, even strenuous self-criticism—enlivens the on-going search for democratic alternatives and the hope of humanizing possibilities. And so it is with these aspirations in mind that I find myself among the legion indebted to the inspired legacy of the great spiritual exile Fumitaka Matsuoka.[50]

---

[49] Edward Said, *The World, the Text, and the Critic* (Cambridge: Harvard University Press, 1983), 247.

[50] I am very grateful for the feedback and comments on this essay from Rudy Busto, Eleazar Fernandez, Diane Hoffman-Kim, Jane Iwamura, Sharon Suh, Cornel West, and the external reviewer. An additional word of thanks goes to Eleazar Fernandez for inviting me to contribute to this volume and for the opportunity to honor my dear friend Fumitaka Matsuoka.

www.ingramcontent.com/pod-product-compliance
Lightning Source LLC
Chambersburg PA
CBHW020633230426
43665CB00008B/160